Babies by
the Bay

Babies by the Bay

The Insider's Guide to Everything from Doctors and Diapers to Playgrounds and Preschools in the San Francisco Bay Area

Michelle L. Keene
Stephanie S. Lamarre

WILDCAT CANYON PRESS
A Division of Circulus Publishing Group, Inc.
Berkeley, California

Babies by the Bay: The Insider's Guide to Everything from Doctors and Diapers to Playgrounds and Preschools in the San Francisco Bay Area

Copyeditor: Shirley Coe
Proofreader: Lara Deans Lowe
Cover Design: Mary Beth Salmon
Cover Illustration (skyline): Mike Powell
Art Direction: Leyza Yardley
Interior Design & Typesetting: Margaret Copeland/Terragrafix, Jude Levinson
Typographic Specifications: Body text in Korinna 10/13, headings in Minya-
    Nouvelle.

Printed in the United States of America

Library of Congress Cataloging-in-Publication Data

Keene, Michelle L., 1965–
    Babies by the bay : the insider's guide to everything from doctors and
    diapers to playgrounds and preschools in the San Francisco Bay Area /
    Michelle L. Keene, Stephanie S. Lamarre.
        p. cm.
    Includes bibliographical references and index.
    ISBN 1-885171-78-1 (pbk.)
        1. Infants—Services for—San Francisco Bay Area—Directories.
    2. Toddlers—Services for—San Francisco Bay Area—Directories.
    3. Preschool children—Services for—San Francisco Bay Area—
    Directories. 4. Infant health services—San Francisco Bay Area—
    Directories. 5. Maternal health services—San Francisco Bay
    Area—Directories. 6. Infants' supplies—San Francisco Bay Area—
    Directories. 7. Parents—Services for—San Francisco Bay Area—
    Directories. 8. Family recreation—San Francisco Bay Area—Directories.
    I. Lamarre, Stephanie S., 1966– II. Title.

HQ774.K44.2002
362.7'025'7946—dc21   2002026650

10 9 8 7 6 5 4 3

Acknowledgments

We would like to thank the many people who went above and beyond the call in helping us as we researched and wrote this book: our husbands, Mark Tellini and David Lamarre, for their support and encouragement; all of the parents who responded to our surveys for their invaluable advice and opinions; our entire Wednesday play group —Alix Arndt, Anne Brundige, Christie Carlson, Elizabeth Clark, Amy Culp, Hope Gelbach, Kathy Hoyt, Nicole Klionsky, Anne Nicholson, Amanda Safka, Robyn Sealander, Christine Varon, and Heather Young—for their inspiration; and Mary Asel, Paula Atkinson, Page Barnes, Margaret Bielak, Lesley Brascesco, Sally Brammell, Stephanie Bornstein at Equal Rights Advocates, Wynn Burkett, Genevieve Butcher, Helen Byrne, Irene Byrne, Jeff Byrne, Elizabeth Clark, Pam Clemmons, Dr. Suzanne Cobb-Christie, Susan Condon, Sara Duskin, Carol Egan, Diane Forese, Erin Gilheary, Deborah Klein, Todd Madalone, Cindy Mall, Monica Canty McCarty, Trigg Robinson McLeod, Amy Metzler, Diane Michelsen, Ashley Paff, Barbara Papini, Heather Pedersen, Nancy Pile, Helen Riley, Bonnie Rose, Nishan Shephard, Vena Skolnick, Juliet Tanner, Rose Titcomb, Ashley Tobin, Anne Waltzer, Dr. Donna Wiggins, Kim Yee, and Heather Young for providing much-needed help with research, surveys, leads, and drafts.

Finally, we would like to thank Tamara Traeder at Wildcat Canyon Press for making this book possible.

Table of Contents

A Note from the Authors

Our goal in this book is to present information and when available, "insider information" about parents' experiences of pregnancy and young child resources in the Bay Area. We collected opinions about such resources from several hundred parents in an unofficial survey. The parents' ratings in this book come from our interpretation of the opinions in those surveys, and/or from our own personal experience of the resource. These ratings are merely personal opinions of the authors and their sources and are not official or factual in nature, and should not be looked at as authoritative! Also, the absence of a parent rating carries no negative connotation; it just means that we received no opinions from our surveys, and we have no personal opinion, about a particular resource.

We have tried in each chapter to give you some background material that may help you as you consider the resources in that chapter. Of course, this information is general in nature and should not be construed as medical, legal or other professional advice. We're not doctors, so it's best to consult with your health care provider before acting on any medical decision. And if you have legal questions, you should consult a lawyer about your specific circumstances.

As you may expect, inclusion in this book should not be regarded as a referral to or endorsement of particular doctors, midwives, lawyers, or other service providers, nor a guarantee of the quality of the services they each offer. Similarly, we can't guarantee the quality of any of the products described in this book. Each person needs to make his or her own independent evaluation of all goods and services prior to purchasing or using them.

We do not have any ownership in any of the resources listed in this book. We also did not receive any compensation for including any resource here. We will disclose that our friend and photographer, who is listed in the book, took our author photo as a gift to us! (But we would have recommended her anyway.)

All that being said, we hope that this book is helpful to you, and makes the experience of being an expectant and new parent a little easier. Enjoy!

Introduction

Becoming a parent in the Bay Area catapults you into a new and mysterious world. As we eagerly awaited our first children more than three years ago, we had so many questions about everything, but didn't know where to turn for answers. We wondered how we could have felt so competent in our professional lives, yet feel so incompetent as expectant, and then new, parents. We asked these questions and more:

◆ How do I find the best hospitals and doctors in the Bay Area?
◆ Where can I find great maternity and baby gear at the best prices without driving around the entire Bay Area?
◆ Where can I work out safely during pregnancy, and do any of these clubs have child care?
◆ Where can I meet other new parents?
◆ Which kids' classes are worth the money?
◆ Where can we take our kids on a rainy day?
◆ How do I find a competent doula, baby nurse, nanny, baby-sitter, or day care center near my home?
◆ How do I find, and more importantly, get into, a good preschool in my area?

As we struggled to adapt to life after our first babies were born, we searched in vain for a local baby guide. The phone book was no help—either it did not list the necessary resources, or we had no way of knowing which places other parents liked. More importantly, as new parents we just did not have time to drive in circles around the Bay Area to investigate—and who wants to take a chance on something as important as a baby? We quickly realized that we needed a guide to parenthood in the Bay Area, found there was none . . . and the idea for this book was born.

Our hope is that our work on this book will spare you some of the time and energy we spent finding great resources, and let you enjoy more hours with your children. As we discovered, the Bay Area is full of great resources for parents—so many, in fact, that the trick is to find time to experience them all. During the journey of writing this book, we logged thousands of miles in our cars and strollers, and hundreds of telephone hours. Together we've searched for maternity clothes, baby gear, hospitals, doctors, and preschools. We're both in search of the Holy Grail of postnatal fitness. We've carted our children to museums, libraries, and parks all over the Bay Area. We are both active in several mothers' groups, which keep us sane. Between us we've lived in almost all the local regions, and we've met wonderful parents everywhere we've gone. Along the way, we both somehow managed to find time to have second children, and we have realized again and again that the Bay Area is a great place to raise kids.

We wanted our guidebook to be filled with parents' opinions—a true insider's guide for new parents. And we certainly could not personally experience every single resource in the Bay Area! So before we sat down to write, we surveyed local parents in all six Bay Area counties (Alameda, Contra Costa, Marin, San Francisco, Santa Clara, and San Mateo) about topics ranging from favorite doctors to favorite parks to favorite shopping haunts. We received several hundred enthusiastic responses, including frank opinions on everything from pregnancy through preschool. These parents' opinions, and our own, formed the basis for the ratings and quotes you'll see in this book.

Throughout the book, you'll find a five-star "parent rating" system. Think of it as a report card for baby resources. For those resources we received parent opinions about or have experienced ourselves, we've assigned a rating, ranging from one star (*) at the bottom end, to five stars (*****) at the top. If we have listed no rating, it simply means that we received no comments on the resource from any of the parents surveyed, and have not personally experienced it ourselves. Here is a key to the ratings:

    ☆ I wouldn't send my worst enemy there.

    ☆ ☆ Poor to fair reviews; not the worst, but you can do better elsewhere.

    ☆ ☆ ☆ Satisfactory or mixed reviews.

    ☆ ☆ ☆ ☆ Good reviews; not perfect, but still a great resource.

    ☆ ☆ ☆ ☆ ☆ Excellent; our highest rating.

You won't see many one-and two-star ratings in here, because we wanted to focus on the resources most highly rated (and probably the most useful to users). And of course, ratings are inherently biased, and not gospel. Though we gathered as many viewpoints as possible, our survey process was far from scientific, so take it for what it is: unvarnished personal opinion. (And, if you disagree with any ratings, please let us know! See below for contact information.)

A word on how our book is organized: We've tried to lay out the chapters in the order you'll need them, progressing from pregnancy through postpartum, babyhood, and the preschool years. We discuss healthcare for mom and baby (Chapter 1); fitness and massage (Chapter 2); maternity clothes (Chapter 3); shopping for baby gear (Chapter 4); postpartum help (Chapter 5); play groups and parents' groups (Chapter 6); classes for babies and kids (Chapter 7); fun outings (Chapter 8); child care (Chapter 9); and preschools (Chapter 10). Resources under each topic are divided by locality into San Francisco, the North Bay, the East Bay, and the South Bay (including the Peninsula). Though we've tried to provide up-to-date, complete information about each resource, be sure to call ahead to verify hours, prices, and services, because things always change. Our focus is on the six counties of the Bay Area, but we also discuss some resources in Sonoma (North Bay), Napa (North Bay), and Santa Cruz (South Bay) counties. We had to draw the line somewhere, so we've limited the book to resources for babies through preschoolers, up to about age five. (Talk to us in five years about a guide for older children...)

More than just listing resources, we've endeavored to explain what to look for as a new parent, and how to find it. If we've done our job right, reading this book will be like having a best friend who's gone through everything and who tells it like it is, with no advertising hype or bias. Stick the book in your diaper bag as you explore all the Bay Area has to offer. Keep it by the telephone for those crisis moments when you don't know where to turn for help. Whether you're a new parent or an old hand, we hope this book will help you navigate the unknown, and sometimes surprising, territory of parenthood, while having fun along the way.

We've made every effort to be inclusive, but we may have missed something. Please let us know if you have a new resource, or an opinion on one listed here.

You can write to us care of Wildcat Canyon Press, 2716 Ninth Street, Berkeley, CA 94710, or email us at jacksonstreetpress@yahoo.com. Look for our website, www.babiesbythebay.com, coming soon, with updates on the book and more tips for Bay Area parents.

CHAPTER 1

IN THE BEGINNING . . .
Making Smart Pregnancy, Delivery, and Pediatric Health Care Choices

First things first. If you are thinking of having a baby, or if you are already pregnant, you will need to choose a prenatal care provider and a place to have your baby. You will also need to decide who will help you through labor, how you want to deliver your baby, and who will be your child's primary doctor. This chapter explores Bay Area resources for prenatal health care, delivery, and pediatric health care—from obstetricians, family practitioners, pediatricians, and midwives, to hospitals and birthing centers, doulas, prenatal education, and cord blood banking. Plus we will tell you what is customary in local care during pregnancy and childbirth, so you'll know what to expect. If you are having difficulty becoming pregnant, we will also suggest where to find a fertility specialist. If you are interested in surrogacy or adoption, turn to the section on local resources and legalities. We will also cover resources for babies with special needs. And finally, working parents-to-be will want to check out our discussion of pregnancy discrimination and maternity leave laws.

This chapter will answer the following questions and more:

- Where can I find a good obstetrician, family practitioner, pediatrician, or midwife?
- Are midwives licensed in California?
- What's the best hospital in my neighborhood?
- Can I deliver my baby at home?
- What is a doula, and where can I find one?
- How do I arrange for cord blood banking?
- Where can I take prenatal classes?
- Where can I go for fertility assistance?
- How do I find a surrogate or an adoption agency near me?
- Where can I find help for my baby with special needs?
- Now that I'm pregnant, what are my rights in my workplace in California?

Choosing Care Providers

Choosing people to care for you and your baby are some of the most important decisions you will make. Below we explain the basic choices in prenatal and pediatric care, how to find a care provider, and which local doctors and midwives are parents' favorites according to our surveys.

PRENATAL CHOICES: OB/GYNS, FPS, AND LMS

In California, you have three basic choices in prenatal care and delivery: an obstetrician/gynecologist (OB/GYN), a family practitioner (FP), or a licensed midwife (CNM; LM).

Obstetricians are medical doctors who specialize in caring for women and delivering babies. They have completed medical school, residency, and board certification by the American Board of Obstetrics and Gynecology, and they deliver babies in hospitals. The advantages of choosing an obstetrician are obvious: they are specialists trained to deal with whatever contingency may arise, and they deliver babies all the time. If you have a high-risk pregnancy (previous problematic pregnancies, medical problems, Rh or genetic problems, or are under seventeen or over thirty-five), you will want to see an obstetrician (and perhaps even a subspecialist in high-risk preg-nancies—more on this later).

Family practitioners provide general care for all members of the family. They are medical doctors, have specialty training and board certification in family practice, and practice in hospitals. If you would like one person to care for your entire family, are not high risk, but still want to see a doctor, a family practitioner may be for you.

California licenses two types of midwives: certified nurse-midwives (CNMs) and licensed direct entry midwives (LMs). Both are allowed to provide prenatal and postpartum care, to manage and support normal labor, and to deliver babies of normal spontaneous birth (just about everything short of a cesarean section or vacuum extraction). Both encourage a natural birth process without the use of medical interventions, and they focus on educating the parents for childbirth. Both must arrange for a doctor as a backup in case of emergency, and they practice in hospitals, birthing centers, and homes. The difference is in their training.

Nurse-midwives are registered nurses who also have specialized training in caring for women and babies during the prenatal and immediate postpartum period. A CNM has completed nursing school, hospital training in labor and delivery, a graduate program in nurse-midwifery (from nine months to two years), and a national examina-tion (the American College of Nurse-Midwives certification board exam). Most CNMs practice in hospitals or doctors' offices, although they can establish independent birthing centers or their own practices. They can write limited prescriptions.

In 1993, California also began certifying licensed direct entry mid-wives. LMs are not RNs, but they have passed the Medical Board's licensing exam. To be eligible to take the exam, they must have either graduated from an approved three-year midwifery education pro-gram, successfully challenged courses of an approved program by passing the exams of that program, or been licensed in another state with equivalent standards. LMs generally apprentice with experienced midwives (as opposed to CNMs, who train in hospitals).

Recently, California made some important changes to the mid-wifery laws. Before September 2000, California law required midwives

3

to affiliate with a supervising physician. Now midwives don't need to be supervised, but must make arrangements for medical consultation and referral during the prenatal, delivery, and postpartum periods. Midwives must also tell patients the scope of what they can and cannot do legally, whether or not they carry malpractice insurance, and how to contact the Medical Board if patients have complaints.

If you are healthy, expect a normal, trouble-free pregnancy and delivery, and would like a more natural approach, a midwife may be for you. Local moms report that midwives generally have more time than obstetricians during routine visits and are able to stay with patients during the entire labor and delivery process (and make a number of postpartum visits in many cases). On the other hand, if you expect complications or would like the extra security of a medical doctor, an obstetrician or family practitioner is the way to go.

WHAT KIND OF PEDIATRIC DOCTOR?

Several types of doctors treat children. Pediatricians are medical doctors specializing in children's health. They have completed a three-year pediatric residency after medical school and passed a board examination making them board-certified in pediatrics. Family practitioners, described above, also care for children. Some parents prefer pediatricians because they specialize in taking care of children, while others prefer family practitioners because they can take care of the entire family. Family practitioners are more common in rural areas, but not as popular in metropolitan regions like the Bay Area because of the prevalence of specialists. You may also occasionally see a doctor with the abbreviation "DO" rather than MD. This means "doctor of osteopathic medicine." An osteopathic physician, like an MD, is a licensed doctor. Both attended medical school and completed a residency. But osteopathic medical schools focus on training primary care physicians, osteopathic doctors emphasize a "whole person" approach to medicine rather than treating specific illnesses, and osteopaths are trained to pay special attention to the musculoskeletal system.

HOW TO CHOOSE A CARE PROVIDER

Ideally you have found your own care provider before you get pregnant. Start your search for a pediatric doctor well before your due date, in the beginning of your third trimester, to allow time for research and interviews.

Remember that whomever you choose—an OB, FP, midwife, or pediatrician—you will see this person a lot. Be sure you are comfortable with him or her. Changing care providers in the middle of a pregnancy or after your child becomes accustomed to him or her is not ideal. Get a sense of whether your care provider will take the time to answer your questions.

Your care provider's and your child's doctor's offices should be convenient to your home or work. Remember, you will be going to your care provider once a week toward the end of your pregnancy. Given the number of times babies and toddlers are sick, you'll regret choosing a pediatrician whose office is far away. Personally (and probably because we are always running late), we think location is critical. Free, convenient, and available parking is also a top priority. Those parking fees—and tickets, if you are like us—can add up. If you live in San Francisco, driving may be preferable to taking MUNI in the later stages of pregnancy. (We could tell you horror stories about perfectly healthy people refusing to give up disabled seats to women who looked like they were about to give birth right there on the bus.)

Make sure your insurance covers your provider's fees, or that you can afford them if not. Most California insurance plans provide generous coverage for prenatal visits, at no or low cost to the patient, to encourage healthy pregnancies. We know a mom who paid a grand total of $5 out of pocket to have her first baby. Her HMO picked up the rest of the tab—from initial visit through delivery. What a deal! Insurance companies—particularly HMOs—can be notoriously stingy when it comes to home births. If you plan to use a midwife for a home birth, check with your insurance plan to see whether these expenses are covered and who covers transport, physician, and hospital fees in the event of transfer to a hospital. Most insurance, including Medi-Cal, does cover CNM fees for hospital births.

5

As for pediatric coverage, unfortunately we've heard reports of parents having difficulty finding pediatricians who will accept new HMO patients, particularly in the East Bay. Fortunately, once you have found a physician accepting your insurance, it's likely that your insurance plan will cover well-baby visits at periodic intervals and immunizations. Check to make sure your insurance also covers emergency room visits (without a hefty co-pay), and preferably after-hours clinic care (better than an ER for many reasons, as we'll explain below). You should also make sure the plan includes the hospital to which your physician admits patients (preferably one that specializes in pediatrics), as well as the pediatric specialists to whom you may need referrals. Obviously you can't anticipate all the specialists you may need to see, but make sure the plan includes all the major types of specialties, such as pediatric anesthesiologists, pediatric surgeons, and pediatric ophthalmologists, to name a few. Also, make sure your plan offers good coverage while traveling, such as a nationwide network of physicians.

In searching for a pediatrician, consider whether his or her practice offers access to an after-hours pediatric clinic. As parents, we much prefer pediatric urgent care clinics (except, of course, in life-threatening emergencies, which a clinic is not equipped to handle). At a pediatric clinic, your child will be seen by a pediatrician rather than a generalist. The pediatrician will have the proper child-sized equipment. The clinic visit fees are generally much lower than for an ER visit. And you may actually be able to get an appointment rather than waiting hours in a crowded ER waiting room where your child may be exposed to all sorts of adult diseases. Plus, pediatric clinics are much less frightening places for kids than big ERs. Check with your pediatric doctor for local urgent care clinics. Many pediatricians are affiliated with certain clinics, in which case your insurance is billed for a normal office visit.

WHAT TYPE OF PRACTICE? SOLO VS. GROUPS

In choosing care providers, you also need to decide what type of practice you want to visit. Solo practitioners are reputed to provide more personalized attention to patients, but you may be stuck with a stranger—the on-call doctor or the ER—delivering your baby or car-

Prenatal Testing, Newborn Screening, and Immunizations

If you have concerns about the effects of drugs, chemicals, infectious diseases, and other things that may be harmful to an unborn child (called "teratogens"), ask your care provider or contact:

California Teratogen Information Service and Clinical Research Program
University of California,
San Diego Medical Center
Department of Pediatrics, #8446
200 W. Arbor Dr.
San Diego, CA 92103-8446
619-543-2131 or 800-532-3749

This is a statewide program operated by the UCSD Medical Center to collect, analyze, and disseminate information on known or potential teratogens. It provides confidential counseling and referrals for pregnant women exposed to harmful agents.

At sixteen to twenty weeks of gestation, you may take the California Expanded Alpha Feto-Protein (AFP) test. This is a voluntary, state-administered blood test for spina bifida, Down's syndrome, and certain other birth defects. If results are positive, diagnostic tests will be performed (ultrasound and amniocentesis) and genetic counseling offered. For more information about the AFP test, contact:

California Department of Health Services—Genetic Disease Branch
2151 Berkeley Way, Annex 4, Rm. 300
Berkeley
510-540-2534

Ask for their booklets: *The California Expanded AFP Screening Program* (for women under 35); *Prenatal Testing Choices for Women Thirty-five Years and Older.*

In California, newborns must by law undergo a state-administered Newborn Screening Test for certain diseases, including PKU, galactosemia, hypothryoidism, sickle cell disease, and other hemoglobin diseases. For more information, contact the California Department of Health Services listed above. California has also begun to implement a Newborn Hearing Screening Program. For more information, contact:

California Newborn Hearing Screening Program
1515 K St., Rm. 400
Sacramento, CA 94234-7320
916-322-5794
www.dhs.ca.gov

For immunization requirements for school and child care entry, see:

California Department of Health Services—Immunization Branch
2151 Berkeley Way, Rm. 712
Berkeley
510-540-2065
www.dhs.ca.gov

ing for your child if your doctor is unavailable when you deliver or in an urgent care situation. In a group OB/GYN practice, you typically see each member of the group at different prenatal visits. This can be somewhat disjointed (and frustrating if you prefer one doctor), but at least you are guaranteed to have met the person delivering your baby. The nature of pediatric care being what it is (unpredictable), many pediatricians practice in groups so patients can be assured of seeing *someone* in the group whenever the need for urgent care arises.

Questions to Ask a Potential Care Provider

Schedule an interview appointment with each candidate, by telephone if not in person. If a candidate objects to an interview, you don't want to see that person anyway. Here are some questions you might ask a candidate. In addition to their answers, also consider *how* they approach your questions. This can be a good indication of how they will respond to you as a patient or parent!

♦ What is your background, training, and experience?
♦ (If it is a group practice) How many doctors are in your practice, and how do you divide responsibilities? Who will I see at my regular visits? Who will deliver my baby? Under what circumstances would another member of the practice deliver my baby or see my child? Can I request appointments with you?
♦ Will nurse practitioners or physician assistants see me at my visits? (If important to you: Can I opt to see a doctor instead?)
♦ What are your opinions on: (choose any important to you)
  ✧ Use of pain medication and anesthesia in delivery
  ✧ Episiotomies
  ✧ Having support persons in the delivery room
  ✧ Birth plans
  ✧ Inducing labor
  ✧ Circumcision (in California, this is usually performed by the obstetrician if done in a hospital)
  ✧ Breastfeeding
  ✧ Immunizations
  ✧ Antibiotics
  ✧ Child-rearing philosophies in general

- Who do I call in an emergency? What is the procedure if I think I'm in labor?
- What are your after-hours policies? Is there an advice nurse available to answer questions 24/7?
- Are you available by telephone if I want to speak with you directly?
- Where do you have hospital or birthing center privileges?
- (For prenatal care providers) What experience do you have with high-risk pregnancies? How many babies have you delivered/do you deliver per year?
- (For midwives) Where and how long did you apprentice? With which doctors and hospitals are you affiliated, in case of complications? What conditions require transport? Do you have current CPR certification, and what medications and equipment do you have for emergencies?
- (For pediatric doctors) Will you come to the hospital or home to examine my baby after delivery? What tests do you do at that point? Do you offer same-day appointments for sick children? Do you have special provisions for sick children (e.g., a separate waiting room)?

In the end, your decision probably will come down to a gut feeling. You should not feel rushed or as if you are asking "stupid" questions. Having a baby is a very intimate, personal experience. You need to trust this person with your lives, and you should feel very comfortable with him or her.

How to Find a Care Provider

So now you are thinking: all those questions are great, but how do I actually find this person? We have found the most reliable sources are personal referrals—the good old word-of-mouth method. Start with friends, colleagues, and neighbors. Find out how they like their doctors or midwives. Check out our list of favorite doctors and midwives. Check with nurses, lactation consultants, and staff at your local hospital's perinatal or women's center. They regularly interact with doctors and midwives and their patients, and know which providers are good (and which are not!). Of course, once you have found a doctor or midwife for yourself, he or she will likely be able to recommend a pediatrician for your baby.

If you are not having any luck with the old-fashioned method, here are some good referral sources:

San Francisco Magazine (formerly *San Francisco Focus*)

PARENT RATING: ☆ ☆ ☆ ☆

This magazine annually publishes a list of the "best" Bay Area doctors, by type of practice. We have found that this list, while not always comprehensive, includes many popular doctors. The source for that article, Castle Connolly Medical, a New York-based research firm, has put together a book titled *Top Doctors: San Francisco Bay Area.*

Birth and Bonding Family Center

1126 Solano Ave.
Albany
510-527-2121
www.birthbonding.org

PARENT RATING: ☆ ☆ ☆ ☆

This resource center and retail store in the East Bay maintains professional listings of hospitals, doctors, and midwives based on parents' recommendations (with an East Bay focus, but some greater Bay Area listings).

Birthways

478 Santa Clara Ave., 3rd Fl.
Berkeley
510-548-0845
www.birthways.org

PARENT RATING: ☆ ☆ ☆ ☆ ☆

This grassroots, nonprofit, volunteer-supported organization maintains referral lists of hospitals, doctors, and midwives (accessible in the center or by phone). The website features classified ads for midwives.

Natural Resources

1307 Castro St.
San Francisco
415-550-2611
www.naturalresourcesonline.com

PARENT RATING: ☆ ☆ ☆ ☆ ☆

A pregnancy, childbirth, and parenting center in the Noe Valley neighborhood, this store maintains binders of information about doctors, midwives, pediatricians, and doulas (some advertising, and some consumer feedback). Although the feedback on doctors is quite dated, there are many current opinions on local midwives. If you are planning a home birth in San Francisco, this is the place to start your research.

The Nurture Center

3399 Mt. Diablo Blvd.
Lafayette
925-283-1346
www.nurturecenter.com

PARENT RATING: ☆ ☆ ☆ ☆ ☆

This Contra Costa County parenting center run by two local moms features professional listings of obstetricians and midwives.

UC Berkeley Parents Network

http://parents.berkeley.edu

PARENT RATING: ☆ ☆ ☆ ☆ ☆

This invaluable website is filled with parents' uncensored opinions about doctors, midwives, hospitals, insurance companies, and just about anything else related to parenting. Though the focus is the East Bay, parents occasionally mention resources in other parts of the Bay Area. Note: this website is scheduled to merge with the Neighborhood Parents Network website, www.parentsnet.org, by the end of 2002.

American Academy of Family Physicians

11400 Tomahawk Creek Pkwy.
Leawood, KS 66211-2672
913-906-6000
www.aafp.org

PARENT RATING: ☆ ☆ ☆ ☆

This national association of family doctors offers a searchable database of family practitioners' websites (by state), as well as a very useful website for family health information.

American Academy of Pediatrics

Attn: Pediatrician Referral Service
141 Northwest Point Blvd.
Elk Grove Village, IL 60007-1098
847-434-4000
www.aap.org

PARENT RATING: ☆ ☆ ☆ ☆

You may write this national association of pediatricians with the name of your desired geographic area and a self-addressed, stamped envelope. They will send you a list of pediatricians and/or specialists, depending on your needs. Their website features very useful articles on pediatric health.

American College of Obstetricians and Gynecologists

www.acog.com

PARENT RATING: ☆ ☆ ☆

This website provides a physician directory and health information.

www.healthgrades.com

PARENT RATING: ☆ ☆ ☆

This is an on-line national database of physicians and hospitals. You can search by geographic area, specialty, or name, and it will give you information about a doctor's education and hospital affiliations. For some (not all) doctors, you can also view the results of patient satisfaction surveys.

Your insurance plan's referral service

PARENT RATING: ☆ ☆ ☆

Most insurance plans, particularly HMOs and PPOs, have telephone or on-line referral services. The insurers won't provide subjective information, but they will let you search by objective criteria like neighborhood, specialty, and school attended.

For *midwives*, the search may be a bit more difficult. In addition to the foregoing, try the following organizations for referral lists, but bear in mind that inclusion on these lists is largely voluntary and does not reflect any kind of selection process.

California Association of Midwives

P.O. Box 460606
San Francisco, CA 94146-0606
800-829-5791
midwives@wenet.net

This is a professional organization of California midwives. For a list of midwives practicing in your area, call or e-mail.

Midwives' Alliance of North America (MANA)

4805 Lawrenceville Hwy., Ste. 116-279
Lilburn, GA 30047
888-923-6262
www.mana.org

This is a national midwives' organization; call for referrals to midwives by state.

www.birthpartners.com

This is an on-line directory of midwives and doulas run by midwives, which allows searching by zip code.

www.gentlebirth.org

This site lists South Bay midwives and other home birth resources and includes anecdotal reviews of South Bay hospitals' attitudes toward midwives and natural childbirth.

www.withchild.org

This site lists midwives, doulas, and childbirth educators around the Bay Area.

CHECKING CREDENTIALS

Once you have several candidates, narrow them down by checking their credentials with the appropriate licensing agencies. Be sure to find out whether the provider is licensed, board certified (in the case of OB/GYNs), and has no history of malpractice claims. Popularity alone provides no assurance of competence.

Medical Board of California

1426 Howe Ave.
Sacramento, CA 95825-3236
916-263-2382 (for doctors)
916-263-2393 (for LMs, the Midwifery Licensing Program)
www.medbd.ca.gov

PARENT RATING: ☆ ☆ ☆ ☆

This board can tell you: whether a doctor or LM is licensed, what school he or she attended and the year he or she graduated, whether there are any disciplinary charges pending or any completed disciplinary actions against him or her (if charges have been filed by the Board), and whether any malpractice judgments or felony criminal actions have been reported to the Board. Get a free pamphlet, *Services to Consumers from the Medical Board of California,* on how to choose a doctor or check credentials.

American Board of Medical Specialties (ABMS)

1007 Church St., Ste. 404
Evanston, IL 60201-5913
866-ASK-ABMS (phone verification)
847-491-9091
www.abms.org

PARENT RATING: ☆ ☆ ☆ ☆

This organization can tell you whether an OB is board certified (the California Medical Board does *not* have this information).

Directory of Medical Specialists

This directory is published by Who's Who (available in most public libraries).

California Board of Registered Nurses

400 R St., Ste. 4030, P.O. Box 944210
Sacramento, CA 94244-2100
916-322-3350
www.rn.ca.gov

This board licenses CNMs in California.

American College of Nurse-Midwives (ACNM)
818 Connecticut Ave., NW, Ste. 900
Washington, DC 20006
202-728-9860
www.acnm.org
This group administers board examinations for CNMs and maintains a database of CNMs searchable by zip code.

North American Registry of Midwives (NARM)
888-842-4784
www.narm.org
This group administers an international competency certification program and grants the title Certified Professional Midwife (CPM). However, note that the CPM title does *not* grant legal status to practice in California; a midwife must still pass the California board exam.

Doctors and Midwives: Survey Favorites

We hesitate to name favorite doctors, practice groups, or midwives. The criteria are often highly subjective, personal reactions can vary widely, and we don't want to create a land rush to certain providers. That said, our survey revealed some consistent favorites, and we thought we should share that information with you. Of course, the fact that a particular person is not on this list does not mean he or she is not a great care provider. As we have said, our survey was far from scientific! See the Introduction for an explanation. And remember, always check credentials with the Medical Board (see above) before selecting a doctor or midwife.

And the top picks from our survey are ...

OBSTETRICIANS

For ease of reference, we have noted the hospitals at which each doctor has privileges.

San Francisco

Karen Callen, Jane Fang, Katherine Liniecki, Fung Lam, and Donna Wiggins, MDs
3838 California St., Ste. 812
415-666-1250
California Pacific Medical Center (CPMC)

Margaret Chen, Cynthia Farner, Bernard Gore, Jordan Horowitz, Joanne Kim, and Frederica Lofquist, MDs
415-668-1010
• 3625 California St.
• 525 Spruce St.
CPMC

Elena Gates, MD
UCSF/Mt. Zion Women's Health Group
2330 Post St., Ste. 220
415-885-7788

13

Laurie Green, MD
3838 California St.
415-379-9600
CPMC

Holly Holter, MD
• 3838 California St., 415-668-1560
• 909 Hyde St., 415-673-6522
CPMC

Perinatal Services
Michael Katz, Elliott Main,
Kimberley Susan, and Tom Musci,
MDs
• San Francisco
3700 California St., 5th Fl.,
415-750-6388
• Burlingame
1783 El Camino Real
650-696-5548
CPMC and Peninsula Medical
Center
Perinatology (high-risk) services.

North Bay

Stephen Bearg and LizEllen
LaFollette, MDs
1260 S. Eliseo Dr.
Greenbrae
415-461-7800
Marin General Hospital

Brian DeMuth, MD
1000 S. Eliseo Dr.
Greenbrae
415-464-0184
Marin General

David Galland, MD
5 Bon Air Rd., Ste. 117
Larkspur
415-924-4870
Marin General

Richard Printz, MD
599 Sir Francis Drake Blvd., Ste. 202
Greenbrae
415-461-8636
Marin General

Gerald Wilner, MD
5 Bon Air Rd., Ste. 117
Larkspur
415-924-9770
Marin General

East Bay

F. Ryan Anderson, MD
909 San Ramon Valley Blvd., Ste. 214
Danville
925-820-9898
John Muir Medical Center

Monica Brar, Robert Cole, and
Stephen Wells, MDs
110 Tampico, Stes. 200, 210, and 220
Walnut Creek
925-932-7494, Monica Brar
925-935-6952, Robert Cole
925-935-5356, Stephen Wells
John Muir

John Girard, Marilyn Honegger,
James Sakamoto, and Kurt
Wharton, MDs
• Berkeley
2999 Regent Street, Ste. 701,
510-845-4200
• Orinda
12 Camino Encinas, Ste. 15,
925-254-9000
Alta Bates Medical Center

Elizabeth Kanwit and Katarina
Lanner-Cusin, MDs
2915 Telegraph Ave., Ste. 200
Berkeley
510-845-8047
Alta Bates

14

Hank Streitfeld, MD
3000 Colby St., Ste. 303
Berkeley
510-644-0110
Alta Bates

South Bay

Maurice Druzin, MD
Chief of Maternal-Fetal Medicine
and Obstetrics
Lucile Packard Children's Hospital
at Stanford, Clinic A
725 Welch Rd.
Palo Alto
650-725-8623 or 650-498-4069

Nancy Mason, MD
1101 Welch Rd.
Palo Alto
650-329-1293
Stanford Medical Center

Kathryn Matthews, MD
1101 Welch Rd.
Palo Alto
650-328-5141
Stanford

Menlo Medical Clinic
1300 Crane St.
Menlo Park
650-498-6500
www-med.stanford.edu/shs/
PrimaryCare/menlo.html
Stanford

Palo Alto Medical Foundation, Palo Alto Clinic
795 El Camino Real
Palo Alto
650-321-4121
www.pamf.org
Stanford

Peninsula Women's Health and Medical Group
1828 El Camino Real, Ste. 805
Burlingame
650-692-3818
Peninsula Medical Center

Jagdip Powar, MD
1101 Welch Rd., Ste. A-7
Palo Alto
650-328-1420
Stanford

Women's Health Medical Group, Portola Valley Center
(affiliated with Palo Alto Medical
Foundation)
3250 Alpine Rd.
Portola Valley
650-851-6650
Stanford

MIDWIVES

Where it is not obvious, we have
noted whether the midwife offers
home birth, hospital birth, or both.

San Francisco

Bay Area Home Birth Collective
415-273-5185

Maria Iorillo, LM, CPM
526 Liberty St.
415-285-9233
Home birth

Judith Loebensteen-Tinkelenberg, CNM
See the listing under "Bay Area Birth
Centers"—Sage Femme Midwifery
Service.

Angelika Nugent, LM, CPM
1447 34th Ave., 415-242-0517
Home birth

UCSF Faculty OB/GYN Group

400 Parnassus St.
415-353-2223
Hospital practice includes CNMs.

North Bay

Circle of Life Midwifery Center

145 Bolinas Rd.
Fairfax
415-456-2961
Home birth or birthing center

East Bay

Bay Area Home Birth Collective

415-273-5185

Hsiu-Li (Sho-Li) Cheng, CNM

East Bay Perinatal Medical
Associates
350 30th St., Ste. 205
Oakland
510-832-2388
Summit Medical Center

Beah Haber and Jennifer Hess, CNMs

1393 Santa Rita Rd., Ste. C
Pleasanton
925-449-7666
Home birth or birthing center

Lindy Johnson, CNM

2107 Dwight Way, Ste. 102
Berkeley
510-644-0104
Alta Bates Medical Center

South Bay

Kathryn Newburn, CNM

301 Sanchez Ave.
Burlingame
650-347-6943
Home birth

Midwifery Service at Stanford

Linda Walsh, CNM, Director
Stanford Medical Center-OB/GYN
300 Pasteur Dr.
Stanford
800-381-2155

PEDIATRIC DOCTORS

Our survey could not possibly include every wonderful pediatric doctor in the Bay Area, so we advise not limiting your search to those listed here!

San Francisco

Jane Anderson and William DeGoff, MDs

UCSF/Mt.Zion Pediatric Primary
Practice
2330 Post St., Ste. 320
415-885-7478

Eileen Aicardi, Martin Ernster, William Gonda, Robert Patton, John Piel, and Mary Piel, MDs

- San Francisco
  3641 California St., 415-668-0888
- Orinda
  61 Camino Alto, 415-388-6303

Brock Bernsten, Marta Kozinski, Steven Rosenbaum, Robert Saffa, and Carolyn Wright, MDs

- San Francisco
  3838 California St., Ste. 111,
  415-666-1860
- Mill Valley
  61 Camino Alto, Ste. 105,
  415-383-0918

Katherine Crosby, Susan Dab, Gary Gin, Alan Johnson, Richard Leonards, and Margaret Miller, MDs
- San Francisco
  525 Spruce St., 415-668-8900
- Tiburon
  21 Main St., 415-435-3154

Gianna Frazee and James Schwanke, MDs
3700 24th St.
415-641-1019

Martin Fung, Colleen Halloran, Mitchell Sollod, and Nanci Tucker, MDs
Stonestown Medical Building
595 Buckingham Way, Ste. 355
415-566-2727

Sonja Huie and Diana Tang, MDs
3905 Sacramento St.
415-379-6700

Daniel Kelly, MD, Barry Rostek, DO, and William Solomon, MD
45 Castro St., Ste. 232
415-565-6810

Martha Taylor, MD
UCSF Pediatric Primary Care Clinic
400 Parnassus St.
415-476-4988

North Bay

See above for San Francisco practices with Marin offices.

Melissa Congdon, Richard Dow and Michael Harris, MDs
1206 Strawberry Village
Mill Valley
415-388-3364

John Harvey, Erin Heath, Jan Maisel, and Stewart Rowe, MDs
- Greenbrae
  599 Sir Francis Drake Blvd.,
  415-461-0440
- Novato
  1615 Hill Rd., Ste. 11, 415-892-0965

Martin Joffee, Kathryn Sexton, and Katrina Urbach, MDs
- Greenbrae
  1000 S. Eliseo Dr., Ste. 1-A,
  415-461-5436
- Novato
  505A San Marin Dr., Ste. 260,
  415-898-5437

Scott Werner, MD
1100 S. Eliseo Dr., Ste. 106
Greenbrae
415-461-8828

East Bay

Myles Bruce Abbott, Marcia Charles-Mo, Mary Jones, and Richard Oken, MDs
- Berkeley
  2999 Regent St., Ste. 325,
  510-841-6451
- Orinda
  96 Davis Rd., Ste. 2, 925-254-9203

Ralph Berberich, Steve Kowaleski, and Petra Landman, MDs
Pediatric Medical Group
2320 Woolsey St., Ste. 301
Berkeley
510-849-1744

Philip Chamberlain, Seymour Harris, Kimberly Mar, and Lloyd Takao, MDs
4 Country Club Plaza
Orinda
925-254-9500

James Cuthbertson, Annemary Franks, Howard Gruber, and Olivia Lang, MDs
Berkeley Pediatrics
1650 Walnut St.
Berkeley
510-848-2566

Bruce Gach, MD
- Livermore
  1171 Murrieta Blvd., Ste. 8,
  925-455-5050
- Pleasanton
  5575 W. Las Positas, Ste. 340,
  925-847-9777

Juliet Patricia Granberg, MD
2915 Telegraph Ave.
Berkeley
510-843-4077

Colleen Hogan and Tracy Trotter, MDs
San Ramon Valley Primary Care
Medical Group
200 Porter Dr., Ste. 300
San Ramon
925-838-6511

Montgomery Kong, MD
1822 San Miguel Dr.
Walnut Creek
925-934-9339

Andrew Nash, Margaret Saltzstein, and Lynne Whyte, MDs
Muir Primary Care
- Alamo
  1505 St. Alphonsus Way
- San Ramon
  5201 N. Canyon Rd., 925-837-4225

Frederick Osborne, MD
4725 First St., Ste. 100
Pleasanton
925-462-7060

Daniel Robbins, MD
930 Dewing Ave.
Lafayette
925-284-1800

South Bay

Bay Area Pediatric Medical Group
www.bayareapediatrics.com
- Belmont
  2100 Carlmont Dr., Ste. 2,
  650-591-3937
- Daly City
  1800 Sullivan Ave., Ste. 202,
  650-756-4200
- Daly City
  1500 Southgate Ave., Ste. 104,
  650-992-4200
- San Mateo
  29 Baywood Ave., Ste. 1, 650-343-4200

Donna Chaet and Penny Loeb, MDs
842 Altos Oaks Dr.
Los Altos
650-940-7177

Alger Chapman, MD
ABC Pediatrics
50 S. San Mateo Dr., Ste. 260
San Mateo
650-579-6500

Brian Drucker and Christine Halaburka, MDs
250 Blossom Hill Rd.
Los Gatos
408-354-7910

Remington Fong, Kim Harvey, Annette Hwang, and Judith Murphy, MDs
1101 Welch Rd., Ste. A-1
Palo Alto
650-329-0300

18

Albert Kasuga, MD
Peninsula Pediatric Medical Group
1720 El Camino Real, Ste. 205
Burlingame
650-259-5050

Menlo Medical Clinic
Nancy Adelman and James Cisco, MDs
1300 Crane St.
Menlo Park
650-498-6500
www-med.stanford.edu/shs/
PrimaryCare/menlo.html

Palo Alto Medical Foundation
795 El Camino Real
Palo Alto
650-853-2992
www.pamf.org

Pediatric Dentists

Sooner or later, you will have to make that much-feared first dental appointment. The American Academy of Pediatrics recommends that children get regular dental checkups after age three or when all twenty baby teeth have come in. If possible, see a pediatric dentist, who has an additional two to three years of training in treating children. You can find a referral to a pediatric dentist either through the American Dental Association (www.ada.org) or the American Academy of Pediatric Dentistry (www.aapd.org), both of which have useful websites with lots of publications and searchable databases of pediatric dentists.

Health Care Coverage When You Cannot Afford It

Pregnant and uninsured? The State of California administers several programs for families having difficulty getting health insurance:

Access for Infants and Mothers (AIM)
P.O. Box 15248
Los Angeles, CA 90015
800-433-2611
www.mrmib.ca.gov

This program provides low-cost health insurance coverage to low- to moderate-income pregnant women and their families (who do not qualify for Medi-Cal). It covers mother during pregnancy, childbirth, and sixty days postpartum, and covers child from birth to age 2. After a low-cost contribution, you receive health care coverage from one of nine participating health plans. It is administered by the California Managed Risk Medical Insurance Board.

Healthy Families Program (HFP)

888-747-1222

www.mrmib.ca.gov or
www.healthyfamilies.ca.gov

This program provides low-cost health, dental, and vision coverage for children in low-wage families who do not qualify for Medi-Cal. In 2001, premiums were $4-9 per child per month (with a maximum of $27 per family per month). There is a choice of several insurance plans.

Major Risk Medical Insurance Program (MRMIP)

800-289-6574

www.mrmib.ca.gov

By contracting with six insurance plans, this program provides health insurance to those who are unable to obtain coverage in the individual health insurance market. Participants contribute to the premiums.

Medi-Cal

916-657-1460

www.medi-cal.ca.gov

California's version of the U.S. Government's Medicaid program, eligibility depends on income and family size. Medical, dental, and vision care are provided at no cost. Visit or call your local county's department of health, human, or social services.

Child Health and Disability Prevention Program (CHDP)

California Department of Health Services

916-654-0364

www.dhs.ca.gov

This program provides regular check-ups, immunizations, and specialist referrals to children in families meeting certain financial eligibility guidelines. Every California local health department has a CHDP program. For more information, contact your county health department or the California Department of Health Services.

County hospitals and health services also run low-cost clinics. Check with your local county.

Choosing Where You Will Deliver

From hospitals to birthing centers to home birth, the Bay Area offers many delivery options.

HOSPITALS

Forty hospitals in the Bay Area deliver babies. But don't be overwhelmed. Use the following list to find a nearby hospital offering the services you want. Within the list you'll find hospitals that received consistent high praise from the Bay Area parents we surveyed, designated with parent comments. If you're deciding between a few hospitals, *be sure* to take a tour to see for yourself and ask questions, and check the following key attributes:

Problems with Managed Care Health Insurance?

Is your HMO giving you a hard time? California has an innovative new program to help patients deal with managed health care. The state created the Department of Managed Health Care (DMHC) in January 2000 to "ensure high quality prevention and health care for Californians enrolled in managed care plans." The DMHC is charged with licensing managed health plans, enforcing quality of care laws, educating the public on health care rights, providing an annual report card on quality of care under managed care, and implementing a third-party review system for patient grievances and coverage disputes. Contact:

Department of Managed Health Care
980 Ninth St., Ste. 500
Sacramento, CA 95814-2725
888-HMO-2219 (consumer HMO complaints)
916-322-2078 (general)
www.dmhc.ca.gov

Location. You don't want to be stuck on a bridge or in a tunnel delivering your baby. On the other hand, many suburbanites bypass more convenient hospitals to travel to San Francisco's California Pacific Medical Center (CPMC) because of the highly touted doctors and the Level III nursery.

Level of neonatal intensive care. Hospital nurseries are classified as either Level I, II, or III (according to the American Academy of Pediatrics and the American College of Obstetrics and Gynecology). A Level I nursery is for healthy newborns. A Level II nursery is an intermediate care or "special care" nursery for premature or ill infants. A Level III neonatal intensive care unit (NICU) admits more serious cases (from other hospitals as well) who can't be cared for in the other two types of nurseries. In any facility, look for 24/7 coverage by perinatologists (OBs with specialized training in high-risk pregnancies and deliveries) and neonatologists (pediatricians specializing in caring for sick newborns).

Who practices there? No surprise—highly rated doctors seem to congregate at certain highly rated (generally private or university-run) hospitals. Compare our list of doctors to the list of hospitals. (That does not mean there are not some great doctors at other hospitals.)

Private postpartum rooms. This may seem like a petty concern. But think about spending the most intimate, physically uncomfortable forty-eight hours of your life with a total stranger and her family (not to mention two screaming newborns) and then take our advice: if you can afford it, get a private room! Sometimes this means paying extra if your insurance does not cover it. You are not going to get much sleep at home during the first few weeks postpartum, so try to get as much as possible at the hospital.

Accreditation and awards. The Joint Commission on Accreditation of Healthcare Organizations (JCAHO) evaluates and accredits U.S. hospitals and other health care organizations. A JCAHO accreditation means that the hospital meets certain performance standards. All of the hospitals listed below were accredited as of 2001. Also, an independent organization, HCIA-Sachs, annually publishes a list of the "100 Top Hospitals" nationally. See www.100tophospitals.com. We've noted the Bay Area hospitals making the grade in recent years. However, making this list depends on the entire hospital, not just the labor and delivery department.

Other amenities. A Jacuzzi tub in the labor and delivery room sounds nice, but like us, you may be too busy during labor to remember it's even there. More important to your husband or partner may be a cot for him or her to spend the night. Most hospitals allow a husband or partner to spend the night in a private room, but not in a semiprivate one. Note that some hospitals do not allow children, even siblings. Also, hospitals are generally flexible about having support people in the delivery room, but if you absolutely must have your entire extended family in the delivery room filming the event, you may want to check the hospital's policy.

The following list provides facts and figures about each hospital, largely supplied by the hospitals themselves. In addition to the key attributes identified above, the list also includes the following information:

Type of hospital: This includes each hospital's size, ownership (private or public), and any affiliation with large health care systems, HMOs, or universities. Bear in mind that teaching hospitals are just that; although they are known for top-notch research, you may work with interns and residents (though supervised).

Number of births annually: All figures are from 2001, unless noted.

Cesarean section rate: A higher rate of cesarean or "C"-sections does not necessarily indicate poor care. Indeed, many of the best hospitals have higher C-section rates simply because they attract more high-risk patients. If you are looking for a less medically managed orientation, however, be sure to ask about attitudes toward C-sections and VBACs (vaginal birth after cesareans). Your care provider is the place to start this discussion.

Rooms: An LDR (labor, delivery, and recovery) room is the modern maternity ward standard. It means you will labor, deliver, and spend your initial recovery in the same room. This is very convenient, considering you won't be able to walk if you have an epidural. (Some hospitals have separate ORs or C-section suites for C-section deliveries.) In an LDRP (LDR plus postpartum) room, you'll also spend the rest of your visit in the same room. This is even more convenient, but most hospitals don't have LDRPs. To facilitate early breastfeeding and mother-baby bonding, most hospitals today allow (and encourage) healthy moms to keep their healthy babies in their rooms ("rooming-in"), rather than whisking them away to the nursery. You may want to take advantage of the nursery to get some shut-eye, however! Since every hospital responding to our survey encouraged rooming-in, we did not include it as a separate item in our list.

Are midwives on staff? What percentage of deliveries do midwives perform? If having a midwife deliver your baby is important to you, find a hospital that has midwives on staff or allows them privileges. Some hospitals have lots of experienced midwives; others don't allow them at all.

Breastfeeding rate: Many hospitals do not keep figures on the number of women breastfeeding (or intending to breastfeed, if their milk has not come in) upon discharge from the hospital. We've given you the hospital-supplied estimates, if no hard figures were available.

Perinatal classes: Most hospitals offer classes for expectant and new parents ("perinatal classes"). We recommend you take a newborn care class, a breastfeeding class, a childbirth preparation class, and an infant CPR class, at the minimum. See additional resources for perinatal classes after the hospital list.

San Francisco Hospitals

California Pacific Medical Center (CPMC)
3700 California St.
415-600-6000
415-600-BABY (Newborn Connections, 3698 California St.)
www.cpmc.org

Type: Large, private, nonprofit medical center and Sutter Health affiliate. Level III nursery.

Births and C-section rate: 5,448; 24%

Rooms: 19 LDR rooms; 50 (of 54) postpartum rooms are private.

Midwives on staff: Yes. Midwives perform less than 10% of deliveries.

Breastfeeding: 93%

Perinatal classes: Healthy pregnancy, preterm labor, childbirth preparation, mindfulness-based pain reduction, multiples, newborn parenting and breastfeeding, sibling preparation, infant massage, and infant CPR.

Amenities: CPMC has perinatologists and neonatologists on staff and features a prenatal diagnosis and genetic counseling program and an antenatal testing center. The hospital recently opened a remodeled postpartum care floor with an additional nursery.

PARENT RATING: ☆ ☆ ☆ ☆ ☆
CPMC is regarded as the leading private hospital in San Francisco, and parents gave CPMC universally excellent reviews for doctors and advanced care. The labor and delivery nurses were praised as "professional" and "top notch." Parents also love the Newborn Connections center with its myriad classes, support groups, and lactation consultants. In post partum care, the nurses received reviews ranging from "I felt well taken care of," "fabulous," and "orderly," to "hit or miss." Some recent patients noted a decline in numbers of postpartum nurses and level of responsiveness since several years ago. The postpartum nursing shortage may be offset by the lactation center and excellent labor and delivery nurses.

Kaiser Permanente San Francisco Medical Center
2425 Geary Blvd.
415-833-2000
415-833-4120 (classes, tours)
www.kaiserpermanente.org

Type: Large, private, nonprofit HMO. Must be a Kaiser HMO member to deliver at a Kaiser hospital. Level III nursery.

Births and C-section rate: 2500; 21%

Rooms: 8 LDR rooms. All but one postpartum room is private

Midwives on staff: No

Breastfeeding: Figure not available, but hospital promotes breastfeeding.

Perinatal classes: Pregnancy, childbirth preparation, breastfeeding, parenting, expectant fathers, sibling preparation, infant CPR, and infant massage.

Amenities: Kaiser Permanente is a group practice HMO, and the largest nonprofit HMO in the U.S. Kaiser-SF also serves many of Kaiser's Marin patients, as there is no Kaiser hospital delivering babies in Marin.

St. Luke's Hospital
3555 Cesar Chavez St.
415-647-8600
415-626-BABY (maternity services, education, and tours)
www.stlukes-sf.org

Type: Private, nonprofit hospital. Level II nursery.

Births and C-section rate: 1,100; 13%

Rooms: 3 LDR rooms; 3 labor rooms; 2 ORs; 1 recovery room; 6 (of 28) postpartum rooms are private.

Midwives on staff: Yes. Midwives perform 35% of deliveries.

Breastfeeding: 75%

Perinatal classes: Childbirth preparation, breastfeeding, well-baby care, and infant CPR. Classes and materials are also available in Spanish.

Amenities: St. Luke's serves all of San Francisco, but primarily residents from the Mission, Bernal Heights, Bayview Hunters Point, Excelsior, Ingleside, Glen Park, and Noe Valley neighborhoods. There is 24/7 neonatologist coverage, as well as a breastfeeding center. Staff is multilingual.

San Francisco General Hospital
1001 Potrero Ave.
415-206-8000
415-206-5302 (Women's Health Center)
www.dph.sf.ca.us/chn/SFGH

Type: Large public hospital run by the City and County of San Francisco. Level III nursery.

Births and C-section rate: Not available.

Rooms: 7 labor and delivery rooms.

Midwives on staff: Not available.

Breastfeeding: Figure not available.

Perinatal classes: Classes are open only to Department of Public Health patients.

Amenities: S.F. General is a public hospital serving all patients needing emergency services regardless of their ability to pay. General services are available to all county residents. It is a teaching hospital for UCSF and a state-designated trauma center.

Seton Medical Center
1900 Sullivan Ave.
Daly City
650-992-4000
650-992-6435 (classes)
www.dochs.org

Type: Private, nonprofit medical center run by Daughters of Charity Health System. Level II nursery.

Births and C-section rate: 1,128; 18%

Rooms: 5 LDR rooms; 2 C-section rooms. No private postpartum rooms, but most are private rooms if ward is not full.

Midwives on staff: No.

Breastfeeding: About 90%

Perinatal classes: Childbirth preparation, breastfeeding, baby care, parenting, women's health issues, post-partum care, and infant CPR.

Amenities: Seton's nursery is staffed by San Francisco Neonatology Services. Before leaving the hospital, parents attend a mom and baby care class.

University of California at San Francisco Medical Center (UCSF)

505 Parnassus St.
415-476-1000
415-353-1787 (Birth Center)
415-353-2667 (classes and tours, Women's Center, 2356 Sutter St.)
415-476-1817 (CPR classes)
www.ucsf.edu

Type: Large state university hospital. Level III nursery.

Births and C-section rate: 1,965 (2000); 15%

Rooms: 6 LDR rooms. All 22 (of 22) postpartum rooms are private.
Midwives on staff: Yes.
Breastfeeding: 95%

Perinatal classes: Pregnancy, child-birth preparation, breastfeeding, parenting, baby care, infant health, and infant CPR.

Amenities: Some of the rooms feature city views. UCSF's Women's Center offers Great Expectations classes, breast pump rentals and sales, and a lending library. UCSF is also home to many highly regarded groups of doctors, including the members of its OB-GYN department, its reproductive endocrinologists specializing in fertility treatments, and its pediatric surgeons and anesthesiologists. UCSF is Northern California's only nationally designated Center of Excellence in Women's Health.

PARENT RATING: ☆ ☆ ☆ ☆ ☆
UCSF—one of the leading academic hospitals on the West Coast—garnered high praise from parents, particularly for C-sections and high-risk deliveries, as well as pediatrics. Patients noted no decline in service since the UCSF/Stanford merger collapsed several years ago. Patients found the nurses "particularly wonderful," and the level of care excellent. Several patients who were transferred to UCSF after attempting home birth reported that the hospital staff was open to their preference for home birth.

North Bay Hospitals

Kaiser Permanente Santa Rosa Medical Center

401 Bicentennial Way
Santa Rosa
707-571-4000
707-571-4167 (classes)
www.kaiserpermanente.org

Type: Large, private, nonprofit HMO. Level II nursery.

Births and C-section rate: 1,561; 24%

Rooms: 9 LDRP rooms; 1 OR dedicated for labor and delivery. All 14 (of 14) postpartum rooms are semi-private.
Midwives on staff: Yes. They perform all low-risk deliveries 8 a.m.-6 p.m.
Breastfeeding: 88%

Perinatal classes: Childbirth preparation, breastfeeding, and sibling preparation.

Amenities: Kaiser Santa Rosa is the only Kaiser hospital delivering babies in the North Bay.

Marin General Hospital

250 Bon Air Rd.
Greenbrae
415-925-7000
415-925-7450 (classes)
www.maringeneral.sutterhealth.org

Type: District hospital (acute-care facility) owned by the publicly elected Marin Healthcare District. A Sutter Health affiliate. Level II nursery.

Births and C-section rate: 1,808; 26%

Rooms: 8 LDR rooms; 1 recovery room. 16 (of 22) postpartum rooms are private.

Midwives on staff: Yes. Midwives perform 33% of all deliveries.

Breastfeeding: 94%+

Perinatal classes: A five-week series in prenatal education, including parenting, baby safety, breast and bottle feeding, labor and delivery, C-sections, and postpartum care.

Amenities: The labor and delivery rooms were renovated recently and are extremely spacious. Some rooms feature Mt. Tamalpais views. The hospital offers an on-site lactation center and a doula service, and is a state-designated trauma center.

PARENT RATING: ☆ ☆ ☆ ☆

Patients praised the hospital's labor and delivery facilities and nurses, while some cautioned that the postpartum care was "not as great as expected."

Petaluma Valley Hospital

400 N. McDowell Blvd.
Petaluma
707-778-1111
707-778-2502 (classes)
www.stjosephhealth.org

Type: Small, private, nonprofit hospital run by the St. Joseph Health System. No intensive care nursery (ICN).

Births and C-section rate: 580; 16%

Rooms: 3 LDR rooms. All 5 postpartum rooms are semiprivate, but the staff tries to give patients private rooms whenever possible.

Midwives on staff: Yes. Midwives perform 20% of all deliveries.

Breastfeeding: 90%

Perinatal classes: Childbirth preparation, childbirth refresher, and sibling preparation.

Amenities: Petaluma Valley's sister hospital is Santa Rosa Memorial, home of a Level II Intensive Care Nursery run by UCSF. Breast pump rentals are available. Rooms feature sleeping accommodations for significant others.

St. Helena Hospital and Health Center

650 Sanitarium Rd.
Deer Park
707-963-3611
707-963-1912 (classes, tours)
www.sthelenahospital.org

Type: Small, private, nonprofit hospital run by Adventist Health System. Level I nursery.

Births and C-section rate: 382; 12%

Rooms: 6 LDRP rooms. All are private.

Midwives on staff: Yes. Midwives perform 25% of all deliveries.

Breastfeeding: 90%

Perinatal classes: Most classes are free and cover topics including pregnancy, childbirth preparation, breastfeeding, newborn care, sibling preparation, and infant CPR.

Amenities: St. Helena Hospital features views of Napa Valley. Every mother who lives in Napa County receives a postpartum home visit, regardless of her ability to pay. There is a child safety seat technician on staff.

Santa Rosa Memorial Hospital

1165 Montgomery Dr.
Santa Rosa
707-546-3210
707-571-7011 (classes, tours)
www.stjosephhealth.org

Type: Private, nonprofit, acute-care hospital run by the St. Joseph Health System. Level II nursery.

Births and C-section rate: 1,554; 21%

Rooms: 7 LDR rooms. 5 (of 10) postpartum rooms are private.

Midwives on staff: Yes. Midwives perform 14% of all deliveries.

Breastfeeding: 95%

Perinatal classes: Classes include pregnancy, breastfeeding, childbirth preparation, newborn care, sibling preparation, infant CPR, and infant massage.

Amenities: Santa Rosa Hospital's ICN is affiliated with UCSF and is expected to upgrade to Level III. Lactation consultants are on staff.

Sutter Medical Center Santa Rosa

3325 Chanate Rd.
Santa Rosa
707-576-4600
707-576-4800 (Women's Health Resource Center)
www.sutterhealth.org

Type: Private, nonprofit medical center and Sutter Health affiliate. Level III nursery.

Births and C-section rate: 4,800; 18%

Rooms: 9 LDR rooms. 7 (of 18) postpartum rooms are private.

Midwives on staff: Yes. Midwives perform 15-20% of deliveries.

Breastfeeding: Figure not available.

Perinatal classes: Pregnancy, childbirth preparation, breastfeeding, infant care, multiples, sibling preparation, and infant CPR. Classes are also taught in Spanish.

Amenities: The Women's Health Resource Center offers classes, lactation consultation, and breast pump rentals.

East Bay Hospitals

Alta Bates Medical Center

2450 Ashby Ave.
Berkeley
510-204-4444
510-204-1334 (classes, tours)
510-204-1507 (perinatal center)
www.altabates.com
www.babies.sutterhealth.org

Type: Large, private, nonprofit hospital and Sutter Health affiliate. Level III nursery.

Births and C-section rate: 7,600; 21%

Rooms: 24 LDR rooms. 18 private postpartum rooms.

Midwives on staff: No.

Breastfeeding: 85%

Perinatal classes: Healthy pregnancy, childbirth preparation, pain management, breastfeeding, baby care, sibling preparation, father preparation, and infant CPR.

Amenities: Alta Bates recently merged with Summit Medical Center and says it delivers "more babies than any other hospital in California." The hospital also provides labor and delivery facilities for Kaiser's Oakland and Richmond patients (those Kaiser sites don't do deliveries anymore). The facility offers 24/7 coverage by perinatologists and neonatologists, and a respected in vitro fertilization program. A postpartum nurse follows up with a telephone call to the patient.

PARENT RATING: ☆ ☆ ☆ ☆ ☆

Parents responding to our survey gave Alta Bates very positive reviews as a "fantastic" facility, agreeing that the hospital has the reputation as "the best" in the East Bay, with particularly excellent high risk care. Most found the labor and delivery doctors and nurses to be "superb," "caring," and "professional." Those with difficult deliveries seemed to get the best care. One patient saw a lactation consultant in the hospital who was "excellent." Unfortunately (and this is echoed with respect to other hospitals as well) postpartum nurses are reportedly overworked and the hospital somewhat understaffed. Overall, parents advised shelling out the extra money for the quiet of a private room, being proactive with the nursing staff, and hiring a doula or other experienced support person as an advocate and teacher in the hospital.

Contra Costa Regional Medical Center

2500 Alhambra Ave.
Martinez
925-370-5000
925-370-5200 (classes)
www.co.contra-costa.ca.us

Type: Public hospital run by Contra Costa County. A teaching hospital for UC Davis Medical School. Level II nursery.

Births and C-section rate: 1,560; 19%

Rooms: 8 LDR rooms. Postpartum rooms are semiprivate.

Midwives on staff: No.

Breastfeeding: 85%

Perinatal classes: Childbirth preparation and breastfeeding classes in English and Spanish.

Amenities: Contra Costa Medical Center was completely rebuilt and reopened in January 1998. The majority of patients have health coverage through public sources. Lactation educators are on staff.

Doctors Medical Center

2000 Vale Rd.
San Pablo
510-970-5000
www.tenethealth.com/
pinole&sanpablo

Type: For-profit hospital. Part of Tenet Health Systems. Levels I and II nurseries.

Births and C-section rate: About 60 births per month.

Rooms: 7 LDR rooms (including 2 large remodeled birthing rooms). 9 private postpartum rooms.

Midwives on staff: Not available.

Breastfeeding: Figure not available.

Perinatal classes: Classes are open only to current patients of affiliated physicians and include basic childbirth preparation, breastfeeding, and newborn care topics.

Amenities: The maternity ward was remodeled three years ago. Recently purchased by for-profit Tenet Health Systems, the hospital is in the process of revamping its program.

Eden Medical Center

20103 Lake Chabot Rd.
Castro Valley
510-537-1234
510-727-2715 (classes, tours)
www.edenmedcenter.org

Type: Private, nonprofit hospital and Sutter Health affiliate. Level II nursery.

Births and C-section rate: 1,135; 24%

Rooms: 3 LDR rooms; 2 labor rooms; 1 C-section room; 3-bed recovery room; 2 (of 13) postpartum rooms are private.

Midwives on staff: None on staff. One midwife works with an affiliated physician.

Breastfeeding: 85%

Perinatal classes: In addition to a monthly "Pregnancy Forum," the hospital offers classes on childbirth preparation, breastfeeding, baby care, and sibling preparation.

Amenities: Eden is a state-designated trauma center. Cots are available for spouses/partners. The director of the nursery is a neonatologist. Newborns requiring advanced care are usually sent to Alta Bates (a Sutter affiliate). A lactation consultant is on staff.

Highland Hospital (Alameda County Medical Center)

1411 E. 31st St.
Oakland
510-437-4800
888-774-BABY (Bright Beginnings Family Birthing Center, classes, tours)
www.acmedctr.org

Type: Public hospital owned by Alameda County. Level II nursery.

Births and C-section rate: 1,281; 20%

Rooms: 6 LDR rooms; 1 C-section OR. All postpartum rooms are semi-private.

Midwives on staff: Yes (24-hour coverage). Midwives perform 54% of deliveries.

Breastfeeding: 86%

Perinatal classes: Classes are open only to current patients and include prenatal care, breastfeeding, baby care, and car seat safety.

Amenities: Highland Hospital is part of the Alameda County Medical Center, serving the medically indigent population of the county regardless of their ability to pay. It is a state-designated trauma center. The spouse/partner may stay overnight on a cot in the patient's room if space is available. A free doula program is offered (student doulas in training). They provide breastfeeding counselors to assist patients.

John Muir Medical Center

1601 Ygnacio Valley Rd.
Walnut Creek
925-939-3000
925-941-7900 (classes, Women's Health Center, 1656 N. California Blvd., Walnut Creek)
www.johnmuirmtdiablo.com

Type: Large, private, nonprofit acute-care medical center. Part of the John Muir/Mt. Diablo Health System. Level III nursery.

Births and C-section rate: 3,500; 18%

Rooms: 10 LDR rooms; 2 ORs; 2 recovery rooms; 2 testing rooms. All 24 (of 24) postpartum rooms are private. 15 antepartum high-risk rooms.

Midwives on staff: No.

Breastfeeding: 94%+

Perinatal classes: Pregnancy, childbirth preparation, newborn care and breastfeeding, sibling preparation, father preparation, multiples, grandparenting, car seat safety, infertility, parenting, and infant CPR.

Amenities: The hospital features a Level III nursery, 24/7 coverage by in-house perinatologists and neonatologists, and lactation consultants on staff for inpatient consultation. The New Women's Health Center in downtown Walnut Creek offers classes, support groups, exercise programs, and a lactation center. Each new mother receives a home visit from a RN. The hospital is the only state-designated trauma center for Contra Costa County.

PARENT RATING: ☆ ☆ ☆ ☆

Parents praised John Muir as being a comfortable place to deliver—with nice amenities and less of a crowd than bigger hospitals. High-risk patients favored John Muir over other Contra Costa County hospitals.

Kaiser Permanente Hayward Medical Center

27400 Hesperian Blvd.
Hayward
510-784-4000
510-784-4531 (classes)
www.haykaiser.org

Type: Large, private, nonprofit HMO. Level III nursery.

Births and C-section rate: About 3,200; 16%

Rooms: 2 ABC rooms (alternative birth center, meaning labor, delivery, and sometimes recovery); 9 labor rooms. All postpartum rooms are semiprivate.

Midwives on staff: Yes. Midwives perform all low-risk deliveries and are available 24/7.

Breastfeeding: 92%

Perinatal classes: Free classes include fitness and nutrition, childbirth preparation, breastfeeding, newborn care, and parenting. Some classes are provided in Spanish.

Amenities: Kaiser Hayward has a perinatologist and lactation consultants. Patients who check out of the hospital early (before 48 or 96 hours) may go to a postpartum care center. A weekend pediatric clinic is available to Kaiser members. Remodel plans include 10 LDRs. The hospital was the first California Kaiser Permanente facility to be designated Baby-Friendly™ by the World Health Organization, United Nations Children's Fund, and Baby-Friendly™ USA in 2001.

Kaiser Permanente Vallejo Medical Center

975 Sereno Dr.
Vallejo
369-651-1000
369-651-2692 (classes)
www.kaiserpermanente.org

Type: Large, private, nonprofit HMO. Level I nursery.

Births and C-section rate: About 2,400.

Rooms: 10 LDR rooms. 12 (of 22) postpartum rooms are private.

Midwives on staff: Yes (one). She handles normal deliveries only.

Breastfeeding: 70%

Perinatal classes: Classes include childbirth preparation, breastfeeding, and newborn care.

Amenities: Newborns requiring advanced care are transported from Vallejo to Walnut Creek (a Level III nursery).

Kaiser Permanente Walnut Creek Medical Center

1425 S. Main St.
Walnut Creek
925-295-4000
925-295-4040 (classes)
www.kaiserpermanente.org

Type: Large, private, nonprofit HMO. Level III nursery.

Births and C-section rate: 3,606; 23%

Rooms: 11 LDR rooms. 20 (of 26) postpartum rooms are private.

Midwives on staff: Yes. Midwives handle 52% of deliveries and most low-risk deliveries.

Breastfeeding: 90%

Perinatal classes: This Kaiser hospital offers the most extensive array of classes of any of the Kaiser facilities in the East Bay, including many free classes. Classes include pregnancy, childbirth preparation, breastfeeding, newborn care, sibling preparation, multiples, and premature infant development.

Amenities: Kaiser Walnut Creek's labor and delivery floor is only three years old. Sleep chairs for significant others are available in labor and delivery and some postpartum rooms. Lactation educators are on site every day.

St. Rose Hospital

27200 Calaroga Ave.
Hayward
510-264-4000
510-264-4044 (classes)
www.strosehospital.org

Type: Private, nonprofit acute-care hospital. Part of the Via Christi Health System. Level I nursery.

Births and C-section rate: 1,416 (1999); 17.7%

Rooms: 9 LDRP rooms. 2 ORs. 9 (of 11) postpartum rooms are private.

Midwives on staff: One midwife on staff.

Breastfeeding: 80-85%

Perinatal classes: Natural family planning, childbirth preparation, infant care, sibling preparation, and infant massage.

Amenities: St. Rose was founded by an order of Catholic nuns and retains a Christian orientation (according to its website). A larger VIP suite is available on a first-come, first-served basis. A Jacuzzi tub is also available.

San Ramon Regional Medical Center

6001 Norris Canyon Rd.
San Ramon
925-275-9200
925-275-8230 (classes, tours)
www.sanramonmedctr.com

Type: Private acute-care medical center. Part of Tenet Health Systems. Level II nursery.

Births and C-section rate: 814; C-section rate not available.

Rooms: 10 LDRP rooms. 2 ORs. All 18 (of 18) postpartum rooms are private.

Midwives on staff: No.

Breastfeeding: 98%

Perinatal classes: Childbirth preparation, breastfeeding, newborn care, sibling preparation, and infant safety.

Amenities: SRRMC offers 24/7 coverage by neonatologists and anesthesiologists. A lactation consultant is on staff. The Breastfeeding Resource Center offers consults, support groups, and breast pump rentals.

Summit Medical Center

350 Hawthorne Ave.
Oakland
510-655-4000
510-869-6777 (classes)
www.summitmed.com

Type: Large, private, nonprofit medical center and Sutter Health affiliate. Merged with Alta Bates Medical Center. Level II nursery.

Births and C-section rate: 3,000; 20%

Rooms: 9 LDR rooms. 1 OR. 25 (of 28) postpartum rooms are private.

Midwives on staff: Yes. Midwives perform almost half of all deliveries.

Breastfeeding: 70%

Perinatal classes: Childbirth preparation, breastfeeding, newborn care, sibling preparation, and infant CPR.

Amenities: Summit has a relationship with Children's Hospital Oakland for acute-care of newborns (with both on-site neonatologist coverage and transfer if necessary). Perinatologists specializing in high-risk deliveries and lactation consultants are on staff. The hospital focuses on natural birthing. A home nursing visit is available postpartum. Two LDR rooms have Jacuzzis.

Sutter Delta Medical Center

3901 Lonetree Way
Antioch
925-779-7200
925-779-7230 (birthing center, classes)
www.sutterdelta.com

Type: Nonprofit hospital and Sutter Health affiliate. Level I nursery.

Births and C-section rate: 1,000; 21%

Rooms: 6 LDR rooms. 6 private postpartum rooms.

Midwives on staff: No.

Breastfeeding: 75%

Perinatal classes: Childbirth preparation, breastfeeding, postpartum care, sibling preparation, and infant CPR.

Amenities: Sutter Delta has a lactation nurse on staff.

Valleycare Medical Center

5555 W. Las Positas Blvd.
Pleasanton
925-847-3000
925-416-3475 (classes, tours)
www.valleycare.com

Type: Small, nonprofit community hospital. In the process of affiliating with Stanford Medical Center. Level II nursery.

Births and C-section rate: 1,600; C-section rate not available.

Rooms: 9 LDRP rooms. 2 ORs. 8 (of 10) postpartum rooms are private.

Midwives on staff: No.

Breastfeeding: 90%

Perinatal classes: Childbirth preparation, breastfeeding, newborn care, sibling preparation, and infant CPR. There is a special class for moms on bedrest.

Amenities: Valleycare was recently remodeled. Neonatologist consultants are available. Lactation educators are on staff. LDRP rooms have whirlpool tubs. A new pediatric unit was scheduled to open in spring 2002.

Washington Hospital

2000 Mowry Ave.
Fremont
510-797-1111
510-791-3423 (birthing center, classes, tours)
www.whhs.com

Type: Nonprofit district hospital run by Washington Township Health Care District. Level II nursery.

Births and C-section rate: About 3,000; about 17%

Rooms: 22 LDR rooms. 15 private postpartum rooms.

Midwives on staff: No.

Breastfeeding: 90%

Perinatal classes: Childbirth preparation, an infertility lecture, a diabetes and pregnancy program, a parenting workshop, sibling preparation, infant and toddler safety, and a pediatric asthma class.

Amenities: Washington's ICN is run by Lucile Packard Children's Hospital with a neonatologist and lactation consultants on staff.

Community Hospital of Los Gatos

815 Pollard Rd.
Los Gatos
408-378-6131
408-866-3905 (classes, tours)
www.tenethealth.com/Los Gatos

Type: For-profit acute-care hospital. Part of Tenet Health Systems. Level II nursery.

Births and C-section rate: 821; 19%

Rooms: 6 LDR rooms. All 8 postpartum rooms are private.

Midwives on staff: Yes. Midwives perform 35% of all deliveries.

Breastfeeding: 95%

Perinatal classes: Childbirth preparation, breastfeeding, newborn care, sibling preparation, and infant CPR.

Amenities: The hospital has a Jacuzzi available and provides cots for spouse/partner to spend the night.

El Camino Hospital

2500 Grant Rd.
Mountain View
650-940-7000
800-216-5556 (Maternal-Child Health Center)
650-940-7302 (classes, tours)
www.elcaminohospital.org

Type: Large, nonprofit district hospital run by the hospital board. Level III nursery.

Births and C-section rate: 4,200; 26%

Rooms: 10 LDR rooms. 28 (of 40) postpartum rooms are private.

Midwives on staff: No.

Breastfeeding: 90%

Perinatal classes: Childbirth preparation, breastfeeding, newborn care, sibling preparation, infant massage, and infant CPR.

Amenities: The labor and delivery rooms overlook a garden, and the hospital offers sleep chairs for patients' spouses or partners. The hospital has perinatologists available for consultation in the Prenatal Diagnostic Center (in conjunction with Stanford). Along with the Level III nursery, neonatologists (members of Stanford's neonatology department) are on staff. Two rooms are available in the neonatal intensive care unit for parents to visit and feed newborns. The Maternal Connections lactation center features eleven staff lactation consultants, a store, and a library. The hospital received a best birthing facility award from *Bay Area Parent* Magazine in April 1999, and made the HCIA-Sachs "100 Top Hospitals" national benchmarks list in 1993 and 1994. See www.100tophospitals.com.

PARENT RATING: ☆ ☆ ☆ ☆

Parents responding to our survey praised El Camino as a "pleasant, patient-friendly" place to deliver a baby.

Good Samaritan Hospital of Santa Clara Valley

2425 Samaritan Dr.
San Jose
408-559-2011
408-559-BABY (classes)
www.goodsamsj.org

Type: Large, investor-owned, acute-care hospital run by HCA Health Care. Level III nursery.

Births and C-section rate: 4,400; 25%

Rooms: 15 LDR rooms. 34 private postpartum rooms.

Midwives on staff: Midwives work with affiliated physicians and perform 2% of deliveries.

Breastfeeding: 99%

Perinatal classes: Classes include pregnancy, childbirth preparation, breastfeeding, newborn care, sibling preparation, and infant CPR.

Amenities: Good Samaritan features 24/7 neonatologist coverage in the NICU and provides high-risk perinatal services and fertility services. It has a breastfeeding center with lactation consultants. It made the HCIA-Sachs "100 Top Hospitals" national benchmarks list in 1995.

Kaiser Permanente Redwood City Medical Center

1150 Veterans Blvd.
Redwood City
650-299-2000
650-299-2433 (classes)
650-299-2692 (Breastfeeding Center, 610 Walnut St., Redwood City)
www.kaiserpermanente.org

Type: Large, private, nonprofit HMO. Level II nursery.

Births and C-section rate: 1,200; 14%

Rooms: 6 LDR rooms. All 15 postpartum rooms are semiprivate.

Midwives on staff: Yes. Midwives perform 45% of deliveries.

Breastfeeding: 85%

Perinatal classes: Nutrition, childbirth preparation, breastfeeding, and newborn care.

Amenities: Kaiser Redwood City has lactation consultants on staff. The Breastfeeding Center provides pump rentals.

Kaiser Permanente Santa Clara Medical Center

900 Kiely Blvd.
Santa Clara
408-236-6400
www.kaisersantaclara.org

Type: Large, private, nonprofit HMO. Level III nursery.

Births and C-section rate: 3,141; 17%

Rooms: 11 LDR rooms. All 26 post-partum rooms are private.

Midwives on staff: No.

Breastfeeding: Figure not available.

Perinatal classes: Prenatal nutrition, childbirth preparation (in English and Spanish), breastfeeding, newborn care, and sibling preparation.

Amenities: Not available.

Kaiser Permanente Santa Teresa Medical Center

250 Hospital Pkwy.
San Jose
408-972-3000
408-972-6715 (classes)
www.kaiserpermanente.org

Type: Large, private, nonprofit HMO. Level II nursery.

Births and C-section rate: 2,728; 18.4%

Rooms: 6 LDR rooms. No private postpartum rooms.

Midwives on staff: Yes.

Breastfeeding: 95%

Perinatal classes: Classes (most in English and Spanish) include nutrition, labor preparation, breastfeeding, and infant care.

Amenities: Not available.

O'Connor Hospital

2105 Forest Ave.
San Jose
408-947-2500
408-947-2699 (classes)
www.dochs.org

Type: Private, nonprofit hospital run by Daughters of Charity Health System. Level II nursery.

Births and C-section rate: 3,212; 24%

Rooms: 12 LDR rooms; 2 C-section suites; 17 (of 24) postpartum rooms are private.

Midwives on staff: Yes, there are two midwives on staff.

Breastfeeding: 60%

Perinatal classes: Natural family planning, childbirth preparation, breastfeeding, parenting, and infant CPR.

Amenities: O'Connor offers perinatal consultation for high-risk pregnancies and coverage by neonatologists. There is a lactation consultant on staff, plus a breast pump rental station.

Peninsula Medical Center (Mills-Peninsula Health Services)

1783 El Camino Real
Burlingame
650-696-5400
650-696-5600 (classes, tours)
www.mills-peninsula.org

Type: Nonprofit, community acute-care hospital and Sutter Health affiliate. Level II nursery.

Births and C-section rate: 2,272; 21%

Rooms: 15 LDR rooms; 2 C-section suites. 18 private postpartum rooms.

Midwives on staff: Yes. Midwives perform 33% of deliveries.

Breastfeeding: 95%

Perinatal classes: Childbirth preparation/Lamaze, breastfeeding, newborn care, and sibling preparation.

Amenities: The hospital offers staff lactation consultants and a Prenatal Diagnosis Program in conjunction with CPMC perinatologists, as well as a diabetics and pregnancy program. The hospital made the HCIA-Sachs "100 Top Hospitals" national benchmark list in 1998 and 1999.

PARENT RATING: ☆ ☆ ☆ ☆

A perennial favorite for San Mateo County moms, Peninsula is said to provide "lots of amenities," from private rooms with refrigerators and rocking chairs to sleeper sofas for spouses and partners. Most reported they had a "great experience." Parents raved about the many classes and support groups.

Regional Medical Center of San Jose

225 N. Jackson Ave.
San Jose
408-259-5000
www.hcahealthcare.com

Type: Large, private, for-profit medical center run by HCA Health Care. Level II nursery.

Births and C-section rate: 3,070; 20.75%

Rooms: 10 LDR rooms. Only 3 (of 32) postpartum rooms are private, but the staff tries to give each patient a private room whenever possible.

Midwives on staff: No.

Breastfeeding: 75%

Perinatal classes: Classes (many in Vietnamese and Spanish) include childbirth preparation, breastfeeding, newborn care, and father preparation.

Amenities: Regional Medical Center was formerly known as Alexian Brothers Hospital. A perinatologist and neonatologist group is associated with the hospital. There are two lactation consultants on staff, plus a breastfeeding clinic for postpartum support. Sleep chairs are available for spouses/partners.

St. Louise Regional

9400 No Name Uno
Gilroy
408-848-2000
408-848-8601 (classes)
www.dochs.org

Type: Small, private, nonprofit hospital run by Daughters of Charity Health System. No ICN.

Births and C-section rate: 800; C-section rate not available.

Rooms: 4 LDR rooms. All 9 postpartum rooms are technically semiprivate but are usually private when ward is not full.

Midwives on staff: Yes (2). Approximately one-third of deliveries are performed by midwives.

Breastfeeding: Figure not available.

Perinatal classes: Childbirth preparation and breastfeeding.

Amenities: St. Louise was formerly known as South Valley Regional Hospital. It features a newly remodeled LDR. There is a lactation consultant on staff.

Santa Clara Valley Medical Center

751 S. Bascom Ave.
San Jose
408-885-5000
408-885-6400 (maternity)
www.scvmed.org

Type: Large, public hospital owned and operated by Santa Clara County. Level III nursery.

Births and C-section rate: 4,020; 16%

Rooms: 11 LDR rooms. 3 private postpartum rooms, of 44 postpartum beds.

Midwives on staff: No.

Breastfeeding: 70-80%

Perinatal classes: Offers a five-week prenatal class in English and Spanish

Amenities: Santa Clara Valley Medical Center has an open-door policy, meaning it serves those needing medical care regardless of their ability to pay. It is a state-designated trauma center. There are board-certified lactation consultants on staff.

Sequoia Hospital District

170 Alameda de las Pulgas
Redwood City
650-369-5811
650-368-BABY (birth center, classes, tours)
www.chwbay.org/sequoia

Type: Community hospital. A Catholic Healthcare West affiliate. Level II nursery.

Births and C-section rate: 1,300; 25%

Rooms: 13 LDRP rooms; 2 C-section rooms. All rooms are private.

Midwives on staff: Yes. Midwives perform 5% of deliveries.

Breastfeeding: 99%

Perinatal classes: Childbirth preparation, breastfeeding, infant care,

sibling preparation, infant massage, and pediatric first aid and CPR.

Amenities: Sequoia has cots available for spouses/partners. All new patients receive a Sequoia *Baby's First Months* video as well as a monthly parenting newsletter during the baby's first year. The Lactation Education Center offers in- and outpatient consultations and a "CalmLine" for questions.

Lucile Packard Children's Hospital at Stanford Medical Center

725 Welch Rd.
Palo Alto
650-497-8000
650-723-4600 (classes, tours)
650-498-KIDS (Parent Information and Referral Center)
www.lpch.org

Type: Large, private university hospital. Levels I, II, and III nurseries.

Births and C-section rate: 5,245; 20.5%

Rooms: 10 LDR rooms; 1 early labor room; 2 surgical suites. 16 (of 52) postpartum rooms are private.

Midwives on staff: Yes. See "Midwifery Service at Stanford" above under midwives.

Breastfeeding: Figure not available.

Perinatal classes: Stanford's "Becoming Parents" program is extremely popular, so sign up early. The hospital offers a full set of classes, including childbirth preparation, breastfeeding, newborn care, multiples, grandparenting, sibling preparation, infant safety, infant CPR, infant massage, and lectures on many parenting topics.

Amenities: The Johnson Center for Pregnancy and Newborn Services combines the perinatal services of Stanford Hospital with the neonatal medicine services of Lucile Packard Children's Hospital at Stanford. The hospital offers neonatologists and perinatologists on staff, as well as genetic testing, diagnosis, and counseling. The Perinatal Diagnostic Center provides services for high-risk patients. There are nineteen physician faculty members (Stanford is a teaching hospital); private practice physicians also deliver babies at Stanford. Lactation consultants are available, and the prenatal/postnatal education program is highly rated. The Children's Hospital is world-renowned. UCSF/Stanford Health Care (it has since split) is the only hospital system in the Bay Area to land on the HCIA-Sachs "100 Top Hospitals" national list four times in recent years, 1994-1997. See www.100tophospitals.com.

PARENT RATING: ☆ ☆ ☆ ☆ ☆

Parents rated Stanford as *the* place to have a baby in the Peninsula/ South Bay area. Nurses received excellent reviews, as did the level of advanced care for high-risk deliver-ies. "I had a great experience in delivery," said one patient. Though the level of care was universally praised, the hospital was sometimes criticized in more detailed areas. One parent said that it "can be a bit disorganized" since it is a very large place, and one can easily get "lost in the crowd." "The birthing/recovery rooms were pretty disappointing," noted another parent. As at other hospitals, parents advised patients to be proactive—order your anesthesia early and be a squeaky wheel.

—⁓—

Finally, we would be remiss if we did not mention the largest and most comprehensive pediatric medical center in Northern California, Children's Hospital Oakland. Many parents praised its specialized departments and services, as well as its telephone advice line.

Children's Hospital Oakland
747 52nd St.
Oakland
510-428-3000
800-400-PEDS (child health resource line)
www.childrenshospitaloakland.org

BIRTH CENTERS

Independent birth centers are run by doctors and midwives outside of hospitals. They target low-risk patients who prefer a more natural, minimal intervention, drug-free approach in a home-like environment, but who want the extra security of a birth center. Local birth centers charged $2,000-3,000 per birth in 2001. Check with the California Office of Statewide Health Planning and Development, www.oshpd.cahwnet.gov, for a list of licensed birth centers. Be sure to check whether the birth center is accredited according to national standards developed by:

Commission for the Accreditation of Birth Centers
3123 Gottschall Rd.
Perkiomenville, PA 18074
215-679-4833
www.birthcenters.org

BAY AREA BIRTH CENTERS

The Birth Home
4441 Railroad Ave.
Pleasanton
925-447-1010
www.birthhome.com
PARENT RATING: ☆ ☆ ☆

We received largely positive reviews of this center, although one patient complained of not being told ahead of time that a physician rather than a midwife would attend the birth. Since opening in 1997, the center has had over 130 births. The center features two birthing rooms, a Jacuzzi tub, and water birth facilities. The facility is staffed by both a physician and a midwife, and focuses on natural childbirth and nonintervention. Hospital backup is at Valleycare Medical Center three miles away. The center accepts insurance.

Sage Femme Midwifery Service/ Community Childbearing Institute Judith Loebensteen-Tinkelenberg, CNM
877 Bryant St., Ste. 210
San Francisco
415-552-6600
PARENT RATING: ☆ ☆ ☆ ☆

Ms. Tinkelenberg, a CNM since 1991, performs deliveries at this center, which has two birth rooms and a tub for water birth if desired. She also rents water birth tubs. She adjusts her fees for Medi-Cal and HMO patients, accepts PPO insurance, and offers doula services and childbirth preparation classes.

Women's Health and Birth Center
583 Summerfield Rd.
Santa Rosa
707-539-1544
www.birthcenters.org

Run by CNMs, this center features two birthing rooms and two birthing tubs. CNMs and physicians with delivery privileges perform deliveries. Doulas and lactation consultants are available. Each patient receives a home visit from a nurse. The center is licensed and accredited, and is certified by the Baby-Friendly Hospital Initiative, a breastfeeding initiative of UNICEF/WHO. The center accepts insurance and arranges backup care at Santa Rosa Memorial Hospital in case of complications. It also offers classes in pregnancy, childbirth preparation, and breastfeeding.

HOME BIRTH

Contrary to popular myth, home birth *is* legal in California. People who choose home birth say it increases intimacy, privacy, and control over the birthing experience. They choose it because they want a natural, drug-free childbirth experience. To deliver at home, refer to the section on midwives, above, to find a competent midwife. Check the credentials of your midwife carefully, and make sure he or she is trained in emergency measures and has the right equipment for such an eventuality (typically, a fetal stethoscope or doppler, oxygen, suturing materials, medicine to control bleeding, IVs, and newborn resuscitation equipment). It goes without saying that you must be healthy and expecting a normal delivery to deliver at home (C-sections are only done in hospitals). Make sure you have arranged for medical transport to a nearby hospital in case of emergency.

Midwives' fees for a typical home birth—including prenatal care, delivery, and postpartum visits—averaged about $2,000-3,000 in California in 2001. Many insurance companies, particularly HMOs and including state-subsidized Medi-Cal, will not cover home birth fees, so some patients see a doctor for prenatal care, lab tests, and ultrasounds, and then see the midwife during the third trimester and delivery.

For local water tub rental, home birth information, and referrals, contact Natural Resources in San Francisco or Birthways or Birth and Bonding Family Center in the East Bay, all listed above under Choosing a Care Provider. For further information, check out the following:

Midwifery Today Magazine
P.O. Box 2672
Eugene, OR 97402
800-743-0974 or 541-344-7438
www.midwiferytoday.com
This magazine and affiliated website provide information about midwifery and home birth.

Global Maternal Child Health Association/Waterbirth International
P.O. Box 1400
Wilsonville, OR 97070
503-682-3600
www.waterbirth.org
This group provides water birth information, tub rentals, and referrals to local waterbirth resources.

Informed Homebirth/Informed Birth and Parenting
P.O. Box 1733
Fair Oaks, CA 95628
916-961-6923
This national nonprofit organization is dedicated to educating parents on birth alternatives and home birth; ask for their *Informed Homebirth* pamphlet. They provide referrals to midwives, doulas, and childbirth educators.

Prenatal Education

Before you deliver or adopt a baby, you should educate yourself on childbirth, breastfeeding, and newborn care. You should also consider taking an infant CPR class to learn specialized techniques for emergencies. Check out the classes at your local hospital, above, or see the following independent entities for more classes. If you are short on time, and money is not an issue, hospitals and parenting centers can also provide lists of nurses or childbirth educators who will give private classes in your home. Parents raved about these private classes. For infant CPR and first aid courses, in addition to the resources listed below, try your local fire department. We've heard reports of several fire stations offering free classes! Nurses or certified childbirth educators usually teach the classes. Note that several organizations provide educator certification, sometimes resulting in a flood of different acronyms after educators' names (CCE, ICCE, LCCE, etc.). For more parenting classes and groups after you have the baby, check out chapter 6.

GENERAL RESOURCES

Association of Labor Assistants and Childbirth Educators (ALACE)
P.O. Box 382724
Cambridge, MA 02238
888-22ALACE or 617-441-2500
www.alace.org

A nonprofit association certifying childbirth educators and doulas, ALACE focuses on natural childbirth and home birth, and provides referrals to local childbirth educators and doulas.

American Red Cross Bay Area
85 2nd St., 7th Fl.
San Francisco, CA 94105
415-427-8000
www.bayarea-redcross.org
PARENT RATING: ☆ ☆ ☆ ☆

The Red Cross offers low-cost classes in CPR and first aid, including infant and child CPR.

Bradley Method of Natural Childbirth

(American Academy of Husband-Coached Childbirth)
Box 5224
Sherman Oaks, CA 91413-5224
800-4-A-BIRTH (800-422-4784)
www.bradleybirth.com

The Bradley Method is a system of husband-coached natural childbirth and emphasizes breathing and relaxation. Classes are typically held in small groups over the course of twelve weeks, beginning in the sixth month. The website provides referrals to local instructors.

Childbirth and Postpartum Professionals Association (CAPPA)

P.O. Box 491448
Lawrenceville, GA 30043
888-548-3672
www.childbirthprofessional.com

A membership and certification organization for childbirth professionals including educators and doulas, CAPPA encourages natural childbirth. The website lists members by state.

International Childbirth Education Association (ICEA)

P.O. Box 20048
Minneapolis, MN 55420
952-854-8660
www.icea.org

This group grants professional certification to childbirth educators (ICCE designation) and doulas. The website features a database of certified instructors and doulas.

Lamaze International

2025 M St., Ste. 800
Washington, DC 20036
800-368-4404
www.lamaze-childbirth.com

Lamaze International's mission is to promote normal, natural, and healthy childbirth. The website provides referral to local Lamaze-certified instructors.

San Francisco

Bay Area Home Birth Collective

415-273-5185
PARENT RATING: ☆ ☆ ☆ ☆

This organization offers a "Homebirth Education Series" for couples planning to give birth at home.

Day One

3490 California St., Ste. 203
(entrance on Locust St.)
415-440-3291
www.DayOneCenter.com
PARENT RATING: ☆ ☆ ☆ ☆ ☆

A new privately run center for new and expectant parents in Laurel Village, Day One offers popular classes in healthy pregnancy, childbirth preparation, newborn parenting, breastfeeding, infant safety, and infant CPR.

Natural Resources

1307 Castro St.
415-550-2611
www.naturalresourcesonline.com
PARENT RATING: ☆ ☆ ☆ ☆ ☆

This pregnancy, childbirth, and parenting center in Noe Valley offers a lending library and classes in childbirth preparation, pregnancy, infant care, breastfeeding, and infant CPR, among others.

Pillowtalk
415-456-8188
PARENT RATING: ☆ ☆ ☆ ☆
This private organization holds classes in San Francisco and Marin, including baby care, childbirth preparation, breastfeeding, and infant CPR and safety. Parents universally recommended them, citing the emphasis on "realistic and practical" childbirth preparation.

San Francisco Paramedic Association
657 Mission St., Ste. 302
415-543-1161
www.sfparamedics.org
This group offers basic CPR and first aid classes for the public, and it will customize classes for groups.

North Bay

A.P.P.L.E. Family Works
4 Joseph Ct.
San Rafael
415-492-0720
www.familyworks.org
PARENT RATING: ☆ ☆ ☆ ☆
This nonprofit organization offers classes in childbirth preparation, sibling preparation, and CPR. Private home or hospital childbirth preparation classes are available for moms on preterm bed rest.

Bug a Boo
14 Bolinas Rd.
Fairfax
415-457-2884
This children's store offers infant massage, infant and child CPR, and positive parenting courses.

Center for Creative Parenting
Pacheco Plaza
446A Ignacio Blvd.
Novato
415-883-4442
PARENT RATING: ☆ ☆ ☆ ☆
This parents' center with a holistic emphasis offers classes in pregnancy, childbirth preparation, newborn care, infant CPR, first aid, infant massage, and other parenting topics.

Luray Eshelman, MA, RPT, ACCE
Marin Orthopedic Rehabilitation Center
650 E. Blithedale, Ste. C
Mill Valley
415-388-5690
PARENT RATING: ☆ ☆ ☆ ☆
This popular certified childbirth educator has taught childbirth preparation classes in Marin for the past twenty-seven years. Her series includes newborn care and breastfeeding.

Gheri Gallagher, RN
415-457-6865
PARENT RATING: ☆ ☆ ☆ ☆ ☆
Parents gave these in-home CPR and child safety classes rave reviews. Gallagher teaches three-hour private classes scheduled at the client's convenience.

Maternity of Marin
874 4th St.
San Rafael
415-457-4955
PARENT RATING: ☆ ☆ ☆ ☆
This parents' resource center offers classes in childbirth preparation, breastfeeding, newborn care, infant CPR, and infant massage.

Moms on the Move

510-234-1629

www.momsonthemove.net

PARENT RATING: ☆ ☆ ☆ ☆ ☆

A local labor and delivery nurse and certified childbirth educator offers a one-day intensive or a five-week series of childbirth preparation classes in Marin. Comment: "A basic unbiased introduction to childbirth."

Sarah McMoyler's Birth University
(formerly The Lamaze Intensive Course)

707-746-7783

www.birthu.com

PARENT RATING: ☆ ☆ ☆ ☆ ☆

Parents lauded these one-day intensive Lamaze courses, taught by a local labor and delivery nurse. She also offers classes in newborn care, breastfeeding, and infant safety. All classes are held in Marin.

East Bay

Birth and Bonding Family Center

1126 Solano Ave.

Albany

510-527-2121

www.birthbonding.org

PARENT RATING: ☆ ☆ ☆ ☆

This resource center offers childbirth preparation (with a natural birth focus), breastfeeding, and newborn parenting classes.

Birthways

478 Santa Clara Ave., 3rd Fl.

Berkeley

510-869-2797

www.birthways.org

PARENT RATING: ☆ ☆ ☆ ☆

This nonprofit organization offers its own childbirth preparation classes focusing on natural birth, and provides a referral list of educators offering private classes. Other classes include infant CPR, first aid, newborn care, postpartum realities, mindfulness-based pain reduction, infant massage, and child rearing.

Janaki Costello, ICCE, IBCLC

510-525-1155

PARENT RATING: ☆ ☆ ☆ ☆

This educator offers private childbirth preparation classes in the East Bay with an "eclectic" approach.

The Nurture Center

3399 Mt. Diablo Blvd.

Lafayette

925-283-1346

www.nurturecenter.com

PARENT RATING: ☆ ☆ ☆ ☆ ☆

This parenting center offers classes in newborn care, breastfeeding, childbirth preparation, infant massage, and postpartum adjustment.

Christine Vida, RN

510-841-1291

berkeleynurse@mindspring.com

PARENT RATING: ☆ ☆ ☆ ☆

This former emergency room nurse offers private classes and in-home tutoring in baby care and infant CPR/first aid.

South Bay

Blossom Birth Services

1000 Elwell Ct.

Palo Alto

650-964-7380

www.blossombirth.com

This nonprofit education, resource, and training center offers small group classes in childbirth preparation, newborn care, breastfeeding, sibling preparation, and massage.

Patty Dougherty

831-475-0451

pattyd@aawsom.com

PARENT RATING: ☆ ☆ ☆ ☆

This certified childbirth educator offers childbirth preparation classes either in a group setting in Redwood City or in a private class at the client's home.

Metropolitan Adult Education Program

1224 Del Mar Ave.

San Jose

408-947-2304

This organization offers classes in childbirth preparation and Lamaze, newborn care, and infant CPR.

Palo Alto Medical Foundation, Education Division

795 El Camino Real

Palo Alto

650-853-2960

www.pamf.org

PARENT RATING: ☆ ☆ ☆ ☆

This medical group offers classes in breastfeeding, pregnancy and newborn care, and childbirth preparation.

Santa Clara Adult Education

1840 Benton St.

Santa Clara

408-423-3500 or 408-984-6220

www.scae.org

This community group offers CPR and first aid for parents and daycare providers, as well as many parenting programs for after your baby's birth.

LABOR DOULAS

A labor doula, also called a labor assistant or labor coach, can help mothers before, during, and after birth. Before birth, a doula will meet with the family to decide on a birth plan. During labor, the doula generally comes to the home and then the hospital to help you relax and get through labor, using massage and relaxation techniques. In addition, the doula can serve as your advocate at the hospital, especially when hospital staff members change shifts. Most doulas focus on a natural, nonmedicated approach to labor. Some doulas also work with families in the postpartum period—doing everything from helping with breastfeeding, to cleaning, doing laundry, running errands, caring for older siblings, and cooking. Some also do pre- and post-natal massage. For more on postpartum doulas, see chapter 5. In the Bay Area, fees averaged $500-800 for labor support in 2001.

Doulas are not licensed or regulated by the state. And unless they also have a nursing or midwifery background, they do not have medical training. They have learned by attending many births over the years, and that's why it's important to find one with a lot of experience. Before hiring a doula, make sure you are very comfortable with her on a personal level. Obviously, it's a rather personal decision to have a doula in addition to your partner in the delivery room. If it's the right fit, however, many moms reported it was a nice treat to have someone taking care of *them* during the birth and postpartum.

To learn more about doulas, local moms recommend reading *Mothering the Mother: How a Doula Can Help You Have a Shorter, Easier, and Healthier Birth*, by Marshall Klaus, MD, John Kennell, MD, and Phyllis Klaus, MEd.

How do you find a doula? Again, word of mouth is probably the best method. As in a child care provider search, be sure to check at least three references, particularly since no government agency regulates doula services. Ask the prospective candidates about their backgrounds, experience, and philosophies. National organizations such as ALACE, CAPPA, and ICEA, listed above under prenatal education, can help you find local labor doulas. You may also contact DONA, listed below, for local referrals. For more information and local doula resources, check out chapter 5.

Doulas of North America (DONA)
P.O. Box 626
Jasper, IN 47547
801-756-7331 or 888-788-DONA
www.dona.com
PARENT RATING: ☆ ☆ ☆ ☆

This professional association includes doulas who have completed training and agreed to the DONA Code of Ethics and Standards of Practice. The website lists doulas by region.

CORD BLOOD BANKING

Cord blood banking is a relatively new phenomenon. In this procedure, cells from a newborn's umbilical cord are collected immediately after the baby and placenta have been delivered. Then the blood is either donated to a blood bank for public use or stored at a private blood bank for future personal use. Because cord blood has a high percentage of stem cells (the cells that create other cells and are found in bone marrow), it has been used instead of marrow for people needing transplants for diseases like cancer, leukemia, and sickle cell anemia. Cord blood cells also appear to pose fewer transplant barriers than bone marrow, allowing a greater number of potential recipients.

Particularly for those with a family history of such diseases (e.g., with an older child suffering from leukemia), banking a younger sibling's cord blood may make sense. However, the American Academy of Pediatrics has concluded that there is not enough evidence to warrant the *routine* collection and storage of cord blood. Cord blood banked for personal use is handled by private companies. Currently the industry is unregulated, and some private cord blood banks have gone bankrupt. The cost of private banking for one year ranged from $275-1,500 in 2001. The National Institute of Health (NIH) nonprofit cord blood banks are solely for public donation. Either way, you need to plan early (at least two months before delivery for some banks) if you would like to have your baby's cord blood collected. The research on this topic is evolving, so talk to your doctor about the latest pros and cons in your particular circumstances and about the current transplant success rates.

PUBLIC CORD BLOOD DONATION

American Red Cross Cord Blood Program of Children's Hospital Oakland
510-450-7647
The Red Cross operates a public cord blood donation program with collections at Alta Bates Medical Center in Berkeley.

Children's Hospital Oakland Children's Research Institute Western Area Community Cord Blood Bank
510-450-7605
Children's Hospital is home to a sibling cord blood donation program funded by the NIH.

Cord Blood Donor Foundation
1200 Bayhill Dr., Ste. 301
San Bruno
650-635-1456
www.cordblooddonor.org
This nonprofit wing of the private Cord Blood Registry provides collection kits for donors. They do not take donations; check first.

National Marrow Donor Program
800-654-1247
Call to find out about the current locations and status of cord blood donation programs in the Bay Area.

PRIVATE CORD BLOOD BANKS

California Cryobank, Inc.
3228 Nebraska Ave.
Santa Monica, CA 90404
800-400-3430
www.cryobank.com
Accredited by the American Association of Blood Banks, this company operates nationwide and stores blood in a company-owned laboratory in California.

Cord Blood Registry (CBR)
1200 Bayhill Dr., Ste. 301
San Bruno, CA 94066
888-267-3256
www.cordblood.com
This company bills itself as the largest processor of cord blood cells in the world.

Cryo-Cell International
3165 McMullen Booth Rd., Bldg. B
Clearwater, FL 33761
800-786-7235
www.cryo-cell.com
This company's fees are among the lowest we found.

Viacord
131 Clarendon St.
Boston, MA 02116
800-998-4226
www.viacord.com
Accredited by the American Association of Blood Banks, this nationwide company stores cord blood at the University of Cincinnati's Hoxworth Blood Center.

Infertility and Third-Party Reproduction

Over six million American women and their partners suffer from infertility—that's about 10 percent of the U.S. population of reproductive age. Fortunately, medical advances have made it possible for many of those couples to have children. Techniques range from surgically correcting problems with the male or female reproductive system, to prescribing drugs to stimulate ovulation, to employing assisted reproductive technologies (ART). The most well-known ART is in vitro fertilization (IVF). Techniques are evolving, so be sure to check with your doctor for the latest developments.

If you are experiencing fertility problems, first talk to your OB/GYN. He or she may give you some tests and/or prescribe medication, or may directly refer you to a reproductive endocrinologist. For more on how to find a specialist locally, see below. For male fertility issues, see a urologist with a subspecialty in andrology. Be sure you see a genuine board-certified specialist and not merely a physician with an interest in fertility. To check a doctor's credentials, see the *Directory of Medical Specialists*, published by Who's Who (available in most public libraries) or the American Board of Medical Specialties (www.abms.org). Always check a physician's background with the California Medical Board (www.medbd.ca.gov).

You can also check the success rates of potential clinics. The Society for Assisted Reproductive Medicine (SART) and the Center for Disease Control (CDC) report live birth data. Visit the CDC's website at www.cdc.gov/nccdphp/drh/art.htm to see the report, or call the CDC at 770-488-5372 to get a printed copy.

The costs for these procedures vary widely. The U.S. average cost of an IVF cycle in 2000 was $7,800. Locally, patients report spending $10,000-15,000 or more for a full cycle at a private clinic. A large part of that cost is the medication, and some local parents report purchasing the drugs outside the U.S. at substantially reduced prices. California law requires group health insurers covering hospital, medical, or surgical expenses to *offer* employers coverage for infertility diagnosis and treatment. But nothing requires employers to buy the coverage. And IVF is not a covered treatment under the law. Check your insurance plan carefully. In addition, some clinics offer package plans for a flat fee, in which some of the fee will be refunded if the treatment is not successful. These outcome-based plans have raised ethical questions in the medical community. For more information, contact RESOLVE, see resources below.

Third-party reproduction uses eggs, sperm, embryos, or a uterus donated by a third person (donor) to allow an infertile person or couple to have children. Donors may be known or anonymous. Either way, experts advise consulting an attorney familiar with the legal issues. Most of the time, contracts need to be signed before these procedures are done, and sometimes adoption needs to take place afterward. Experts also recommend seeing a professional counselor to help with the psychological issues of third-party reproduction. Many of the clinics listed below have counselors on staff or provide referrals. Costs of these procedures are generally higher than for traditional IVF because third-party donors must be compensated for their expenses and inconvenience. Many expenses will not be covered by your own health insurance since the procedures involve treatment of a third party. For example, local parents estimate spending as much as $75,000 in the surrogacy process on agency fees, legal work, and the surrogate's expenses and fees. Going solo eliminates the agency fee, but local parents report it's a long, difficult process to find a qualified surrogate on one's own. They found agencies provided more qualified surrogates and helped greatly with the administrative process, which otherwise can be a huge headache.

REGULATION OF FERTILITY PROGRAMS

Fertility clinics, laboratories, and donor programs are regulated by voluntary professional organization guidelines and some federal and state laws. Federal law requires ART clinics to report their success rates to the CDC, see above, and also requires andrology labs to register with the Health Care Finances Administration (HCFA) and to adhere to strict standards. Surrogacy agencies, however, are *not* regulated, so be sure to check references carefully given what is at stake—and the amount of money you will be entrusting to them! Here are some places to seek advice about clinical practices and ethics:

American Association of Tissue Banks (AATB)
1350 Beverly Rd., Ste. 220-A
McLean, VA 22101
703-827-9582
www.aatb.org
This professional organization publishes a list of sperm banks meeting its guidelines for donor testing, screening, and specimen storage.

American Society for Reproductive Medicine (ASRM)
1209 Montgomery Hwy.
Birmingham, AL 35216
205-978-5000
www.asrm.com
This professional organization publishes minimum standards for ART programs as well as guidelines for laboratories and donation programs.

California Department of Health Services
714 P St., Rm. 440
Sacramento, CA 95814
916-654-0357
This department licenses fertility clinics in California.

College of American Pathologists
325 Waukegan Rd.
Northfield, IL 60093
800-323-4040
www.cap.org
About one-third of all clinics reporting statistics to SART are accredited voluntarily by this lab accreditation program.

QUESTIONS TO ASK ABOUT FERTILITY PROGRAMS

In selecting a fertility program, you'll want to consider not only the physicians' experience, but also the clinic's location (it's important for some procedures that the clinic be located close to your home), cost (since treatment may not be covered by insurance), and success rates. In general, you will want to ask all of the questions you would ask a prospective obstetrician, as discussed earlier, plus the following:

◆ What are the physicians' credentials and experience?

◆ Is the doctor a member of the American Society for Reproductive Medicine? Is the clinic a member of the Society for Assisted Reproductive Technologies (SART)? Does the program meet the ASRM guidelines? Is the lab accredited?

◆ What is the fee structure? Are payment plans available? Does insurance cover the fees?

◆ Are the lab and ultrasound open on weekends and holidays? Can procedures be done on weekends? (This may be important to your treatment.)

◆ What procedures does the doctor perform?

◆ What are the clinics' success rates?

◆ What tests will the doctor do before recommending ART?

◆ Does the clinic have counselors available?

◆ Does the clinic freeze extra embryos? If yes, what are the fees?

◆ If you are considering third-party reproduction, be sure to ask about affiliated donation banks, referrals to potential surrogates, donor and surrogate selection and screening, consent, compensation, and confidentiality.

GENERAL INFERTILITY RESOURCES

American Society for Reproductive Medicine

PARENT RATING: ☆ ☆ ☆ ☆ ☆

See the listing under "Regulation of Fertility Programs," above. This professional organization has a comprehensive website featuring fact sheets, lists of member physicians by geographic area, and links to other resources (notably the affiliated Society of Reproductive Surgeons, www.reprodsurgery.org).

Organization of Parents Through Surrogacy (OPTS)

P.O. Box 611
Gurnee, IL 60031
847-782-0224
www.opts.com

This national surrogacy support group provides information, networking, support, and referrals.

RESOLVE

1310 Broadway
Somerville, MA 02144
617-623-0744
www.resolve.org

PARENT RATING: ☆ ☆ ☆ ☆ ☆

Local parents highly recommend this national nonprofit infertility association and its local chapter. It provides advice, publications, and referrals to specialists. The website provides a wealth of information and links to other resources; it's a great place to start your research.

RESOLVE of Northern California

312 Sutter St., Ste. 405
San Francisco
415-788-6772
415-788-3002 (telephone assistance program)
www.resolvenc.org

PARENT RATING: ☆ ☆ ☆ ☆ ☆

This local chapter offers a telephone assistance program to speak confidentially with a peer counselor and obtain professional referrals. It also offers monthly workshops, support groups, infertility awareness meetings, preadoption meetings, symposia on infertility and adoption, a newsletter, and a library.

Society for Reproductive Endocrinology and Infertility

www.socrei.org

The website of this national professional organization of board-certified reproductive endocrinologists lists members by geographic area.

CLINICS AND DOCTORS

Alta Bates Medical Center In Vitro Fertilization Program
Ryszard Chetkowski, MD

2999 Regent St., Ste. 101-A
Berkeley
510-649-0440

Marin Fertility Medical Group
Sae Sohn, MD

1100 S. Eliseo Dr., Ste. 107
Greenbrae
415-464-8688
www.marinfertility.com

Pacific Fertility Center (PFC)
Carolyn Givens, Isabelle Ryan,
and Eldon Schriock, MDs
55 Francisco St., Ste. 500
San Francisco
415-834-3000
PFC is owned by the San Francisco
Center for Reproductive Medicine.

Reproductive Science Center
Susan Willman, MD
• Orinda
  89 Davis Rd., Ste. 280, 925-254-0444
• San Ramon
  3160 Crow Canyon Rd., Ste. 150,
  925-867-1800

San Francisco Center for
Reproductive Medicine
Philip Chenette and Carl Herbert,
MDs
390 Laurel St., Ste. 205
San Francisco
415-771-1483
www.Sffertility.com
This group owns Pacific Fertility
Center. Another affiliate, Pacific
Fertility Parenting Center, is a third-
party agency specializing in ovum
donation services.

Stanford Medical Center
Reproductive Endocrinology and
Infertility (REI) Division
300 Pasteur Dr.
Stanford
650-725-5983
www.stanford.edu/dept/GYNOB/rei

UCSF Fertility Clinic and In Vitro
Fertilization Program
350 Parnassus Ave.
San Francisco
415-476-2224

Wu's Healing Center
703 Clement St.
San Francisco
415-752-0170
This alternative medicine center provides infertility evaluations and pre-
and post-natal treatments with
acupuncture, acupressure, and
Chinese herbs.

AGENCIES AND ATTORNEYS

Center for Surrogate Parenting
15821 Ventura Blvd., Ste. 675
Encino, CA 91436
818-788-8288
www.creatingfamilies.com

Family Fertility Center
2855 Mitchell Dr., Ste. 104
Walnut Creek
925-977-4850
www.surromother.com

Law Offices of Diane Michelsen
3190 Old Tunnel Rd.
Lafayette
800-877-1880
www.lodm.com

Woman to Woman Fertility Center
3201 Danville Blvd., Ste. 160
Alamo
925-820-9495

Adoption

Adoption is another option for those who cannot or choose not to have children. There are basically four different approaches to adoption in California: private agency adoption, public agency adoption, independent adoption, or international adoption.

In a *private agency* adoption, the agency helps you through the application process, does the home study, offers parent education, locates a child, places the child, does post-placement follow-up, and helps finalize the adoption. (In a home study, a social worker meets with and assesses the prospective parents. You'll need to provide income and medical histories, and undergo background checks.) You may also locate a birth mother on your own and have the agency do everything else. Either way, you will need an attorney to do the legal end of the work, and you should have your own attorney represent you even if the agency has its own. Make sure the agency is licensed by the State of California and has no consumer complaints filed against it. (Check with the Adoptions Branch of the California Department of Social Services.) Also, check to see that the agency is accredited by the Council on Accreditation for Children and Families Services. Your attorney should be in good standing with the State Bar of California and preferably a member of a specialized association of adoption attorneys. Local families say the process takes at least a year from home study to a child's placement. Costs range from $5,000-30,000, with local families reporting spending about $10,000-15,000. The main cost variable is how much of the birth mother's expenses you pay. (California law allows the adopting family to pay certain medical and living expenses, but not to pay placement fees.) The private agency's advantage is its experience and resources, but its disadvantage is that the wait may be longer than in independent adoption.

In a *public agency* adoption, the agency performs functions similar to those of a private agency. But public agencies, run by the California Department of Social Services, work to place children who are already in the system, meaning their parents' rights have been involuntarily terminated for one reason or another. Generally, this means older children rather than newborns, and may mean children with special needs. The chief advantage of working with a public agency is the cost—it is nominal (zero to $2,500), and financial assistance or subsidies may be available. The disadvantages are having to deal with bureaucracies (and if you wish to adopt a newborn, there are very few available).

In *independent* adoption, you hire a facilitator to do the search (or you conduct a search on your own), a social worker or agency to do the home study, and an attorney to finalize the adoption. You gain a greater degree of control over the process (and you may shorten the time to adopt), but a search on your own requires a lot of time, you won't have post-adoption follow-up, and it may be more expensive ($8,000-30,000+). In addition, facilitators (unless they are also attorneys) are not licensed, so there is no governmental oversight.

In *international* adoption, you will also work with an agency, but to adopt a child from overseas. This usually means the domestic agency (working with foreign agencies or facilitators) will help you go through home study, locate a child, get INS approval to bring the orphan back to the U.S., and finalize the adoption overseas. Costs range from $7,000-25,000, not including travel costs, but they depend on the country. The most popular countries for adoption locally are China and Russia. Adopting internationally is generally a more predictable (and faster) process than domestic adoption. But the information you receive about the child's medical and social history may be limited, and some countries restrict certain people from adopting (such as single parents or same sex couples).

No matter which approach you take, check with the IRS and your tax adviser regarding the current status of tax credits for adoption expenses (www.irs.ustreas.gov) and your employer for adoption benefits and leave policies. The Family and Medical Leave Act does cover adopting parents, and many employers are offering adoption benefits.

QUESTIONS TO ASK AN ADOPTION AGENCY OR ATTORNEY

Be sure to check references of anyone you hire, preferably by contacting parents who have already gone through the process. Most reputable agencies and attorneys will provide you a list of references.

◆ How many years have you been in business? How many adoptions do you do per year? What is your accreditation and licensure (agencies)? Are you a member of the bar (attorneys)?

◆ What types of services do you offer (domestic, international, birth mother search, open adoption, pre- and post-adoption support and education)?

◆ How long does an adoption take?

◆ How much does it cost (ask for it to be itemized)?

◆ What do you need to do the home study and to approve parents?

◆ Are there age, religion, or race restrictions for prospective parents, or restrictions on single parents, working parents, parents with other children, or same-sex couples?

◆ What kind of information will I receive about the child and the birth parents?

GENERAL ADOPTION RESOURCES

www.Adoptionprofessionals.com

This website features state-by-state adoption laws and a searchable database of agencies.

www.Adopting.org
www.Adoption.com

These websites offer searchable directories of adoption resources.

Bananas

510-658-0381

This family resources organization in Oakland offers a workshop on adoption and fostering. See under referrals in chapter 9.

Council on Accreditation for Children and Family Services, Inc.

120 Wall St., 11th Fl.
New York, NY 10005
212-797-3000
www.coanet.org

This organization accredits adoption agencies.

National Adoption Information Clearinghouse

330 C St., SW
Washington, DC 20447
888-251-0075
www.calib.com/naic

PARENT RATING: ☆ ☆ ☆ ☆ ☆

This congressionally established agency provides an invaluable website that should be your first step in researching adoption. They provide information on every conceivable aspect of adoption and list local resources.

Natural Resources

1307 Castro St.
San Francisco
415-550-2611
www.naturalresourcesonline.com

PARENT RATING: ☆ ☆ ☆ ☆ ☆

This center offers a workshop on adoption featuring local attorneys, social workers, and facilitators.

PACT, An Adoption Alliance

1700 Montgomery St., Ste. 111
San Francisco
415-221-6957
www.pactadopt.org

This nonprofit organization provides adoption-related services for children of color and their families. This is not a licensed adoption agency, but they facilitate adoptions and offer educational events, counseling, and post-adoption services.

RESOLVE

PARENT RATING: ☆ ☆ ☆ ☆ ☆

See the listing under "General Infertility Resources," above. National and local chapters provide useful publications and highly recommended local workshops on adoption.

U.S. Immigration and Naturalization Service

800-375-5283
949-831-8427 (California Service Center)
www.ins.usdoj.gov

Get their publication M-249, "The Immigration of Adopted and Prospective Adoptive Children."

U.S. Department of State, Office of Children's Issues

202-736-7000
www.travel.state.gov

This agency provides information about international adoption (by country) and U.S. visa requirements.

AGENCIES

ACCEPT

www.acceptadoptions.org
- Los Altos
  339 S. San Antonio Rd., Ste. 1A,
  650-917-8090
- San Francisco
  1500 Noriega St., Ste. 110,
  415-681-4957

PARENT RATING: ☆ ☆ ☆ ☆ ☆

Parents called ACCEPT "efficient, supportive, and helpful." This licensed nonprofit agency for international adoption works throughout the Bay Area. They provide counseling, home study, country selection, child referral, and post-placement services. They will also do home study and post-placement services for independent domestic adoptions.

Adopt International

www.adopt-intl.org
- Redwood City
  121 Springdale Way, 650-369-7300
- Oakland
  160 Santa Clara Ave., 510-653-8600

This licensed nonprofit agency operates throughout the Bay Area. They offer international and domestic adoption, outreach services, counseling, birth parent screening services, education, home study, post-placement services, and social activities for adoptive families.

Adoption Connection (Jewish Family and Children's Services)

3272 California St., 2nd Fl.
San Francisco
415-202-7494
www.adoptionconnection.org
PARENT RATING: ☆ ☆ ☆ ☆ ☆

This licensed nonprofit, nonsectarian agency works throughout the Bay Area on domestic adoptions only. They are open to same-sex couples and offer many helpful workshops.

Bay Area Adoption Services, Inc. (BAAS)

465 Fairchild Dr., Ste. 215
Mountain View
650-964-3800
www.baas.org
PARENT RATING: ☆ ☆ ☆ ☆

Parents called this licensed nonprofit agency for international adoptions "experienced and ethical."

California Association of Adoption Agencies (CAAA)

www.california-adoption.org

This professional association of California adoption agencies lists its members on its website.

California Department of Social Services, Adoptions Branch

744 P St.
Sacramento, CA 95814
800-KIDS-4-US
www.ChildsWorld.ca.gov

This bureau licenses adoption agencies, and its website has a directory of licensed agencies. Its Oakland District office can provide a list of public agencies (510-622-2650).

The Family Network, Inc.

307 Webster St.
Monterey
831-655-5077
www.adopt-familynetwork.com

This licensed nonprofit agency for international adoption works throughout the Bay Area and will also do home study, counseling, and post-placement services for domestic adoption (no placement).

Future Families, Inc.

www.futurefamilies.org
• San Jose
1671 The Alameda, 408-298-8789
• Aptos
3233 Valencia Ave., Ste. A-6,
831-662-0202

This licensed nonprofit agency works with families in the 408, 415, 510, 650, and 831 area codes only. They provide domestic adoption and foster care services, focusing on fost-adopt (foster care leading to adoption), foster parent adoption, or concurrent (open) adoption. Their fees are minimal for fost-adopt services (and a stipend may be available). They also provide home study, training, therapy, and support services.

Kinship Center

22 Lower Ragsdale Dr., Ste. B
Monterey
831-649-3033
www.kinshipcenter.org

This licensed agency works statewide. They have a small infant adoption program but focus on fost-adopt for special needs children already in the system (fees may be waived or a subsidy available). They will also do home study for independent adoptions.

Partners for Adoption
4527 Montgomery Dr., Ste. A
Santa Rosa
707-539-9068
www.sonic.net/adoptpfa

This licensed nonprofit agency works in all Bay Area counties except Santa Clara and south. They perform domestic and international adoptions, and offer classes, counseling, home study, searching, post-placement services, foster family certification, and birth parent services.

ATTORNEYS

American Academy of Adoption Attorneys
Box 33053
Washington, DC 20033-0053
202-832-2222
www.adoptionattorneys.org

This is a professional organization of adoption attorneys providing referrals.

Academy of California Adoption Lawyers
www.acal.org

The website of this specialized bar association lists members.

Gradstein and Gorman
Marc Gradstein, Attorney-at-Law
1204 Burlingame Ave., #7
Burlingame
650-347-7041

Law Offices of Diane Michelsen
See listing above under "General Infertility Resources."

State Bar of California
180 Howard St.
San Francisco
415-538-2000
www.calbar.org

This organization licenses and disciplines attorneys. Check to make sure your attorney does not have a history of complaints or malpractice suits filed against him or her.

SUPPORT GROUPS FOR ADOPTIVE PARENTS

Families for Russian and Ukranian Adoptions (FRUA)
650-941-9497, Susan Lobo

Families with Children from China
FCC-Northern California
415-751-2724, Terry M. Fry
www.fcc.org
terry_fry@stanfordalumni.org
Prospective parents are welcome

Families Adopting in Response (FAIR)
650-328-6832

Las Madres
408-868-9310, Anne Kay

This group provides support for all types of adoptions.

Neighborhood Parents Network
510-527-MOMS

This East Bay parents group has an extensive offering of volunteer support groups, including ones for adoptive families. See in chapter 6 under "Mothers' and Parents' Groups and Clubs"—East Bay.

Parents Place San Francisco Adoptive New Mother New Baby Group
1700 Scott St.
San Francisco
415-359-2454
www.jfcs.org
This discussion group focuses on issues unique to adoptive mothers of infants newborn to twelve months. Bring your baby!

Single Adoptive Parents
Esther Zack
ezack20@hotmail.com
Prospective parents are welcome

Help for Kids With Special Needs

Parents of children with special needs will want to tap into the many local resources, from medical to educational programs, designed especially for children facing physical, psychological, or developmental challenges. We've listed some places to start, below. In addition, here are some tips from local parents of children with disabilities:

◆ Contact your local school district for special education programs and testing (free and mandated by law).

◆ Check out your local library for books on tape and other resources for the disabled.

◆ Parent-run Family Resource Centers, see below for listing, are great places to find out about local resources and parent support groups.

◆ State-funded Regional Centers, see below for listing, are also helpful places for children with developmental disabilities.

◆ Learn about the federal and state laws regarding the rights of the disabled. An advocacy organization such as CASE, see below, can provide guidance.

◆ Find a pediatrician specializing in developmental or behavioral pediatrics, or whichever specialty applies to your child's disability. Your local Family Resource Center or Regional Center is a great place to find referrals. You can also check out the pediatric departments of three leading hospitals: Children's Hospital Oakland, Lucile Packard Children's Hospital at Stanford, and the University of California at San Francisco.

◆ Be proactive. You are your child's best advocate!

California Department of Developmental Services

P.O. Box 944202
Sacramento, CA 94244-2020
800-515-BABY (2229)
(Early Start Program)
www.dds.ca.gov

PARENT RATING: ☆ ☆ ☆ ☆ ☆

This state agency provides services and support to children with developmental disabilities. The agency operates seven Developmental Centers throughout California for inpatient treatment, and funds nonprofit, private Regional Centers to help families access local resources. Local Regional Centers are listed below. The agency also administers the "Early Start Program" of early intervention, information, and referrals for babies and toddlers with developmental disabilities, offered through a variety of public and private organizations.

Golden Gate Regional Center

www.ggrc.com
• Corte Madera
  5725 Paradise Dr., Ste. 100 (Building A), 415-945-1600
• San Francisco
  120 Howard St., 415-546-9222
• San Mateo
  3130 La Selva Dr., Ste. 202, 650-574-9232

North Bay Regional Center

www.nbrc.net
• Napa
  10 Executive Ct., 707-256-1100
• Santa Rosa
  2351 Mendocino Ave., 707-569-2000

Regional Center of the East Bay

www.rceb.org
• Concord
  2151 Salvio St., Ste. 365, 925-798-3001
• Oakland
  7677 Oakport St., Ste. 300, 510-383-1200

San Andreas Regional Center

www.sarc.org
• Campbell
  300 Orchard City Dr., Ste. 170, 408-374-9960
• Gilroy
  7855 Wren Ave., Ste. A, 408-846-8805

California Department of Health Services—California Children Services (CCS)

185 Barry St., Lobby 6, Ste. 255
San Francisco
415-904-9699 (Northern California regional office)
www.dhs.ca.gov

This state program provides medical services for physically disabled children in California. Services include diagnostic evaluation, treatment, referrals to specialists, and therapy. Families meeting certain income guidelines receive free or low-cost care; others pay based on a sliding scale. Every county has a CCS office.

California Department of Health Services—Medically Vulnerable Infant Program

916-323-3541
www.dhs.ca.gov

This state program provides home visits to families with "medically fragile" infants to minimize developmental delays. Services include case management, referrals, intervention, support, counseling and education, health and developmental assessments, and therapeutic consultation.

Center for Access to Resources and Education (CARE) Parent Network

1350 Arnold Dr., Ste. 203
Martinez
925-313-0999
www.contracostaarc.com/html/care.html

This Family Resource Center provides support groups, a warm line, education, referrals, and resources for Contra Costa County families of children with special needs. They offer an Early Start program from newborn to age 3.

Children's Council of San Francisco

445 Church St.
San Francisco
415-276-2900
www.childrenscouncil.org
PARENT RATING: ☆ ☆ ☆ ☆ ☆

This nonprofit resource and referral agency offers free information, training, and consultation to parents and caregivers of children with emotional and behavioral problems, and regularly publishes a list of local resources.

Children's Health Council

650 Clark Way
Palo Alto
650-326-5530
www.chconline.org

This organization provides programs and services for children with learning, behavioral, or developmental difficulties, including diagnosis, evaluation, therapy, research, parent education, and outreach.

Community Alliance for Special Education (CASE)

1500 Howard St.
San Francisco
415-431-2285

This nonprofit organization provides information and advocacy services for children needing special education.

Family Resource Network

5232 Claremont Ave.
Oakland
510-547-7322
PARENT RATING: ☆ ☆ ☆ ☆ ☆

This highly recommended Family Resource Center provides advocacy, support groups, training, and resources for families with children with disabilities.

Matrix

94 Galli Dr., Ste. C
Novato
415-884-3535
www.matrixparents.org
PARENT RATING: ☆ ☆ ☆ ☆ ☆

This nonprofit Family Resource Center provides support, information, training, and referrals for families of children with disabilities.

MORE Family Resource Center
1764 Marco Polo Way
Burlingame
650-259-0189
PARENT RATING: ☆ ☆ ☆ ☆ ☆
Run by parents, this Family Resource Center provides support and education to families of children with special needs in San Mateo County. They publish a useful special needs resource directory for San Mateo County.

Parents Helping Parents
3141 Olcott St.
Santa Clara
408-727-5775
www.php.com
PARENT RATING: ☆ ☆ ☆ ☆ ☆
This highly recommended nonprofit organization for parents of children with special needs offers an Early Intervention Program for infants and toddlers newborn to 3 years old, help with special education programs, support and information groups, a mentor parent program, an assistive technology center, a siblings program, parent training, and play groups.

Support for Families of Children with Disabilities
2601 Mission St., Rm. 804
San Francisco
415-282-7494
PARENT RATING: ☆ ☆ ☆ ☆ ☆
This Family Resource Center offers support groups, peer counseling, and a warm line for families of children with disabilities. They publish a useful directory of local resources.

Your Rights in the Workplace

If you are a working parent-to-be, you should be aware of your rights in the workplace during pregnancy and after giving birth (or adopting a child). The following information incorporates only the minimum legal requirements; be sure to check your individual employment agreement or policies, which may be more generous.

Federal and state laws prohibit employment *discrimination on the basis of pregnancy*. Thus, generally an employer can't fire or demote you, or refuse to hire you, because you are pregnant. A new state law requires employers to provide pregnant employees with "reasonable accommodations" related to pregnancy. For example, you may be able to transfer to a less strenuous position during pregnancy. If you can't do your job, you must be offered the same benefits as your employer offers other disabled workers (e.g., disability leave or easier duties).

- The federal Family and Medical Leave Act of 1993 (FMLA) and a similar state law (the California Family Rights Act) allow employees to take up to twelve weeks of *unpaid family and medical leave* when the employee is "unable to work because of a serious health condition" (including pregnancy or a family member's illness). Only public agencies and private employers with fifty or more employees are required to comply, and you must have worked for the employer for a year before you are eligible (and put in at least 1,250 hours during that year). Medical leave can be taken intermittently or on a reduced work schedule (e.g., for prenatal care, if you have periods of morning sickness rendering you unable to work, or if you are undergoing a series of fertility treatments requiring bed rest). Your employer must continue to maintain your group health insurance coverage and other benefits during your leave (on the same terms as if you had continued to work).
- Under the FMLA and state law, eligible employees may take up to twelve weeks of *unpaid leave* (in a twelve-month period) for the *birth, adoption, or foster placement* of a child. This law applies to both men and women.
- In California, FMLA leave for the birth of a child can be *added* onto any *pregnancy disability leave*. California law allows women to take up to four months of *unpaid*, doctor-certified pregnancy disability leave before or after a child is born. In effect, then, you could take up to seven months off for the birth of a child, provided you were actually "disabled" for four of those months. This disability law applies to employers with five or more employees, a significant benefit for California families.
- *California State Disability Insurance* (SDI) covers most nongovernment employees for pregnancy disability. SDI provides partial wage replacement during disability, from $50-490 per week in 2001. In most cases, the disability period for a normal pregnancy is up to four weeks before the due date and six weeks afterward. But your doctor may certify you for a longer period (e.g., for a cesarean section).

- Under the Family Medical Leave Act and state law, eligible employers must give employees taking FMLA leave their old job or an *"equivalent" job* with "equivalent" pay, benefits, and working conditions *upon return from leave.*
- If you intend to take leave, you should give your employer reasonable notice. Most experts advise telling your employer at the beginning of your second trimester. Be sure to review your leave and benefits plans with your human resources department (including getting your baby on your insurance plan), and make arrangements with your supervisor for someone to cover your responsibilities while you are gone.

WHERE TO GET HELP

If you feel your rights have been violated, or have questions about your individual situation, here are some organizations that can help:

Equal Employment Opportunity Commission (EEOC)
1801 L St., NW
Washington, DC 20507
800-669-EEOC
This federal agency enforces federal pregnancy discrimination laws.

Equal Rights Advocates
1663 Mission St., Ste. 250
San Francisco
415-621-0672
800-839-4ERA (4372) (advice and counseling hotline)
www.equalrights.org
PARENT RATING: ☆ ☆ ☆ ☆ ☆
This is a women's public interest law center engaged in litigation and pub-

lic advocacy. The website has useful information about the FMLA and other pregnancy-related laws, and the hotline provides free assistance to women facing pregnancy discrimination and medical leave issues.

Legal Aid Society of San Francisco/ Employment Law Center
1663 Mission St., Ste. 400
San Francisco
415-864-8848
800-880-8047 (hotline)
www.las-elc.org
PARENT RATING: ☆ ☆ ☆ ☆ ☆
This public interest law center specializes in employment discrimination law, particularly family and medical leave issues. The center offers free advice and information through its hotline, limited representation, workshops to parents' groups, impact litigation, and lobbying and legislative work. Call for brochures on your workplace rights.

State of California, Department of Fair Employment and Housing

800-884-1684
www.dfeh.ca.gov
- Oakland
  1515 Clay St., Ste. 701, 510-622-2941
- San Francisco
  455 Golden Gate Ave., Ste. 7600,
  415-703-4175
- San Jose
  111 N. Market St., Ste. 810,
  408-277-1277

This department enforces state discrimination and medical leave laws.

State of California, Employment Development Department
SDI Program Offices

800-480-3287 (statewide)
www.edd.ca.gov
- Oakland
  7700 Edgewater Dr., Ste. 210
- San Francisco
  745 Franklin St., Ste. 300
- San Jose
  297 W. Hedding
- Santa Rosa
  50 D St., Rm. 325

The EDD administers the SDI program; get forms and apply for SDI benefits here.

U.S. Department of Labor– Women's Bureau

71 Stevenson St., #927
San Francisco
415-975-4750
www.dol.gov

This federal agency enforces the FMLA and informs the public on working women's rights. Get a fact sheet on the FMLA.

CHAPTER 2

TAKING CARE OF YOURSELF: Pre- and Post- Natal Fitness

Regular, physician-approved exercise can be a great benefit to healthy women with low-risk pregnancies—it can increase energy levels, aid in sleeping and maintaining an appropriate weight gain, relieve many of the physical discomforts of pregnancy, and help the body prepare for labor and delivery. Exercise can also help speed up the postpartum recovery period. Many new moms, eager to shed those pregnancy pounds, reclaim their body through exercise. Of course, if you are pregnant, you should check with your physician before beginning any new exercise program. Many medical professionals say that pregnancy is not the best time to begin a new routine.

From pre- and post-natal aerobics, yoga, and swimming, to personal trainers with a special certification in working with pre- and post-natal women—there are plenty of exercise options for moms-to-be and new moms. In this chapter, we'll tell you about those that Bay Area parents have shared with us. We will help you answer the following questions:

◆ Where can I find a prenatal or postpartum exercise, yoga, or aqua-aerobics class?

- Where can I find a personal trainer who has experience working with prenatal and postpartum women?
- Where can I find a fitness center that offers child care?
- What are some good walks or hikes for me to take with my baby?
- Where can I get a prenatal or postpartum massage?

TIPS FOR PRE- AND POST- NATAL EXERCISE
- Always get your physican's approval before exercising during pregnancy or after delivery. Don't be surprised if many classes and fitness centers ask you for a note from your physician approving your exercise routine, especially if you are pregnant.
- Be sure to find out what credentials and experience your fitness instructor has in working with pregnant and postpartum women. There are several different certifications available, including Dancing Through Pregnancy, Moms in Motion, and Healthy Moms Fitness, which are recognized as industry leaders in providing training and certification to fitness instructors to teach pre- and post-natal exercise. The Aerobics and Fitness Association of America also offers a certification. For yoga certification, Whole Birth Yoga is a locally offered certification program for pre- and post-natal yoga instruction.
- Each trimester of your pregnancy brings its own demands, requiring you to modify your exercise. Be sure to check in with your instructor and physician and let them know where you are in your pregnancy and any special concerns you may have.
- Don't get overheated—drink lots of water and stop before the point of sweating profusely. Drink, drink, drink, and drink plenty of water before, during, and after exercising.

Pre- and Post-Natal Aerobics, Yoga, and Fitness Classes and Personal Trainers

Listed below are fitness centers that pregnant and postpartum women have recommended to us. Many of these centers offer drop in classes, while some offer a series that requires advance registration, so be sure to call ahead first. Prices vary, but group exercise classes run from approximately $7-20 per class and personal trainers run from $40-95 per session. You can often buy a package of classes that reduces the individual price of each class or training session. Since class schedules, hours, and fees change frequently, please call ahead for up-to-the-minute information, or check the website (if available).

San Francisco

Body Kinetics
2399 Greenwich
415-931-9922
Body Kinetics specializes in one-on-one fitness training. They have several trainers who have pre- and post-natal fitness and Pilates certification.

Castro Yoga
4450 18th St.
415-552-9644
They offer pre- and post-natal yoga classes.

Day One
3490 California St., 2nd Fl.
415-440-3291
PARENT RATING: ☆ ☆ ☆ ☆ ☆

This stunning, state-of-the-art center for new and expectant parents offers a prenatal yoga class. Instructors are nationally certified and have extensive experience in teaching prenatal yoga. Day One supplies yoga mats, bolsters, and eye pillows. One mother commented, "One prenatal class in this serene setting was just what I needed to stretch out my sore back and limbs in my last trimester!"

Ellie Herman Studios
3435 Cesar Chavez
415-285-5808
www.ellie.net

This popular Pilates studio doesn't offer anything specifically for pre- or post- natal women, but rather offers many different levels of Pilates workouts (both mat work and equipment), which pregnant and postpartum women often attend.

Firststeps Fitness
415-380-1877
susan@firststepsfit.com
This pre- and post-natal outdoor fitness class for moms and babies takes a unique approach by incorporating outdoor elements into the workout with baby. For instance, they work with resistance bands around trees, do push ups with babies underneath, and do lunges with their strollers. It is a complete body workout, including cardio vascular and strength training, focusing on strengthening the abdominal muscles and improving flexibility. They vary their workout venues depending on what suits the interests of the group.

Integral Yoga Institute
770 Dolores St.
415-821-1117
The institute offers a prenatal Hatha yoga class. They also offer a parent and baby yoga class for newborns and pre-crawling babies. This class includes gentle stretching, chanting, breathing, deep relaxation, and discussion.

Iyengar Yoga Institute

2404 27th Ave.
415-668-1736
www.iyisf.org

Featured in the December 2000 issue of *American Baby Magazine*, This studio offers a popular prenatal yoga class and a parent/baby class for postpartum women or dads and their pre-crawling infants. Classes are open to all levels; no previous experience is necessary.

The Mindful Body

2876 California St.
415-931-2639
www.themindfulbody.com

PARENT RATING: ☆ ☆ ☆ ☆ ☆

Voted as the "Best Yoga Studio" by *The San Francisco Chronicle*, The Mindful Body offers prenatal and postpartum yoga classes, specifically designed for pregnant and postpartum women to enhance the body's ability to move comfortably through the different stages of pregnancy and to recuperate from childbirth.

Open Door Yoga

1500 Castro
415-824-5657
www.opendooryoga.com

This is a relatively recent addition to the yoga scene in Noe Valley, opened in May 2001. They offer a Mommy and Me yoga class where drop ins are welcome or where you can buy a package. They also offer a preparing-for-childbirth yoga class.

OutFit Fitness

1505 Northpoint St.
415-441-4631
www.outfitfitness.com

Get ready for childbirth or get back into shape with this outdoor fitness training bootcamp. Owner and certified personal trainer Jennifer Jolly leads a one-hour-and-fifteen-minute outdoor fitness program at Kezar Stadium specifically for pregnant women and new moms and their babies. The "Baby Boot Camp" workout varies according to the fitness level of participants and includes cardio and strength training. They also offer a baby-sitter to watch the babies, as needed. The locale is a very contained space, so it is ideal for older children as well as babies. They also have an inclement weather meeting spot in the neighborhood. Bring your baby and a jogger, stroller, or baby carrier and prepare for a challenging workout!

Presidio YMCA

Lincoln Way at Funston (Building 63)
415-447-9622

PARENT RATING: ☆ ☆ ☆ ☆ ☆

This YMCA offers a popular prenatal and postpartum aerobics class consisting of an intense step aerobic workout, hand weights, and floor work. The instructor is especially good at tailoring the exercise to your stage of pregnancy and your fitness level. She also encourages networking among other city moms in this very social class! Non-crawling or walking babies are welcome. If you want to try the class before joining the Y, you can purchase a "day pass." Comments: "This is an amazing workout—even for non-pregnant women." "I go for the exercise, but also to socialize and get caught up in the world of urban moms and babies!"

Purely Physical Gym

1300 Church St.
415-282-1329

This friendly neighborhood gym permits strollers, so you can park your baby in front of your stairmaster.

San Francisco Buddhist Center

37 Bartlett St.
415-282-2018
www.sfbuddhistcenter.org

This center offers a prenatal yoga class of gentle stretches for pregnant women to prepare for a relaxed labor and birth. They also offer mommy and baby yoga that includes gentle stretching to help replenish your body and focus on strengthening your pelvic floor and abdominal muscles.

San Francisco Kaiser Permanente

415-202-4120

Prenatal exercise and yoga classes are held at 2425 Geary Blvd., in the Mezzanine, Conference Rm. 4. Drop ins welcome. See Whole Birth Yoga below.

Strong Heart Strong Body

3556 Sacramento St.
415-353-5616

PARENT RATING: ☆ ☆ ☆ ☆ ☆

This posh Pacific Heights studio recently moved to a larger space and offers more options than ever before. They offer one-on-one personal training, Pilates, and one-on-one yoga, and they have pre- and postnatal certified trainers on staff. It is possible to bring infants to workout sessions, as long as they are in a stroller and not mobile. They also offer a variety of group fitness classes, including pre- and post-natal yoga.

Studio Valencia

See under "Individual Pre- and Postnatal Fitness Instructors"—Elizabeth Bessamir.

University of California, San Francisco

Millberry Union
500 Parnassus Ave.
415-476-1115

This group offers a prenatal and postpartum exercise class called Fit for Two. This class is designed to condition your body during pregnancy and prepare for delivery by stimulating circulation, building strength and flexibility, and increasing stamina. This is also a great class for getting back into shape after childbirth. Babies are welcome.

Urban Body Works

2501 Lake St.

415-831-0727

This state-of-the art (opened in 2001) Pilates, yoga, and fitness center specializes in one-on-one training. They have a staff member with considerable experience and certification in pre- and post-natal fitness. Appointment required.

Whole Birth Yoga

831-425-7731 (Robin Sale, founder)

www.wholebirthresources.com

wholebirth@earthlink.net

Whole Birth Yoga offers unique pre-natal yoga and support classes at several area hospitals including San Francisco Kaiser and South San Francisco Kaiser. For a schedule, fees, and registration, contact each hospital directly. For full description, see under South Bay.

Yoga Tree

www.yogatreesf.com

• 1234 Valencia, 415-647-9707
• 780 Stanyan, 415-387-4707
• 519 Hayes, 415-626-9707

Yoga Tree has three San Francisco locations that offer prenatal and mom and baby postpartum yoga.

North Bay

Baby Boot Camp

Blackie's Pasture

Tiburon Blvd. (at Trestle Glen)

Tiburon

415-290-2764

www.babybootcamp.net

This 75-minute group fitness class led by Kristen Horler (who has certifications in pre- and post-natal fitness) consists of strength training, muscle toning, stretching, and functional exercises for motherhood. The class meets two mornings per week at Blackie's Pasture in Tiburon. At press-time, plans are being made for the class to meet in Mill Valley as well. Bring water and either a yoga mat or blanket suitable for exercising on the grass. The class is compatible for babies either in a stroller, front carrier, or by the side of your mat. Participants are free to take care of their babies as needed.

Elan Health and Fitness Center

www.elanfitness.com

• San Anselmo
  230 Greenfield Ave., 415- 485-1945
• Petaluma
  1372 N. McDowell Blvd.,
  707-765-1919

This family-run health and fitness center offers exercise classes and a well-equipped exercise facility exclusively for women. In addition they offer one-on-one certified trainers. Child care arrangements are available. They also sponsor the Moms on the Move post-natal exercise classes. See below.

Fairfax Health Club and Aerobic Center
713 Center Blvd.
Fairfax
415-459-1030
This club offers personal trainers and certified fitness specialists who have extensive experience working with pregnant women.

Gold's Gym
10 Fifer Ave.
Corte Madera
415-924-4653
This gym offers certified personal trainers who are experienced in working with expecting mothers. Child care is available. They also sponsor Moms on the Move classes. See below.

Marin YMCA
1500 Los Gamos Dr.
San Rafael
415-492-9622
While not specifically offering prenatal classes, this YMCA offers low-impact aerobics, stretching and toning, and yoga classes that many pregnant women attend. They also offer one-on-one fitness training and child care.

Mill Valley Recreation Center
180 Camino Alto Ave.
Mill Valley
415-383-1370
PARENT RATING: ☆ ☆ ☆ ☆ ☆
This state-of-the-art community center offers a popular combined pre- and post-natal exercise class three mornings a week, which includes strength training and flexibility exercises.

Moms on the Move
510-234-1629
www.momsonthemove.net
- Mill Valley
  RoCo Dance & Fitness,
  237 Shoreline Hwy.
- San Anselmo
  Elan Fitness Center,
  230 Greenfield Ave.
- Corte Madera
  Gold's Gym, 10 Fifer Ave.

PARENT RATING: ☆ ☆ ☆ ☆ ☆
Moms on the Move is an innovative exercise program, offering pre- and post-natal exercise and yoga classes for the expectant and new mom at three Marin locations. You don't have to be a member of the facility to attend classes. Babies are welcome in classes and child care is available at all locations. Classes consist of cardio (step aerobics) and strength training (hand weights). They also offer Moms Mat classes that target core strengthening, stretching, and mind-body awareness through Pilates and yoga poses. Segments of all classes may be modified to suit your fitness level. Directed by an obstetrical nurse, all instructors are trained and certified by the internationally recognized Moms on the Move certification teacher training.
Comment: "Though the pace is a bit slower than a regular aerobics class, it's still a good workout and a nice transition between doing nothing and a full workout in a very supportive environment."

Mt. Tamalpais Racquet Club

1 Larkspur Dr.
Larkspur
415-924-6226

PARENT RATING: ☆ ☆ ☆ ☆ ☆

Enjoy this neighborhood fitness facility's group exercise classes from yoga to step aerobics to aqua aerobics and cycling. Child care is available for children 3 months and up at reasonable rates.

Osher Marin Jewish Community Center

200 N. San Pedro Rd.
San Rafael
415-444-8038
www.jccmarin.org

This center offers a water exercise class for pregnant and postpartum women members. They also offer a one-on-one pre- and post-natal resistance training program. A personal trainer with experience in training pregnant and postpartum women provides a supportive and motivated environment to prepare your body for the physical demands of pregnancy and childbirth and to strengthen and tone your body afterwards. This fitness training includes using bands, floorwork stretching, resistance training, free weights, and machines. Infants are welcome to accompany moms in either a car seat or a stroller. Training is by appointment only.

Roco Dance and Fitness

237 Shoreline Hwy.
Mill Valley
415-388-6786
www.rocodance.com

This award-winning dance and fitness center offers Pilates, spinning, aerobics, and yoga. Child care is available. They also sponsor Moms on the Move classes. See above. Roco members receive 50 percent off these classes.

Ross Recreation

The Stress Management Center of Marin
1165 Magnolia Ave.
Larkspur
415-461-2288
www.SMCmarin.com

This community recreation center offers both pre- and post- natal yoga classes. They also offer a yoga class for parents of preschool-age children called Yoga for Moms and Dads. Child care is available for children one-5 years old.

Santa Rosa YMCA

1111 College Ave.
Santa Rosa
707-545-9622

This YMCA offers a pre- and post-natal aqua aerobic class.

Strawberry Recreation Center

118 E. Strawberry Dr.
Mill Valley
415-383-6494

This center offers a great water aerobics class in their wonderful outdoor pool. While it isn't a class specifically for pregnant women, many do attend.

Terra Linda Community Center

670 Del Ganado Rd.
San Rafael
415-485-3344

The pool is open from March through October and offers an aquatic exercise program during that time.

X Gym

401B Tamal Plaza Dr.
Corte Madera
415-924-9496

PARENT RATING: ☆ ☆ ☆ ☆ ☆

Short on time? X Gym is the answer! This one-on-one personal training center has a unique program where you go twice a week for a twenty-minute strength training workout. Comment: "It's very effective and great for people (with babies and young children) with a limited amount of time." Training sessions are by appointment only.

Yoga Center of Marin

142 Redwood Ave.
Corte Madera
415-927-1850
www.yogacenterofmarin.com

This center offers two prenatal yoga classes a week. Drop ins welcome.

Yoga Garden

412 Red Hill Ave., Ste. 12
The Essex Center Building
San Anselmo
415-485-5800
www.yogagardenstudio.com

This popular yoga studio offers ongoing pre- and post-natal yoga classes that provide a supportive environment for both pregnant women and new mothers. The prenatal class includes postures and breath awareness that will help maintain your well-being through pregnancy and will enhance your endurance, strength, and flexibility in preparation for birth. Both of these classes are ongoing, but registration is suggested.

The Yoga Source

8 Mariposa Ave.
San Anselmo
415-460-1232

PARENT RATING: ☆ ☆ ☆ ☆ ☆

This small yoga studio offers yoga for moms and babies classes from time to time. Class size is limited to ten, so call in advance to reserve your spot. Drop ins (if space is available) are welcome.

Yoga Studio

650 E. Blithedale Ave.
Mill Valley
415-380-8800
www.yogastudio.com

PARENT RATING: ☆ ☆ ☆ ☆ ☆

This wonderful and popular yoga studio offers ongoing pre- and post-natal yoga classes. Classes are taught by an instructor who is certified in yoga, massage, and acupressure for pregnant women. The prenatal class helps you cultivate health and prepare for birth through gentle yoga postures and breath awareness in a supportive environment. The postnatal class, Mom and Baby Yoga, helps you get back in shape with yoga poses designed for strengthening and toning your body after giving birth. The studio offers community and support for new moms, playful interactions with babies, and lively discussions to help you experience parenting as a joyful meditation. Comment: "Very relaxing with lots of stretching...avoids holding poses for long periods of time, which is difficult when pregnant!"

Albany YMCA

921 Kaines St.
510-525-1130
Albany

PARENT RATING: ☆ ☆ ☆ ☆ ☆

This YMCA offers prenatal and post-partum aerobics classes two mornings a week. Comment: "Great way to meet other pregnant and new moms—the teacher is great too!"

Berkeley YMCA

2001 Allston Way
510-848-9622
www.berkeley-ymca.org

The Berkeley YMCA offers three classes for pre-and post-natal needs, including step aerobics, yoga, and water exercise. Child care is available. Besides being a great workout, the prenatal water aerobics includes time to socialize with other moms-to-be. Comment: "The prenatal yoga class resulted in my being able to sleep better than I have in months."

Berkeley Yoga Center

1250 Addison St., Ste. 209
510-843-8784
www.BerkeleyYoga.com

PARENT RATING: ☆ ☆ ☆ ☆ ☆

This beautiful yoga center overlooks Strawberry Creek Park in a converted warehouse with brick walls and hardwood floors. The center offers both prenatal yoga classes and postnatal classes. In the prenatal class, she prepares pregnant women for labor and delivery through postures, breathing exercises, and relaxation. The postpartum class is oriented to the special needs of new mothers.

Non-mobile babies (pre-crawling) are welcome; an assistant is available to help with all babies. Comment: "This class gave me not only the physical conditioning that I needed before going into labor, but also [taught me] meditation and conscious relaxation."

Karen Casino

1432 Derby St.
Berkeley
510-644-2066

Karen offers a pregnancy workout and a new mother's workout in her home studio. Her pregnancy workout includes Pilates, pelvic tilts, and exercises for the entire body that aim to ease pregnancy and labor as well as postpartum recovery. The new mother's workout is a ten-session class designed to remodel your body after childbirth, focusing on the muscles affected during pregnancy and childbirth. Babies are welcome, and there is a baby-sitter on hand. The pregnancy class is ongoing and pregnant women may join at any time. A sliding fee schedule is available.

Club One

1200 Clay St.
Oakland
510-895-1010

This full-service fitness center offers group exercise classes as well as all the standard gym equipment. They also have a personal trainer on staff with experience in working with pre-and post-natal women. Child care is available.

Courthouse Gym

2985 Telegraph Rd.
Oakland
510-834-5600

This full-service fitness center offers group exercise classes as well as a well-equipped gym for members. Child care is available.

Ellie Herman Studios

3929 Grand Ave.
Oakland
510-594-8507
www.ellie.net

See under San Francisco.

Fit Mama

510-601-8558
www.fitmama.com

Fit Mama offers a special ongoing class for new moms at The Mind-Body Connection at 5255 College Ave. in Oakland. Each class includes a cardio warm up, strength training, lots of abdominal work, and flexibility and relaxation training. Babies up to 7 months are welcome. She will help you incorporate your baby's needs into the exercises, if necessary. Comments: "Fun and low-key!" "A great way to meet other new moms!"

Fourth Street Yoga

1809C 4th St.
Berkeley
510-845-YOGA
www.4thstreetyoga.com

PARENT RATING: ☆ ☆ ☆ ☆ ☆

Serving the Berkeley community for almost ten years, Fourth Street Yoga offers both pre- and post-natal yoga classes. The prenatal class is a beginning class designed for pregnant women who want to increase awareness of their bodies. The post-natal class aims to bring the body back to its original strength and tone. Infants are welcome at this class. Many moms commented on how much they enjoy the prenatal class: "It flowed well, and she had a great way of working with us in our growing bodies." "She is very clear in her direction and is very knowledgeable about how pregnancy changes your ability to move." Since this class is so popular, it is reportedly a little crowded.

Helene Byrne's Post Pregnancy Exercise

Montclair Women's Cultural Arts Center
1650 Mountain Blvd.
Oakland
510-530-5710

Author of *Exercise after Pregnancy: How to Look and Feel Your Best,* Helen Byrne has become one of the Bay Area's own expert on postpartum exercise. A mother herself, she offers a six-week, post-pregnancy exercise workshop that uses the Pilates method of body conditioning to restore alignment and balance during the postpartum period. Helen has a professional background in dance and Pilates training. Babies are welcome at the class.

John Muir/Mt. Diablo Health System Women's Health Center

1656 N. California Blvd.
Walnut Creek
925-947-3331

This center offers a pregnancy yoga class and a Mommy and Me yoga class. Prenatal yoga explores postures for pregnancy, labor, and delivery, including deep breathing, stretching, strengthening, and relaxation. Mommy and Me yoga is offered to moms and their pre-crawling infants. Yoga postures and breathing techniques are taught to help restore and rebuild your body, mind, and spirit.

Oakland YMCA

2350 Broadway
Oakland
510-451-9622

The YMCA offers many group exercise classes appropriate for moms-to-be and new mothers, including low-impact water aerobics and water walking. Child care is available.

Physiotherapy Associates

3031 Telegraph Ave.
Berkeley
510-644-3031

This one-on-one fitness training group has a staff member who is experienced in developing fitness programs for pregnant women.

Seventh Heaven Body Awareness Center

2820 7th St.
Berkeley
510-665-4300
www.7thheavenyoga.com

This full-service yoga center offers a combined pre- and post-natal class to support women through the phases of pregnancy, birthing, and post-delivery. Emphasis is placed on gentle postures to create ease, build strength, and deepen the connection between the expectant mother and her baby. All levels are welcome.

Synergy Fitness

1124 Solano Ave.
Albany
510-527-9005

This center offers one-on-one personal fitness and Pilates training with trainers who are experienced in working with pre- and post-natal women.

Yogalayam

1723 Alcatraz Ave.
Berkeley
510-655-3664

PARENT RATING: ☆ ☆ ☆ ☆ ☆

Saraswathi Devi offers ongoing pre- and post-natal yoga classes that you can join at any time. Babies are welcome at the postnatal class. She offers a sliding fee schedule. She also offers a popular yoga course that complements childbirth preparation instruction, as well as couples yoga and massage for childbirth, pregnancy, and postpartum periods. Moms swear by her classes: "She knows a lot about how the body changes when pregnant, and her class really resulted in my aches and pains diminishing." "Her class is gentle, nurturing, and restorative."

The Yoga Room
The Julia Morgan Center
2540 College Ave.
Berkeley
PARENT RATING: ☆ ☆ ☆ ☆ ☆

The Yoga Room is a yoga co-op, with several teachers offering classes for varying fees. Barbara Papini (510-601-1883) offers an ongoing prenatal beginning yoga class to assist women in preparing for childbirth. Her class emphasizes the Iyengar style, which stresses a healthy alignment of the spine and increased self-awareness. No previous yoga experience is necessary. Everyone seems to love this class! Debbie Gillman (510-655-9813) offers a postpartum Yoga for Moms and Babies class, which is an Iyengar style yoga class for moms and their pre-crawling babies. The class is designed with the early postpartum months in mind and incorporates interaction with the babies.

Betty Wright Swim Center
Community Association for Rehabilitation Inc.
3864 Middlefield Rd.
Palo Alto
650-494-1480
PARENT RATING: ☆ ☆ ☆ ☆ ☆

This center offers prenatal aquatic exercise classes in an indoor pool twice a week. Drop ins are welcome.

Blossom Birth Services
1000 Elwell Ct.
Palo Alto
650-964-7380
www.blossombirth.com
PARENT RATING: ☆ ☆ ☆ ☆ ☆

This resource center offers prenatal yoga classes that aim to enhance awareness of the body and its dramatic changes during pregnancy. They also offer a mother-baby yoga class, where new moms bring their babies and join others in stretching, relaxing, and rejuvenating! In a Moving with Baby class, new moms learn exercises and stretches that incorporate interacting with their baby. No previous experience is necessary for the yoga classes.

California Yoga Center
570 Showers Dr., Ste. 5
Mountain View
650-947-9642
www.californiayoga.com

The center offers a prenatal Iyengar yoga class. Drop ins are welcome. Pregnant and recently postpartum women are also welcome to attend several Level I classes.

Can Do Yoga

3636 Florence St., Ste. A
Redwood City
650-368-5727

They do not offer a specific class for pregnant or postpartum women, but rather welcome and integrate them into regular classes with the instructor modifying their sequences.

Center for Spiritual Enlightenment

1146 University Ave.
San Jose
408-283-0221

This center offers prenatal and postpartum yoga classes. Yoga for the mother is the focus of the first part of the postpartum class, followed by a second part for mom and baby together. Non-crawling babies are welcome.

Devine Design

3199 S. Bascom Ave.
Campbell
408-371-5313
www.devinedesignfitness.com

They offer personal fitness training with trainers who have prenatal and postpartum experience.

El Camino YMCA

2400 Grant Rd.
Mountain View
650-969-9622

In addition to a full offering of group exercise classes and a state-of-the-art fitness center, this Y offers three specific classes for prenatal and postpartum women that are quite popular. They offer a pre- and post-natal exercise class, which consists of modified low-impact aerobics and strength training. They also offer a pre- and post-natal aquatics exercise class as well as a prenatal yoga class.

Kaiser Permanente

* Redwood City
  Redwood City Medical Center,
  Health Education Center,
  1150 Veterans Blvd., 650-299-2433

This hospital offers a six-week prenatal yoga class for women during any stage of pregnancy. They teach yoga postures for strength, tone, balance and agility to enhance comfort during pregnancy and to prepare body and mind for childbirth. No previous yoga experience is necessary.

* Santa Clara
  Santa Clara Medical Center,
  900 Kiely Blvd., 408-885-5000

This hospital offers a prenatal yoga class.

Menlo Park Recreation Center

700 Alma St.
Menlo Park
650-858-3470
www.menlopark.org

PARENT RATING: ☆ ☆ ☆ ☆

This community center has myriad fitness options for pregnant and postpartum women. They offer a full aquatics exercise program as well as aerobics, including the Stretch and Firm class which is popular with pregnant women. Sessions run eight weeks. The center also offers a pre- and post-natal yoga class.

Mills-Peninsula Health Center Community Education

Garden Room
100 S. San Mateo Dr.
San Mateo
650-696-5600 (The Wellness Center)
www.mills-peninsula.org

Mills-Peninsula offers a prenatal yoga class that aims to increase relaxation, flexibility, and strength. Previous yoga experience is required. They also offer a popular water aerobics class for pre- and post partum women.

Mills-Peninsula Health Center

Mack E. Mickelson Arthritis and Rehabilitation Center
75 El Camino Real
San Mateo
650-696-4315

PARENT RATING: ☆ ☆ ☆ ☆ ☆

This center offers Aquatic Stretch and Tone, a low-intensity aquatic exercise program geared toward pregnant women and new mothers. Mills-Peninsula also offers a full aquatic exercise program that includes other low to moderate workouts. This class is *very* popular!

No Excuses, Your Fitness Partner

543 Addison Ave.
Palo Alto
650-325-1273
www.noexcusesfitness.com

This fitness center offers one-on-one personal training, with trainers and Pilates instructors who have experience in working with prenatal and postpartum women.

Palo Alto YMCA

3412 Ross Rd.
Palo Alto
650-856-9622 (general numbers)
650-842-7162 (Director, group exercise)

Modified low impact classes specifically intended for pregnant and post-partum women are held twice a week. Babies are welcome.

Peninsula Family YMCA

1877 S. Grant St.
San Mateo
650-286-9622
www.peninsulafamilyYMCA.org

In the past, the Peninsula Y offered a prenatal and postpartum exercise class. At presstime, however, they do not have an instructor for this class. They do plan to offer this popular class again. In the meantime, the Peninsula Y offers a Low Impact/Gentle Aerobics Class for pregnant and postpartum women in addition to many other classes. Child care is available.

Reach Fitness Club

707 High St.
Palo Alto
650-327-3224

This club offers personal trainers who are experienced in working with pregnant and postpartum women.

San Carlos Parks and Recreation Department

1017 Cedar St.
San Carlos
650-802-4382

They offer a twice-weekly prenatal fitness class that incorporates low impact aerobics, muscle toning, light weight training and supportive tips and advice for expectant mothers.

Sequoia Hospital

Health & Wellness Services
702 Marshall St.
Redwood City
650-482-6065

PARENT RATING: ☆ ☆ ☆ ☆ ☆

They offer a prenatal yoga class that features postures to ease labor discomfort and strengthen the abdominal muscles.

Stanford Hospital
Lucile Packard Children's Hospital

Perinatal Education
650-723-4600

Stanford offers several options for maternity fitness. The Fit for Two Prenatal Program is designed for the healthy pregnant mother. This class includes aerobic exercise, floor work, and stretching. They also offer Prenatal Yoga which emphasizes body awareness and focused breathing for use in pregnancy, labor, and postpartum recovery. They also offer a Stroller Fitness class from time to time.

Whole Birth Yoga

831-425-7731 (Robin Sale, founder)
www.wholebirthresources.com
wholebirth@earthlink.net

Whole Birth Yoga trains instructors to offer unique prenatal, postpartum and couples yoga, and support classes. These instructors offer classes at several area hospitals, including the Community Hospital of Los Gatos (408-866-3905), Santa Cruz Dominican Hospital (831-462-7700), Kaiser Permanente South San Francisco (650-742-2439), Sequoia Hospital in Redwood City (650-368-2229), Kaiser Permanente Pleasanton (925-847-5172), and Valley Care Health Services in Livermore (800-719-9111). They also offer classes at Blossom Birth Services, see above, Palo Alto Recreation Department (650-493-4900), the Yoga Center of Las Gatos (408-857-0901), and Downtown Yoga in Pleasanton (925-463-YOGA). The prenatal class is a two-hour-and fifteen-minute class that includes time for checking in with one another. The postnatal class incorporates pre-crawling babies into postures and movement, and includes time for mothers to share stories and advice.

The Yoga Solution, Marti Foster

Menlo Park
408-323-8833
www.yogasolution.com

In this pre- and post-natal yoga class for couples and pregnant women, you learn special yoga postures to practice during the changing phases of your pregnancy as well as calming breathing techniques. The couples class focuses on creating a nurturing bond between you and your baby and allows you to share this experience with your partner. Workshops are held on weekend days at the Peninsula School in Menlo Park. Foster also offers in-home instruction.

The Yoga Wellness Center
35 N. San Mateo Dr.
San Mateo
650-401-6423
www.yogawellnesscenter.com
The Yoga Wellness Center offers a class for pregnant women called Yoga for Pregnancy. Drop ins are welcome.

Individual Pre- and Post-Natal Fitness Instructors

Listed below are some personal trainers and fitness instructors who work as free-lancers in several different locations and studios. Contact them directly or check their website (if available) for venues, schedules, and fees.

San Francisco

Elizabeth Bessamir
415-931-7291
Elizabeth teaches pre- and post-natal yoga in various locations in San Francisco, including Studio Valencia (a studio space for free lance instructors located at 455A Valencia St.).

Tracy Hartway
650-557-1434
Offering personal training and yoga for moms and moms-to-be, Tracy combines nearly ten years of experience in fitness, yoga, and childbirth education. She is a recent mom herself. A former pre- and post–partum yoga instructor at The Mindful Body in San Francisco and The Mill Valley Yoga Studio, Tracy currently offers her one-on-one personal training out of the Strong Heart, Strong Body studio. See above. "Amazing teacher...the best!"

Julie Rappaport
415-263-3940
www.yogabliss.com
Julie teaches pre- and post-natal yoga in various studios in San Francisco, Berkeley, and Oakland. She also offers private or semiprivate classes.

East Bay

Jane Eversole, RPT
510-538-2586
Jane offers prenatal and postpartum exercise classes through the Hayward Area Recreation Department at the Kenneth Aitken Senior and Community Center,

17800 Redwood Rd, Castro Valley. The prenatal class focuses on conditioning and relaxing the body while strengthening the key muscles used in childbearing. The postpartum class is a six-week session that helps new mothers gain control of muscles affected during pregnancy and delivery. Jane offers lots of education about muscles, saving your back and relaxation in both classes. Pre-crawling babies are welcome.

Kim Frank

510-526-4619
learnmatwork@yahoo.com

Kim offers private (in your home) one-on-one training in Pilates mat work for new mothers. Her fee depends on the frequency of the training sessions.

Julie Rappaport

415-263-3940
www.yogabliss.com
See above.

Susan Schreier Williams

510-482-2276

Susan is an Alexander Technique certified teacher who works with pre- and post-natal women who want to reduce tension and pain by learning a "relaxed state of attention." She offers small, ongoing classes. Babies are welcome in the postpartum class.

South Bay

Mara Cohen

650-379-2764

She offers private and semiprivate pre- and post-natal yoga classes.

Julia Roberts

408-746-2752

She offers Iyengar yoga classes in Sunnyvale and Mountain View where she welcomes pregnant and postpartum women.

Favorite Fitness Facilities with Child Care

The facilities listed below are some of parents' favorite fitness centers that offer child care, in addition to those noted under "Classes," above. Reservations are required in most clubs, and the services are for members only. Child care arrangements in fitness centers are typically available for a limited time, depending on the age of your child, usually for one-half hour up to two hours, at varying costs. Most are quite reasonable and a few are free. If you plan on using child care at a gym, your best bet is to observe the child care room before you join and to talk to some of the parents who use it.

Bar Method Exercise Studio

3333 Fillmore St.

415-441-6333

www.barmethod.com

PARENT RATING: ☆ ☆ ☆ ☆ ☆

Opened in summer 2001, the Bar Method is all the rage! The owners of this posh Marina exercise studio promise to tone your body and elongate muscles with their rigorous one-hour workout. They have an attractive child care room with many wooden toys and even a teepee for toddlers to play in! The best part is that there is no need to make a reservation! Comments: "I feel good when I arrive in this serene studio, but oh so much better afterwards!" "I really look forward to these workouts, even though they are tough!"

Bay Club

150 Greenwich St.

415-433-2200

PARENT RATING: ☆ ☆ ☆ ☆ ☆

According to many parents, the Bay Club, an upscale full-service fitness club, has a great child care program where the child care providers really make an effort. You can book up to two weeks in advance and they accept infants as young as 6 weeks old.

Presidio YMCA

Lincoln Way at Funston (Building 63)

415-447-9622

PARENT RATING: ☆ ☆ ☆ 1/2

While the Y is among parents' favorites for the breadth of their offerings, their "childwatch" room is small and can be crowded during the popular morning hours. (There's also a small, fenced outdoor area.) Overall, the childwatch staff does a good job. It can be difficult to get reservations for infants, especially during the morning aerobic classes. Infants must be at least 3 months old. The Y starts taking reservations for any particular day two days in advance (and not sooner).

Richmond YMCA

360 18th Ave.

415-666-9622

This is a smaller facility than the Presidio Y, but also offers group exercise classes and more. This Y offers childcare from 3 months and up during the day only.

Bay Club

221 Corte Madera Town Center

Corte Madera

415-945-3000

San Francisco's famed Bay Club is scheduled to open in August 2002 with all the same great amenities, including child care.

Elan Health and Fitness Center

• San Anselmo
  230 Greenfield Ave., 415-485-1945
• Petaluma
  1372 N. McDowell Blvd., 707-765-1919

Gold's Gym

10 Fifer Ave.

Larkspur

415-924-4653

Marin YMCA

1500 Los Gamos Dr.

San Rafael

415-492-9622

Meridian Sports Club
1299 4th St.
San Rafael
415-459-8668

Mt. Tamalpais Racquet Club
1 Larkspur Dr.
Larkspur
415-924-6226
Infants must be at least 3 months old.

Osher Marin Jewish Community Center
200 N. San Pedro Rd.
San Rafael
415-444-8038

Rolling Hills Club
351 San Andreas Dr.
Novato
415-897-2185

Santa Rosa YMCA
111 College Ave.
Santa Rosa
707-545-9622

East Bay

Albany YMCA
921 Kaines St.
Albany
510-525-1130
This YMCA usually has one child care provider in a small room adjacent to the gym. Care is fine according to most, but the linoleum floors can be a bit rough for toddlers who aren't quite walking. Child care providers here are not licensed to change diapers, so they'll come get you from your workout to do this. Comment: "Very caring staff, mostly experienced moms."

Berkeley YMCA
2001 Allston Way
510-848-9622
Parents who are Y members staff the "childwatch" room. They take infants as young as 8 weeks. The room is reportedly busy, but there's a great kindergym that young children love with lots of toys and art, and even a computer!

Blackhawk Pinnacle Fitness
3464 Blackhawk Plaza Cir.
Danville
925-736-0898

ClubSport
• San Ramon
350 Bollinger Canyon Rd.,
925-735-8500
Comment: "Child care is super here!"
• Pleasanton
7090 Johnson Dr., 925-463-2822

Courthouse Gym
2985 Telegraph Rd.
Oakland
510-834-5600
Child care is staffed by members; reduced membership rates are given in return.

Harbor Bay Club Gym
200 Packet Landing Rd.
Alameda
510-521-5414

Jazzercise, Castro Valley
Kenneth C. Aitken Community Center
17800 Redwood Rd.
Castro Valley
510-537-6824
www.jazzercise.com

87

Mariner Square Athletic Club

2227 Mariner Square Loop
Alameda
510-523-8011

This is a nice, clean child care facility with a play fort, play kitchen, and more for kids. Best of all it is free to members!

Oakwood Athletic Club

4000 Mt. Diablo Blvd.
Lafeyette
925-283-4000

Schoeber's Athletic Club

• Pleasanton
  5341 Owen's Ct., 925-463-0950
• Fremont
  3411 Capital Ave., 510-791-6350

Walnut Creek Sport and Fitness

1908 Olympic Blvd.
Walnut Creek
925-932-6400

South Bay

Courtside Club

14675 Winchester Blvd.
Los Gatos
408-395-7111

El Camino YMCA

2400 Grant Rd.
Mountain View
650-969-9622

Infants must be at least 3 months old.

Decathlon Club

3250 Central Expwy.
Santa Clara
408-738-2582

Los Gatos Swim and Racquet Club

14700 Oka Rd.
Los Gatos
408-356-2136

Pacific Athletic Club

200 Redwood Shore Pkwy.
Redwood Shores
650-593-4900

This club will take infants as young as 6 weeks old.

Palo Alto YMCA

3412 Ross Rd.
Palo Alto
650-856-9622 (general number)
650-842-7162 (Director, group exercise)

Infants must be at least 3 months old.

Peninsula Covenant Community Center

3623 Jefferson Ave.
Redwood City
650-364-6272

Comment: "All of their classes are great, especially the water aerobics, and they offer excellent child care!"

Peninsula Family YMCA

1877 S. Grant St.
San Mateo
650-286-9622

Infants must be at least 3 months old.

Favorite Walks and Hikes

There are many wonderful places to walk and hike with a baby or young child in the Bay Area. Here are a few favorites:

San Francisco

Baker Beach

A walk on this beach is best on a warm day, with a front or back pack. If you are really up for exploring, there are a couple of dirt trails in the Presidio that lead down to the beach.

City Guides: Free Walking Tours

www.sfcityguides.org

Learn a little history about your city with baby by taking a San Francisco Public Library-sponsored City Guide walk. They offer twenty-seven different walks each week. Just meet your badge-wearing guide at the designated venue. Walks are free and usually last between one-and-a-half to two hours. Not all walks are stroller friendly, so either bring baby in a front pack or other carrier or call in advance. Visit their website for a complete schedule of walks.

Crissy Field (Marina)

Enjoy a walk or jog all the way from St. Frances Yacht Club to Fort Point. While a good portion of this trail is paved, some of it is loose gravel, so a jog stroller is recommended. Don't forget to bring a windbreaker and to stop off at the Warming Hut Café and Bookstore, located about three-quarters of the way to Fort Point.

Fort Funston

Skyline Blvd. (about one mile south of Sloat Blvd.)
415-556-8371
There are great walking paths and hang glider viewing here.

Additional Resources for Walks and Hikes in San Francisco

◆ *Skating Unrinked in the San Francisco Bay Area* by Richard Katz features paved trails which are not only great for skaters, but also for strollers!

◆ *Hidden Walks in the Bay Area* by Stephen Altschuler is a great guide to many walks in San Francisco.

◆ *Stairway Walks in San Francisco* by Adah Bakalinsky is a great guide to getting to know your city while your baby is still in a front carrier!

Golden Gate Park

http://www.civiccenter.ci.sf.ca.us/recpark/location.nsf

The nation's largest urban national park offers many hikes and walks appropriate for babies and strollers. A fun and easy one is around the Rodeo Lagoon. Or take a stroll around Stow Lake at John F. Kennedy Dr. and feed the ducks with your little one. Or watch model boat sailing at Spreckels Lake. The Strybing Arboretum and Botanical Gardens both offer walking tours.

Lake Merced

Skyline Blvd. at Lake Merced Blvd.
415-831-2700

Great paved paths go around the perimeter of the reservoir. Perfect for strollers!

Mountain Lake Park Loop

Lake St. and 12th Ave.

Part of this under-a-mile loop is paved and the other part is gravel. One of the nice things about this walk is that it ends up at Mountain Lake Park's playground which features a little lake where you can feed the ducks—if the pigeons let you!

Noe Valley Stroller Group

www.noestrolls.com

This play group on wheels meets at various locations in the city to take stroller walks with their little ones. It's a great way to exercise, meet new moms, and enjoy our wonderful city with your baby! They have regular strolls, a jogging group, and much more. The walks are geared for kids (newborn to age 3) who are in strollers. The group also has Fitness Fridays, which features a workout with a group member who is also a personal trainer. To join, all you have to do is e-mail your first name and your baby's name and age to their website, or visit their website for venues and show up at one of their strolls. Membership is free.

Wednesday Stroller Walks in Golden Gate Park

415-750-5105 (Friends of Recreation and Parks)
www.frp.org

Enjoy fresh air and exercise, meet other parents, and learn a little Park history. These walks are designed for parents with strollers, as guides stay on paved paths. They meet the first and third Wednesday of every month, rain or shine. A free one-hour stroll begins at 10 a.m.

North Bay

Angel Island

Kids will love taking the ferry to Angel Island from San Francisco, Tiburon, Oakland, or Vallejo. Once you are there, chose a five-mile perimeter loop, which takes you past Camp Reynolds, a Civil War-era garrison with spectacular views. A less rigorous route is the 3.7-mile loop up to Mount Livermore, which also has great views.

Blackie's Pasture, Tiburon

This park offers plenty of parking, with paved flat trails, perfect for strollers, offering great bay views. The path will take you all the way to downtown Tiburon. There is a nice playground on the way.

Creekside Path (from Corte Madera to Ross)

This is a nice hiking or biking trail that runs along a creek past Corte Madera Town Park, Piper Park in Larkspur, and Creekside Park in Greenbrae. It's great for strollers. Take it to the College of Marin or all the way to Ross.

Indian Valley, Novato

This valley has a wide, flat, and shady trail.

Muir Woods

415-388-2595
www.visitmuirwoods.com/trails.htm
Muir Woods has a couple of easy to moderate trails that work well with a

---

Additional Resources for Walks and Hikes in the North Bay

◆ www.marintrails.com/Kids/kidsintro.html
Marin trails offers three types of hikes, with babies, toddlers, and children. The website provides a great deal of information, including how much shade each hike typically has, approximate mileage, and good directions.

◆ www.plumsite.com/bayareamoms/outandabout/naturetrails/trails.htm

◆ www.bahiker.com/kids.html
For rougher terrain trails that are suitable for jogging strollers or baby backpacks, visit these websites.

◆ *Best Hikes with Children: San Francisco's North Bay*, by Bill McMillon and Kevin McMillon.

◆ *Easy Hiking in Northern California*, by Ann Marie Brown, contains fourteen hikes in Marin, four in the East Bay, and many in Yosemite and Tahoe, which are suitable for preschoolers.

◆ *Hiking in Marin, 133 Great Hikes in Marin County*, by Don and Kay Martin.

◆ *Skating Unrinked in the San Francisco Bay Area,* by Richard Katz features paved trails that are not only suitable for skaters, but also for strollers!

baby in either a jog stroller or front- or backpack. The Main Trail Loop from the Visitor Center to Cathedral Drive is an easy one-hour, one-mile round trip unpaved trail. The Fern Creek Trail, a moderate three-mile trail, takes about two hours.

Phoenix Lake Loop, Ross

This scenic loop starts at Natalie Coffin Greene Park in Ross and goes through the watershed lands around Phoenix Lake.

Point Reyes National Seashore

415-464-5100
www.trails.com

The park has over 140 miles of trails and three visitor centers. There are short, scenic hikes from the Bear Valley Visitor Center. The Earthquake Trail starts across the street from park headquarters; it is flat and paved. Call ahead for park maps.

Samuel P. Taylor State Park, Lagunitas

415-488-9897

This park has several flat paved trails that go through stunning redwood groves. It is suitable for jog strollers or backpacks.

Tennessee Valley (Golden Gate National Recreation Area)

This lovely one-mile unpaved trail is fairly flat and leads out to the ocean and a protected cove. Bring your baby in a jog stroller or front or backpack and a picnic for the beach.

East Bay

Briones Park, Lafayette and Martinez

www.ebparks.org/parks/briones.htm

Two trails suitable for front- and backpacks or jog strollers are Old Bear Creek Rd. (which is nearly flat) and Alhambra Creek Valley.

Cesar Chavez Park, Berkeley

This is a nice mile-and-a-half-paved loop next to San Francisco Bay. It is great for strollers, but not on windy days!

East Bay Moms

6000 Contra Costa Rd.
510-653-7867

Among other events and outings, this popular mothers group offers weekly hikes and power stroller walks with other parents and their little ones. There is a $75 annual membership fee that includes a newsletter and unlimited participation in scheduled events. See chapter 6.

Huckleberry Regional Preserve, Oakland

www.ebparks.org/parks/huck.htm

There is a 1.9-mile loop suitable for front- or backpacks. There is beautiful vegetation with plenty of shade for the little ones.

Mount Diablo, Danville

www.ebparks.org/parks/irontr.htm

Although much of Mt. Diablo is rugged terrain, the gentle .7-mile loop Fire Trail near the summit makes a nice family hike. Rock City is a beautiful hiking area with lots of rocks for kids to climb. There is a moderate trail from here that takes about ninety minutes round-trip with a baby in a front- or backpack. **Iron Horse Trail** is also a great 12.7-mile hike for either a jog stroller or front- or backpack.

Lafayette-Moraga Trail
www.ebparks.org/parks/lafmotr.htm
This fairly flat three-mile paved trail is perfect for strollers. There's a picnic area and playground adjacent to the parking lot that makes this walk popular among mothers' groups.

Tilden Park (Berkeley Hills)
510-525-2233
www.ebparks.org/parks/bot.htm
This is one of the best parks for children in the Bay Area! Pony rides, team trains, and beach swimming are offered. The Nimitz Trail to Inspiration Point on Wildcat Canyon Rd. is a popular mile-long paved trail that is suitable for strollers. For backpackers, the Lone Oak Trail is a 2.9-mile dirt trail with a fairly gentle climb. The Environmental Education Center offers outings for Tilden Tots for children ages three and four. Outings feature a nature hike with parents that focus on a theme, such as spiders or leaves. These walks are quite popular, so call to register in advance. The Tilden Park Botanical Garden is also a great place for walking; kids can either explore or look at plants from the stroller.

Additional Resources for Walks and Hikes in the East Bay

◆ www.ebparks.org/parks/htm
   This great website gives all the particulars on East Bay parks and trails.

◆ www.bahiker.com/kids.html
   This site gives details for eleven East Bay hikes suitable for young children.

◆ *Best Hikes with Children: San Francisco's South Bay*, by Bill McMillon (includes the East Bay).

◆ *Easy Hiking in Northern California*, by Ann Marie Brown, contains fourteen hikes in Marin, four in the East Bay, and many in Yosemite and Tahoe, which are suitable for preschoolers.

◆ *Skating Unrinked in the San Francisco Bay Area,* by Richard Katz features paved trails that are not only suitable for skaters, but also for strollers!

Alum Rock Park, San Jose

408-259-5477

Alum Rock was a spa with mineral baths 100 years ago. Today it is a nature preserve with thirteen miles of trail, many of which are suitable for young children.

Alviso Slough Trail

408-262-5513

This flat nine-mile trail built around salt ponds at the tip of San Francisco Bay is a good choice for young children, with stunning views of the East Bay Hills and Santa Cruz Mountains on clear summer days.

Blossom Birth Moms' Walk

650-964-7380

Join expectant and new moms for an hour "Moms' Walk" every Tuesday morning at 9:30. They meet at the eastern most end of San Antonio Rd.—the Palo Alto entrance to the Shoreline Path.

Coyote Creek Parkway

408-225-0225
www.parkhere.org/prkpages/coyote.htm

This fifteen-mile long, paved, mostly level multi-use trail runs along Coyote Creek from South San Jose, through the Coyote Valley, and ends at Anderson Lake in Morgan Hill.

Hidden Villa Ranch (in Los Altos Hills near San Jose)

650-949-8650 (administration)
650-949-8641 (camping)

There are more than seven miles of trails to roam, in addition to an actual working farm with farm animals, oak-studded grasslands, organic gardens, and Adobe Creek's woodland watershed.

Los Gatos Creek Trail, Los Gatos

408-356-2729 (park office)
www.parkhere.org/prkpages/lgcreek.htm

This is a nicely paved trail—7.4 miles from Leigh Ave. to Main St. Perfect for a stroller!

Moms and Tots Hiking Club, El Camino YMCA

650-969-9622

This popular group of moms and babies ages 3-8 months meets each Wednesday in a six-week series for progressive hikes through Rancho San Antonio State Park. Trails are suitable for a jog stroller or a front- or backpack.

Additional Resources for Hikes and Walks in the South Bay

◆ www.bahiker.com

This is a great website with information on fifteen popular family hikes in the South Bay.

◆ www.parkhere/org/map.htm

Includes specifics about parks and trails in Santa Clara County.

◆ *Best Hikes with Children-San Francisco's South Bay* by Bill McMillon.

◆ *Skating Unrinked in the San Francisco Bay Area* by Richard Katz features paved trails that are not only suitable for skaters, but also for strollers!

Additional Fitness Resources

◆ *Strollercize*, by Elizabeth Trindade and Victoria Shaw offers stroller based strength training, stretching and cardiovascular workouts, with an emphasis on safety for mom and baby.

Comment: "A great way to bond with your baby and shed those pregnancy pounds!"

◆ www.workoutsforwomen.com

Can't afford a personal trainer? This website offers personal fitness training for women, including a pregnancy workout.

◆ www.expectingfitness.com

This website describes itself as "your source on pre-and post-natal fitness."

◆ www.strollerfit.com

This is the official Strollerfit website. They promise to teach you how to "turn your stroller into a portable fitness machine!"

◆ www.fitmaternity.com

This website sells maternity fitness wear.

408-867-3654 (park office)
www.parkhere.org/prkpages/rancho.htm

One of the Bay Area's most popular hikes, this park includes twenty-six miles of trails, meadows and an educational working farm that is open for observation year-round. Summer weekends get very crowded. The Rancho San Antonio Trail is a paved three-quarter-mile trail.

Shoreline Park, Palo Alto

Offers a smooth flat trail with interesting birds to see.

Pregnancy and Postnatal Massages

Having a massage can help stave off those pregnancy aches and pains and also help restore and rejuvenate your body after delivery. Other benefits of pre-and post-natal massage therapy may include improving circulation, directing blood flow and nutrients to mother and baby, increasing metabolism rates, ensuring the production of vital hormones and the elimination of toxins, promoting relaxation, reducing stress and anxiety, and calming the mind and body.

When making an appointment for a pregnancy massage be sure to ask if a note with your physician's approval is required. You should also ask whether the masseuse is a licensed professional (a Certified Massage Therapist, CMT), and what kind of experience he or she has in working with pregnant or postpartum women. In addition, you may want to inquire about whether they use a special massage table that is often used for pregnant women to allow for a full body and back massage. On this table, you lie comfortably on your stomach—the table has a hole in it and a mesh basket to support the belly. Some practitioners do not use these tables because they believe that lying on your stomach in this manner places an unhealthy strain on abdominal muscles. Instead, they perform a prenatal massage in a side-lying position with many pillows and wedges for your comfort.

The following are some spas and professionals specializing in pre-and post-natal massages in the Bay Area whom we have heard about from other parents—this list is by no means complete, as many more full-service spas, salons, and individual practitioners offer these types of massages. Prices are usually dependent on the length of your massage, but they still vary from one professional or organization to another, so be sure to inquire before your appointment.

San Francisco

California Pacific Medical Center Women's Health Resource Center
3698 California St.
415-600-0500
They also give massages in hospital rooms! Comments: "CPMC is a true bargain—a great massage at an affordable price." "A real treat during my ninth month!" "Just what I needed to get rid of my neck and shoulder muscle aches from nursing and carrying my baby."

Heaven Center for Wellness
2209 Chestnut St.
415-749-6414

LaBelle Day Spa
133 Kearny St.
415-433-7644

The Mindful Body
2876 California St.
415-931-2639
www.themindfulbody.com

Novella Spa and Salon
2238 Union St.
415-673-1929

Renew Bodyworks
Ellin Pearlman, CMT
2295 Chestnut St., Ste. 3
415-577-6000
Ellin will do home visits to mothers on bed rest.

Spa Nordstrom
San Francisco Center, 5th Fl.
865 Market St.
415-977-5102
Comment: "Couldn't have made it through the third trimester without Nordstrom's pregnancy massage!"

Spa Radiance
3061 Fillmore St.
415-346-6281
Comments: "The best of the best massages ever!" "A real postnatal treat!"

Zendo Urban Retreat
256 Sutter St., 2nd Fl.
415-788-3404
Comment: "The ultimate maternity massage!"

North Bay

Aase Lium-Hall, CMT
415-332-7042

Asanté Day Spa
18 Mary St.
San Rafael
415-460-6506

Espirit Skin Care
36 Tiburon Blvd.
Mill Valley
415-383-3534
A favorite in Southern Marin!

Labor Support Services
203 Devon Dr.
San Rafael
415-451-7287

Samantha Stormer
645 Tamalpais Dr.
Corte Madera
415-924-9096
PARENT RATING: ☆ ☆ ☆ ☆ ☆
Comment: "Samantha gives a very
intense but relaxing postpartum massage...teaches you about pressure
points to relieve pain."

Tea Garden Springs
38 Miller Ave.
Mill Valley
415-389-7123

**Whole Health Associates Center
for Integrative Medicine**
Dolores Caruthers, CMT
1368 Lincoln, Ste. 109
San Rafael
415-454-4325

East Bay

**Bodywork Central Massage
Supply**
5519 College Ave.
Berkeley
510-547-4313

Bridget Scadeng
2421 4th St., #B
Berkeley
510-526-3493

Claremont Resort and Spa
41 Tunnel Rd.
Berkeley
800-551-7266

Face and Body Magic
1009 Solano Ave., #A
Berkeley
510-526-3223

Mama Massage
Christina Del Gallo, CMT
510-531-5963
Motherwit
Lisa Rasler, LM, CPM, CMT
510-530-1178
**Moving Light Massage and Body
Works**
510-841-6263 or 510-525-8539

South Bay

AvantGard Day Spa
1224 El Camino Real
San Carlos
650-591-1498

Body Presence
904 Laurel St.
San Carlos
650-593-9652

Body Therapy Center
368 California Ave.
Palo Alto
650-328-9400
www.bodymindspirit.net

Blossom Birth Services
1000 Elwell Ct.
Palo Alto
650-964-7380

Can Do Yoga
3636 Florence St., Ste. A
Redwood City
650-368-5727

Center for Therapeutic Massage
1905 Palmetto Ave., Unit E
Pacifica
650-359-3921

Integrated Health Care Center for Wellness
2290 Birch St.
Palo Alto
650-321-7193

LaBelle DaySpa
- Palo Alto
  95 Town and Country Village,
  650-327-6964
- Stanford
  36 Stanford Shopping Center,
  650-326-8522

Peninsula Covenant Community Center
3623 Jefferson Ave.
Redwood City
650-364-6272

Sandra Caron European Spa
105 E. 3rd Ave.
San Mateo
650-347-9666
www.sandracaron.com

CHAPTER 3

OUTFITTING YOURSELF:
Finding Stylish
Maternity Clothes
without Breaking the Bank

Let's face it: maternity clothes are expensive and, until recently, not very attractive. Few *want* to wear them; fewer still can afford to drive around the Bay Area looking for stylish and affordable options. To make your life easier, we've sorted out the best and worst of Bay Area maternity clothes shopping. We'll tell you what (and what not) to buy and when to buy it, and give you the lowdown on where to find good values and clothes you'll actually want to wear (at least for a few months…). Check out our list of Bay Area moms' favorite on-line sources too. Happy shopping! This chapter answers the following questions and more:

◆ What kinds of maternity clothes should I buy, and when should I buy them?

◆ Where can I find the best deals on maternity clothes?

◆ What kinds of clothes are a waste of money?

◆ Where can I find gently used maternity clothes?

◆ I'm overwhelmed by the choices on-line. What do parents recommend?

100

When to Buy

If you are like we were during our first pregnancies, you probably think you'll need maternity clothes from the first month on. Relax. Don't rush out and buy *anything* until you need it, or you may end up not wearing it at all when the seasons change. For first-time moms, this could be anywhere from the fourth to the sixth month. Second timers, unfortunately, will need things a bit sooner.

For the first few months, you'll want clothes that expand comfortably, but maternity clothes will look ridiculous. For this awkward in-between stage, when your normal size does not fit but you're too small for maternity clothes, local moms recommend loose dresses (waistless sundresses and sweater dresses with cardigans worked for us), pants and skirts with elastic waistbands (leggings are great), overalls, and shirts that don't tuck in. You can get by with borrowing clothes from friends who are slightly larger than you are. You can also try the old "leave the top button open" trick. In the meantime, start asking friends and relatives for hand-me-downs—our favorite source of maternity clothes!

Sometime in the second trimester, you'll probably need some maternity clothes, and that's when you should shop. Realistically, you may only wear these clothes for four to six months, so think carefully before you spend a lot of money. Remember, it's best to borrow, borrow, borrow! And when you are finished, lend, lend, lend.

What to Buy and Where to Buy It

What should you buy? If you need to dress up for work, start with a couple of black or khaki pants suits. Local moms recommend pants because: it's a rare Bay Area workplace where you need to wear a skirted suit, and you can then wear the pants without the jacket on the weekends. Buy basic colors and stay away from trendy looks, which may not look so great in your next pregnancy a few years down the road. For suits, your basic shopping choices are chain stores like Pea in the Pod/Mimi (high-end), Motherhood (low-end), a few of the local boutiques noted below (also high-end, but you may find a knockout suit), or Japanese Weekend or Belly Basics on-line or in boutiques (our best recommendation, see below).

For casual clothes, Bay Area moms recommend a few staples: seasonless khaki pants, a pair of comfortable jeans, a white cotton button-down shirt, a couple of T-shirts, and a cotton cardigan in a basic color. You can expand on that repertoire as you see fit and according to the season. (Remember, if you live in the city it will never be "summer" so don't worry about shorts or sundresses unless you plan weekends in Sonoma.) For sweatshirts, T-shirts, and button-down shirts, raid your husband's closet. Keep it simple: buy clothes in coordinating colors so you can mix and match. Now is not the time to take on an entirely new style or color scheme; you want to be able to blend in elements of your existing wardrobe (e.g., your regular shirts under overalls or jumpers, or your existing scarves). The best thing to hit casual maternity wear in recent years is on-line shopping at The Gap or Old Navy, where you can find fashionable items that won't break your budget. If you would like to hit the stores, try Target or Motherhood first for weekend basics, then supplement with a few splurges at the boutiques if you can afford it.

Probably the most important thing to buy is a couple of good support bras to fit your expanding bust. Smaller women may not need maternity bras at all; just find a good supporting bra in a larger size (usually a cup size larger and one to two inches larger in diameter). Nordstrom's lingerie department is a great place to get fitted for regular bras; according to local moms, the salespeople seem to be more knowledgeable than at your average department store. Most larger women will want real maternity bras, which you can find at maternity stores (high-end) or Mervyn's/Target (low-end). Either way, you'll need at least two (one to wash and one to wear).

When you get to the ninth month, shop for some nursing bras, preferably at a lactation center where the salespeople know how to fit nursing moms. Believe it or not, you'll get even bigger while you nurse, so you'll need to buy a size or two larger than your pregnancy size! This is why buying nursing bras as maternity bras probably won't work. The absolute best nursing bra, by common consensus among local moms, is the Japanese Weekend Hug bra. There are no annoying hooks or buttons to deal with, and it's built like a comfortable jogging bra, albeit with narrow straps, so you can even wear it while you sleep. (Yes, you may need it then too.) Another great cotton nursing bra is the Bravado, which comes in several different colors. While it has hooks, it's also very comfortable and provides more support than the Japanese Weekend version.

Whether to buy maternity underwear is a personal decision. Some moms did without it altogether and just wore their normal bikini bottoms under the belly. Others found it more comfortable to go the "over the belly" maternity underwear route. The best options for underwear shopping, according to local moms, are Japanese Weekend (high-end) or Target, JC Penney, or Mervyn's (low-end).

You may or may not need a maternity swimsuit, depending on your lifestyle or the season. The first time around, we wore regular swimsuits one size up and let them stretch. Obviously, you shouldn't try this with a suit you really care about wearing again postpregnancy! The second time, we were just too big for regular suits and went straight to maternity. Our advice: wear a regular suit (J. Crew makes a good tank with underwire support) until you really need a maternity suit, skip the high-priced suits and then shop for an inexpensive one.

Your feet will undoubtedly swell during pregnancy. Don't stretch and ruin expensive shoes if you anticipate wearing them again postpregnancy. We found we either had to buy bigger shoes or wear mules or tennis shoes during the last trimester. (Skip laces, though, because at the end you won't be able to bend down to tie them!)

Opinions (even between us) are sharply divided on nursing shirts and dresses. Some of us found them a waste of money in the Bay Area, where we never faced any kind of hostility to nursing in public. Some thought it was more time consuming to find the special openings in nursing shirts than just to undo a few buttons on a normal button-down shirt, or put the baby under a big shirt or sweater, and still discreetly nurse. Nursing shirts are also notoriously unfashionable (some would say hideous). Recent advances in maternity wear seem to have missed the nursing side of things, with the exception of the attractive clothes in the Motherwear catalog, see below. Others thought the nursing shirts were helpful, easier to nurse in since the baby's head wasn't hidden up a large shirt, and more discreet. Our advice: try both and see what works for you, but don't buy a bunch of nursing shirts until you figure it out.

Overall, we recommend looking for clothes that will stand up to a lot of wear (including many washings) over a short period of time. Cotton is best because of its durability and breathability; pregnant women tend to get overheated. Skip anything that must be dry cleaned; you'll spend enough just buying the clothes themselves!

What about used clothing? There are many good local resale stores selling maternity clothing; most are children's resale boutiques with small selections of maternity wear. Unfortunately, selection varies a great deal. Sometimes you can find bargains on barely worn high-end clothing (usually priced at one-half to one-third of the new retail price). Suits and dresses often fall into this category. On the other hand, we have seen a lot of low-end casual wear priced the same as it would be new, in which case you are better off just buying it new! Our advice is to know the brand names and new clothes prices before you hit the resale stores. That way, you will know whether you are really buying a bargain. Don't forget to consign your maternity clothes when you are done with them!

Top Five Sources for Maternity Clothes

1. **Gap or Old Navy** (on-line at www.gap.com or www.oldnavy.com)

2. **Japanese Weekend** (San Francisco boutique, on-line at www.japaneseweekend.com, or in other local boutiques)

3. **Mom's the Word** (San Francisco and Walnut Creek boutique)

4. **Target Stores**

5. **Hand-Me-Downs!**

Best Ways to Save Money on Maternity Clothes

1. **Borrow clothes from friends and family who have just given birth.**

2. **Scour the resale stores for bargains on high-end merchandise.** (Just beware of paying too much for low-end brands.)

3. **Shop Target Stores for casual wear.** You'll be surprised at what you find for $20 and under.

4. **Hop in the car and go to the Motherhood outlets in Gilroy, Vacaville, or Petaluma for career and evening wear at drastically reduced prices.**

5. **Wear nonmaternity clothes as much as possible.** Clothes for larger women are much less expensive than maternity clothes. Try long sweaters, sweater dresses, overalls, and elastic waistbands, particularly for those in-between stages when you aren't big enough for maternity clothes.

What Not to Buy

Here's what *not* to buy, unless money is not an issue:

◆ Special occasion dresses (borrow them instead). If you must, buy a simple black seasonless number that can be dressed up or down as necessary.

◆ Outerwear (except perhaps the Japanese Weekend "mommy and baby" coat that can be zipped up postpartum around a baby in a front carrier).

◆ Sleepwear, except maybe nursing pajamas. You can borrow your husband's pajamas or wear T-shirts or nightgowns during pregnancy. Some found it easier just to wear old T-shirts at night during nursing; when they got soiled they could throw them in the wash and get another. Others really appreciated the convenience of nursing pajamas. Some moms though found the nursing slits in the nursing pajamas were a little *too* revealing.

◆ Anything really trendy (you'll feel ridiculous wearing it again in subsequent pregnancies).

◆ Anything in horizontal stripes (why do so many manufacturers make maternity clothes in stripes?) or loud patterns. Black or navy is best.

◆ Anything that looks like it will not withstand a lot of washing.

DEPARTMENT AND CHAIN STORES

These stores all have more than one Bay Area location. If the address is not listed below the store name, check the website for local stores.

JC Penney Company
www.jcpenney.com
PARENT RATING: ☆ ☆

Penney's prices are very reasonable, and selection is fairly broad, particularly in the catalog. You can find mainly casual clothes, as well as a few career and dress items, swimsuits, and bras. Unfortunately, however, the clothes look much better in the catalog than they do in person. We were disappointed in what we saw: clothes tended to be oversized, fabrics cheap, and styles a bit outdated. The five-piece knit set at $80 is less expensive than the Belly Basics "pregnancy survival kit" it mimics, but the quality of the Penney version is much poorer. However, this is a good place to pick up inexpensive maternity hose and underwear. Lines include: Duo.

Mervyn's California Stores
www.mervyns.com
PARENT RATING: ☆ ☆

Owned by Target Stores, Mervyn's is a department store with locations throughout California. Like Target, it has a small selection of well-priced casual maternity clothes. Almost everything retailed for under $50. Unlike Target, however, its styles are outdated, and clothes look cheap. Shorts and T-shirt sets and rompers were made of nonbreathable polyester blends, T-shirts featured horizontal stripes, jeans and khakis sported huge panels, even on the rear, and leggings were baggy. Stick to the inexpensive cotton maternity underwear and (if you've been fitted elsewhere and know your size) cotton nursing bras by Leading Lady. Lines include: Oh Mamma, Due Date, and Baby's Nest.

Mimi Maternity
• Corte Madera
  The Village at Corte Madera,
  415-927-3500
• Walnut Creek
  Broadway Plaza, 2 Broadway,
  925-932-8863
• Santa Clara
  Valley Fair Shopping Center,
  408-249-2244

PARENT RATING: ☆ ☆ ☆ ☆

Like its sister store Pea in the Pod, Mimi is at the high end of the price spectrum, according to local moms. But its prices are a bit lower than Pea in the Pod's, many times for the same items. The best value is the Mimi Essentials line of basic shirts and pants, with T-shirts at $20-25 and pants at $50. You'll also find a decent selection of stylish dresses and suits, bathing suits, lingerie, and pajamas. Insider advice: hit the periodic sales. Designer lines that don't sell at Pea in the Pod are often sent here for markdown.

Motherhood Maternity

www.motherhood.com

PARENT RATING: ☆ ☆ ☆ ☆

Motherhood is the low-priced end of the Pea in the Pod/Mimi/Motherhood national chain stores. Don't expect high-quality stuff (but what maternity clothes are?). But you can find "decent, inexpensive" casual basics like cotton shirts, shorts, pants, and casual dresses for under $30. This is definitely the place to buy your weekend T-shirts, shorts, and jeans, and well-priced maternity bathing suits. The store also offers a selection of cotton nursing pajamas and shirts. Word to the wise: petite women may find even the smallest sizes run very large, so be sure to try clothes on for fit. Comment: "Excellent product for the price... A lifesaver."

Motherhood Maternity Outlets

- Petaluma
  Petaluma Village Factory Outlets, 707-763-3261
- Vacaville
  Factory Stores at Vacaville, 707-446-4792
- Milpitas
  Great Mall of the Bay Area, 408-262-0950
- Gilroy
  Gilroy Premium Outlets, 408-847-7560

PARENT RATING: ☆ ☆ ☆ ☆ ☆

Overstock and out-of-season Pea in the Pod/Mimi/Motherhood clothes are sent to these outlets for markdown. Selection varies according to the season, but generally you can find everything from basics to career to special occasion outfits. A great place to find big-ticket items like suits, this outlet also carries the regularly priced Motherhood line. "Lifesavers...well worth the drive... the best for me," raved local moms.

Nordstrom

www.nordstrom.com

PARENT RATING: ☆ ☆ ☆ ☆

Famous for its customer service, this department store carries the full line of Belly Basics maternity wear, one of our favorites. They also feature Kate Spade and Nicole Miller diaper bags, as well as Mustela skin products for those inevitable stretch marks. Nordstrom's lingerie department is also a good place to find supportive bras during pregnancy. We like Nordstrom for its generous no-questions-asked return policy.

A Pea in the Pod

- San Francisco
  290 Sutter St., 415-391-1400
- Palo Alto
  74 Stanford Shopping Center,
  650-323-7343

PARENT RATING: ☆ ☆ ☆

This chain is at the high end of the Pea in the Pod/Mimi/Motherhood group, with stores all over the country. It's great if you want designer labels; Lilly Pulitzer, Anna Sui, Vivienne Tam, and Nicole Miller were all featured when we visited. The store features a good selection of work clothes and special occasion outfits, and if you need to wear a nice suit to work, you'll find it here. But almost everyone we surveyed had the same reaction: it's "expensive." You may find T-shirts and khakis elsewhere at lower prices, but if you're in search of upscale labels, and good service, start here.

Ross Dress for Less Stores

www.rossstores.com

PARENT RATING: ☆ ☆

This national chain of discount stores features a sporadic stock of maternity clothes. Selection is limited to casual shirts, pants, and dresses. We noticed most of the "designer labels" were inexpensive Sears, JC Penney, and Mervyn's brands. On the plus side, prices were very low; everything was priced under $15. But don't expect great customer service. Our salesperson did not speak English, and we had to point to our enormous bellies to find the maternity clothes rack. Lines include: Oh Mamma, Due Date, Take Nine, Duo.

Target Stores

www.target.com

PARENT RATING: ☆ ☆ ☆ ☆ ☆

We were pleasantly surprised by Target's small selection of *100 percent cotton*, attractive maternity clothing at *very* reasonable prices. We found great solid-color cotton twill shorts for $15 and twill pants for $20. T-shirts were $10, and Target even offered some decent denim shirts and cotton sweaters for $20. You won't see work clothes here, or special occasion outfits, but this is a great place for weekend basics. We also appreciate the "no hassle" return policy. "Great and inexpensive… a surprising place to find knockabout maternity clothes," say local moms. Lines include: In Due Time.

LOCAL BOUTIQUES AND RESALE STORES

San Francisco

CPMC Newborn Connections
(formerly the Perinatal Center)
3698 California St.
415-600-BABY (2229)

PARENT RATING: ☆ ☆ ☆ ☆

This location doesn't carry maternity clothes, but it offers a small selection of nursing wear, mainly casual cotton shirts, and dresses. You will find an extensive array of nursing bras, with "helpful and knowledgeable" salespeople (often lactation consultants) to assist with sizing.

Day One

3490 California St., Ste. 203

415-440-3291

www.dayonecenter.com

PARENT RATING: ☆ ☆ ☆ ☆ ☆

This attractive, organized, new center features a great selection of upscale, fashionable maternity and nursing wear. Prices are not inexpensive, but comparable to other boutique pricing. You can find everything from casual to career wear, and even some dressy outfits. The center also offers swimsuits and exercise gear, a large selection of nursing wear, and nursing bras (with very helpful salespeople, often lactation consultants). Lines include: Japanese Weekend, Belly Basics (the full line), Duet, Rumble, Olian, and Maxi-Mom.

Dress

2271 Chestnut St.

415-440-3737

PARENT RATING: ☆ ☆ ☆ ☆

This upscale Marina-district boutique features "urban chic" maternity clothes—think lots of black and Lycra—and "great service." Waistbands tend not to include the ugly maternity panel (helpful if you are trying not to look so "maternity," but watch for fit in the final months). Prices are comparable to other boutiques. Local moms recommend treating yourself to a new Dress outfit when you're having a bad day and don't feel like being pregnant! Lines include: Belly Basics, Pumpkin, Zoe, Amy Zoller, and the owner's own designs under the Dress label.

Japanese Weekend

500 Sutter St.

415-989-6667

www.japaneseweekend.com

PARENT RATING: ☆ ☆ ☆ ☆ ☆

Consistently the most popular brand of maternity clothes in the Bay Area, JW offers great basic cotton suits, pants, skirts, and shirts. The Sutter Street store is this local manufacturer's only storefront, but you can also find the clothes at other local boutiques and on-line. Casual and career clothes are "very convertible from day to evening to weekend." Some pants feature the underbelly "OK" waistband, which many found very comfortable. Others have the "during and after" expandable waistband (useful for those first few months after giving birth when you aren't quite back to your old size). The JW nursing bras (Hug or jog bra style) are the best we've found—they are comfortable enough to sleep in, and allow easy access with no snaps. Most found the clothes "expensive" but "durable," "comfortable," and a "good value." Styles are usually very current. Check out the seasonal sales for great bargains. A city mom's favorite!

Minis

2278 Union St.

415-567-9537

PARENT RATING: ☆ ☆ ☆ ☆

This Union Street kids' clothier also offers stylish maternity wear for mom. Selection consists largely of basic cotton and cotton/Lycra casual wear, with a few very nice suits and dresses. Again, prices are not inexpensive, but they are comparable to other boutiques carrying the same brands. Moms found the staff "very helpful." Lines inlcude: Belly Basics, Minis (house label), Duet, Olian.

Mom's the Word

3385 Sacramento St.
415-441-8261

PARENT RATING: ☆ ☆ ☆ ☆ ☆

This Presidio Heights boutique, now with a Walnut Creek branch, is a favorite of city moms. The store features "nice choices" of upscale career and casual maternity clothing, as well as special occasion dresses, lingerie, sleepwear, swimsuits, and some nursing wear. We found nothing we wouldn't want to wear (which says a lot for a maternity store!). Prices are high-end but not as high as Pea in the Pod, and selection is more stylish. Moms report sales associates are "very helpful" and pay customers a great deal of "personal attention." Lines include: Belly Basics, Japanese Weekend, Pumpkin, Hayley Michaels, Linique, Mommy Chic, Maxi-Mom.

Natural Resources

1307 Castro St.
415-550-2611
www.naturalresourcesonline.com

PARENT RATING: ☆ ☆ ☆ ☆

This birthing resource center located in the heart of Noe Valley has a nice selection of new and used maternity and nursing wear. New clothes prices are comparable to other local boutiques. This is the only place to find used maternity clothes in the city, and the selection is fairly ample. When we visited, we saw higher-end brands like Japanese Weekend and

Pea in the Pod among the used clothes. Your best bet is the sale rack, where almost everything is in the $10 range. Used clothes are purchased on consignment (50 percent cash or 60 percent store credit, paid when clothes sell). New clothes lines include: Japanese Weekend, Belly Basics, Zero-to-Nine.

North Bay

Glow Girl

7 Throckmorton Ave.
Mill Valley
415-383-4141
www.glowgirlmaternity.com

PARENT RATING: ☆ ☆ ☆ ☆ ☆

This new upscale boutique, opened in March 2002, is the only of its kind in Marin. Now Marin moms-to-be need not journey to the city for urban chic maternity clothes. The store focuses on affordable casual wear and attractive accessories such as diaper bags, jewelry, hats, scarves, and shoes. Stay for tea and lollipops in the store's big comfortable chairs. Lines include: Adidas athletic wear, L'Attesa, Belly Basics, Chaiken, Duet, Japanese Weekend, Nicole Miller, Mothers-in-Motion athletic wear, Olian, and Pumpkin.

MOM (Maternity of Marin)

874 4th St.
San Rafael
415-457-4955

PARENT RATING: ☆ ☆ ☆ ☆

This independent resource center and store offers a good selection of new and used maternity clothes. It's one of the few maternity boutiques in Marin. New clothes prices are comparable to other boutiques. The store also offers a decent selection of new nursing bras (and expert help with fitting), swimsuits, nursing pajamas, nursing shirts, and exercise clothes. This is a great place to sell your maternity clothing; used clothes are taken on consignment (60 percent to the store, 40 percent to the consignor, paid when clothes sell). Unlike many resale shops, the store is nicely arranged by style and color so you don't have to wade through piles of unattractive clothes. The store's owner is selective about what she buys, so used clothes are in season and include many high-end brands such as Japanese Weekend, Mimi, and Pea in the Pod. You will pay for this selection, but you may score a great deal on the sale rack, where prices are 50 percent off. New clothes lines include: Japanese Weekend, Belly Basics, Olian.

Outgrown

1417 4th St.
San Rafael
415-457-2219

PARENT RATING: ☆ ☆ ☆ ☆

This long-time kids' resale store also features a rack of consignment maternity wear. Moms say the store features "sporadic stock" but "good prices" and call it the "best" resale store in Marin for that reason. While you won't find a lot of high-end brands, most shirts and pants were priced under $10. Consignors receive 40 percent of the sales price when the items sell.

Play It Again Kids

508 4th St.
San Rafael
415-485-0304

PARENT RATING: ☆ ☆ ☆

This kids' resale shop offers a very small selection of maternity clothes. Prices are very reasonable—$5-10 for most items—but brands tend to be low-end and stock limited. The store offers a 40 percent split to consignors.

East Bay

Baby World

- Oakland
  6000 College Ave., 510-655-2828
- Oakland
  3923 Piedmont Ave., 510-547-7040

PARENT RATING: ☆ ☆ ☆

Baby World is a general baby gear retailer (part of the Baby News chain) and it offers a very small selection of maternity clothes. Basic clothes are well-priced (e.g., cotton shorts for $15), but you won't find a huge variety.

Bearly Worn

1619 N. Broadway
Walnut Creek
925-945-6535

PARENT RATING: ☆ ☆ ☆

This kids' resale store carries a small selection of used maternity clothes on consignment. When we visited, the selection was varied and included some high-end brands like Mimi (with higher prices to match) and some lower-end brands like Motherhood (in the $10 range). The store offers a 50 percent split to consignors on maternity wear.

Birth and Bonding Family Center

1126 Solano Ave.
Albany
510-559-5516
www.birthbonding.org

PARENT RATING: ☆ ☆ ☆ ☆

This perinatal resource and lactation center features a small but quality selection of maternity clothes, including cotton basics. The center also carries cotton nursing shirts and sleepwear. It's a good place to get fitted for a nursing bra, as salespeople are "knowledgeable," and you can also pick up other lactation supplies. You can also shop for the Belly Basics line on the Birth and Bonding website. Lines include: Dax & Coe, Belly Basics.

Cotton & Company

• Oakland
    5901 College Ave., 510-653-8058
• Lafayette
    3535 Mt. Diablo Blvd., 925-299-9356

PARENT RATING: ☆ ☆ ☆ ☆ ☆

One of the few upscale boutiques in the East Bay, Cotton & Company offers an excellent selection of chic maternity clothes amid a general baby store. Prices are on par with other boutiques offering the same lines. This is a great source for a nice suit or blouse. Lines include: Japanese Weekend, Ran Designs, Hayley Michaels, Belly Basics.

Crackerjacks

14 Glen Ave.
Oakland
510-654-8844

PARENT RATING: ☆ ☆ ☆ ☆ ☆

Crackerjacks offers new and used maternity clothes (within a kids' consignment store). The selection of new clothes is limited (mainly Dax & Coe label and nursing bras), but the store offers a *huge* selection of well-priced, used maternity wear in good condition, including name brands like Belly Basics, Motherhood, and Maternite. Look carefully and you may find a high-quality used outfit at a reasonable price. The store purchases used clothes outright for 50 percent of the used price, and salespeople are very helpful.

Fashion After Passion

1521 Webster St.
Alameda
510-769-MOMS

PARENT RATING: ☆ ☆ ☆

A maternity and kids' store, this boutique offers new and used maternity and nursing wear, nursing bras, and breast pump rentals.

Finders Keepers

1581 Olivina Ave.
Livermore
925-449-7793

PARENT RATING: ☆ ☆ ☆

This kids' resale store also features used maternity clothes in its well-organized layout. The owner accepts many different brands and everything from casual to career and evening wear. Consignors receive 50 percent of the sales price after the clothing sells.

Kids Again

6891 Village Pkwy.
Dublin
925-828-7334

PARENT RATING: ☆ ☆ ☆ ☆

This children's resale store also sells used maternity clothes on consignment. Many different brands are featured, and clothes are priced accordingly. Consignors receive 50 percent of the sales price. The store features a play area for kids.

Laura's Closet

2926 College Ave.
Berkeley
510-845-3157

Formerly a branch of Lauren's closet, see below, this resale store features used maternity clothes on consignment.

Lauren's Closet

- Alameda
  1420 Park St., 510-865-2219
- Lafayette
  3484 Mt. Diablo Blvd., 925-299-1475

PARENT RATING: ☆ ☆ ☆ ☆ ☆

This local kids' resale store has three branches and offers used maternity clothes on consignment. Alameda is the largest store. The selection of maternity clothes is decent and well priced. The store offers a 50 percent split to consignors. The store's play area will entertain the kids while you shop.

Marino's Second Time Around

17279 Hesperian Blvd.
San Lorenzo
510-276-8705

PARENT RATING: ☆ ☆ ☆

This kids' resale store buys and sells used maternity clothing. Representative brands are mainly lower-end Sears and Target labels, and prices are fairly low. The store pays cash for used maternity clothing, usually 30-40 percent of the used sales price.

The Nurture Center

3399 Mt. Diablo Blvd.
Lafayette
925-283-1346
www.nurturecenter.com

PARENT RATING: ☆ ☆ ☆ ☆ ☆

This resource and lactation center offers a small selection of maternity clothes and a large array of nursing bras. Owner Meri Levy says she chooses affordable, comfortable clothes. She carries the Bravado nursing bra, one of our favorites. Nursing clothes and quality nursing supplies (such as Medela and Avent) are also available. Lines include: Zero-to-Nine, Rebel, Belly Basics.

Mom's the Word Maternity

1628 N. Main St.
Walnut Creek
925-937-6818

PARENT RATING: ☆ ☆ ☆ ☆ ☆

This upscale boutique, see San Francisco listing, offers a large selection of fashionable casual, career, and special occasion maternity clothing, nursing clothing, sleepwear, and swimwear. Prices were surprisingly reasonable, with many dresses under $100. There is even a small play area for the kids while you shop. Lines include: Japanese Weekend, Belly Basics, Zoe, Olian, Duet, Rebel.

Snickerdoodles

442 Hartz Ave.
Danville
925-820-4956

PARENT RATING: ☆ ☆ ☆ ☆ ☆

This popular kids' resale store also carries a selection of used maternity clothing on consignment. Brands range from Motherhood to Mimi to Pea in the Pod, and selection usually includes career as well as casual styles. Prices for brand-name suits in excellent condition can be high, but you can also find low-priced casual wear. Consignors receive 40 percent of the sales price after goods sell.

They Grow So Fast
3413 Mt. Diablo Blvd.
Lafayette
925-283-8976
PARENT RATING: ☆ ☆ ☆ ☆ ☆

This constantly expanding kids' resale store also offers consignment used maternity clothes. The owner is selective about what she buys, and better brands are represented. You can find quality used clothing at about one-third of the new retail price, depending on condition. The store accepts clothing on consignment according to the season, and consignors receive 40 percent of the sales price.

South Bay

Baby on the Way Maternity Fashions
Vallco Fashion Park
10123 N. Wolfe Rd.
Cupertino
408-253-4675
PARENT RATING: ☆ ☆ ☆ ☆

This boutique carries everything from casual to evening wear, in a wide range of sizes from petite through 3X. The store also has a good selection of nursing bras. Over forty brands are represented, including Japanese Weekend.

Bearly Worn
35 W. Manor Dr.
Pacifica
650-355-5089
PARENT RATING: ☆ ☆ ☆ ☆

This children's consignment store also offers used maternity clothes. Representative brands include Gap Maternity, Pea in the Pod, and Mimi, and prices are about half of new retail prices. The store purchases clothing outright and accepts consignments.

Dimples
5965 E. Almaden Expwy.
San Jose
408-323-0360
www.edimples.com
PARENT RATING: ☆ ☆ ☆ ☆

Dimples focuses on upscale, name-brand used maternity clothes. All of its clothing is used, but the store is very selective about what it accepts, so better brands are represented. The store buys used clothing outright and pays 30 percent of the selling price in cash or 40 percent of the selling price in store credit.

Ricochet
1610 S. El Camino Real
San Mateo
650-345-8740
PARENT RATING: ☆ ☆ ☆ ☆ ☆

This resale store features high-end used maternity clothing at reasonable prices, usually one-third to one-fourth of retail prices. Representative brands include Mimi Maternity, Pea in the Pod, and imaternity, all in excellent condition. The store also offers monthly rentals of maternity wear, and has a $10-and-under sale rack.

On-line and Catalog Shopping for Maternity Clothes

In this age of the Internet, don't forget twenty-four-hour shopping from home—a favorite choice for busy people. Parents we surveyed shared their favorite catalog and on-line maternity shopping sources. Here they are:

www.babystyle.com
PARENT RATING: ☆ ☆ ☆ ☆

This stylish site features a large selection of high-end designer clothing. You'll find everything from casual to career to special occasion outfits on this site. Some complain customer service is "horrible" (why this site did not receive a five-star rating) so choose carefully. Prices for the designer wear (e.g., Liz Lange) are high, but check out the sale page for discounts. This is a great option for those in outlying areas who can't make the drive to the San Francisco boutiques but must have designer clothing. Lines include: babystyle (house label), Liz Lange, Japanese Weekend, Pumpkin, Belly Basics, Mothers-in-Motion, Mammaluna, and Zoe.

www.bellybasics.com
PARENT RATING: ☆ ☆ ☆ ☆ ☆

Home of the four-piece "pregnancy survival kit" created by two pregnant fashion executives (a dress, a shirt, pants, and a skirt in cotton solid colors), the Belly Basics website offers up-to-date and comfortable cotton clothes, including basics like cotton shirts, T-shirts, suits, dresses, and swimsuits. We like this line for its comfortable waistbands (the "best" according to local moms), durability, and style. Belly Basics' clothes are also available at local boutiques, see above.

www.fitmaternity.com

This website sells maternity fitness wear.

Garnet Hill
800-870-3513 (catalog)
www.garnethill.com
PARENT RATING: ☆ ☆ ☆ ☆

This high-end cotton specialty catalog offers a very small, but high-quality, selection of stylish cotton casual maternity clothing at mid-range prices.

www.Gap.com
PARENT RATING: ☆ ☆ ☆ ☆ ☆

Gap Maternity is only available on-line, but it's the best thing to hit maternity wear in recent years. The site features well-priced, fashionable basics like stretch pants, stretch capris, jeans, cotton shirts, and sweaters. We love these clothes for reasonable prices, style, and comfort! These were by far our most-worn outfits. They have a great return policy—they'll take back anything, no questions asked, at any Gap store or via mail.

www.littlekoala.com
PARENT RATING: ☆ ☆ ☆ ☆

This site features Belly Basics and Japanese Weekend lines, Kenneth Cole diaper bags, and lots of nursing and maternity bras.

Liz Lange Maternity

888-616-5777 (catalog)
www.lizlange.com

PARENT RATING: ☆ ☆ ☆ ☆ ☆

This may be the closest place to the Bay Area to get Liz Lange's full line of upscale, tres chic maternity clothes; as of this writing her only retail stores are in New York and Los Angeles. A former fashion editor, Liz Lange designs very current clothes that "fit very well." Prices are "obscenely high" (what do you expect?), but if you can afford it and want to wear the very latest, this is it.

Mothers-in-Motion

877-512-8800 (catalog)
www.mothers-in-motion.com

PARENT RATING: ☆ ☆ ☆ ☆

This site offers a good selection of hard-to-find upscale maternity athletic wear.

Motherwear

800-950-2500 (catalog)
www.motherwear.com

PARENT RATING: ☆ ☆ ☆ ☆

Motherwear offers fashionable, non-matronly nursing wear for discreet nursing in public. Though we don't usually like nursing wear, this catalog made us reconsider.

Naissance on Melrose

800-505-0517 (catalog)
www.naissancematernity.com

PARENT RATING: ☆ ☆ ☆ ☆

This is the on-line and catalog version of ultra-hip Naissance on Melrose, a popular Los Angeles maternity emporium. You must be very comfortable with your body to wear these belly-baring styles, and money must not be an object, but if you can pull it off, great. You'll look like a celebrity mom! Lines include: designers such as Magda Berliner, Anja Flint, and Tova Celine.

www.oldnavy.com

PARENT RATING: ☆ ☆ ☆ ☆ ☆

It's finally here—Old Navy for moms-to-be! Old Navy's Mom-to-Be collection is available only on-line, but we love it. Prices are very reasonable (everything under $40 when we shopped recently), but styles are fashion-forward and fun, and feature natural fibers (thank you!). Example: the summer 2001 collection included simple capri pants in solids or plaids. The collection consists mainly of casual clothes, with a few dresses and swimsuits. Returns are easy: mail it back or take it to your local store.

www.pumpkinmaternity.com

PARENT RATING: ☆ ☆ ☆ ☆

This is the on-line store for the popular Pumpkin line of maternity wear (also found at local boutiques). Clothes are stylish and upscale, with prices to match (e.g., $130 cardigans). Most of the line features casual cotton or cotton/Lycra blends.

Title Nine Sports

800-609-0092 (catalog)
www.title9sports.com

PARENT RATING: ☆ ☆ ☆ ☆ ☆

A favorite for workout-crazed moms-to-be, this East Bay sportswear company—catalog and on-line—offers a great cotton nursing bra, as well as under-the-belly maternity cotton/spandex workout pants and shorts.

ALL THAT BABY "STUFF":
Shopping for Gear, Nursery, Clothes, Toys, Photography, and Childproofing

There are probably few things that are more life changing than having a baby. With your newfound responsibilities and role as a parent, your life isn't the only thing that feels a change; your pocket book will too! In this chapter, we will introduce you to Bay Area parents' favorite baby gear retailers. This chapter will answer the following questions and more:

◆ What is some general shopping advice for preparing for the baby's arrival?
◆ Which items are essential and which ones are not?
◆ Where can I go to buy basic baby gear?
◆ Where can I find stores to furnish the baby's nursery?
◆ Where can I find the best baby clothes and shoes?
◆ Where are some good resale shops?
◆ Where can I go to buy great baby toys and books?
◆ Where can I find a great baby photographer?
◆ How can I get my home childproofed?

Baby Gear and Nursery Essentials
Baby gear, equipment, and furniture can be purchased at baby superstores, specialty stores, mail order catalogs, and on-line.

Superstores offer unparalleled one-stop shopping for new parents. Some Bay Area parents' favorites are a consortium of retailers that operate under the name Baby News. These stores are owned and operated individually, but they are associated in that they buy together from the same distributor. The collective buying results in better wholesale prices for them. There are also less expensive superstores, such as Toys "R" Us, that carry a vast collection of moderate and low-end brands of baby gear. Specialty stores are often locally owned and run and tend to offer a smaller selection of higher end products. On-line sources and mail order catalogs offer the convenience of shopping from home. Some on-line sites offer great discounts on name brand gear—we've listed some at the end of this section.

General Shopping Advice

◆ To help ensure your baby's safety and comfort, do your homework before shopping. We suggest reading the book *Baby Bargains* by Denise and Alan Fields in which the authors review products by manufacturer and style, and share parents' opinions on the pros and cons of each.

◆ Before your baby arrives, visit a few baby gear stores to get a sense of what you need to buy and which brands and models you like. Find a store that has a lot of equipment on the floor and is service-oriented so a salesperson can demonstrate how to use the equipment, and you can actually try everything out too. Take it from us, knowing how to set up the crib or fold a stroller is better learned before your baby arrives!

◆ Focus on one or two products per visit to avoid baby gear burnout.

◆ Baby gear retailers are great places to survey other parents as to what products they like or don't like and why.

CAR SEAT

If there is one thing that you should do before your baby's arrival, it is to purchase and install your infant seat. By state law, hospitals may not permit you to drive home with your baby unless you have a properly installed infant car seat. Safety experts agree you should *never* buy or use a previously owned car seat, as you won't know

Carseat Safety

The world of car seats can be one of the most overwhelming and confusing safety issues for parents. With conflicting advice and recommendations, it's not easy to sift through all the information out there on car seat safety, never mind properly installing and using the car seat. The National Highway Traffic Safety Administration estimates that up to 85 percent of infant and child car seats are incorrectly installed, putting children at greater risk in a car accident. Safety experts can't stress enough the importance of following manufacturer's directions. When in doubt, it is a wise idea to have the installation and use of the seat checked.

Many baby superstores that sell car seats will help install or check your car seat, and often will do so for free. In addition, local police departments, such as the ones listed below, often sponsor such programs. For other areas, call your police department or the National Safe Kids Buckle Up Campaign (800-441-1888) and inquire.

Child Passenger Safety Program
San Francisco Police Department
415-575-6363 (Information and Appointment Phone Line)

California Highway Patrol
Corte Madera
415-924-1100

NEW CALIFORNIA BOOSTER SEAT LAW

As of January 1, 2002, children must be secured in an appropriate safety seat until they are 6 years old or weigh at least 60 pounds (prior regulations only applied to children up to age 4 or who weigh at least 40 pounds).

whether the car seat has been in an accident. If it has, it could be unsafe. Also, car seat specifications are always being improved, so a car seat purchased only a few years ago may not meet current safety standards. Infant car seats are generally around $50-75, and we advise spending the money and buying a new one. Infant seats (for infants and babies up to 20 pounds) must be rear facing, preferably in the middle of the back seat and never in the front seat of a car, especially a car with front seat passenger airbags.

www.aap.org/family/carseatguide.htm

The American Academy of Pediatrics website offers a "family shopping guide" to car seats. They concisely explain the different types of car seats and their features, as well as height and weight requirements. They have detailed information about almost every car seat out there—truly a great resource for parents!

www.chp.ca.gov/html/safetyseats.html

This website offers detailed information on California's requirements for infant and child car seats.

www.safewithin.com/childsafe/child.seats.cgi

This website offers basic car seat safety information and advice.

www.nhtsa.dot.gov

800-424-9393

This is the website for the National Highway Safety Traffic Administration. It features a list of car seat inspection stations by zip code.

www.safekids.org

The National Safe Kids Campaign's website offers an excellent car seat locator feature on picking the best car seat for your child.

www.carseatdata.org

This website has an interactive compatability database that allows you to search for which seats work best in which cars.

BASSINET, MOSES BASKET, AND SIDECAR

After a car seat, the next most important item is a comfortable place for the baby to sleep when you bring her home. Many newborns prefer the cozy confines of a bassinet, Moses basket, or sidecar (a three-sided bassinet that attaches to your bed to accommodate co-sleeping). However, most babies outgrow a bassinet by 3-4 months, so it's a great idea to borrow one if you can, provided it is in good condition and safe (no loose pieces of wicker that the baby can pick off). If you decide to buy one, these items run from $90-300 for a Moses basket with linens (sheets, liners, decorative skirts, and hoods), and up to $400 for an heirloom quality wicker bassinet. Alternatively, many babies sleep in a crib from day one and do just fine.

INFANT BATHTUB

An infant bathtub is a little plastic tub that is placed inside your tub. It allows the baby to recline and lets you have both hands free to wash him. When your baby can sit up well enough on his own (around 6–8 months) he can use a bath seat that is also placed inside your tub. Even with these helpful tools, however, *never* leave a baby or small child unattended in any amount of water for even a second! Infant bathtubs and seats run around $20-40.

STROLLER

When out and about, babies depend on either Mom's or Dad's bulging biceps or a sturdy stroller to get around. Even tired toddlers and preschoolers often favor a stroller over walking. What style you choose—whether it's a stroller that fastens an infant car seat to either a metal frame (such as Baby Trend's Snap and Go LX) or stroller (most of the high-end brands offer this feature); a lightweight easily collapsible umbrella stroller; or a more rugged carriage or pram—

What You Really Need

- ◆ Infant car seat and head and neck support insert
- ◆ Crib or bassinet
- ◆ Changing table or dresser combination
- ◆ Bouncy seat
- ◆ Infant bath tub
- ◆ Diaper pail
- ◆ Diapers, either cloth with wraps or covers or disposable
- ◆ If bottle feeding: four bottles and slow-flow nipples, pediatrician recommended formula, and bottle brush
- ◆ Two to four pacifiers for newborns
- ◆ Toiletries and health items (thermometer, baby Tylenol, baby shampoo and wash, nail clipper, nasal aspirator)
- ◆ Diaper bag
- ◆ Stroller
- ◆ Basic baby parenting book
- ◆ Highchair (not until 5-6 months)
- ◆ Baby spoons and feeding accessories
- ◆ Bibs

depends on your lifestyle and needs. Options to consider are whether or not the stroller converts to a carriage, where the baby faces, ease of folding, weight, whether the seat reclines, and if there is a sunshade and ample size storage basket. Given the variety of features and models available, the wide price range of strollers is similar to that of the car market—from $50 for your basic bare bones to over $500 for a fancy imported pram.

BOUNCY SEAT

A bouncy seat is undeniably a necessity. It's a great place to set your baby down when you need to shower, answer the phone, eat dinner, or just take a break from holding your baby. It also gives your baby a view of the world other than the one seen when lying on his back. If you don't receive one as a shower gift, go ahead and buy one—you won't regret spending the $30-45.

DIAPER BAG

Take your time in selecting a diaper bag, as it will be with you every day for the next couple of years! This is a personal item with many different styles to chose from—a backpack may appeal to one person while a messenger bag is better for another, and a stylish shoulder tote works for yet another. Be sure to try out several styles and think about how they will work with your lifestyle. Diaper bags come in all price ranges, and don't forget you can always make your own out of your favorite bag or backpack.

BABY CARRIER

Carrying a baby either in a front pack or a sling has become very popular. Babies love to be carried close to your body, and a baby carrier lets your hands be free. Your baby will love going on walks with you and taking in his surroundings. Bay Area parents' favorites include the Baby Bjorn carrier and Nojo Baby Sling. Parents said that their babies either loved or loathed the sling, so try to borrow one first. Baby carriers are great, but they are useful for a limited time, as once baby is a certain weight and length, it won't be comfortable for you to carry him tied on to you. They range from $40-80.

What Would Be Nice to Have

- ◆ Breast pump (if breastfeeding)
- ◆ Baby carrier or sling
- ◆ Glider or rocker
- ◆ Baby monitor
- ◆ Black and white toys and small baby board books
- ◆ Mobile
- ◆ Baby gym
- ◆ Cell phone for Mom! (to have your spouse or partner, caregiver, and pediatrician a dial away!)
- ◆ Exersaucer (not until 4-5 months)
- ◆ Portable crib or play yard
- ◆ Shelving or a closet organizer
- ◆ Tape or CD player and lullaby tapes and CDs
- ◆ Breastfeeding pillow (if breastfeeding)

BABY MONITOR

Baby monitors are a great way of hearing your baby without actually being in her room. They are especially useful if you live in a two-story house or a large home. Many are battery operated and can be carried from room to room. Monitors range from $25-65.

BABY SWING

Most parents say that their baby either loved or hated a swing. Don't rush out and buy one—borrow one from a friend first to see whether your baby likes it. Baby swings range from $75-170.

PORTABLE CRIB

A portable crib is great to have for travel as well as when your baby becomes mobile and you need to step away from her for a minute. Choose carefully. Focus on the size and weight, rather than the color scheme, if you plan on traveling a lot with the baby. Portable cribs range from $60-150, depending on manufacturer and features.

CRIB

By 3-4 months of age, your baby will have outgrown his bassinet. Unless you are embracing the concept of co-sleeping in a family bed, your baby will likely be transitioning to a crib. Order a crib before your baby arrives, because many stores don't stock a lot of models, and an order may take six to eight weeks to fill, and sometimes longer! Delivery and setup usually costs $50 extra, but is worth it when you discover in the process that you are missing a part or, worse, that the crib is defective.

Like car seats, safety experts agree that you should *never* buy or use an old crib, which may present safety hazards, including spindles not being spaced narrowly enough, lead paint, and turned posts. Cribs sold today are certified by the Juvenile Products Manufacturers Association (JPMA), which sets standards for most baby products, including cribs, strollers, high chairs, and portable cribs. Cribs come in all different types of styles, finishes, and prices—from $100 for a metal one from a discount retailer like Target to designer imported models for close to $1,000! Happily, most hardwood cribs made by quality domestic manufacturers cost between $250-500.

CRIB MATTRESS AND BEDDING

The most important considerations for crib mattresses and bedding have to do with safety. You want a tight fit between the mattress and crib. Essential pieces of bedding include a crib sheet and a mattress pad. A dust ruffle is purely for decor, and a baby quilt and pillows are safety hazards. If you buy bumpers, they should by tied on by snaps or short ties. However, some babies may think about using bumpers in ways that they were not intended for, such as climbing out of the crib. Also, some people think bumpers are a suffocation hazard since a mobile baby may be inclined to explore between the bumper and the crib. Basic mattresses start at $50 and go up to $150. Crib bedding (sheets, bumpers, and crib skirt) range from $100-800 depending on whether you opt for ready-made or custom-made pieces.

CHANGING TABLE

Changing tables, made at a comfortable height for your back when changing your baby, range from basic no frills models to fancy ones that match cribs or are combined with a dresser and are priced between $90-500. These can take as long as cribs to order, so it's a good idea to order one when you are still pregnant and also to set it up with some of baby's clothes and diapers *before* you have the baby. The last thing you'll feel like doing when you come home from the hospital is setting up a changing table and stocking your diaper station!

HIGH CHAIR

Once you begin to feed your baby solids (4-6 months), you'll need a high chair. There are many wonderful styles on the market today—from black leather-look vinyl seats to classic wooden high chairs. Select one with a wide base to prevent it from tipping over and with an easy tray release mechanism that can be managed with one hand. A five-point harness is also a good safety idea. High chairs cost from $50-220.

ROCKER AND GLIDER

A rocker or glider is a luxurious gift if you are lucky enough to receive one! They are a wonderful place to feed your baby and to help put her to sleep as well as to read to her when she is a bit older. However, it may be difficult to use a glider with a breastfeeding pillow, as it's a tight fit. Gliders retail for $250-500.

CLOSET ORGANIZER

You can store the baby's first clothes in baskets under a changing table or in dresser drawers. If using a closet, small shelves and cubbyholes, or rods at varying heights, will maximize your baby's closet space. Instead of buying a separate dresser, build a set of drawers in the closet—either ready-made closet storage pieces or, if you want to spend the money, a custom-built storage unit.

NATIONAL CHAINS

Here is what Bay Area parents have to say about several national chains. Call the toll free numbers listed, check the yellow pages, or visit their websites for a store location near you.

Baby Superstores

Babies "R" Us
888-BABYRUS
www.babiesrus.com
PARENT RATING: ☆ ☆ ☆ ☆

While this store is owned by Toys "R" Us, this baby superstore offers surprisingly better quality merchandise, including moderate to some upscale baby gear. Service is only slightly better than at Toys "R" Us. They carry almost all the major brands of car seats, cribs, and strollers, and a nice selection of infant clothing as well as many other baby accessories. One San Francisco mom's comment (who had to drive almost an hour to the closest Babies "R" Us) is, "well worth the drive!"

Baby Depot at Burlington Coat Factory
800-444-COAT
www.coat.com
PARENT RATING: ☆ ☆

This store is known for having a great selection of high-end brands of baby gear, including strollers, car seats, cribs, changing tables, and dressers, at discounted prices. However, most agree that staff is neither helpful nor knowledgeable. Several parents reported mix-ups in ordering items and long and agonizing delays. Their return policy is also undesirable—they offer no cash refunds under any circumstances (even if a product breaks or is defective, they only offer store credit). Bottom line: Don't set up a gift registry here and don't buy from them unless it is off the floor.

Specialty Chains

Pottery Barn Kids
800-430-7373
www.potterybarnkids.com
PARENT RATING: ☆ ☆ ☆ ☆ ☆

Pottery Barn Kids is the latest retailer to dive into the juvenile products market. Many moms wonder how mothers before them decorated their kids' rooms! They offer traditionally designed cribs, beds, and desks, and other furnishings and accessories for baby's room at prices that aren't cheap, but aren't ridiculous either.

They have a wonderful selection of matching bedding and accessories for cribs and beds that changes several times a year. Products are also available via their website and mail order. Order early, or you may have to wait for back-ordered items. At press-time, Pottery Barn Kids is rapidly expanding with plans to open stores in Emeryville and Palo Alto in addition to their Corte Madera and San Jose locations.

The Right Start
800-548-8531
www.rightstart.com

PARENT RATING: ☆ ☆ ☆ ☆ 1/2

The Right Start offers a choice selection of high-end baby gear (strollers and car seats) and travel, feeding, health, and bath accessories, and specializes in carrying developmentally oriented toys and educational videos and books for infants and young toddlers. They carry an extensive selection of smaller baby gear items and accessories such as booster seats, teethers, Mustela toiletries, and potty training accessories. They also have a large selection of nursing products, including pillows and pumps. They often offer a 10-15 percent discount if you order on-line.

Discounters

Target
www.target.com

PARENT RATING: ☆ ☆ ☆ ☆

This mega store offers a decent selection of moderate-end baby gear, including bassinets, strollers, high chairs, decor for baby's nursery, and many baby accessories. Service is lacking, but good buys can be found.

BEST BUYS FOR DIPES AND WIPES

Bay Area moms agree that Costco and Target have the best prices on disposable diapers and wipes. If you can stand trekking out to these mega stores, the savings are worth the trip. Target is also great for basic baby equipment, which they often put on sale to get you there.

Toys "R" Us
800-869-7787
www.toysrus.com

PARENT RATING: ☆ ☆

New and expectant parents can stock up on baby gear here, including strollers, cribs, car seats, and diapers at moderate prices. However, they don't carry any of the high-end brands. Service is lacking, so if you have questions, go to a more service-oriented retailer.

Department Stores

JC Penney
www.jcpenney.com

JC Penney offers great deals on moderate-end brands of baby gear, nursery furnishings, bedding, and accessories. Goods are available on-line if there isn't a store nearby you.

Sears
www.sears.com

Sears offers all the baby gear and equipment that you need. You'll find brands such as Cosco, Graco, and Evenflo at moderate prices.

BAY AREA RETAILERS

Here is what Bay Area parents have to say about their favorite local stores for all of their baby gear:

Citikids

152 Clement St.
415-752-3837

PARENT RATING: ☆ ☆ ☆ ☆ ☆

Part of the consortium of Baby News retailers, Citikids is San Francisco's primary full-service baby gear retailer offering everything that new and expectant parents will need for the first couple of years of their baby's life. They have one of the largest displays of strollers in the Bay Area including many high-end brands. They also have many top-quality car seats, gliders, swings, baby carriers, diaper bags, high chairs, portable cribs, nursing and bottle feeding accessories, childproofing items, and more. They offer a wonderful selection of baby furniture, including high-end baby cribs, wicker bassinets, coordinating bedding, changing tables, dressers, and lamps, as well as upscale baby clothing and developmental toys. You might find better bargains elsewhere, but this friendly family-run business wins the prize for service. They will gladly demonstrate equipment and tell you the pros and cons of each. They also will check on the proper installation of your car seats without asking whether you bought it from them. The friendly and helpful staff is unparalleled in the area and well worth it!

Country Living–Unique and Natural Furniture

1033 Clement St.
415-751-1276

PARENT RATING: ☆ ☆ ☆ ☆ ☆

Known to San Francisco parents as a great place to get bargains on unpainted furniture, Country Living carries changing tables, cribs, dressers, rockers, children's tables and chairs, bookshelves, desks, and bunk beds. All of their furniture is made of solid wood and can be bought either finished or unfinished if you want to save some money and do it yourself. Service is friendly and helpful.

Day One

3490 California St.
415-440-3291
www.dayonecenter.com

PARENT RATING: ☆ ☆ ☆ ☆ ☆

This state-of-the-art parenting center has a wonderful boutique that includes smaller baby gear items and accessories such as high-end high chairs, diaper bags, baby carriers, and mobiles, as well as all the nursing supplies you could ever need. They also carry a great bassinet that is lightweight and portable. See also in chapter 5.

Not there

Jonathan Kaye   *NICE SMALL*

3548 Sacramento St.
415-563-0773

PARENT RATING: ☆ ☆ ☆ ☆ ☆

The original store (they opened a baby store in 2000, see below) is now exclusively devoted to young children's high-end bedroom furnishings and accessories. They feature hand-painted toy chests and tables, lamps, nightlights, and bookends, as well as unique wall hangings and handmade quilts. They also offer a wonderful selection of classic toys that feature Curious George and Madeline as well as educational and developmental toys.

Jonathan Kaye Baby

3615 Sacramento St.
415-922-3233

PARENT RATING: ☆ ☆ ☆ ☆ ☆

Among San Francisco's most elegant baby boutiques, Jonathan Kaye Baby is a block away from the original store. This store (opened in 2000) is devoted exclusively to babies, offering customized nursery design services including furniture featuring whimsical designs, and painted wall murals. They carry beautiful wicker bassinets and Moses baskets, high-end cribs and chests, and an elegant selection of high-end custom or ready-made crib bedding, as well as unique accessories to complete your baby's nursery. We've heard from one Bay Area mom that this tony boutique will match prices for nursery furnishings at Lullaby Lane in San Bruno! They also carry a choice selection of upscale clothing and developmental toys.

Karikter

418 Sutter St.   *Too modern*
415-434-1120

This fun European comic and design boutique is of interest to adults and children alike! The shop carries unique accessories including bookends, lamps, clocks, posters, feeding accessories, towels, and occasionally bedding, that feature characters including the Little Prince, Babar, Wallace and Gromit, Elmer and Noddy, and Tintin.

 # Most Useful Baby Gear for City Life

- ◆ Baby Bjorn baby carrier
  - ◆ A stroller with a car seat attachment bar or Baby Trend's Snap and Go LX metal stroller frame
- ◆ Lightweight reclinable stroller (many like the Maclaren, Combi Savvy Z, and Peg Perego Pliko strollers)
- ◆ Baby jogger
- ◆ Backpack diaper bag or messenger bag-style diaper bag

Maison de Belles Choses

3623 Sacramento St.

415-345-1797

Owner Ellen Fletcher-Kelly carries an elegant selection of imported caned beds from France for your toddler when she is ready to transition out of the crib. See a full description and rating under the "Baby and Children's Clothing" section of this chapter.

Mudpie Homeworks

1750 Union St.

415-673-8060

PARENT RATING: ☆ ☆ ☆

Right down the street from its clothier, Mudpie Homeworks offers designer quality and designer-priced baby furnishings, including antique reproduction cribs, beds, changing tables, and dressers, as well as crib sheets, customized bedding, matelasse bumpers, handmade quilts, rugs, and lights. In-home designer services are also offered by appointment. This talented team will gladly assist you in creating a one-of-a-kind nursery or room for your baby or young child. Just be prepared to pay the bill! *Expensive, custom*

Scheuer Linens

340 Sutter St. *No more baby*

415-392-2813

PARENT RATING: ☆ ☆ ☆ ☆

A San Francisco institution, Scheuer Linens carries, among their elegant selection of linens, beautifully detailed crib bedding, including fitted sheets, comforters, quilts, and bumpers. They also offer custom-made bedding and accessories for the baby's room. Scheuer offers stellar service and a friendly attitude.

Baby News Outlet

1445 Santa Rosa Ave.

Santa Rosa

707-542-1006

PARENT RATING: ☆ ☆ ☆ ☆ ☆

Baby News Outlet is part of the consortium of Baby News Bay Area baby gear retailers. Like its sister retailers, it carries high-end baby gear and clothing. However, Baby News Outlet is distributor owned unlike the other Baby News stores, which means it carries discontinued models of many items at great prices. Their staff is helpful and knowledgeable.

Goodnight Moon

117 Corte Madera Town Center

Corte Madera

415-945-0677

PARENT RATING: ☆ ☆ ☆ ☆ ☆

One of Marin's best baby boutiques, Goodnite Moon carries high-end furnishings for your baby's nursery and child's room, including handpainted dressers, lamps, toddler beds, custom-made bedding, and many wonderful accessories from bookends to lamps. Prices for custom bedding compare favorably to other retailers.

Heller's for Children

514 4th St.

San Rafael

415-456-5533

PARENT RATING: ☆ ☆ ☆ ☆ ☆

Part of the Baby News consortium of baby retailers and in business since 1958, Heller's is a Marin parent's staple. They have a large store filled with almost everything you'd ever need for

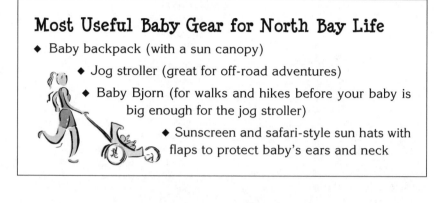

Most Useful Baby Gear for North Bay Life

- ◆ Baby backpack (with a sun canopy)
  - ◆ Jog stroller (great for off-road adventures)
  - ◆ Baby Bjorn (for walks and hikes before your baby is big enough for the jog stroller)
    - ◆ Sunscreen and safari-style sun hats with flaps to protect baby's ears and neck

your baby's first two years, including a large selection of high-end strollers, car seats, joggers, gliders, high chairs, diaper bags, baby carriers, toys, baby books, and baby clothing and sleepwear. The second floor has an extensive collection of furnishings for baby's room, including cribs, dressers, changing tables, and bassinets. They also have a nice selection of developmental toys for infants, including colorful, multisensory toys, mobiles, and activity gyms. The staff is knowledgeable and friendly.

Sanders Furniture
825 W. Francisco Blvd.
San Rafael
415-459-5757
This furniture store offers finished wood beds for children, as well as a great selection of bookcases, dressers, children's table and chair sets, and nightstands. They also have another store in the same shopping center (Anderson Dr.) that offers unpainted furniture, including many items for a child's room.

Babies 2 Kids
4807 Davenport Ave.
Fremont
510-797-5437
Part of the Baby News association of Bay Area baby retailers, Babies 2 Kids has recently shifted its focus from baby gear to baby and children's furniture, including cribs and bunk beds.

Baby World—The Children's Place
- Berkeley
  6000 College Ave., 510-655-2828
- Oakland
  3925 Piedmont Ave., 510-547-7040

PARENT RATING: ☆ ☆ ☆

Also part of the Baby News consortium of baby retailers, Baby World is a true baby superstore, carrying an extensive selection of cribs, bassinets, strollers, car seats, gliders, dressers, and other baby gear. However, the staff is not as knowledgeable about various models of baby gear, and the pros and cons of each, as they might be elsewhere. They also have a nice selection of high-end baby clothing.

Bellini

1651 Botelho Dr.
Walnut Creek
925-274-0829

PARENT RATING: ☆ ☆ ☆ ☆ ☆

Bellini features beautiful cribs, beds, changing tables, and dressers of their label, all direct from Italy. They also carry a large selection of upscale bedding, strollers, car seats, portable cribs, high chairs, and many other baby accessories.

Berkeley Kids' Room

2474 Shattuck Ave.
Berkeley
510-841-5068

Berkeley Kids' specializes in bedroom furnishings for young children, including beds, dressers, bunk beds, rugs, lamps, and bedding. They also carry a small selection of cribs and changing tables for infants.

Cartan's

2085 San Ramon Valley Rd.
San Ramon
925-820-3440

Part of the Baby News association of Bay Area baby retailers, Cartan's is a baby superstore, offering a vast selection of strollers, car seats, baby carriers, cribs, and bedding among all the other gear new parents need. The also offer a nice selection of upscale baby clothing up to size 24 months. They also carry christening gowns.

Earthsake

1772 4th St.
Berkeley
510-559-8440

This store offers natural products for a baby's nursery, including maple cribs, organic cotton crib mattresses and bedding, receiving blankets and towels, and laundry flakes.

Most Useful Baby Products for Life in the East Bay

- ◆ Jog stroller
- ◆ Quality car seat and good car toys (such as a Magna Doodle and books)
- ◆ Large blanket for the park, picnics, and other outings
- ◆ Insulated lunch bag
- ◆ Wagon for neighborhood rides and to load up with stuff to take to cook-outs

Goodnite Room

1848 4th St.
Berkeley
510-548-2108

This Rockridge neighborhood store specializes in building both classic and whimsical wood furniture for your child's room.

Jacadi Paris

3435 Blackhawk Plaza Cir.
Danville
925-736-5600
www.jacadiusa.com

This small upscale French boutique offers exquisite coordinating fabrics, bedding, wallpaper, and nursery accessories. Most of the nursery furnishings and decor are not in the store (which primarily carries a high-end line of imported clothing from France) and can only be viewed and ordered from a catalog. At press time, Jacadi is planning on opening stores in Walnut Creek and San Jose.

Kids N' Cribs

1820 A St.
Antioch
925-778-2229
www.kids-n-cribs.com

Kids N' Cribs, a family-operated business, specializes in carrying furniture for your baby's nursery and child's room. They have more than fifty cribs and beds on display. They also offer bedding and accessories, reams of basic baby gear, including car seats, strollers, and breast pumps, developmental toys for infants and toddlers, and a nice line of baby clothing, including sizes for newborns and preemies.

Kids Room

40524 Albrae St.
Fremont
510-490-1313
www.Kids-Room.com

The Kids Room offers an extensive selection of twenty-five different children's furniture lines, including bunk beds, dressers, twin beds, toddler beds, mattresses, lamps, and bean bag chairs. The large showroom features furnishings in solid hardwoods, including oak and maple, as well as a variety of color laminates. Owner Lanny Witt will match any price in the Bay Area. Another added bonus is that unlike most other furniture stores, Lanny can get you many items within a week. They do not carry cribs or any baby furnishings.

Leonard's Tot Shop

- Pleasant Hill
  548 Contra Costa Blvd., 925-682-5888
- Concord (Outlet store)
  1281 Challenge Drive, 925-363-9756

Leonard's specializes in baby and children's furniture and has been in business for more than fifty years. They feature more than one hundred cribs to choose from, as well as dressers, changing tables, beds, bookshelves, rockers, toy boxes, and coordinating bedding. They also offer baby gear, including car seats, strollers, high chairs, and nursing and bottle feeding supplies. The outlet store hours are often limited to the weekends.

Rockridge Kids

5511 College Ave.
Oakland
510-601-5437

PARENT RATING: ☆ ☆ ☆ ☆ ☆

Located on the same block in Rockridge on the Oakland/Berkeley border for almost twenty-five years, this classic children's department store is an Oakland/Berkeley institution. Nishan Shephard is the proud and helpful owner of this truly special store that offers the very best of basic baby gear. They also carry baby clothing up to size 3T, including preemies, unique bedding for babies and children, and a thoughtful selection of classic toys, featuring Radio Flyer wagons and Kettler Trikes. Rockridge Kids also has one of the best car seat installers around town; the highway patrol sends people to him to have their car seats properly installed. The store is as service-oriented and as kid friendly as you can get. Sales people are eager to offer you useful information about specific products, and the owner encourages little shoppers to play with the train tables. The store is also very involved in the community of Rockridge, and they are playing a large role in helping build a park. In addition, 10 percent of all profits is given to the schools in the community.

South Bay

Baby Land Furniture ✗

1990 W. San Carlos St.
San Jose
408-293-1515

Baby Land offers a large selection of moderately priced wooden furniture for babies and toddlers, including cribs, cradles, and dressers. They also offer moderately priced strollers, car seats, and other baby gear and accessories.

Baby Super Store and Rocker ✓ World and Furniture for Kids

1523 Parkmoor Ave.
San Jose
408-293-0358

Baby Super is true to its name—a true baby superstore. It's actually three stores in one and offers everything from cribs, beds, and bedding, to strollers, car seats, high chairs, gliders, and rockers. Their best feature is the numerous displays of infant and kids' rooms, which help you visualize your baby's or child's room.

Bellini ✗

1910 W. El Camino Real
Mountain View (CLOSED)
650-567-9891

See the description and rating under East Bay.

Earthsake ✗

230 University Ave.
Palo Alto
650-322-9505

See under East Bay.

Hoot Judkins

- Redwood City
  1269 Veterans Blvd., 650-367-8181
- San Bruno
  1400 El Camino Real, 650-952-5600

While these stores are not exclusively devoted to children's furniture, they carry solid wood baby furniture, including beds, rockers, toy boxes, bunk beds, step stools, rocking horses, and dollhouses. Items come unfinished, but special orders may be placed to have items finished for you.

Jacadi Paris

1215 Burlingame Ave.
Burlingame
650-558-1122

See under East Bay

Juvenile Lifestyles, Inc.

654 Santa Cruz Ave.
Menlo Park
650-322-3500

PARENT RATING: ☆ ☆ ☆ ☆ ☆

Juvenile Lifestyles is a dream come true for any parent who desires to transform her little one's room into a magical kingdom. For over ten years, Juvenile Lifestyles has excelled in offering hand-painted, exclusively designed furniture and custom bedding for the little prince or princess in your life as well as a wide variety of beautiful accessories in fanciful designs, including hand-painted high chairs, clocks, lamps, and unique rugs and books. They also carry hand-knit sweaters and hats by Jelly Beenies. Truly an exquisite baby boutique!

X Kiddie World Furniture

150 N. San Thomas Aquino
Campbell
408-370-3550
CLOSED
www.kiddieworldfurniture.com

They offer every piece of furniture that you could ever need for your baby's or child's room, including cribs, changing tables, gliders, dressers, beds, and desks. They also offer a selection of car seats, strollers, baby clothing, and toys.

Laura Ashley Home

• Burlingame *CLOSED*
  1375 Burlingame Ave., 650-344-1774
• Palo Alto
  12 Stanford Shopping Center,
  650-328-0560

PARENT RATING: ☆ ☆ ☆ ☆

Laura Ashley Home offers ready-made crib bumpers, crib sheets, and other bedding and nursery decor that coordinates with borders, lamp-shades, picture frames, and other accessories for your baby's room. Or choose among the wonderful fabrics of The Mother and Child Collection to customize your baby's bedding and room decor.

Lullaby Lane ✓

556 San Mateo Ave.
San Bruno
650-588-7644
www.lullabylane.com

PARENT RATING: ☆ ☆ ☆ ☆ ☆

Family-owned and operated for over fifty years, Lullaby Lane offers one-stop shopping for all of your baby's needs. This store has a large floor space covered with an extensive selection of strollers, joggers, car seats, high chairs, baby carriers, baby furniture, and bedding at some of the Bay Area's most competitive prices. They also have a nice selection of baby clothing. Lullaby Lane has a small clearance center just down the street (570 San Mateo Ave., 650-588-4878) where real bargains can be found. The retail store has a semi-annual closeout sale, but you need to get there before the doors open. Lullaby Lane also offers a free seminar almost every month on selecting and using baby gear. It's a great way to learn about what to look for in quality and safety. They also demonstrate car seat installation, strollers, high chairs, and cribs. Bay Area moms say that "The Lane" "stands out for knowledgeable staff and excellent customer service." "You really get the sense that it's family run and owned." "I liked everyone I dealt with there."

Planet Kids

1145 El Camino Real
Menlo Park
650-329-8488

A member of the Baby News consortium of baby superstores, Planet Kids offers high-end infant and children's furniture, a large selection of ready-made and customized bedding, high-end baby gear, including strollers, car seats, and high chairs, and child-proofing products. They also offer individual design services by appointment. They carry a nice selection of developmentally oriented toys for infants and toddlers. The staff is friendly and knowledgeable. Planet Kids features built-in entertainment for your little one in its Galaxy Playroom.

Talbot's Toyland

445 South B St.
San Mateo
650-342-0126

PARENT RATING: ☆ ☆ ☆ ☆

In business for more than fifty years, Talbots "has it all" in baby gear. They carry an enormous selection at good prices, including medium- and high-end strollers, bassinets, car seats, and baby carriers, along with other baby accessories and a wonderful selection of toys.

Most Useful Baby Gear for South Bay Life

- ◆ Car seat gallery and other toys for the car

- ◆ A stroller with a car seat attachment bar or Baby Trend's Snap and Go LX metal stroller frame (great for mall shopping).

- ◆ Baby sun block and safari-style sun hat with flaps to protect baby's ears and neck

INDIVIDUAL NURSERY DESIGNERS AND MURALISTS

We know this doesn't come under the heading of necessities, but the Bay Area offers many talented designers and muralists who specialize in making a one-of-a-kind nursery or child's room.

Elizabeth Brownrigg

415-440-1271

Elizabeth Brownrigg offers hand-painted furniture and one-of-a-kind murals for your baby's nursery or child's room.

A Child's Eye View

510-653-3304

This talented team of interior designers specializes in creating nurseries and children's rooms.

Croworks Decorative Painting

415-454-6809

Victoria Bohlman does beautiful faux, painting, and glazing designs for a baby's or child's room, especially girls' rooms.

Kim Curtis

415-221-2255

Kim Curtis offers custom baby decoration and specializes in painting favorite nursery rhymes and stories by hand on your baby's nursery walls.

Tori Debella

PARENT RATING: ☆ ☆ ☆ ☆ ☆

415-258-8123

Parents love the work of this talented muralist!

The Flying Brush

415-285-0322

Teresa O'Connor offers unique painting for kids, including custom murals and furniture.

Juvenile Lifestyles, Inc.

654 Santa Cruz Ave.
Menlo Park
650-322-3500

For a full description, see above under "Bay Area Retailers." This team of talented interior designers has been in business for more than seventeen years. They offer full design services and will work with you for all of your needs in designing the ultimate nursery or child's room, including customized bedding, window treatments, and providing muralists to transform your baby's room. They offer complimentary in-store advice and at-home consultations by appointment.

Masterpiece Murals

800-242-2003

June Workman will transform your baby's or child's room into an enchanted environment.

Mommy's Murals

925-820-7235

Sylvia Pillsbury, a former children's book illustrator, offers painted murals and faux painting to transform a child's room. She prefers serving Pleasanton, Danville, and Walnut Creek, but will travel to other areas.

Novak Art Studio

800-550-5322

They specialize in creating walls, tiles, and furniture for kids' rooms.

Diane Pizzoli
415-775-6434
PARENT RATING: ☆ ☆ ☆ ☆ ☆
Parents rave about Diane's murals!

Jane Resnick, Interior Design
415-641-4858
Jane Resnick specializes in designing baby's and children's rooms. She has clients all over the Bay Area.

Vacationing or Visiting Baby

Are you wondering where your sister's eight-month old baby is going to sleep when he visits you next month? Or, now that you have your vacation booked, are you wondering how you are going to lug all that baby gear with you? Leave it behind, and let a baby equipment rental agency be your answer. These companies rent a large inventory of strollers, car seats, portable cribs, swings, joggers, high chairs, cribs, and much more. You either make your reservation via phone or their website. Within a couple of days, a representative will call you to confirm and make delivery or pickup arrangements.

Little Luggage
877-FLYBABY
www.littleluggage.com
This San Francisco based company rents baby gear in the Bay Area for your visiting friends and relatives with babies. They will come to your house and set up a crib or drop off a stroller with friendly and reliable service. They are also planning to offer the option of picking up baby equipment at SFO airport.

Baby's Away
800-571-0077
www.babysaway.com
Baby's Away is the largest baby and child gear rental service in the country with thirty locations. At press-time, they do not have a Bay Area location, but serve parts of Hawaii and other popular vacation destinations. Call or visit their website for locations and details.

Lullaby Lane
650-588-7644
This full-scale baby superstore located in San Bruno also rents baby equipment.

138

BUYING BABY GEAR ON-LINE AND THROUGH MAIL ORDER

There are myriad websites that sell baby gear and accessories, some at great prices. Here are several recommended to us by parents. However, remember that saving $50 on a stroller purchased on-line might not be worth it when it breaks or arrives defective, rather than buying from your neighborhood retailer that may offer repairs! Also, be sure to get all the details on delivery charges and arrangements before you place your order—some parents have reported high shipping costs and deliveries of nursery furniture that only went as far as their front door.

*These sites also carry baby clothing:
www.babybundle.com*
www.babycenter.com*
www.babyproductsonline.com
www.babysupercenter.com
www.babysupermall.com
www.babystyle.com*
www.babycollection.com

The above are comprehensive on-line baby retailers that offer specialty items for baby as well.

Baby Catalog of America
800-PLAYPEN (catalog)
www.babycatalog.com
This comprehensive on-line and mail order baby boutique offers the "lowest advertised price" of all baby gear, many of which are high-end brands. Join the "Baby Club" for $25 the first year and receive an additional 10 percent discount.

Kids Club
800-363-0500 (catalog)
www.kidstuff.com
Kids Club offers deep hard-to-beat discounts on high-end baby equipment and accessories to club members. Membership is $18 a year and well worth it if you plan on buying a lot of baby gear. Non-club members may purchase items, but at slightly higher prices.

Stroller Depot
www.strollerdepot.com
They offer great discounts on name brand strollers, including many high-end brands.

One Step Ahead
800-274-8440 (catalog)
www.onestepahead.com
This store is similar to Right Start, offering select major baby gear items such as strollers, high chairs, and car seats and specializing in smaller baby accessories for use around the house or when traveling, such as monitors, and bathing, feeding, and childproofing items.

Right Start
800-LITTLE-1 (catalog)
www.rightstart.com
See description under "Baby Gear" retailers. They often offer a 10-15 percent discount if you order on-line.

Toys "R" Us

www.toysrus.com

Babies "R" Us

www.babiesrus.com*

Two sane alternatives to these mega stores!

eBay

www.ebay.com

Baby product makers and stores are quietly selling overstocked, new items on eBay at prices that are much lower than most major retailers.

ON-LINE BABY PRODUCT REVIEWS

The following websites offer reviews of baby gear and equipment:

- www.babycenter.com
- www.epinions.com
- www.deja.com
- http://parents.berkeley.edu (by end of 2002 will be replaced by www.parentsnet.org)

HELPFUL SHOPPING TIPS FOR CLOTHING

- Wait until after your baby shower to buy, as you may receive several gifts of clothing.
- Unless your doctor expects that you are having a small baby, don't buy too many things in the newborn size, 0-3 months. Most of these items won't fit a baby larger than ten to twelve pounds.
- Keep track of how many gifts you receive in what sizes and save gift receipts. You may want to exchange some gifts for different sizes.
- Do exchanges as soon as you can. If you're like most new moms and put it off, you'll find the unworn outfit with tags still on it hanging in your baby's closet a year later!
- European-style boutiques often have strict return and exchange policies, often requiring that they be done within two weeks.

Department stores offer the most liberal return and exchange policies.

- Buy cotton—it's the most comfortable fabric for babies. Their delicate skin knows the difference between natural and synthetic fibers. Cotton is also easier to wash than many synthetics. The only exception to this is sleepwear, which must be 100 percent polyester to be flame retardant.
- Buy only machine-washable clothing. If you didn't have time to do your own hand-washing before your baby was born, you definitely won't have time to do it after your baby's arrival!
- One-piece outfits such as stretchy suits and rompers are best for babies, since two-piece outfits tend to "ride up" each time you lift your baby.

On-Line and Mail Order Resources for Nursery Bedding and Accessories

Baby Bedding Online
www.babybeddingonline.com

Best for Babies
www.bestforbabies.com

Baby Style
www.babystyle.com

Company Kids
800-323-8000 (catalog)
www.companykids.com

Garnet Hill
800-622-6216 (catalog)
www.garnethill.com

Graham Kracker
800-489-2820 (catalog)
www.grahamkracker.com

Linens for Us
www.linensforus.com

Land's End
800-345-3696 (catalog)
www.landsend.com

The Land of Nod
800-933-9904 (catalog)
www.landofnod.com

Pottery Barn Kids
800-430-7373 (catalog)
www.potterybarn.kids.com

Stephanie Anne
888-885-6700 (catalog)
www.stephanieanne.com

Warm Biscuit Bedding Co.
800-231-4231 (catalog)
www.warmbiscuit.com

You may also want to check out websites of individual designers and manufacturers of baby and children's bedding.

Baby and Children's Clothing

Everyone loves baby clothing, and you'll love it even more when you have a baby! To make buying baby clothing even more irresistible, the Bay Area has some of the best baby clothing retailers in the country. We've done our best to peruse the Bay Area and ask moms and dads about their favorite baby and children's clothiers. Many baby superstores carry wonderful selections of clothing and shoes, so be sure not to miss those listed in the "Baby Gear" section above. We've also included some Bay Area parents' favorite places to shop for children's clothing on-line and through mail order catalogs.

Favorite Mail Order Catalogs and On-Line Resources for Baby and Children's Clothing

Baby Gap
www.babygap.com

BabyoBaby
www.babyobaby.com (monogramed baby blankets and accessories)

Old Navy
www.oldnavy.com

The Wooden Soldier
800-375-6002 (catalog)

Children's Wear Digest
800-242-5437 (catalog)
www.cwdkids.com

Hanna Andersson
800-222-0544 (catalog)
www.hannaandersson.com

Land's End
800-963-4816 (catalog)
www.landsend.com

L.L. Kids (catalog)
800-552-5437
www.llbean.com

Talbot's Kids
800-543-7123 (catalog)
www.talbots.com

Biobottoms
800-766-1254 (catalog)
www.biobottoms.com

Patagonia Kids
800-638-6464 (catalog)
www.patagonia.com

www.agingerhouse.com
www.gigglesandcurls.com
www.redapple1.com
www.precious-child.com
www.babyultimate.com
www.babystyle.com
www.oneofakindkid.com

NATIONAL CHAINS

Here is what Bay Area parents have to say about several national chains. Check the yellow pages or each chain's website for a store location near you.

Specialty Chains

Baby Gap
www.babygap.com
PARENT RATING: ☆ ☆ ☆ ☆ ☆

This locally-headquartered chain is a favorite among Bay Area parents. Even though you may see many other babies in the same outfit, this doesn't seem to stop most Bay Area parents from buying here. Lines change about every eight weeks, after which whatever is left goes on sale at a deep discount. Their flagship store in downtown San Francisco has an entire floor for babies and kids. Most Gap Kids also carry a selection of the current baby line of clothing. Goods are also available on-line.

The Children's Place

www.childrensplace.com

PARENT RATING: ☆ ☆ ☆

This national chain offers moderately priced playwear and dressier wear, as well as outerwear and sleepwear for infants and young children.

Gymboree

www.gymboree.com

PARENT RATING: ☆ ☆ ☆ ☆

A Bay Area-based designer and company popular with many Bay Area moms, Gymboree offers colorful coordinating ensembles for infants and children. Clothing lines change about every eight weeks. What's left goes on sale at great savings.

Old Navy

www.oldnavy.com

PARENT RATING: ☆ ☆ ☆ ☆

If you and your baby can stand the blaring music and football-field size of the store, Old Navy offers moderately priced basics for babies, toddlers, and kids. Bay Area moms generally agree that Old Navy's styles aren't quite as cute or stylish as their sister company Baby Gap, and the selection isn't as large either; however, they certainly are less expensive. They offer affordable prices and hip styles of decent quality clothing that don't have to last more than one season anyway! Items are also available on-line.

Department Stores

Bloomingdale's

www.bloomingdales.com

Bloomies has an extensive upscale infant and children's department, featuring designer labels including

DKNY and Ralph Lauren—what else would one expect?

JC Penney

www.jcpenney.com

Penney's offers moderately priced playwear and dressy wear for infants and children, including labels such as Carter's and Health Tex.

Macy's

www.macys.com

PARENT RATING: ☆ ☆ ☆

While the service could use improvement, Macy's infant department offers one of the largest selections of moderately priced infant and toddler clothing through size 4T.

Nordstrom

www.nordstrom.com

PARENT RATING: ☆ ☆ ☆ ☆ ☆

Nordstrom has a great infant and children's department, with a variety of designer playwear clothing. Popular lines/products: Hartstrings, Little Me, Ralph Lauren, Tommy Hilfiger, Mulberribush, and their own moderately priced Baby N label. They also carry special occasion wear from newborn on up. Popular lines/products: Imps Original suits (boys); Florence Eiseman dresses; and Posie hand-sewn christening gowns. The staff is very service oriented.

Neiman Marcus

www.neimanmarcus.com

PARENT RATING: ☆ ☆ ☆ ☆

Neiman's has a small but unsurprisingly upscale baby and toddler's department, featuring designer playwear and elegant special occasion wear. Popular lines/products: Florence Eiseman party dresses; Posie christening gowns.

Babies "R" Us

www.babiesrus.com

PARENT RATING: ☆ ☆ ☆ ☆

This store has an impressive selection of moderate name–brand clothing such as Carter's and Little Me at discounted prices (30 percent or more off retail) for newborns, toddlers, and children. They carry all the baby basics, such as sleepers, rompers, and Ts, as well as more hip styles for your preschooler and beyond.

Marshall's

PARENT RATING: ☆ ☆ ☆ ☆

This national discount department store is well known for its quality and name–brand labels at deep discounts. Inventory varies with store location, but their infant and children's department is usually worth checking out.

Mervyn's California

www.mervyns.com

PARENT RATING: ☆ ☆ ☆

Mervyn's offers moderately priced baby and children's clothing at great savings, especially when on sale. Mervyn's is a great place to stock up on basics such as Ts, socks, and sleepers. You can also occasionally find great designer knock-offs.

Favorite local baby and children's clothiers in San Francisco

Most Hip Baby Clothing
Kids Only
Baby Gap

Best Sales
Dottie Dolittle
Baby Gap

Most Traditional Baby Clothing
Dottie Dolittle
Mudpie
Maison de Belles Choses

Special Occasions (Christenings, Weddings, and Parties)
Dottie Dolittle
Mudpie
Neiman Marcus
Nordstrom

Halloween Costumes
1887 Dance Shop
Tuffy's Hopscotch
Baby Gap
Mervyn's
Old Navy
The Disney Store

Ross Dress for Less

www.ross.com

This discount department store offers a selection of infant and toddler clothing at great values. Selections tend to vary by each store location, but it is worth checking out.

Target

www.target.com

PARENT RATING: ☆ ☆ ☆ ☆

You can get great buys on Target's own line of 100 percent cotton baby and toddler clothing, under the Cherokee label. Many Bay Area moms buy all of their kid's play clothes here at low prices.

BAY AREA RETAILERS

Here is what Bay Area parents have to say about their favorite local baby and children's clothiers:

San Francisco

1887 Dance Shop

2206 Union St.

415-441-1887

1887 Dance Shop specializes in carrying dancewear for young children as well as many costumes and dress-up clothes year-round.

Day One

3490 California St., Ste. 203

415-440-DAY1 (3291)

www.dayonecenter.com

PARENT RATING: ☆ ☆ ☆ ☆ ☆

This new parents' resource center runs a fabulous boutique that carries an upscale selection of baby clothing as well as developmental toys for babies. They feature beautiful chenille and fleece baby blankets, as well as a nice selection of comfy clothing and caps for preemies. Popular lines/products: Victoria's Kids sweaters, Zutano (100 percent cotton ensembles), Oink Pig.

Dottie Doolittle

3680 Sacramento St.

415-563-3244

PARENT RATING: ☆ ☆ ☆ ☆ ☆

This one-of-a-kind store is a long-time favorite among San Francisco moms, as owner Maggie Chafen has been in business for twenty-seven years! Dottie carries exquisite clothing, for both play and special occasions, featuring many traditional-style designers, for newborns through 12 years. They offer beautiful baby sweaters and blankets and adorable ensembles for your toddler or preschooler too. Dottie is best known for its wonderful little girls' party and special occasion dresses. Service is always friendly and helpful. Be sure to get on their mailing list to be notified of their semi-annual sales that always draw crowds. Popular lines/products: Sophie Dess of France (smocked dresses), Imp Originals (boys suits), Carriage House, Gordon & Co., Hartstrings, Le Top, Petit Bateau, Hearthside Handworks (custom hand-knit sweaters), and Posie christening gowns.

Jean Marie—La Boutique Pour Bébés

11 Clement St.

415-379-1111

PARENT RATING: ☆ ☆ ☆ ☆

Owner Monica Labbe offers an elegant collection of European imports and high-end domestic clothing for infants and young toddlers. She is friendly and helpful and often has her own little ones in the store helping her! They also carry a small selection of unique imported toys, including those by the French company, Vilac. Popular lines/products: Sophie Dess ensembles for baby girls and boys; Absorba; Le Top; Catamini, Petit Bateau.

Kids Only

1608 Haight St.

415-552-5445

Kids Only remains true to the Haight/Ashbury neighborhood's reputation by featuring some of the hippest babywear in town. They feature tie-dye and Batik outfits made by local artists for newborns and young children. They also have a small toy selection, including developmental and wooden toys and stuffed animals featuring Curious George, Madeline, and Pooh. Popular lines/products: Baby M (animal print blankets/ensembles); Baby Lula; and Cherry Pie outfits (reportedly bought by Madonna in bulk for her daughter).

Kidiniki

2 Embarcadero Center

415-986-5437

PARENT RATING: ☆ ☆ ☆ ☆ ☆

While the financial district isn't the most likely place for such an elegant baby boutique, Kidiniki offers upscale shopping for many mom execs. The owner proudly offers a variety of price points for shoppers to choose from in infant and toddler playwear and dressier wear up to size 4T. They have a wonderful selection of baby blankets, sweaters, and hats, as well as small toys (including Thomas the Tank Engine trains) and accessories that complete any gift. Popular lines/products: Le Top, Chicken Noodle, Victoria's Kids; Confetti; Absorba.

Kindersport

3566 Sacramento St.

415-563-7778

PARENT RATING: ☆ ☆ ☆ ☆ ☆

Kindersport carries wonderful top-quality outdoor gear for infants to preteens, including swimsuits with built-in polyfloats for the new swimmer, and ski outfits for toddlers and children. They also carry a great assortment of coordinating gloves, hats, and boots. Watch for end-of-the-season sales for great savings. Popular lines/products: Spyder and Cacao ski suits; Mystic swimsuits with UV protection; Jet Pilote wet suits and life vests; Boeri ski helmets; Dale of Norway ski sweaters.

Maison de Belles Choses

3263 Sacramento St.

415-345-1797

PARENT RATING: ☆ ☆ ☆ ☆ ☆

We all know how the French love to dress their babies in their finest, and now San Francisco parents are doing the same. Shop owner Ellen Fletcher-Kelly, an avid Francophile, travels to France several times a year and brings back wonderful treasures, among them exquisite baby clothing featuring hand-smocked dresses and outfits for boys, cozy velour rompers, one-of-a-kind sweaters, hats and coats, beautiful bibs, and much more. She also carries unique baby gifts such as French baby dolls and teddy bears dressed in smocked dresses that coordinate with baby's, miniature Moses baskets for dolls lined in French toile, cloth activity books in French and English, and a wonderful selection of locally painted framed prints for your baby's nursery. Ellen also carries a fine selection of French furniture, each piece selected by her, including smaller proportioned armoires and caned beds for when your petit pois is ready to transfer out of the crib. Ellen says these pieces of furniture are for the parent who wants to give her child something that can be passed down for generations.

Lit'l Lizards
3961A 24th St.
415-641-6261
PARENT RATING: ☆ ☆ ☆ ☆

This sweet Noe Valley neighborhood store opened its doors in August 2001. Owner Liz Terbolizard carries casual baby and toddler playwear with her own label—she sews the vibrantly colored ensembles in her Noe Valley home with her 4-year old daughter by her side. Her designs are made with baby and kid's lifestyles in mind—they are all durable and machine washable. She takes custom orders; you pick the fabric and design and she'll make the outfit!

She also carries play costumes year-round such as angel wings and fairy costumes. Lit'l Lizards offers a fun and inviting atmosphere for little shoppers with a large play area in the back of the store, including a play kitchen, drawing pads and crayons, and lots of books. Thankfully, she also has a convenient changing table in the bathroom.

Mini's—Kids and Maternity Wear
2278 Union St.
415-567-9537
PARENT RATING: ☆ ☆ ☆ 1/2

Mini's carries its own line of clothing. It is moderately priced with European styling and is all made in San Francisco. They carry sizes for newborns through 10 years. Minis has a nice selection of educational and classic toys and carries a small selection of Elefanten shoes.

Mudpie
1694 Union St.
415-771-9262
PARENT RATING: ☆ ☆ ☆ ☆ ☆

Among San Francisco's choicest baby boutiques, Mudpie offers beautifully designed clothing for infants, much of which is imported from France and Italy. Mudpie is where you might shop for the dressy ensemble that a christening, wedding, or party calls for. They carry wonderful classic toys, including china tea sets, small metal carousels, and other old-world inspired toys, as well as wonderful puzzles, books, costumes, and special accessories for your baby's or child's room. Popular lines/products: Petit Bateau;

Magil; Bon Point; Bains-Plus; Posie hand-sewn christening gowns.

Small Frys
4066 24th St.
415-648-3954
PARENT RATING: ☆ ☆ ☆ ☆

This sweet Noe Valley boutique offers a wide selection of wonderful infant and children's clothing in sizes newborn to 7 years. They also have a wonderful collection of toys, quilts, and accessories. Popular lines/products: Osh Kosh; Absorba; Kushies; and Chicken Noodle.

Talbots Kids
126 Post St., 2nd Fl.
415-398-8881
PARENT RATING: ☆ ☆ ☆

This well-known women's clothier also houses Talbots Kids on the second floor. They offer a traditional line of clothing for girls, ages 6 months to 7 years. Boys items are available through their mail order catalog or online.

Thursday's Child
1980 Union St.
415-346-1666
PARENT RATING: ☆ ☆ ☆

This children's store carries cute essentials, such as ladybug slickers and boots and colorful Ts. They also carry clothing for girls from newborn to age 14 and for boys from newborn to 7 years old.

Tuffy's Hopscotch
3307 Sacramento St.
415-440-7599
PARENT RATING: ☆ ☆ ☆ ☆

While best known for their high-end children's shoes, including European imports, Tuffy's also carries exquisite clothing for infants and children from newborn to size 10. Much of the clothing is European-designed playwear as well as elegant dressy wear for your little one. They also carry a select line of high-end Halloween costumes for infants and toddlers. The store is quite kid-friendly, offering a large hopscotch pattern in the entryway for kids to jump around on while trying out their new shoes. While most of the staff is knowledgeable and helpful, we've heard that their customer service could use improvement. Popular lines/products: shoe brands including Elefanten, Brakkies, Aster, Mod 8, Shoe-be-Do, New Balance, and Stride Right; clothing brands Catimini and Petit Bateau.

Yountville Clothes for Children
2416 Fillmore St.
415-922-5050
PARENT RATING: ☆ ☆ ☆ ☆ 1/2

Pacific Height's neighborhood baby boutique, Yountville carries largely upscale European imported baby and toddler clothing. Watch for their occasional sales when real bargains can be found. It is a great place to shop for special occasion outfits. While it offers a small selection of ensembles, they are unique and as one Pacific Heights mom said, "made to last—the kind you keep in storage for your next baby." "This is the kind of store where the sales people will recognize you if you shop there once a month or so, which makes it even nicer!"

Favorite local baby and children's clothiers in the North Bay

Most Hip Baby Clothing
Bug a Boo

Best Sales
Baby Gap
Riley's
Mervyn's
Old Navy

Most Traditional Baby Clothing
Riley's

Special Occasions (Christenings, Weddings, and Parties)
Riley's
The White Rabbit (christening)
Nordstrom

Halloween Costumes
Baby Gap
D'Lynnes Dancewear
Noodle Soup

North Bay

Bella Bambino
823 Grant Ave.
Novato
415-898-6453
PARENT RATING: ☆ ☆ ☆ ☆ ☆

Bella Bambino offers a fun selection of upscale playwear for babies and toddlers, up to size 4T. Popular lines/ products: Baby Lulu; Zutano; Pepper Toes; Baby Rhino; and Bella Note.

Bug a Boo
14 Bolinas Rd.
Fairfax
415-457-2884
PARENT RATING: ☆ ☆ ☆ ☆

This unique store carries infant and children's clothing, specializing in offering brightly-colored clothing for newborns up to size 6x. You won't find those traditional soft pastels for baby here! They also carry outerwear as well as developmental toys and whimsical rainboots. In addition to children's clothing, Bug a Boo offers a new mother's group and parenting classes such as CPR, first aid, and infant massage. See chapter 6. Popular lines/products: Zutano playwear; Molehill outerwear (for little skiers); Manhattan Toy Co.

Carter's Childrenswear
Factory Stores of Vacaville
Vacaville
707-447-5755 (general mall information)
(Other outlet locations: Folsom, Gilroy, Milpitas, and Pacific Grove.)

This outlet offers 30 percent off retail prices for first quality Carter's playwear, sleepwear and layettes, sizes newborn to 6X. Irregulars are also available at deeper discounts.

Ciao Ragazzi

532 San Anselmo Ave.
San Anselmo
415-454-4844

PARENT RATING: ☆ ☆ ☆ ☆ ☆

This upscale baby boutique opened its doors in March 2001. They offer a variety of clothing for infants, toddlers, and young children (up to size 8 for boys and size 12 for girls). They also have an impressive selection of children's shoes to chose from, including many European imports. In addition, they have a nice selection of unique toys, games, and other accessories. Popular lines/products: Benedict Boys, Cotton Caboodle, One Kid for Boys, and Zyno for boys; Confetti; Three Palm; and Shortcakes for girls. Shoes include Aster; Buckle My Shoe; Naturino; and Primigi.

Cubby House

107 Plaza St.
Healdsburg
707-433-6861

This moderate-to-high-end baby and children's clothing store has consistently been voted "Best Baby Gift Store" and "Best Kids Clothing" by locals. In business for more than twenty-five years, Cubby House carries a nice selection of children's clothing from infants up to size 6x for girls and boys. They carry mostly 100 percent cotton items that are made in the U.S. They also offer a good selection of baby blankets, buntings, and darling coordinated sibling outfits. Popular lines/products: Le Top; Little Me.

D'Lynnes Dancewear

1435 4th St.
San Rafael
415-456-4747

D'Lynnes has every costume, either for dress-up or Halloween, that your little one could ever dream of. From Cinderella to pirates and Pokeman, they carry an extensive selection of costumes as well as dancewear for young children year-round.

Half Pint

450 1st St. E.
Sonoma
707-938-1722

PARENT RATING: ☆ ☆ ☆ ☆ ☆

Half Pint carries a nice selection of upscale American and European playwear and dressy wear for babies and children sizes newborn to size 10 for boys and size 16 for girls. They carry some of the more trendy items for young children such as sparkly shoes and Doc Martins, and distinguish themselves from other children's clothiers with their large inventory for boys. They also carry a thoughtful selection of nursery accessories including Moses baskets, prints for the nursery, and classic toys. Popular lines/products: Catamini; Jean Borget; Miniman; Baby Lula; Flapdoodles; Flowers by Zoe; Charlie Rocket.

Mill Valley Mercantile

167 Throckmorton Ave.
Mill Valley
415-388-9588

PARENT RATING: ☆ ☆ ☆ ☆ ☆

Family–owned and operated, Mill Valley Mercantile (formerly only a women's clothier, which is now next door) opened its doors for babies and young children in September 2000. Since then, it has quickly become a Marin and Bay Area favorite for outfitting babies and toddlers in upscale playclothes. The sisters who manage the store for their parents, are both moms and offer lots of friendly advice about everything from parenting to kids' clothing. They also carry beautiful baby blankets, a wonderful collection of children's books, wooden toys, and developmental toys. Popular lines/products: Zutano; Cotton Caboodle; Petit Bateau; Shortcakes; Dogwood; Cherry Pie; Rico; Under the Nile; Little Chum; and Manhattan Toy Co.

Noodle Soup

- San Anselmo
  718 San Anselmo Ave., 415-455-0141
- Corte Madera
  117 Corte Madera Town Center,
  415-945-9683

PARENT RATING: ☆ ☆ ☆ ☆ ☆

Noodle Soup's two locations offer an adorable selection of infant and children's clothing. They also carry a great selection of unique toys, puppets, and Halloween costumes, including infant sizes. Popular lines/products: Flapdoodles; Baby Lulu; Sweet Potatoes.

Play Mates

31 Sunnyside Ave.
Mill Valley
415-381-3047

PARENT RATING: ☆ ☆ ☆ ☆

Playmates is a cute children's store in downtown Mill Valley that carries moderate-to-high-end clothing. They also have a small and thoughtful selection of toys. The staff is quite friendly and customer service-oriented. Popular lines/products: Baby Lulu; Kissy Kiss; Zutano.

Riley's

310 Strawberry Village
Mill Valley
415-388-2446

PARENT RATING: ☆ ☆ ☆ ☆ ☆

Riley's is a Marin mom's favorite and also attracts many city moms since it is only a quick jaunt over the bridge. Riley's carries a nice selection of upscale infant and children's clothing and a choice selection of quality shoes. They also carry an array of toys with a retro flair, as well as beautiful accessories for babies on up, including sun hats, theme socks (such as fire trucks and trains), and hand-made hair bows and barrettes. The staff is friendly and helpful, and there is a train table set up in the store, on the boy's side, to entertain your toddler while you shop. Watch for end-of-the-season sales for great bargains! Popular lines/products: Sophie Dess, Hartstrings; K.C. Parker, Zutano; Zyno; At Home; Catamini; Little Me; Baby Lulu; Cach Cach; Flowers by Zoe; Dale of Norway (in season).

Tapioca Tiger

1234 Adams St.
St. Helena
707-967-0608

Tapioca Tiger is a fun infant and children's clothier, specializing in casual playwear for boy and girls. Popular lines/products: Monkey Monkey; Lauren Celeste; Charlie Rocket; Zutano; Baby Lulu; Pepper Toes; Mini Rocket; Flapdoodles; Petit Bateau.

The White Rabbit

601 San Anselmo Ave.
San Anselmo
415-456-1938

PARENT RATING: ☆ ☆

In business for more than twenty-five years, The White Rabbit could use a little updating. They offer traditional baby and children's clothing, including some smocked dresses and English coats. They do better in the nonclothing area and carry beautiful baby blankets and silver cups and spoons. They also carry traditional christening gowns.

Trumpette Outlet

108 Kentucky St.
Petaluma
707-769-1173

Trumpette is the label behind the "Got Milk?" infant suit. Many other clever sayings are silk-screened across their 100 percent cotton rompers, dresses, and Ts. Savings are about 40 percent off retail of first-quality overruns.

East Bay

Chicken Noodle Outlet

954 60th St.
Oakland
510-658-5880

This line of adorable children's playwear is known for their witty 100 percent cotton prints. This outlet offers 40-70 percent off previous season's overruns.

A Child's Place

1898 Solano Ave.
Berkeley
510-524-3651

A Child's Place offers a wonderful selection of fun, comfortable, and casual clothing for infants and children at moderate to high-moderate prices. They feature many 100 percent cotton items. They have a few dressier things for girls, but for boys the main style is casual. They also carry some thoughtful accessories and toys for babies and young children. Popular lines/products: Flapdoodles; Charlie Rocket.

Cotton and Company

- Oakland (Rockridge)
  5902 College Ave., 510-653-8058
- Lafayette
  3535 Mt. Diablo Blvd., 925-299-9356

PARENT RATING: ☆ ☆ ☆ ☆ ☆

This adorable baby and children's clothier offers some of the most upscale ensembles for little ones in the East Bay. They also carry children's shoes, including European imports, and have wonderful accessories as well as hats, mobiles, and layette items. They offer high-end bedding, and their sales force is friendly and helpful. They also have a train table set up for children to play with while Mom shops. Popular lines/products: Clothing: Hartstrings, Sophie Dess, Florence Eiseman, Mulberribush, Flapdoodles, LeTop, as well as several French imports.

Cotton Kids

2112 Vine St. #B
Berkeley
510-665-8133

This "very Berkeley" shop (as the store manager likes to describe it) carries its own 100 percent cotton playwear for infants and children,

Favorite local baby and children's clothiers in the East Bay

Most Hip Baby Clothing
Cotton Kids
Sioban Van Winkel Functional Art
Tadpoles and Frogs

Special Occasions (Christenings, Weddings, and Parties)
Cotton & Company
Freckles and Frills
Lil' Ladies & Gents

Best Sales
Baby Gap
Sara's Prints
Sweet Potatoes Outlet

Most Traditional Baby Clothing
Cotton & Company
This Little Piggy Wears Cotton

Halloween Costumes
Sweet Potatoes

---

which is made right in Oakland. The ensembles are all very casual (leggings and coordinating Ts) and are coordinated by color and patterns. They offer some funky styles for girls, including twirly skirts and beaded clothing. For active boys, they feature double-knit pants and good-quality corduroys. They carry newborn sizes through size 10.

Freckles and Frills Children's Shop
590 Dutton Ave.
San Leandro
510-638-1622

This traditional children's clothier specializes in outfitting school children in their uniforms, but they also have a wonderful selection of moderate-to-high-end clothing for infants and young children. Most of their items are for dressier occasions, but they also carry a nice variety of playwear, especially for infants. They

have a large selection of christening gowns and outfits too. Popular lines/products: Hartstrings; Alexi; Heart Togs; BT Kids; Castro.

Kids Are People Too
• Pleasanton
  537 Main St., 925-462-5974
• Castro Valley
  3356 Village Dr., 510-247-1258

This cute baby clothing store carries moderately-priced quality clothing for preemies, infants, and toddlers, plus some young children's sizes up to size 6x. They carry a broad selection of sleepers, buntings, night-gowns, and other infant and toddler wear. They specialize in clothing for special occasions such as christening gowns and outfits and wedding attire, including dresses for flower girls and tuxedos for toddlers and little boys. They also carry an extensive selection of holiday dresses for girls, including the smocked variety, as well as a small selection of wooden toys, including blocks and carpenter's sets. Popular lines/products: Alexis; Buster Brown; Baby's Own; Baby Dove; Lito; Alexandra.

Lil' Ladies and Gents

12901 Alcosta Blvd.
San Ramon
925-901-0970

PARENT RATING: ☆ ☆ ☆ ☆ ☆

This special occasions clothier for infants and young children offers a large selection of traditional clothing for dressy occasions, such as christenings, weddings, birthdays, and baby's "coming home from the hospital." They carry miniature tuxes, suits for boys with dress shirts, sweater vests and ties, and special-occasion dresses for girls, including flower girl, holiday, and smocked dresses. The friendly and helpful shop owner describes her clothing as what "could have been worn forty years ago and God willing can be worn forty years from now!" They also have a nice selection of "casual dressy" ensembles, such as white linen and cotton outfits, which are popular for outdoor professional photographs. They try to carry a lot of things that you don't see in department stores. In fact, Nordstrom sends business here. Parent comment: "Excellent dress-up clothes at reasonable prices." Popular lines/products: Strausbourg (smocked dresses).

Noodles for Kids

725 Main St.
Martinez
925-210-1006

The Swedish-born owner of this infant and children's shop designs and makes a unique line of European-inspired funky baby and kid's clothing with her own label, Noodles. She chooses 100 percent cotton fabrics that are vibrant and whimsical and transforms them into fun playwear and some dressier ensembles for the holidays. She also laminates her fabrics and turns them into one-of-a-kind raincoats. She sells all over the country as well as to other Bay Area children's shops, including Dottie Dolittle in San Francisco and This Little Piggy Wears Cotton in Berkeley.

The Nurture Center

3399 Mt. Diablo Blvd.
Lafayette
925-283-1346

PARENT RATING: ☆ ☆ ☆ ☆ ☆

This resource center for new parents has a pleasant retail store that sells hand-made quilts and lovely baby clothing. It's a good place to pick up an exta outfit or a gift, especially if you are already there for one of their many great new parents' support groups. See chapter 6. Popular lines/products: Kushies; Sweet Potatoes; Le Top.

Pickles and Ice Cream

1677 Shattuck Ave.
Berkeley
510-540-7210

PARENT RATING: ☆ ☆ ☆ ☆

This combination baby clothier and new parent resource center has much to offer many new East Bay moms! See chapter 6. The front of the store carries a good selection of upscale outfits for babies, newborn to 24 months. Popular lines/products: Zutano; Kushies.

Sara's Prints (factory outlet)

3018A Alvarado St.
San Leandro
510-352-6060
www.sarasprints.com

Sara's Prints is best known for their quality sleepwear and playwear for infants and children, made from 100 percent long staple cotton, imprinted with some of the cutest designs you have ever seen! Four times a year, the outlet is open for one- to two-week factory sale events where over-stocks and last season's items are sold for at least 50 percent off retail.

Siobhan Van Winkel Functional Art

6371 Telegraph Ave.
Oakland
510-652-1415

This unique children's clothing and gift shop offers some of the funkiest and most darling clothing for new-borns to 6-year-olds in the East Bay! Siobhan's carries handmade items from over thirty local artists, includ-ing one-of-a-kind fleece hats and sun hats, hand-knit sweaters, silk-screened onesies, reversible dresses (including one that is shaped like a spaceship!), panchos, dolls, and puppets, as well as jewelry and bags for mom.

Sweet Potatoes, Inc.

1799A 4th St.
Berkeley
510-527-5852

PARENT RATING: ☆ ☆ ☆ ☆ ☆

Start your shopping from the back of this outlet, where the modest bargains may be found, to the front, where full-priced new collections are pre-dominantly displayed. A Bay Area mom's favorite, Sweet Potatoes offers a collection of comfortable cotton infant and children's coordi-nating outfits with its own label for newborns and toddlers, including S.P.U.D.Z. for boys (Sweet Potatoes' sportswear line for newborns to size 7) and Yams for girls (size 4-14). They also offer locally made party dresses in infant and girl's sizes, as well as comfortable and good quality Halloween costumes for babies and toddlers—a rare find! The store fea-tures a small enclosed play area, which makes shopping with a toddler manageable.

Tadpoles and Frogs

1506 Walnut St.
Berkeley
510-848-2678

Tadpoles and Frogs offers unusual clothing for infants and children made from African fabrics, cottons, and fleece. All styles are unisex. They also carry a nice selection of velour receiving blankets and fleece baby slings and a small selection of shoes.

Teddy's Little Closet

- Berkeley
  2903 College Ave., 510-549-9177
- Orinda
  2 Theater Sq., 925-254-6672

Independently owned and operated, this shop carries moderate- to high-priced quality clothing for infants and young children. They also carry unique accessories for babies, including nightlights, one-of-a-kind receiving blankets, quilts, and classic toys. They own Sweet Things, a children's toy store which is connected to the Orinda store, and offer all the classics. Popular lines/products: Clothing: Cotton Caboodle; Mulberribush; Sweet Potatoes; OshKosh; Flapdoodles; Kushies; Oink Pig. Toys: Lego; Playmobil; Barbie; Brio; Thomas the Tank Engine.

This Little Piggy Wears Cotton

1840 4th St.
Berkeley
510-981-1411
PARENT RATING: ☆ ☆ ☆ ☆ ☆

This sweet boutique carries a select line of infant and children's clothing (up to size 8), accessories, and toys. Labels feature the store's own brand, which is a 100 percent high grade yarn dyed cotton, and includes leggings and matching Ts, rompers, and dresses. Most of the clothing is casual playwear, but they also carry a nice selection of dressier clothes, especially for little girls. They offer a thoughtful selection of interesting toys for babies and toddlers too. Popular lines/products: Flapdoodles; Baby Lulu; Charlie Rocket; Flowers by Zoe; Petit Bateau; Hawk and Hurleyware.

South Bay

The Children's Shoppe

325 Sharon Park Dr.
Menlo Park
650-854-8854
PARENT RATING: ☆ ☆ ☆ ☆ ☆

This elegant and upscale infant and children's boutique carries imported fashions for your little one's dressier occasions. They carry a wonderful assortment of carefully selected clothing from France, Italy, Germany, and Denmark. They also carry hard-to-find European christening gowns and outfits. The Children's Shoppe also offers beautiful baby blankets, as well as dressier European-made shoes. They also carry a small but thoughtful selection of toys for infants and toddlers. This is definitely a special shop that caters to those who appreciate elegant old-world-inspired styles for their children. Popular lines/products: Clothing: Petit Bateau; Bon Point; Sonia Rykiel; Cacherel; Florian; Babar; Mini Man; Arctic Kids; Cacherel; Sophie Dess. Shoes: Baby Botte; Aster; Naturino; More 8. Accessories: Curchill Weavers; Pappa and Ciccia (baby blankets).

Deborella Per Bambini

1414 Burlingame Ave.
Burlingame
650-348-8956

Deborah Woodman runs a beautiful European-inspired baby boutique that specializes in high-end European designs for babies and toddlers. She carries it all—from hand-smocked dresses from France to natural silk-rimmed fleece baby blankets from Italy. She also carries some moderate to high-end American labels. In addition, she offers vintage pieces of furniture, such as cribs and dressers, that are all refurbished and painted in shades of white—no two are the same. Popular lines/products: Jean Bourget; Mini Man; Catamini; Barefoot Dreams; Fattamano; Sophie Dess; Le Top; Zutano.

Howard's Children's Shop

115 E. 4th Ave.
San Mateo
650-343-1518

This elegant specialty shop has a beautiful collection of dresses, jackets, and rompers for babies, toddlers, and children.

Jacadi Paris

1215 Burlingame Ave.
Burlingame
650-558-1122

PARENT RATING: ☆ ☆ ☆ ☆

This boutique chain offers traditional European baby clothing, featuring

handcrafted and embroidered designs. See a complete description under the "Baby Gear" section.

The Kids Company/Footsteps Shoe Store

1201 San Carlos Ave.
San Carlos
650-595-7745

PARENT RATING: ☆ ☆ ☆ ☆ ☆

This lovely clothier for children, in the words of the owner, is "very traditional" and "offers nothing hip-hop or trendy." They feature upscale quality infants and children's clothing up to sizes 12-14, including sweaters, shorts, sleepwear, and layette items. They also have a huge selection of special occasion attire, including christening gowns and outfits, tuxes for little boys, and flower girls' dresses. At the back of the store is a large children's shoe store which is run by the clothing store owner's daughter—

many say that the selection is better than Nordstrom's! They also have a thoughtful selection of toys for babies and toddlers, including cloth books and development toys. This may be among the best places for one-stop upscale clothing shopping for little ones in the South Bay! Popular lines/products: Clothing: Hartstrings; K.C. Parker; Petit Bateau; Impact; Sweet Potatoes; Chicken Noodle; Sara Louise (christening gowns) and Petit Bateau (christening gowns). Shoes: Elefanten; Stride Rite; Doc Martens; K-Swiss; Vans; Converse; Birkenstock. Toys: Manhattan Toy Co.

The Oilily Store

186 Stanford Shopping Center
Palo Alto
650-323-1996

Oilily, a Dutch-owned company, offers fun and vibrant ensembles designed mostly in The Netherlands. Their clothing is made from their own one-of-a-kind printed fabrics for infants and children up to size 16, and for women. You either love their fabrics and styles or you don't—it's a definite funky, anything but old-world look!

Oshkosh B'Gosh

Gilroy Premium Outlets
408-842-3280
(Other locations: Napa, Pacific Grove, Petaluma, Vacaville)

Oshkosh B'Gosh offers modest savings at this outlet, but is still a favorite among Bay Area moms. They have a small section where everything is discounted an additional 30-50 percent.

P. Cottontail and Company

527 Main St.
Half Moon Bay
650-726-0200

This store offers attractive baby and preemie basics, as well as top-quality children's shoes, christening gowns and outfits, and accessories for your baby's nursery.

Rebecca Rags, Inc. Outlet

10200 Imperial Ave.
Cupertino
408-257-7884

Rebecca Rags (the girl's line) and Ruff! Rags (the boy's line) offer unique children's clothing, both dressy and casual wear, in bright, cheery velours, knits, and linens. This outlet has a large selection of end-of-season overruns, seconds, and samples at great savings—20 percent off wholesale. They are well known for their fall and spring sales.

Tiny Tots Togs

138 Railway Ave.
Campbell
408-866-2925

Tiny Tots Togs specializes in 100 percent cotton clothes for infants and children. They also carry a wide selection of developmental toys, diaper covers, and breastfeeding supplies, including pump rentals and sales.

Shoes

It may be hard to believe, but before your little bundle of joy reaches his first birthday he'll be on the verge of walking and will need a pair of shoes! When shopping for your child's first shoes, find a store that offers knowledgeable and helpful sales people who know how to measure your child's foot properly. Your baby's first shoes should fit well, as he'll still be learning how to walk. It's also important that his first shoes have a soft and flexible sole. Remember not to go too crazy the first time; children's feet grow fast. You'll be visiting the shoe store in another three or four months to buy the next size up.

We've listed stores that specialize in children's shoes, but be sure to check out the children's clothiers and baby superstores listed in the above sections, as many carry a good selection of children's shoes.

NATIONAL CHAINS

Here is what Bay Area parents have to say about several national chains. Check the yellow pages or their individual websites for a store location near you.

Department Stores

Nordstrom
www.nordstrom.com
PARENT RATING: ☆ ☆ ☆ ☆ ☆

Nordstrom has one of the best infant and toddler shoe departments in the Bay Area, carrying casual and dressy styles and most major brands, such as Stride Rite and Elefanten. In fact, as far as department stores go, it's the tops for baby and children's shoes. The staff is friendly and helpful, and they often offer a balloon to your child and take a polaroid picture of her when you are buying her first pair of shoes.

Discount Stores

Mervyn's California
www.mervyns.com
PARENT RATING: ☆ ☆ ☆

Mervyn's carries a small selection of moderately priced and mostly casual children's shoes. Be sure to come with your child's current shoe size, as you won't receive department store or specialty shoe store service here.

Payless Shoes
www.payless.com
PARENT RATING: ☆ ☆ ☆ ☆

Payless offers great values on moderate–end sneakers and other casual shoes. They often carry a great selection of character or theme shoes (such as Bob the Builder or fire trucks), as well as ballet shoes and sneakers with flashing lights that will delight your toddler or preschooler.

Target
www.target.com

PARENT RATING: ☆ ☆ ☆

Target has a limited selection of mostly casual inexpensive shoes for children, including rainboots and sneakers. Be sure to know your child's current shoe size, as there is no one here offering to measure your child's foot!

Specialty Chains

Baby Gap
www.babygap.com

PARENT RATING: ☆ ☆ ☆ ☆

This ubiquitous chain carries great inexpensive sneakers in a variety of colors for babies and toddlers and occasionally carries other styles of shoes, such as bucks for boys or Mary Janes for girls.

Kids Foot Locker
www.kidsfootlocker.com

PARENT RATING: ☆ ☆ ☆

This store carries a large selection of infant and toddler sneakers, sandals, and boots. Brands include Nike, K-Swiss, Adidas, Timberland, DKNY, Jordan, and Reebok.

Stride Rite
www.striderite.com

PARENT RATING: ☆ ☆ ☆ ☆ ☆

This is a great place to shop for baby's first shoes as well as shoes for the active toddler. Staff is knowledgeable and helpful.

BAY AREA RETAILERS

Here is what Bay Area parents have to say about their favorite local stores for baby and children's shoes:

San Francisco

Cool World Sports
2426 California St.
415-928-3639

This tony Pacific Heights Italian sporting goods store mainly carries shoes for adults, but they also carry a sporty line of unisex designer shoes by Prada if that's what you're looking for! Watch for some great sales from time to time.

Niketown
278 Post St.
415-392-6453

PARENT RATING: ☆ ☆ ☆ ☆

While it may be a hike to go downtown, find parking, and walk to Niketown, it's truly a unique shopping experience. The children's department is on the fourth floor and offers a zillion styles of booties and sneakers specially made for babies and toddlers that are not typically sold at department stores or other shoe stores. Nikes for tots offers more than a name brand; we know a mom whose toddler had a pair of Nikes from Niketown that lasted almost six months and wore beautifully.

Junior Boot Shop

Laurel Village Shopping Center
3555 California St.
415-751-5444

PARENT RATING: ☆ ☆ ☆ ☆ ☆

A San Francisco parents' staple for years now, this down-to-earth shop carries much more than rainboots, including high-end traditional infant and children's shoes. You won't see too many trendy brands and styles here—just the classics. Name brands include K Swiss, Stride Rite, Elefanten, and Jumping Jacks. The store is quite child-friendly with a knowledgeable and helpful staff.

Howard's Shoes for Children

Stonestown Galleria
3251 20th Ave.
415-681-3700

PARENT RATING: ☆ ☆ ☆ ☆ ☆

This local chain of four stores in the Bay Area is a great place to shop for baby's first pair of shoes. They also offer quality shoes for toddlers and young children, including brands such as Stride Rite, Elefanten, Ecco, Vans, Sketchers, Nike, and New Balance. Parent comment: "They have a good selection and friendly, helpful staff."

Tuffy's Hopscotch

3307 Sacramento St.
415-440-7599

See a complete description under "Baby and Children's Clothing."

Wavy Footprints, Inc.

3961 24th St.
415-285-3668

PARENT RATING: ☆ ☆ ☆ ☆ ☆

Wavy Footprints is a Noe Valley mom's favorite place to buy children's shoes. This popular neighborhood shoe store offers quality shoes for children. They carry a large variety of brands and styles, including Aster, Babybotte, Bear Feet, Doc Martens, Elefanten, Goody Goody, Head Dress, Kenneth Cole, Naturino, Primigi, and Stride Rite. They promise great quality shoes and a good fit for your child's healthy feet. They also offer a kid-friendly environment with games and toys to make shoe shopping more fun!

North Bay

Children's Boot Shop

1205 Grant Ave.
Novato
415-897-1460

Offering much more than boots (although they really do carry cowboy boots and rainboots), this traditional children's shoe store carries a wide variety of casual and dressy shoes ranging from sneakers to patent leather Mary Janes. Brands include Stride Rite, Birkenstock, and Reebok.

Reebok Factory Store

Factory Stores of Vacaville
Vacaville
707-452-0235
(Other locations: Gilroy, Pacific Grove, and Petaluma)

This outlet carries sneakers for toddlers and young children at modest savings.

Howard's Shoes for Children

16 Broadway Ln.
Walnut Creek
925-280-8100

See a complete description under
San Francisco.

The Children's Shoppe

325 Sharon Park Dr.
Menlo Park
650-854-8854

This store offers quality shoes for
infants through teens, carrying only
European brands such as Babybotte,
Aster, and Naturino. See a complete
description under "Baby and
Children's Clothing."

Footsteps Children Shoes

1201 San Carlos Ave.
San Carlos
650-654-0277

This wonderfully stocked children's
shoe store is located behind an
equally fabulous infant and children's
clothing store (The Kids Company).
The clothier is run by a mother, and
the shoe store is run by her daughter.
They offer an extensive selection of
quality baby and children's shoes,
including Stride Rite, Elefanten, and
Converse. The knowledgeable and
helpful staff sends a postcard to customers every three months remind-
ing them when they last bought
shoes for their child.

Howard's Shoes for Children

- Palo Alto
  198 Stanford Shopping Center,
  650-325-9300
- Cupertino
  Vallco Fashion Park,
  10123 N. Wolfe Rd., 408-257-6200

See a complete description under
San Francisco.

Manny's Shoes

708 Santa Cruz Ave.
Menlo Park
650-325-5171

PARENT RATING: ☆ ☆ ☆ ☆ ☆

This no-frills children's shoe store
offers shoes for all of your child's
needs. They feature American classics such as Stride Rite, European
styles such as Elefanten, and sportier
styles such as Nike, Reebok, Vans,
Keds, Tevos, and Doc Martens. They
also offer a broad selection of sandals,
boots, ballet slippers, and tap shoes.

Nike Factory Store

Gilroy Premium Outlets
Gilroy
408-847-4300
(Other locations: Folsom,
Vacaville)

This outlet store offers a number of
styles of previous seasons' sneakers
for children at about 30 percent off
retail prices.

Stride Rite Outlet

Gilroy Premium Outlets
Gilroy
408-842-1011

This outlet offers great savings on
discontinued styles, previous seasons' items and slight irregulars.

Toys and Books

The Bay Area abounds with a great variety of toy and book stores. We have included some local favorites and some on-line resources for you to check out. Many of the baby superstores and specialty stores and the baby and children's clothiers offer an array of toys and books, so look for them in the previous sections.

At each stage of your child's development, new skills are emerging and how she plays and what she plays with have a great impact on how she develops these skills. Whether it's simply playing a game of patty-cake or exploring with an elaborate play structure, as a parent, you are the one who determines your baby's environment, which in turn shapes her development. So buy wisely!

One book that we especially like and have found helpful in choosing toys is the *Oppenheim Toy Portfolio* by mother and daughter Joanne and Stephanie Oppenheim. They have published a new 2002 edition in which they review hundreds of toys for babies, toddlers, and preschoolers. They also suggest many fun games to play with your baby that don't require purchasing anything at all. It's a great resource for all new parents! Their website, www.toyportfolio.com, provides updates, reviews of toy award winners, and helpful parenting articles.

NATIONAL CHAINS

Check their individual websites or your yellow pages for the store nearest you:

The Disney Store
www.disney.com

PARENT RATING: ☆ ☆ ☆ ☆

The Disney store offers toys, clothing, and accessories featuring everyone's favorite storybook characters, such as Winnie the Pooh, Pinocchio, Peter Pan, and 101 Dalmatians. They carry great Halloween costumes too!

Imaginarium
www.imaginarium.com

PARENT RATING: ☆ ☆ ☆ ☆ ☆

This fun chain is more like a specialty toy store, featuring an impressive selection of educational and developmental toys for infants on up. They feature Lamaze, Wimmer-Ferguson (well known for their black and white infant developmental toys), Sassy, Brio, Thomas the Tank Engine trains and accessories, Madeline dolls and toys, Clifford, Lego, Felt Kids, outdoor toys such as balls, sand toys, and a toddler's first set of golf clubs, as well as all the traditional items like

Play-Doh. They also stock a few Halloween costumes.

KB Toys

www.kbtoys.com

PARENT RATING: ☆ ☆ ☆

KB Toys is packed with many tempting toys for toddlers and beyond. They carry a small number of toys for babies. While they don't carry most of the higher-end educational toys, there is still something there for almost everyone. Parent comment: "A smaller, more compact version of Toys "R" Us."

Learning Express

www.learningexpress.com

This national chain of franchises specializes in toys with an educational bent for children of all ages, including dress-up and pretend play items, Legos, Thomas trains, and a small selection of developmental toys for infants by Lamaze and Early Years.

Toys "R" Us

www.toysrus.com

PARENT RATING: ☆ ☆

If you don't mind the scale of this mega store and its frequent lack of service, it carries all the major brands of toys and books, including a large selection of baby toys, organized according to stage of development.

Zany Brainy

www.zanybrainy.com

PARENT RATING: ☆ ☆ ☆ ☆ ☆

This national chain is appealing to parents with its vast array of high-end developmental toys for babies and high-quality and educational toys for toddlers and preschoolers. Zany

Brainy features Thomas and Brio trains, many pretend play items such as supermarket carts, plastic fruit and food, play carpenter's kits, Legos, art supplies, musical instruments, a great book department, and much more.

BAY AREA RETAILERS

Here is what Bay Area parents have to say about their favorite local toy stores:

San Francisco

Ambassador Toys

- 186 West Portal Ave., 415-759-8697
- 1981 Union St., 415-345-8697

PARENT RATING: ☆ ☆ ☆ ☆ ☆

Ambassador Toys is a classic toy store, featuring an impressive selection of wooden toys, including Thomas the Tank Engine Trains, wooden doll houses, and all the desired baby dolls, including Corolle and Madame Alexander. They also offer strollers for kids to push their dolls in, kitchen and tea sets, and beautiful kites. Name brands include Bruder trucks, Playmobil toys, Plan Toys, and puzzles. They carry a unique selection of books featuring many foreign language children's books. Toys are arranged according to theme, e.g., there is a fire truck section and a dinosaur section, which makes shopping quick and easy!

The Ark

3845 24th St.

415-821-1257

PARENT RATING: ☆ ☆ ☆ ☆ ☆

This Noe Valley neighborhood store is packed with classic toys that

Favorite Websites and Catalogs for Infant and Children's Toys

Back to Basics Toys
800-356-5360 (catalog)
www.backtobasicstoys.com

Constructive Playthings
800-832-0572 (catalog)
www.constplay.com

Discovery Toys
www.discoverytoysinc.com

Earthwise Toys
www.naturaltoys.com

FAO Schwarz
800-426-8097 (catalog)
www.faoschwarz.com

Hearthsong
800-325-2502 (catalog)
www.hearthsong.com

Imagine the Challenge
800-777-1493 (catalog)
www.imaginetoys.com

Leaps & Bounds
800-477-2189 (catalog)
www.leapsandbounds.com

Lilly's Kids
800-545-5426 (catalog)
www.lillianvernon.com
Great Halloween costumes!

Sensational Beginnings
800-444-2147 (catalog)
www.sensationalbeginnings.com
Great Halloween costumes!

Smarter Kids
www.smarterkids.com

Totally Thomas' Toy Depot
800-30-THOMAS (catalog)
www.totallythomas.com

Thomas the Tank Engine
www.thomasthetankengine.com

Toys to Grow On
800-542-8338 (catalog)
www.toystogrowon.com

continue to delight every child. They feature wooden toys such as play kitchens and smaller items such as toy trains (including Brio and Thomas), beautiful stuffed animals, puzzles, games (including a soft indoor baseball and bat for an active toddler), unusual hand–painted puppets from Germany, and musical instruments for toddlers.

FAO Schwarz
48 Stockton St.
415-394-8700
PARENT RATING: ☆ ☆ ☆ ☆

The authentic children's toy land, FAO Schwarz carries almost every toy, stuffed animal (including Steiff); and doll (including Madame Alexander) imaginable. In recent years they have developed a larger selection of toys for infants and young toddlers.

Best Bets for Children's Books in San Francisco

Alexander Book Company
50 2nd St.
415-495-2992

Borders Books and Music
400 Post St.
415-399-1633
They have an extensive parenting book section.

Bernal Books
410 Cortland Ave.
415-550-0293

Barnes and Noble
2550 Taylor St.
415-292-6762

Books Inc.
• Laurel Village Shopping Center
  3515 California St., 415-221-3666
They have a great parenting book section.

• *2251 Chestnut St., 415-931-3633
They have a large children's section, complete with child–sized chairs.

Booksmith
1644 Haight St.
415-863-8688

*Borders Books and Music
Stonestown Galleria
233 Winston Dr.
415-731-0665
This store has a huge children's section, with lots of room for them to roam!

Browser Books
2195 Fillmore St.
415-567-8027
They have a small children's section, with table and chairs in the back, and an impressive parenting section.

Christopher's Books
1400 18th St.
415-255-8802

City Lights Bookstore
261 Columbus Ave.
415-362-8193

A Clean Well-Lighted Place for Books
601 Van Ness Ave.
415-441-6670
This one-of-a-kind bookstore offers friendly and knowledgeable service.

Cover to Cover Booksellers
3812 24th St.
415-282-8080

Green Apple Books
506 Clement St.
415-387-2272
They have great used books!

Rizzoli Bookstore
117 Post St.
415-984-0225
They have a wonderful selection of classics and hard-to-find foreign language children's books!

Solar Light Books
2068 Union St.
415-567-6082

Waldenbooks
255 West Portal Ave.
415-664-7596

*These stores host a weekly story hour, usually on weekends. Call each store for details.

Growing Up
240 West Portal Ave.
415-661-6304
This neighborhood toy store offers all the classics and more, including wooden toys and puzzles, Brio trains, and Lego.

Jeffrey's Toys
7 3rd St.
415-243-TOYS
Jeffrey's Toys is a traditional toy store, offering developmentally and educationally oriented toys as well as those that are just plain fun, including many stuffed animals and characters.

San Francisco Museum of Modern Art
151 3rd St.
415-357-4035
This museum gift shop offers many unique toys and books for toddlers and children, focusing on the arts, learning, and development. Parent comment: "Not your run-of-the-mill toys and books, truly special items."

Toys and More
1551 Sloat Blvd.
415-665-8921
This small local store carries nothing for infants, but offers some traditional toys such as Lego, stuffed animals, racecars, and plastic models.

Toy Symphony
The Cannery
2801 Leavenworth St.
415-775-7893
www.toysymphony.com
This toy store emphasizes thought by offering toys that use children's imaginations. Favorite toys include wooden and paper dolls and puzzles, Madame Alexander dolls, Vecta Blocks, Radio Flyer wagons, wooden doll houses, and Brio trains.

North Bay

Center for Creative Parenting
The Pacheco Shopping Center
446A Ignacio Blvd.
Novato
415-883-4442
PARENT RATING: ☆ ☆ ☆ ☆ ☆

This center for new parents mainly offers classes and groups, but also houses a boutique that carries an intelligent selection of developmental toys, puzzles, and books.

A Child's Delight
3320 Northgate Mall
San Rafael
415-499-0736
PARENT RATING: ☆ ☆ ☆ ☆ ☆

This upscale toy store offers an inviting array of educational and imaginative toys for infants on up. They specialize in carrying toys that require children to use their minds, including dress-up and pretend clothing and play structures, Thomas and Brio wooden trains, and other wooden toys such as handmade doll houses and rocking horses from France. They also feature all the classics, such as Radio Flyer wagons, Madame Alexander dolls, and other treasures from your own childhood! They have a broad selection of infant toys, including brands such as Papa Gepetto, Lamaze, Sassy, Chicco, Plan Toys, and several independent brands. They pride themselves on carrying many specialty items.

Doll Houses, Trains and More

300 Entrada Dr.
Novato
415-883-0388

This nine thousand square foot store is full of wonderful train tables for preschoolers to adults, including the popular wooden Brio trains. They also have an extensive selection of doll houses and furnishings.

Toy Chest

1000 5th Ave.
San Rafael
415-451-4942

PARENT RATING: ☆ ☆ ☆ ☆ ☆

This upscale toy store carries a vast selection of high-quality toys, such as those by Playmobil and Plan Toys. They also offer many classic toys, featuring Curious George, Madeleine, and Radio Flyer wagons, and educational toys, including Brio and Thomas trains, wooden kitchens, and play food. They also have a great selection of Halloween costumes in season.

Hopscotch Kids

352 Miller Ave.
Mill Valley
415-381-9858

Hopscotch carries a thoughtful selection of toys, including Brio and Thomas wooden trains, Corolle dolls, and high quality infant and toddler toys by Playmobil and Lego among other brands.

Solaria

696 W. Francisco Blvd.
San Rafael
415-459-5160

PARENT RATING: ☆ ☆ ☆ ☆

Solaria is a small, independent toy store jam-packed, albeit slightly chaotic, with all the best toys. Word to the wise, though, leave the stroller at home; it's hard even for the slimmest people to make their way through the overflowing tiny aisles here! They carry all the classics and high-end toys for toddlers and young children, including Brio and Thomas wooden trains, Madame Alexander dolls, Muffy Bears, wooden doll houses, and Playmobil. They have one of the best Brio selections around—so good that many customers come here from San Francisco. They also have an impressive doll and doll house selection.

Toys by Grampa Dean

Kentfield
415-453-2271
http://home.attbi.com/
~toysbygrampadean/

An accomplished woodworker, Grandpa Dean turned his beloved hobby into a business after making several wooden toys for his own grandchildren. Grampa Dean makes unique quality wooden toys that are constructed with dowels and glue to ensure their safety. He works out of his home and makes everything from toy school buses, trains, and cars, to trucks, airplanes, and helicopters. Visit his website for details.

The Toyworks

- Santa Rosa
  2759 4th St. #B, 707-526-2099
- Sebastopol
  6940 Sebastopol Ave., 707-829-2003

In business since 1977, this full-service toy store carries a large selection of developmental toys for babies and toddlers by brands such as Ambi and

Playmobil. They also carry many handcrafted and imported toys from Europe for young children, including wooden trains and wagons.

Best Bets for Children's Books in the North Bay

*Barnes & Noble Booksellers
2020 Redwood Hwy.
Greenbrae
415-924-1016

B. Dalton Bookseller
Corte Madera Town Center
415-927-3226

*Book Passage
51 Tamal Vista Blvd.
Corte Madera
415-927-0960

More of a community center than a bookstore, Book Passage offers all the best for even the tiniest reader in the family, including special children's story hours, sing-alongs featuring the renowned Miss Kitty, and visits from renowned authors.

* Borders Book Store
588 W. Francisco Blvd.
San Rafael
415-454-1400

Copperfield's
- Napa
  1303 First St., 707-252-8002

- Sebastopol
  138 N. Main St., 707-823-2618

- Santa Rosa
  2316 Montgomery St.,
  707-575-0550 or 707-578-8938

- Petaluma
  140 Kentucky St., 707-762-0563
  Parent comment: "Best in the area!"

First Street Books
850 College Ave.
Kentfield
415-456-8770

Great Overland Book Company
215 Caledonia St.
Sausalito
415-332-1532

They have great used books!

*Oliver's Books
645 San Anselmo Ave.
San Anselmo
415-454-4421

They have a great selection of new and used children's books.

A Shop for All Seasons
552 San Anselmo Ave.
San Anselmo
415-454-6018

White's Booksmith
615 San Anselmo Ave.
San Anselmo
415-459-7323

*These stores often host regular story hours. Call the stores for details.

Adventure Toys

3291 Lakeshore Ave.
Oakland
510-452-6470

This quaint neighborhood toy store carries brands such as Lego, Playmobil, Brio, Fisher Price, and Tinker Toys. For infants, they carry a nice selection of Lamaze developmental toys. For a small local store, Adventure has a lovely selection!

Cynthia's Educational Toys and Games

City Center Sq.
501 14th St.
Oakland
510-452-4099
www.cynthiastoys.com

Cynthia's is a small boutique toy store that carries some unique items, such as multicultural toys, as well as general toys, tapes, and books. The owner is very knowledgeable and helpful about age appropriateness of toys, and she offers very personalized service in selecting the right one.

Games Unlimited

Livery and Mercantile Shopping Center
800 Sycamore Valley Rd. W.
Danville
925-838-6358

This independently owned and operated toy store carries "specialty toys," including Playmobil, Brio and Thomas trains, Corolle dolls, Bruder trucks, and Creativity for Kids, along with many other smaller brands.

Golden Apple Learning Store

Rose Pavilion Shopping Center
4240 Rosewood Dr.
Pleasanton
925-460-5163

Golden Apple carries quality toys for newborns, toddlers, and young children, including Brio trains, erector sets, art supplies, developmental toys, books, puzzles, and blocks.

Handlebar Toys

3535 Plaza Way
Lafayette
925-284-4631

Handlebar is a traditional children's toy store, well stocked with all the high-end essentials, including Playmobil, Galt, Brio and Thomas trains, and Madame Alexander Dolls.

Montclair Toy House

6115 La Salle Ave.
Oakland
510-339-9023

In business since 1946, the Toy House is an old-fashioned classic toy store. They offer a nice selection of toys for all ages by the best brands, including Brio and Playmobil.

Mr. Mopps' Children's Books and Toys

1405 Martin Luther King Jr. Way
Berkeley
510-525-9633

PARENT RATING: ☆ ☆ ☆ ☆

In business for more than forty years, Mr. Mopps' is a classic toy store that has become a Berkeley tradition. Despite some complaints we heard about the lack of customer service, Mr. Mopps' is consistently rated "Best Toy Store" in the *East Bay Express*.

Best Bets for Children's Books in the East Bay

Avenue Books, Inc.
2904 College Ave.
Berkeley
510-549-3532

*Barnes & Noble
- Berkeley
  2352 Shattuck Ave., 510-644-0861
- Oakland
  98 Broadway, Jack London Sq.,
  510-272-0120
- Walnut Creek
  1149 S. Main St., 925-947-0373

The Book Tree
6123 La Salle Ave.
Oakland
510-339-0513

Black Oak Books
1491 Shattuck Ave.
Berkeley
510-486-0698

Boadecia's Books
398 Colusa Ave.
Kensington
510-559-9184

*Borders Books and Music
5903 Shellmound
Emeryville
510-654-1633
www.borders.com

Visit their website for other locations.

Cody's Bookstore
- *Berkeley
  1730 4th St., 510-559-9500
- Oakland
  2454 Telegraph Ave., 510-845-7852

The Little Bookshop
3403 Fruitvale Ave.
Oakland
510-530-3946

Mama Bear's Women's Bookstore and Cafe
6536 Telegraph Ave.
Oakland
510-428-9684

Moe's Bookstore
2476 Telegraph Ave.
Berkeley
510-849-2087

Mr. Mopps' Childrens' Books and Toys
1405 Martin Luther King Jr. Way
Berkeley
510-525-9633

Pegasus Books
- Berkeley
  2349 Shattuck Ave., 510-649-1320
- Berkeley
  1855 Solano Ave., 510-525-6888
- Berkeley
  5560 College Ave. (Pendragon Books), 510-652-6259

These stores have an impressive selection of new and used children's books.

Walden Pond
3316 Grand Ave.
Oakland
510-832-4438

*These stores offer story hours or other children's events. Call the stores for details.

Packed with creative toys for all ages in all price ranges, this small toy store has a good children's book section too. They feature infant toys by Lamaze and The First Years, Fisher Price, Barbie, and Lego, as well as high-end toys. Toys are organized according to theme, such as cars and trucks, dress-up, art supplies, and dolls. Mr. Mopps' also carries playhouse furniture, tea sets, pretend food, science and nature toys, games, models, marionettes, and more.

Once Upon a Time

404 Hartz Ave.
Danville
925-820-0182

This independently owned and operated specialty toy store carries all the classics and more that you won't find in mass-market toy stores. They feature dress-up clothing year round; quality Halloween costumes; pretend play toys such as kitchens, vacuums, and tea sets; Brio and Thomas wooden trains; Corolle dolls and strollers; and developmental toys for infants. The staff is friendly and helpful.

Sweet Dreams

• Berkeley
  2921 College Ave., 510-548-8697
• Orinda
  2 Theater Sq., 925-254-6672

PARENT RATING: ☆ ☆ ☆ ☆ ☆

Sweet Dreams is a unique toy store owned by the owners of Teddy's Little Closet, the children's clothier. See under "Baby and Children's Clothing." They offer a wide selection of toys, including high-quality developmental toys for infants by Ambi, and Brio trains, Lego, and Playmobil

for toddlers and preschoolers. They also carry an eclectic variety of novelty and holiday items, including jewelry and barrettes, books, dolls, and sand toys. The Orinda store includes an old-fashioned candy counter with jars brimming with gummies and sour patch kids. The Berkeley store has a separate candy store down the street. Both stores offer friendly and helpful service.

Time Out for Fun and Games

Jack London Sq.
435 Water St.
Oakland
510-444-4386

Time Out carries developmental and educational toys, books, and puzzles.

South Bay

Cheeky Monkey

714 Santa Cruz Ave.
Menlo Park
650-328-7975

PARENT RATING: ☆ ☆ ☆ ☆

Cheeky Monkey is a wonderful toy store that carries high-end toys for infants and beyond. They have a fun costume and dress-up department.

Milo's Toy Chest and Book Store

666 Laurel St.
San Carlos
650-593-8697

Milo's offers an extensive selection of high-end developmental and educational toys and books for infants and toddlers featuring items from Ambi, Lamaze, and Plan Toys. They also have a good selection of wooden toys, including Thomas wooden trains, doll houses, Lincoln Logs, and puzzles.

Best Bets for Children's' Books in the South Bay

Books Inc.
- *Burlingame
  1375 Burlingame Ave.,
  650-685-4911
- Palo Alto
  157 Stanford Shopping Center,
  650-321-0600

Borders Books
322 W. El Camino Real
Sunnyvale
408-730-5050
www.borders.com
Visit their website for other locations.

B. Dalton Bookseller
408 Hillsdale Mall
San Mateo
650-577-0910
Barnes and Noble now owns B. Dalton, so for other locations either visit their website (below) or check the yellow pages.

Barnes and Noble
- Redwood City
  1091 El Camino Real,
  650-299-0117
- *San Mateo
  Hillsdale Mall, 650-341-5560
www.barnesandnoble.com
Visit their website or check the yellow pages for other locations.

Coastside Books
432B Main St.
Half Moon Bay
650-726-5889

*Hicklebee's Children's Books
1378 Lincoln Ave.
San Jose (Willow Glen)
408-292-8880

*Kepler's
1010 El Camino Real
Menlo Park
650-324-4321

Linden Tree Children's Records & Books
170 State St.
Los Altos
650-949-3390

Milo's Toy Chest and Bookstore
666 Laurel St.
San Carlos
650-593-8697

*These stores offer story hours or other children's events. Call the stores for details.

Palo Alto Sport Shop & Toy World

526 Waverly St.
Palo Alto
650-328-8555

PARENT RATING: ☆ ☆ ☆ ☆ ☆

In business since the 1930s, this is one of Palo Alto parents' favorite toy stores. They offer a wide variety of toys for all ages, including Brio and Thomas trains, dolls of all sorts, activity kits such as jewelry making, mini baseball gloves for toddlers, small basketball hoops, Kettler trikes, and a thoughtful selection of developmental toys for infants. The store is noted for its knowledgeable and helpful staff.

The Play Store

508 University Ave.
Palo Alto
650-326-9070
www.playstoretoys.com

PARENT RATING: ☆ ☆ ☆ ☆ ☆

This unique store specializes in carrying high-end wooden toys such as rattles for infants and play kitchens and cradles for toddlers. There is absolutely nothing plastic in the store! The staff is helpful and knowledgeable. Goods are also available via mail order.

Sea Squirts

80R N. Cabrillo Hwy.
Half Moon Bay
650-726-1139

Sea Squirts is a fun-filled toy store for infants and children that is well stocked with a wide variety of developmental toys from Lamaze, Ambi, Plan Toys, Early Years, Tomy, and Brio. They also carry Wedgits (three-dimensional building blocks), wooden puzzles, rocking horses, and much more!

The Wooden Horse

Kings Court Center
796 Blossom Hill Rd.
Los Gatos
408-356-8821

PARENT RATING: ☆ ☆ ☆ ☆ ☆

This specialty toy store offers a thoughtful selection of high-end toys for infants on up. They feature developmental toys for babies, wooden kitchens and play structures, Brio and Thomas trains, Madame Alexander dolls and many other dolls, a "do-it" and "make-it" area full of interactive toys and art projects, as well as an impressive selection of Kettler trikes and Radio Flyer wagons. The staff is helpful and friendly and has a special play area for kids while parents shop.

Resale Shops for Babies and Children (Equipment and Clothing)

If you've never shopped at resale shops before, you might start once you have a baby. Resale shops are great places to clothe your baby, pick up an extra Pack N' Play or stroller, or find a fresh batch of toys or a book or two for your little one—all at great savings. Resale shops are also an excellent way to clean out your house or garage and make a little money too. You can sell your baby's outgrown baby equipment and toys as well as the outfits that no longer fit...when you're ready to let go of them.

The Bay Area abounds with many wonderful resale shops. Many have very helpful and friendly staffs with strong social consciences, donating their unsold items to local charities. We suggest that you call these stores ahead of time to confirm store hours, as many of these shops are owned and run by sole proprietors, resulting in store hours and policies that change periodically.

BAY AREA RESALE SHOPS

Here is what Bay Area parents have to say about their favorite local resale stores for all of their baby gear:

San Francisco

Goodwill Boutique
61 West Portal Ave.
415-665-7291

This traditional secondhand store carries a small selection of children's clothes, but you can usually find a variety of infants' and children's Halloween costumes to chose from in season.

The Junior League's Next-to-New Shop
2226 Fillmore St.
415-567-1627

They only carry a small amount of children's clothing, but it's worth checking out, as the quality and labels are usually quite good.

Peek-A-Boutique
1306 Castro St.
415-641-6192
PARENT RATING: ☆ ☆ ☆ ☆ ☆

Owned and operated by a couple for more than twelve years, this children's clothing and baby gear resale shop is *the* resale shop in San Francisco. They offer parents one of the best venues for finding bargains and getting rid of baby clothing and gear they no longer need. They offer used and some new clothes for infants and young children, as well as shoes, furniture, and basic baby gear, such as cribs, mattresses, bedding, strollers, car seats, baby carriers, swings, and gates. They also carry new smaller baby gear and accessories, such as bathtubs, potties, and childproofing equipment, and new and used toys. Most items are in very good condition and have great prices, and the store is very child-friendly with a small play area.

Town School Clothes Closet

3325 Sacramento St.

415-929-8019

This traditional resale shop offers used children's clothing for infants up to teens, as well as toys that are in very good condition. All proceeds benefit the Town School for Boys.

North Bay

The Kid's Exchange

10 Locust Ave.

Mill Valley

415-388-9068

PARENT RATING: ☆ ☆ ☆ ☆

The Kid's Exchange offers a large selection of high-quality used clothing for infants and toddlers, as well as toys and accessories, in an upscale, boutique-like atmosphere. They also carry some smaller baby gear items, such as car seats, potties, and bouncy seats, as well as parenting books. Some moms think that their prices are on the high side, but owner Jean Gineris justifies this by saying that her consignors expect top dollar for their top-quality merchandise. Jean checks and steams every item as soon as it comes in. She has a large size dressing room and play area to make shopping with little ones easier and entertaining.

Kids Go Round

75 Executive Dr.

Rohnert Park

707-585-8795

They sell a little bit of everything, from secondhand children's clothing to strollers, cribs, toys, and books.

Outgrown

1417 4th St.

San Rafael

415-457-2219

PARENT RATING: ☆ ☆ ☆ ☆ ☆

This large consignment store has been in business for twenty-five years and offers a large selection of children's clothing from infant to teens. Despite its size, it is well organized, making shopping quick and easy. They also carry some basic baby gear items, such as cribs, changing tables, car seats, joggers, and exersaucers. It's a Marin mom's favorite!

Play It Again Kids

508 4th St.

San Rafael

415-485-0304

PARENT RATING: ☆ ☆ ☆ ☆

This popular and successful store has been in business now for more than ten years and specializes in offering top-quality used clothing for infants and toddlers. They also have an extensive selection of used nursery furnishings, such as cribs, changing tables, gliders, and bassinets. They carry baby gear, including gently used swings and bouncy seats, as well as Baby Bjorns, car seats, strollers, high chairs, bedding, books, and toys. They offer new toys, featuring pretend play and science themes. The staff is friendly and helpful and has a special inclination toward customer service—regulars keep wish lists on file and are called when their item comes in the store.

The Second Banana Shop

401C Miller Ave.

Mill Valley

415-383-2699

This store offers a nice selection of used clothing for infants to preteen, as well as toys, books, and basic baby gear, including car seats and strollers.

East Bay

Bearly Worn

1619 N. Broadway

Walnut Creek

925-945-6535

This children's resale shop is jam-packed with decent brands and prices for all kinds of children's clothing. They also carry some baby gear such as strollers and car seats.

Crackerjacks

14 Glen Ave.

Oakland

510-654-8844

PARENT RATING: ☆ ☆ ☆ ☆ ☆

Voted "Best Consignment Store" by the *Oakland Tribune*, Crackerjacks has been in business for more than fifteen years. This boutique-like resale shop carries secondhand name-brand clothing for babies and children. They also have a lot of baby gear, including strollers, high chairs, and toddler beds. Maternity clothing and a few new items for babies are also available. See chapter 3. Customers may ask to be notified when a particular item they are looking for arrives.

Darla's Baby Boutique

10400 San Pablo Ave.

El Cerrito

510-526-KIDS

In business for more than thirteen years, Darla's occupies a huge space; she needs a lot of room to pack in her new and used clothing for infants and children as well as used baby gear, furniture, toys, and books. Her new clothing is discounted since she buys directly from manufacturers. She also maintains a wish book to keep track of customers' desired items.

Finders Keepers

1581 Olivina Ave.

Livermore

925-449-7793

Finders Keepers offers quality infant and children's clothing and an entire room full of baby equipment and furniture (such as cribs and strollers) in a well-organized and kid-friendly environment. Prices are competitive and the staff are all experienced moms, ready and willing to help you shop or lend a hand with your little one.

Hannah's

1871 Solano Ave.

Berkeley

510-525-3488

Hannah's offers quality, used clothing for babies and children, as well as some used toys and accessories.

Kids Again

6891 Village Pkwy.
Dublin
925-828-7334

PARENT RATING: ☆ ☆ ☆ ☆ ☆

Kids Again is part of a large shopping complex that includes a women's clothier and home furnishings store. They carry used clothing for infants and children, baby equipment, and furniture, as well as toys. They also carry a few new items, including cribs, at a discount. They have dressing rooms and a nice play area for little ones. There are many great bargains to be found here!

Laura's Closet

2926 College Ave.
Berkeley
510-845-3157

Recently sold by the owners of Lauren's Closet, this store offers the same items.

Lauren's Closet

• Alameda
  1420 Park St., 510-865-2219
• Lafayette
  3484 Mount Diablo Blvd.,
  925-299-1475

PARENT RATING: ☆ ☆ ☆ ☆ ☆

In business for more than ten years, this store is consistently voted "Best Local Resale Store" by the *Alameda Times Star* and is often featured on local news broadcasts. Known for its high-quality resale items, this well-organized store offers clothing for infants and children, (including brands such as Hartstrings, Gap, and Gymboree) as well as maternity wear, see chapter 3, baby gear (such as Maclaren and Peg Perego strollers, and

exersaucers), furniture (including bassinets, cribs, and changing tables), toys (such as play structures), and books. Family owned and operated, the staff offers excellent customer service, although they are known to be particular when buying used goods. The Alameda store is the larger store.

Lillian's Children's Store

5638 College Ave.
Oakland
510-428-1009

Lillian's carries secondhand children's clothing, baby equipment, furniture, and toys.

Making Ends Meet

3544 Fruitvale Ave.
Oakland
510-531-1135

This secondhand store offers clothing for babies and children, as well as some baby equipment and toys. Customers may ask to be called when a particular item comes into the store.

Marino's Second Time Around

17279 Hesperian Blvd.
San Lorenzo
510-276-8705

Marino's offers great prices on used clothing for infants and children as well as baby equipment and furniture such as cribs, car seats, changing tables, and strollers. They also have a good selection of toys and books.

Silver Moon

3221 Grand Ave.
Oakland
510-835-2229

This charming consignment shop, decorated like a moon with a navy ceiling and silver baskets filled with hats and accessories, carries a nice selection of children's and baby clothes. Everything is in excellent condition. They have baby gear (such as bouncy seats and Pack n' Plays), furniture, and toys.

Snickerdoodles
442 Hartz Ave.
Danville
925-820-4956

PARENT RATING: ☆ ☆ ☆ ☆ ☆

Voted "Best East Bay Consignment Store" by *Diablo Magazine*, this inviting boutique-like resale shop offers children's clothing, brand–name baby equipment (many strollers and cribs), games, books, and quality wooden toys. Prices are very good—about a quarter of retail—and items are in excellent condition.

They Grow So Fast
3413 Mount Diablo Blvd.
Lafayette
925-283-8976

PARENT RATING: ☆ ☆ ☆ ☆ ☆

This local consignment shop cleverly shares a large space with Ponytails Children's Hair Salon. They are well-organized, offering clothing for infants and children, furniture, toys, and books. A very kid-friendly atmosphere makes shopping easier.

Toy Go Round
1361 Solano Ave.
Albany
510-527-1363

PARENT RATING: ☆ ☆ ☆ ☆

In business for more than twenty-five years, Toy Go Round calls itself the Bay Area's first resale toy store. This children's shop carries both new and resale items in excellent condition, featuring Little Tikes play houses and kitchens. They carry a nice selection of new toys such as Brio trains and other wooden toys and blocks. The shop owners keep tabs for regular customers who come in to recycle their children's toys. They offer a very kid-friendly environment, featuring a Brio train table for little shoppers to play with while parents shop. They also carry seasonal items such as rain and snow clothing and a variety of Halloween costumes.

South Bay

Bearly Worn Children's Store
35 W. Manor Dr.
Pacifica
650-355-5089

Bearly Worn offers gently worn clothing for infants and children, as well as books, toys, baby furnishings (such as cribs and changing tables), strollers, and car seats at great prices.

Cottage Collectibles
(formerly Kids Closet)
591 San Mateo Ave.
San Bruno
650-589-6400

This upscale infant and children's resale shop offers well-organized racks of brand-name children's clothing to choose from. They also have a good selection of baby furniture, such as cribs, changing tables, dressers, twin beds, bunk beds, and all the standard baby gear.

Dimples

5965 E. Almaden Expwy., Ste. 145
San Jose
408-323-0360

This upscale resale shops carries a variety of brand-name clothing for infants and children, as well as toys.

Junior League of Palo Alto—Mid Peninsula Shop

785 Santa Cruz Ave.
Palo Alto
650-328-7467

This shop carries a small selection of name-brand clothing for infants and children. They also occasionally have some baby equipment.

Kids' Trading Company

348 N. Santa Cruz Ave.
Los Gatos
408-395-8046

PARENT RATING: ☆ ☆ ☆ ☆ ☆

Kids' Trading Company is located in a small house in downtown Los Gatos and features five neat rooms filled with high-end infant and children's clothing, new toys, and some new articles of clothing such as leggings. Prices are exceptionally low; most items sell for under $10, except for fancy dresses and coats.

The Kidz Shoppe

Cambrian Park Plaza
14454 Union Ave.
San Jose
408-879-0989

In business for more than ten years, The Kidz Shop calls itself the oldest used baby and children's clothing store in Santa Clara County. They also carry previously-owned toys, books, and baby furnishings and equipment, from cribs to car seats. The store is well stocked and caters to all budgets. An attractive feature of this store is that they rent snowsuits. They also have a nice selection of Halloween costumes, in season.

Little Cousins

138 W. 25th Ave.
San Mateo
650-341-8726

This upscale children's resale shop is known for carrying brand–name clothing for infants and young children. They also offer a large selection of baby equipment and toys in excellent condition. The Infant Room in San Mateo hosts a bulletin board advertising recycled items for sale in the neighborhood.

Once Upon a Child

1929 W. El Camino Real
Mountain View
650-960-6822

PARENT RATING: ☆ ☆ ☆ ☆ ☆

They offer great buys on gently worn infant and children's clothing, as well as previously owned baby equipment (including car seats and cribs), toys, and books.

Ricochet Kids Clothing

1610 S. El Camino Real
San Mateo
650-345-8740

PARENT RATING: ☆ ☆ ☆ ☆ ☆

Ricochet sells good-quality traditional children's clothing from newborn to size 14. They offer items that are very casual to dressier classic ensembles such as smocked dresses and European labels. They also carry reasonably priced wooden toys, including wooden trains that are less costly than Brio but are compatible. They carry clothing for all seasons year round so you can shop for the Hawaii-bound vacationing toddler in January! They are very child-friendly and customer service-oriented. The owner, Jill, keeps a running wish list for regulars and calls them when their desired item comes in. She also offers private appointments for families to make it an easy and fun shopping experience!

Too Cute
1375 Burlingame Ave.
Burlingame
650-348-CUTE

Too Cute offers a good selection of previously worn infant and children's clothing and accessories. There is a useful bulletin board for previously owned items for sale in the neighborhood in the Infant Room.

Ubyan
540 Bascom Ave.
San Jose
408-998-1867
This shop offers a large selection of both new and used baby and kids' clothing, shoes, toys, strollers, furniture, and other baby equipment.

Baby and Child Photographers

The Bay Area abounds with many talented photographers who specialize in photographing babies and young children. Be sure to shop around and see their work. Photographers have a wide variety of styles—indoor and outdoor, formal and informal, black and white, color, and hand-tinted. Also, consider your child's age when you are taking professional photographs. Professionals say that the best age for baby pictures is when she can sit up and smile, but can't yet crawl. This is a small window of time, roughly from six to eight months. Many babies begin crawling around nine months, which makes it difficult to capture those classic poses. And once they begin to walk, it's best to wait another year or two!

San Francisco

Martha Bruce
415-822-7581
www.marthabruce.com
Martha specializes in black and white photography of "kids being kids."

Leslie Corrado
415-431-3917
www.lesliecorrado.com
Leslie specializes in black and white photography in outdoor settings and produces spectacular work.

Tami DeSellier
415-668-5930

PARENT RATING: ☆ ☆ ☆ ☆ ☆

Our personal favorite, Tami specializes in black and white photography of babies and children under three years old. We had Tami photograph each of our own children, and were tremendously pleased with the results. Tami really knows how to get your baby to smile and bring out his little personality on film! She is credited with the photo on the back cover of this book.

Katherine Esslinger
415-346-4122

Katherine specializes in black and white photography of children.

Laurel Photography
415-331-1057

Laurel Thornton specializes in black and white children's portraiture.

North Bay

Rana Halprin
415-721-5374

Anna Head
415-332-1210

Anna specializes in black and white candid photography of children, families, friends, and couples.

Chere Pafford
Sonoma
707-695-1508

Chere specializes in photographing children outdoors on black and white film.

David Peters
San Rafael
415-453-2776

Linda Russell
San Rafael
415-459-3639

Mary Small
Sausalito
415-332-5605

East Bay

Dana Davis
Berkeley
510-658-7617

Johannah Hetherington
Oakland
510-663-7408
www.johannahphoto.com

Jonanna specializes in "simple, soulful, black and white hand-printed portraits of children and their kinfolk."

Almudena Ortiz
Berkeley
510-526-0692

Stephanie Tabachnikoff
Oakland
510-632-5886

Carmen Urquiza
Oakland
510-339-3236

Carmen specializes in hand-coloring.

South Bay

Classic Kids
• San Mateo
650-522-9705
• Los Gatos
408-354-9116

Classic Kids is known for their "hip shots" of kids as well as their mantra, "Never try to make a kid sit still!"

Melissa Lynch
408-723-8944

Andrew Michaels
Palo Alto
650-323-6125

Phoenix Studios
Los Gatos
408-354-5667

Portraits by Rebecca
408-848-4555

Deborah Stern
408-997-9250

Childproofing and Home Safety

Just when you think you have this baby thing down to a science, your little bundle of joy starts moving...first creeping, then crawling and then teetering and tottering to full-fledged walking! Congratulations—you have moved into the next stage of parenthood! Now that your little one is free to move about, there's lots of trouble she can get into at home, from electrical outlets to poisons, to unsafe cribs and soft bedding that can suffocate, to dangling window blind cords that can strangle. There is also the potential drowning danger that an accessible toilet poses, furniture that may come crashing down on a toddler if they climb or pull hard enough on it, or that glass framed picture over the baby's crib that could fall in an earthquake.

More than 4.5 million children suffer injuries in the home each year, many of them serious. As a parent, you will certainly need to monitor your mobile child's moves. However, there is a lot that you can do to create a safe environment so that you may also relax a little. There are many retail stores and mail order catalogs where you can buy basic childproofing gear. Home Depot or your local hardware store will often carry many of the basics, like the child safety cabinet locks and other essentials. Almost all the major baby superstores listed earlier in this chapter, under the "Baby Gear" section, carry babyproofing equipment and products.

As an alternative to doing it yourself, an increasing number of Bay Area parents are turning to childproofing services. Rather than poring through those mail order catalogs and spending weekends installing locks and gates, many parents simply hire a professional. After an easy in-home consultation and estimate, the job is done more efficiently than you could imagine! Some will do the home assessment and installation on the same day. Some also will do earthquake and pool safety as well as babyproofing. The general fee for childproofing is about $60 an hour for installation plus the cost of the parts. To follow are some resources for professional childproofers:

The Childproofer
Mark Altman
800-374-2525
www.childproofer.com
PARENT RATING: ☆ ☆ ☆ ☆ ☆

This company offers childproofing product sales, installation, and CPR and safety classes in your home with a minimum of six to eight people. They serve San Francisco, Marin, and some parts of the East Bay. They also offer a home safety assessment for $20, where they'll assess the hazards in your home and advise you on how to minimize them for your baby. They have a great website for safety tips and potential hazards at home for babies and young children. Parent comments: "Experts and very efficient." "Full of wonderful, hard-to-find, real–world advice on babyproofing." "Very knowledgeable about which child-proofing products worked and which ones didn't." "You just can't beat the efficiency in how quickly they install childproof cabinet latches!"

Larry's Baby Safety Services
Larry Mitchell
650-493-4908 or 800-690-7233
Larry's provides all childproofing services including earthquake proofing, as well as car seat installations and checks. They serve the South Bay, San Francisco, and some parts of the East Bay.

Safe and Sound Children
Rachel Murray
510-338-0222
Owner, mother, and civil engineer by training, Rachel Murray of Safe and Sound comes to your home and provides an indoor, as well as outdoor, assessment of the potential hazards to your baby and how you can minimize them. She sells and installs the baby-proofing products herself. Rachel primarily serves the East Bay, but will also service some parts of San Francisco and Marin. Parent comments: "Very knowledgeable, neat, and reasonably priced." "She gets an amazing amount accomplished in an hour!"

Home Safety Services
The Safety Guy
Martin Simenc
888-388-3811 or 650-652-9173
www.homesafety.net
PARENT RATING: ☆ ☆ ☆ ☆ ☆

Martin Simenc, "The Safety Guy," will come to your home for $50 to assess the potential hazards to your baby. You pick and choose which products you want to purchase and have him install. He'll often do the installation of products during the same visit. He also provides earthquake safety and removable pool fencing. Based in Redwood City, he serves almost the entire Bay Area. Parent comments: "Expert advice and workmanship." "Neat, flexible, and efficient."

Protect a Child Pool Fence Company
800-778-8411
www.protectachild.com

This company provides a unique, transparent mesh fence that is strong and secure, climb resistant, and removable in minutes. Call them for a free estimate. They serve the Bay Area.

Safe Solutions
925-735-0700
Safe Solutions sells and installs basic childproofing products.

On-line Childproofing Resources

www.babyproof.com
This website sells childproofing and safety accessories in addition to general baby gear.

www.cpsc.gov
301-504-0580
This is the website for the U.S. Consumer Product Safety Commission. You can register on this website to have current recall information e-mailed to you. To report defective or dangerous products, call 800-638-2772.

www.safetyalerts.com
This website offers an e-mail service where you receive information about infant and children's product recalls.

www.jpma.org
856-439-0500
This is the website for the Juvenile Products Manufacturing Association, which works with the Consumer Products Safety Commission to develop standards for baby gear.

www.safetystore.com
888-723-3897
This website offers convenient one-stop shopping for childproofing products and more.

www.kidsstuff.com
This company says it is the only mail order catalog dedicated to child safety. The catalog, called *Perfectly Safe*, is also available on-line.

www.mommyshelperinc.com
316-684-2229
This website offers shopping for childproofing products and advice.

www.dannyfoundation.org
800-833-2669
The Danny Foundation is a non-profit organization that seeks to prevent injuries from cribs and other baby equipment by conducting research and providing leadership in setting regulatory standards for safe nursery equipment. The foundation was created in memory of 23-month-old Danny, who tragically died because of an unsafe crib.

Other Safety Concerns

Aside from the basic childproofing of your home, parents should be aware of the other potential hazards from which to protect their babies and toddlers. There are many more resources on each of these areas, but we'd like to make you aware of some of them.

EARTHQUAKE PROOFING

As residents of the Bay Area, we all know we have chosen to live in earthquake country. Now that you are a parent, it's even more important than ever to either make an earthquake kit or purchase one. And don't forget to throw in all the essentials for your baby or young child, including extra formula, bottles, water and food, diapers and wipes, and a blanket for that extra person you now have in your life! To follow are a few websites to help you either make or purchase a kit for your family:

www.earthshakes.com
650-548-9065
This Burlingame business (owned by a mother) sells several different ready-made earthquake kits.

www.earthquakesafetykit.com

www.earthquakestore.com

www.iprepare.com

FIRE SAFETY AND ESCAPE PLANS

Now that you are a parent and responsible for another life, there couldn't be a better time to prepare and practice your escape plan in case of a fire. Children under five are more than twice as likely to die in a fire as older children and adults are. Visit the National Fire Protection Association's website at www.nfpa.org for advice on how to put together your family's fire escape plan. Be sure to install smoke detectors inside, and outside, every bedroom and on each level of your home. Also, test your smoke detectors monthly and replace the batteries every four to six months. You may also want to consider installing an automatic sprinkler system in your home.

LEAD POISONING PREVENTION

About one in twenty-two children in the United States have high levels of lead in their blood, according to the Center for Disease Control and Prevention. Children are more susceptible to lead poisoning since their brains and nervous systems are more sensitive to the damaging effects of lead. The long-term health effects of lead for them can be devastating, including damage to the brain and nervous system, and 34 behavioral and learning problems, such as hyperactivity and slowed growth. Lead also poses a significant health hazard to unborn babies, so if you are pregnant, you should pay careful attention to lead hazards.

Lead is often found in the paint of older homes (painted before 1978), as well as in the drinking water as a result of lead plumbing. People most often get lead in their bodies by breathing or swallowing lead dust, or by eating soil or paint chips containing lead. Babies and young children often put their hands and other objects in their mouths, which can have lead dust on them.

Children are often tested for blood lead levels at one year, so be sure to ask your pediatrician about this test. Also, never remove lead paint yourself—many families have been poisoned by the lead dust that is created from scraping or sanding lead paint. If you do hire a professional painter, be sure to hire someone who is lead certified. Finally, the only way to know if you have lead in your water is to have it tested. You can call your local health department or water supplier to find out how to test the water in your home. Be sure to always flush the tap for at least 30 seconds before using water and use cold water when cooking—less lead will leach from any lead plumbing than with hot water. Boiling water does not reduce lead in water.

LEAD POISONING PREVENTION RESOURCES

There are a number of resources where one can learn about lead poisoning prevention. The following are a few such resources:

The U.S. Environmental Protection Agency, National Lead Information Clearinghouse
800-424-5323
www.epa.gov/lead
This agency offers several free lead prevention booklets about testing your home for lead and reducing lead hazards when remodeling your home. Call the toll-free number to obtain copies.

EPA's Safe Drinking Water Hotline
800-426-4791

Childhood Lead Prevention Program San Francisco Department of Public Health
415-554-8930
They offer free lead testing for women, infants, and children.

San Francisco Public Utility Commission
877-737-8297
This organization will test your water for lead for $25.

Other Household Poisoning Prevention Tips

 Have the number of the San Francisco Bay Area Regional Poison Control Center posted near your phone. (800-876-4766)

 Keep a bottle of syrup of Ipecac (it induces vomiting) for each child less than 5 years old. Never use it unless instructed to do so by the Poison Control Center or your doctor.

If you suspect a child has been poisoned, call the Poison Control Center, but dial 911 immediately if the child is unconscious, having convulsions, or having difficulty breathing.

CHAPTER 5

SURVIVING THE
FIRST FEW MONTHS:
Postpartum help

While the first few weeks at home with a newborn are full of joy, this time is often turbulent as well. New parents are typically sleep deprived, having to attend to frequent feedings, diaper changes, and other needs of the baby. Additionally, while both parents may enagage in child care, new mothers may most often feel that their lives are reduced to changing diapers, feedings, and rocking and soothing the baby. As a new mom, you may begin to believe you will never have a normal life again! In addition, giving birth is an emotionally charged experience, and a new mom's hormones fluctuate greatly in the early weeks, resulting in what many call the "baby blues." In some instances, this can escalate into postpartum depression.

Our advice is to anticipate these changes and make a postpartum plan *before* you give birth. This chapter answers the following questions to help you develop such a plan:

- What is a baby nurse and postpartum care doula and where can I find them?
- What is a lactation consultant and what do their certifications mean?
- Where can I join a breastfeeding support group?

189

- How can I get groceries, meals, and other necessities such as baby supplies delivered to my home?
- How can I get professional advice concerning postpartum depression?
- Where can I get access to special "warm" lines and stress lines? (Warm lines are usually for those non-emergency situations when a parent needs special help in anything ranging from breastfeeding to baby-sitting.)
- What are the best places to nurse or change my baby in public?

Baby Nurses and Postpartum Doulas

Many of us live great distances from our families, and the option of having a family member help out in the early weeks of new parenthood isn't available. Hiring a baby nurse has become a popular alternative for gaining an extra pair of hands during this happy but hectic time. Even if you do have family living nearby, you may not want to impose on them—or be imposed upon by them—and may prefer to hire a baby nurse or postpartum care doula, who provides short-term professional help.

In general, the baby nurse and postpartum doula field is unregulated. Practitioners range from having little training and experience to being highly skilled professionals with years of training and experience. It is important to interview candidates and ask about her background, training, and credentials, and you should always check references and work eligibility documentation, see chapter 10. Also, don't forget to ask if she carries insurance should she have an accident in your home.

BABY NURSES

While not always distinguishable, in general a postpartum care doula emphasizes caring for the parents while they are learning to care for their baby, and a baby nurse focuses on caring for the baby. Baby nurses may or may not be registered nurses, but are professionals skilled in newborn care. Baby nurses are usually scheduled to begin working the day you bring your baby home from the hospital.

Tips for New Motherhood Survival

- Stock your freezer before your baby is born and/or order take-out for the first few weeks.

- Plan ahead of time for help, such as a friend, family member, postpartum doula, or lactation consultant.

- Enlist the support of a friend or relative to assist with laundry, meals, and light housekeeping...or simply plan on letting the house get messy. Or, if you already have a regular cleaning person, consider temporarily giving him or her more duties, such as laundry.

- Buy baby supplies (diapers and wipes) in bulk and/or order supplies online, see chapter 4, and have them delivered.

- Put essential baby news (gender, name, date, weight) as well as the state of the parents (for example, we are either nursing or sleeping) on your voice mail to avoid energy and time-con-suming phone calls.

- Sleep when your baby sleeps.

- Let the thank-you notes wait.

- Nurture yourself physically—eat well, sleep, rest, and exercise (with your doctor's approval).

- Develop a support system—get out and meet other new moms by joining a new mothers group, see chapter 6.

- Get outside every day, even if it's only a walk around the block! Vitamin D helps stabilize mood swings.

- Take breaks when you can; a brisk walk, bubble bath, or hour to yourself can make a difference in your attitude and per-spective.

- Keep realistic expectations; your job first and foremost is car-ing for your baby (as well as for yourself).

- Structure your day; list one small errand to do, one person to call, and do something fun for yourself.

They usually work on a full-time schedule, from eight to twelve hours, day or night, and their duties focus exclusively on caring for the baby during the post-delivery period. Many baby nurses do not offer twenty-four hour care. While some new parents do find twenty-four-hour care best fits their needs, keep in mind that the post-birth period is a very intimate time for your family, and you may not want to have any-one—no matter how helpful they are—outside of your family living with you around the clock.

A baby nurse who works at night usually sleeps in the baby's room, or has a baby monitor in her room, and tends to the baby while parents rest. When the baby wakes up, the baby nurse either bottle feeds or brings the baby to her mother to nurse. After the feeding, the baby nurse takes charge of the process of burping, changing and settling the baby back to sleep. Of course, you decide what specific areas you would like assistance with. One of the great services that baby nurses often provide is that they document the baby's eating, sleeping, and diaper patterns to identify any problems. Most importantly, a good baby nurse should be able to teach and support a mother in bonding with her baby, make parents self-supportive, and identify what other kind of help they may need. Baby nurses are usually not responsible for household duties such as housekeeping or for care of other children in the family, although some do offer this service.

Of course, an extra pair of hands can be expensive. Fees range from $15-25 an hour in the Bay Area. The rates are higher for multi-ples, typically $25-35 an hour for twins. Some mothers have been known to fly baby nurses in from other cities where fees are lower. Fees are based on the candidate's training and experience as well as her specific duties. According to Bay Area moms, the best way to find a baby nurse is a referral through a trusted friend. Another good resource is a Bay Area mothers' group newsletter, see chapter 6, which often has baby nurse listings and referrals. The San Francisco Mothers of Twins' Club newsletter is especially helpful.

Personal referrals are generally the best resource in finding a suit-able baby nurse, but agencies can also be a help here. While some agencies specialize in placing baby nurses, most nanny agencies also place them. An agency will send you several prescreened candidates to interview during your pregnancy. After you select one, the agency will reserve the baby nurse and not place her elsewhere within two weeks or so of your due date. Most (but not all) agencies charge a flat registration fee of up to $300 to conduct a search and present candidates to you. Upon hiring an agency's candidate, the agency charges a referral fee that is usually a percentage (20-35 percent) of the baby nurse's total gross income for the assignment.

Although most agencies try to fill immediate needs, baby nurses generally get booked long in advance, so plan early. From what we've learned, starting your search sometime in the first or second trimester is not too early.

When screening and interviewing baby nurse candidates, try to get a clear understanding of the candidate's philosophy with respect to newborn care, such as whether she advocates breast- or bottle feeding, scheduled feedings versus demand feeding, having the baby sleep on her back rather than her side or tummy, and so on. It is important to find someone who's compatible with your approach to newborn care and parenting.

POSTPARTUM DOULAS

A postpartum doula is someone who is trained or experienced in providing postpartum care for a new mother and some newborn care. The word *doula* has a Greek origin, and translates to "mothering the mother." Some postpartum care doulas are also labor and birth doulas, see chapter 1, while others specialize in providing postpartum care, which can include everything from caring for the mother and baby, and breastfeeding assistance, to light housekeeping and meal preparation. A doula's experience may vary greatly, with some doulas better versed in breastfeeding assistance and other aspects of newborn care than others. It is best to discuss your needs thoroughly with an agency and/or with prospective candidates.

The Doulas of North America (DONA) is the primary certification organization for labor and birth doulas, see chapter 1, but until now, postpartum doulas have not been certified by DONA or any other similar entity. (If a postpartum doula says that she is DONA certified, it is likely that she is a certified labor and birth doula.) However, as this book goes to press, DONA is launching a postpartum doula education and certification program which presumably is the first of its kind.

As with finding a baby nurse, your best bet in finding a postpartum doula is through a personal referral. You can also typically find a doula through organizations dealing with childbirth, birth educators, lactation centers and consultants, baby nurse agencies, and the website for Doulas of North America, www.dona.com. (These are DONA labor and birth doulas who also provide postpartum care. At the time that this book goes to press, DONA membership is the only requirement to be listed on the DONA referral list of postpartum doulas.) Doulas are usually hired on a part-time basis, for a minimum number of hours per day (such as three to four hours) and range from $20–80 an hour in the Bay Area. Fees for evening hours can be higher than for day hours.

Most of the major nanny agencies in the Bay Area mentioned in chapter 9 place baby nurses and doulas, so be sure to refer to them. To follow are additional placement agencies that specialize in placing baby nurses and doulas, parent resource centers that offer referrals, and the names of individual doulas and baby nurses that Bay Area parents have shared with us. Since some of these same people and organizations offer labor support services and lactation consulting, we have included these resources here as well.

Bay Area Baby Nurses and Doulas

800-526-9996 or 415-899-1899

Serving San Francisco, Marin, the Peninsula, and the East Bay, Kay Baker, RN places baby nurses and doulas who are matched to a family's needs. Services include guidance on newborn care, breastfeeding support, and help with errands, meals, and light housekeeping. Hourly rates are $22-30, with no referral fee.

San Francisco and North Bay

Day One

3490 California St., 2nd Fl., Ste. 203 (entrance on Locust)
San Francisco
415-440-Day1 (3291)
www.dayonecenter.com

This wonderful state-of-the-art parent resource center offers free referrals in binders for postpartum care and childbirth doulas, as well as night and day nannies.

Labor Support Services

415-451-7287
www.birthdoulas.net

PARENT RATING: ☆ ☆ ☆ ☆ ☆

This group of eight doulas practicing at Marin General Hospital provides support during labor and delivery. Parents may meet them at monthly informational meetings at Marin General. You will be assigned the doula on call for the day you deliver. All doulas are mothers and some are DONA certified.

A Mother's Touch

504 Via Hidalgo
Greenbrae
415-456-9166
amtpps@aol.com

PARENT RATING: ☆ ☆ ☆ 1/2

Calling themselves the Bay Area's "original postpartum care center," we've heard inconsistent reports about this agency that focuses exclusively on newborn care, both preparing for and welcoming baby. They offer baby nurses, labor support doulas, postpartum doulas, and shopping and layette service. Most doulas are also midwives. Owner Judy Kern teaches her doulas to take care of the entire family (mom and baby care, breastfeeding and newborn care instruction, and monitoring postpartum depression) "without interfering in family life." Fees for labor support range from $600-1500, and rates for postpartum care doulas and baby nurses are $25-30 an hour. The agency does not have a registration fee but charges a 20 percent referral fee. They don't offer baby nurses for longer than twelve hour shifts, so if you want round the clock help, you'll need to hire two people from them.

Natural Resources

1307 Castro St.
San Francisco
415-550-2611
www.naturalresourcesonline.com

PARENT RATING: ☆ ☆ ☆ ☆ ☆

They maintain a helpful binder of information about doulas (some containing client feedback) and lactation consultants.

Parents Place

1710 Scott St.
San Francisco
415-202-7454

This full-service parenting center has the city's largest bulletin board where nannies, baby-sitters, and baby nurses advertise.

East Bay

Birth and Bonding Family Center

1126 Solano Ave.
Albany
510-527-2121
www.birthbonding.org

PARENT RATING: ☆ ☆ ☆ ☆

The center maintains binders of listings of doulas recommended by parents. They also offer comprehensive support for the breastfeeding mother, including a quiet, comfortable place to nurse a baby, as well as breastfeeding supplies, bras and clothing, nursing pillows, and breast pumps for sale or rent. They also offer breastfeeding workshops and a referral list of private lactation consultants.

Birthways

478 Santa Clara Ave., 3rd Fl.
Berkeley
510-869-2797
www.birthways.org

PARENT RATING: ☆ ☆ ☆ ☆ ☆

This nonprofit, volunteer organization maintains a list of local baby nurses and doulas and offers lactation consultants, as well as breastfeeding supplies. See their website for a listing of individual postpartum care providers and doulas.

The First Six Weeks

510-232-7678 or 510-540-7210
fst6wks@aol.com

PARENT RATING: ☆ ☆ 1/2

Owner Linda Jones-Mixon provides labor support and postpartum doula services including baby and sibling care, breastfeeding support, meal preparation, grocery shopping, and light housekeeping. Her fees are on a sliding scale for labor support ($750-950), and $25-40 per hour for postpartum support. She works in the East Bay only.

Loving Arms Doula Service

510-525-1155, Janaki Costello
510-563-2831, Alice Elliott
510-527-7210, Carol Shattuck-Rice

This group of three certified doulas each maintains a separate clientele, but they share duties in cases of emergency. They serve the East Bay, and charge $800 for labor support, including meeting before the birth and a postpartum checkup after birth. Costello is also a lactation consultant providing breastfeeding help after birth, and Shattuck-Rice provides postpartum doula services. She gets you off to a good start with your new baby by helping with breastfeeding and basic baby care. She also runs errands, does food shopping, meal preparation, kitchen clean-up, and laundry.

Mother to Mother

510-587-3335

This group offers postpartum care, including freshly prepared organic meals, light house cleaning and laundry, help with meditation and breath work, aromatherapy, foot and leg massage, herbal bathing, and emotional support.

The Nurture Center

3399 Mt. Diablo Blvd.
Lafayette
925-283-1346
www.nurturecenter.com

PARENT RATING: ☆ ☆ ☆ ☆ ☆

This Contra Costa County parenting center run by two local moms maintains listings of professional doulas.

UC Berkeley Parents Network

http://parents.berkeley.edu
(by the end of 2002, this website will be replaced by www.parentsnet.org)

PARENT RATING: ☆ ☆ ☆ ☆ ☆

Parents' uncensored opinions about local doulas (East Bay focus) are listed.

South Bay

Before Birth and Beyond

408-360-0714
This group offers certified postpartum doulas on the Peninsula from Redwood City to Santa Clara, including doulas experienced with twins.

Blossom Birth Services

1000 Elwell Center
Palo Alto
650-964-7380
www.blossombirth.com

This childbirth education and resource center features doula and lactation consultant listings and referrals, as well as doula training classes.

www.gentlebirth.org

This site lists doulas in the South Bay area.

www.withchild.org (under construction)

With Child is a birth support and education group based in Berkeley. Their website includes listings of labor and postpartum doulas for the entire Bay Area.

Individual Postpartum Baby Nurses and Doulas

San Francisco and North Bay

Summer Andreasen

415-753-1314

PARENT RATING: ☆ ☆ ☆ ☆ ☆

She offers new mother and family care, newborn and sibling care, breastfeeding support, light housekeeping, laundry, errands, and meal preparation.

Sara Duskin, CLE, IBCLC

415-386-9250

PARENT RATING: ☆ ☆ ☆ ☆ ☆

This British-trained nurse offers first-rate postpartum assistance, including newborn baby care and breastfeeding consulting. She'll meet you at your home when you leave the hospital and help you and your family embark upon the journey of parenthood in the most positive and nurturing way!

Esther Gallegher
415-821-4490
maymayes@pacbell.net
PARENT RATING: ☆ ☆ ☆ ☆ ☆

Esther offers postpartum care doula services to all of San Francisco proper. With twenty years of experience including work as a childbirth educator and midwife, Esther's services are rated top notch. A firm believer in providing nurture and support to new parents, Esther focuses on postpartum care, coming into your home for a limited number of hours each day and prioritizing your needs as a new parent. She provides lactation consultant services, housecleaning, and meal preparation among her postpartum care services.

Marin Mom and Baby Care
415-472-5934, Debbie Surkhe
415-479-4438, Lynn Gulick

This team of women provide full-service postpartum care, taking care of both mother and baby, and easing the transition into motherhood. Their rate is $25 per hour, and their services are available in San Francisco for full days and for overnights.

Candyce Lawson
415-661-0158

She offers nutritious postpartum meal preparation and full infant care.

Michele Mason, CLE
415-285-5545

She offers infant care and breastfeeding and postpartum support.

Julie Overton
707-762-6702

She offers breastfeeding support, new baby care, and light housekeeping. She also has experience with twins.

Devorah Joy Walder, CMT
415-488-4443

East Bay

Carol Egan
510-528-1694
PARENT RATING: ☆ ☆ ☆ ☆ ☆

Based on what we've heard, Carol offers first rate postpartum care services, including breastfeeding support, baby care, recovery from childbirth, meal preparation, laundry, grocery shopping, errands, and more. She has helped many women in the Bay Area confidently manage their postpartum transition.

Dana Fox, LM
510-530-1963

Her postpartum doula services include new mother care, baby care and light housekeeping. She has experience with multiples.

Teresa McLean
510-581-1013

She offers birth and postpartum doula services, including grocery shopping and in-home meal preparation.

Felicia Roche
510-864-8480
She offers birth doula services.

Constance Williams–My Birth Doula Assistance Services
510-893-3222

**A Good Night with Moon—
Postpartum and Night Care
Lisa Moon, CD, CCE**

510-644-3035

PARENT RATING: ☆ ☆ ☆ ☆ ☆

With over twenty years of experience, Lisa will help you get a restful night's sleep and eat well with healthy home cooking, as well as make your baby comfortable and happy. If she's not available, she offers referrals.

**Doula Service for the Whole Family
Lucia Maya**

510-524-4825

PARENT RATING: ☆ ☆ ☆ ☆ ☆

Lucia Maya offers excellent postpartum care, including newborn and sibling care, breastfeeding support, errand running, grocery shopping and meal preparation, laundry and light housecleaning, and household organization. Lucia also offers reiki energy work for new moms and babies.

South Bay

Elizabeth Greene

650-289-9330

She offers flexible hours as a postpartum doula and will travel from Palo Alto to San Mateo. She has experience working with multiples.

Joanne Hass, CMT

650-726-7528

PARENT RATING: ☆ ☆ ☆ ☆ ☆

She offers first-rate part-time postpartum doula services from South San Francisco to Mountain View. She is experienced with multiples.

Lela Karzian-Banos

408-734-5598

She offers doulas services from Palo Alto to San Jose and is experienced with multiples.

Breastfeeding Assistance and Support

As a new or expectant parent, you have probably been informed about the benefits of breastfeeding. The American Academy of Pediatrics recommends exclusively breastfeeding for the first six months with continuation of breastfeeding for the first year of life for optimal infant health and development. Breast milk helps strengthen a baby's immune system and is the perfect balance of water, fat, protein, vitamins, and minerals that your baby needs. In short, breast milk is designer baby food! Of course, bottle feeding your baby is perfectly fine—after all, you need to do what is best for you.

However, as many mothers can attest, learning to breastfeed can take unanticipated amounts of time and effort. While some mothers have no difficulty breastfeeding, others need help positioning and getting the baby to "latch-on" correctly, and suffer from engorgement and sore nipples. If you are a new mother who has difficulty breastfeeding, you will likely benefit from a professional who specializes in providing breastfeeding support—a lactation consultant.

Many lactation consultants are nurses, although some are not. Some are certified by the International Board of Lactation Consultant Examiners, with the credential "International Board Certified Lactation Consultant" (IBCLC). This is the highest form of certification for a lactation consultant. An IBCLC has passed an independent examination and possesses the necessary skills, knowledge, and attitude to provide quality breastfeeding assistance to mothers and babies. An IBCLC candidate needs a minimum of 2,500 hours of clinical breastfeeding consulting before she can sit for the exam and is required to be engaged in continuing education.

Some lactation consultants are Certified Lactation Consultants (CLC) which means that they have received training and are certified to give one-on-one lactation support. Be aware, however, that there is another "CLC" credential that stands for "certificate as a lactation counselor." These people are not "certified," but rather are issued a certificate of attendance for completing a five-day counselor course. Make sure you ask a lactation consultant exactly which "CLC" credential they have. Other lactation consultants may be Certified Lactation Educators (CLEs). This means that they are qualified to teach breastfeeding classes and field questions over the phone. Certifications are helpful guides in knowing what kind of training a lactation consultant has experienced; however, no credential can ensure the best service. Be sure to interview, or at least speak on the phone, with a lactation consultant before hiring one.

At many hospitals, a certified lactation consultant may visit a new mother in the maternity unit upon request or referral, or you can hire a lactation consultant privately to make a hospital visit. However, since a new mother's milk usually doesn't come in until seventy-two hours after delivery or later (well after discharge from the hospital, unless birth was by cesarean section), assistance may not be needed until arriving at home. A lactation consultant will evaluate any initial breastfeeding challenges, and typically develops a plan for a new mother and baby with one or several follow-up consultations to track progress and the baby's weight.

Lactation consultants are either hospital-based or work in private practices, either individually or in a group. Fees for a hospital-based practitioner's initial consultation, which includes follow-up telephone advice, begin at $35 an hour and go up to about $80. Follow-up visits are usually much less. A private practice lactation consultant's rates range from $85-125 for an initial hour-long consultation. Similar to the hospitals, follow-up visits are much less expensive and telephone advice is usually free. At the more expensive end of this range are lactation consultants who do home visits, which they regard as the best way to help a breastfeeding mother. On a home visit, the lactation consultant gets a chance to see and assess the mother's environment, including the chair in which she is nursing. Some insurance companies cover the cost of these services, so be sure to request an insurance claim form, or a "super bill," at the end of a consultation.

Breastfeeding mothers returning to work, or needing to leave their babies with someone else for a few hours, may want to pump breast milk for the baby to drink in their absence. A breast pump is helpful in relieving fullness as well. Many of the hospitals and lactation centers listed below rent or sell breast pumps, typically by the day, week, or month. Some private lactation consultants also rent them, or at least can help rent one. The most efficient type of breast pump is a hospital-grade electric pump, emptying the breast quickly and comfortably. Other types include a battery-operated pump and a manual pump. While these pumps are less expensive, they are also much less efficient, taking longer to empty the breast. If unsure of your need, we suggest renting a hospital-grade pump to decide whether or not you'd like to buy one.

Joining a group of breastfeeding mothers is a great way to enlist support and share your frustrations and successes. The following Bay Area hospitals and parent resource centers sponsor such groups and offer lactation support. Most hospitals' lactation centers are staffed with board certified lactation consultants and/or certified lactation educators. In addition, some of the nanny agencies mentioned in chapter 9 and postpartum care agencies and parenting resource centers, under the "Baby Nurses and Doulas" section above, offer lactation consultant placements and referrals, so be sure not to miss them!

Bay Area Lactation Associates (BALA)

510-524-5521

PARENT RATING: ☆ ☆ ☆ ☆ ☆

Serving the entire Bay Area, this nonprofit organization is the Bay Area affiliate of the International Lactation Consultants Association. Their membership consists of nearly one hundred breastfeeding professionals, including RNs, IBCLCs, and other licensed health care providers who provide breastfeeding consultations, information, and products, including the sale and rental of breast pumps. They include only those professionals who carry current professional liability insurance.

La Leche League of Northern California

1950 Glen Ave.
San Bruno
650-363-1470 (referral line for local leaders)
800-LA-LECHE (525-3243) (national organization)
www.lalecheleague.org

This international nonprofit group is the mecca of breastfeeding support. Local chapters provide education, information, and support to women who want to breastfeed. La Leche offers free monthly meetings and support groups in various locations throughout the Bay Area, and a popular publication, *The Womanly Art of Breastfeeding*. Babies are always welcome at meetings. They also provide over-the-phone advice and on-line breastfeeding support, tips and information on breastfeeding. Please be aware that the phone numbers listed for La Leche leaders in this section may be home numbers of their volunteers.

California Pacific Medical Center Newborn Connections

3698 California St., 1st Fl.
415-600-BABY (2229)

PARENT RATING: ☆ ☆ ☆ ☆

CPMC's Newborn Connections offers a breastfeeding assistance program, including telephone advice, private one-on-one consultations with board certified lactation consultants, and a weekly breastfeeding mothers' support group. They also offer breast pumps (rentals and sales) and nursing bras and apparel in their boutique. Elaine Jewel, IBCLC, one of the consultants, was highly recommended by several mothers.

Day One

See under "Baby Nurses and Postpartum Doulas"—San Francisco and North Bay.

PARENT RATING: ☆ ☆ ☆ ☆ ☆

There is nothing like this state-of-the-art, privately run center for new and expectant parents, offering everything you need for successful breastfeeding and care for your newborn. Day One offers an inviting and supportive environment to nurse your baby, board-certified lactation consultants and registered nurses, breast pump rentals and sales, an after-hours hotline that you subscribe to on a monthly basis, a current book and video library, and a beautiful boutique that features San Francisco's largest

What You Need to Know About Breastfeeding in the Workplace

If you plan to return to work and wish to continue breastfeeding, a new law is making it easier than before. As of October 2001, all employers in the state of California are required to provide their employees who are nursing mothers with a private place, other than a restroom stall, in close proximity to their work station to pump breast milk. This place may be in the employee's work station. Employers are also required to provide unpaid breaks for these employees to pump milk. (AB 1025).

selection of nursing bras and other nursing and baby accessories and apparel. Ask about their Breastfeeding Value Package, which includes an initial lactation consultation, five breastfeeding support group sessions and baby weight tracking. Day One's breastfeeding support group, "Breastfeeding Connections," meets weekly. Join other nursing mothers to share tips and experiences pertinent to breastfeeding, including expressing and storing breast milk, breastfeeding in public, and taking care of the nursing mother. They also offer many workshops, including one about losing weight while breastfeeding, which is given by a registered dietician. Nancy Held, RN, MS, IBCLC, is the Executive Director of Day One, as well as one of the owners. She is joined by a team of well respected lactation consultants including Laura Alexander, RN, IBCLC, Sara Duskin, CLE, IBCLC, and Patti Neely, RN, CLE. Comments: "First-rate care, service,

and support." "A great place to go to meet other new moms who are going through all the joys and challenges that you are." "The people at Day One couldn't be more supportive and encouraging!"

Kaiser Permanente Breastfeeding Center
2200 O'Farrell St.
415-833-3236 (breastfeeding center)
415-833-BABY (breastfeeding advice and appointments)
PARENT RATING: ☆ ☆ ☆ ☆

The center offers lactation consultations and breast pumps for rent and sale. Comment: "Invaluable!"

La Leche League of San Francisco
415-386-7576
This group holds three meetings per month at various locations in the city. See under Entire Bay Area.

Nursing Mothers Counsel (NMC)

650-327-6455 (referral line for the San Francisco and San Mateo chapter)

NMC is a nonprofit, nonaffiliated volunteer organization whose goal is to help mothers enjoy a positive breastfeeding experience. They have provided free information and support to nursing mothers since 1955. Counselors mainly offer over-the-phone assistance but also will make home visits for difficult situations. NMC also offers breast pump sales and rentals and often sponsors local talks on topics pertaining to breastfeeding.

Silver Avenue Family Health Center

1525 Silver Ave.

415-715-0300

This center offers breastfeeding assistance, including office consultations, home visits, and telephone advice to all clients, including women who are eligible under the federally funded Special Supplemental Nutrition Program for Woman, Infants, and Children known as the WIC program.

St. Luke's Hospital
The Breastfeeding Center

2555 Cesar Chavez St.

415-641-6869

This hospital offers breastfeeding assistance, including office consultations and support groups, as well as breast pump sales and rentals. Ask for Aimee Creelman, MS, IBCLC.

University of California at San Francisco Medical Center
The Women's Health Resource Center

2356 Sutter St.

415-353-2667

At this time, UCSF does not offer out-patient lactation consultations or a breastfeeding support group, but they do offer breast pump sales and rentals at the Women's Health Resource Center.

San Francisco General Hospital Women's Health Center

1001 Potrero Ave.

415-206-5302

www.sfgh.org

The center offers private lactation consultations and breast pump rentals.

North Bay

Center for Creative Parenting

Pacheco Plaza
446A Ignacio Blvd.
Novato

415-883-4442

PARENT RATING: ☆ ☆ ☆ ☆ ☆

Owner Marsha Podd is a certified lactation consultant who offers one-on-one consultations.

La Leche League of Marin

707-789-0894

See under Entire Bay Area.

La Leche League of Sebastopol

707-829-6745

See under Entire Bay Area.

La Leche League of Sonoma

707-823-9480

See under Entire Bay Area.

Marin General Hospital, Lactation Center

250 Bon Air Rd., Rm. 4216
415-925-7522
www.maringeneral.com

PARENT RATING: ☆ ☆ ☆ ☆ ☆

The Lactation Center at Marin General provides counseling and support services for all Bay Area breastfeeding moms. The Lactation Center is located in the pediatric section of the hospital, next to the Family Birthing Center. Chris Costello, IBCLC, runs the center, and survey moms just love her! She and other certified lactation counselors and nurses are available for in-person breastfeeding consultations and education. Telephone advice is also available. The center offers a weekly drop in breastfeeding support group open to all Bay Area nursing moms. The center works in cooperation with the BabyNook store, located next door, which offers breast pump sales and breastfeeding accessories, including nursing bras, nursing pillows, nursing apparel, and baby clothing and products.

Maternity of Marin

874 4th St.
San Rafael
415-457-4955

Roshan Kaderali, RN, CLE, offers lactation advice over the phone as well as one-on-one consultations.

Santa Rosa Memorial Hospital

1165 Montgomery Dr.
Santa Rosa
707-546-3210

This hospital offers free drop in lactation consultations and over-the-

phone advice. It also hosts two weekly breastfeeding support groups.

East Bay

Children's Hospital Oakland Breastfeeding Support Center

5400 Telegraph Ave.
Oakland
510-428-3137

The center offers breastfeeding consultations by appointment. They offer breast pump rentals and a class on returning to work while breastfeeding.

East Bay Breastfeeding Service

510-525-1155, Janaki Costello, IBCLC, ICCE
510-849-1271, Miriam Levitt, IBCLC
510-524-6917, Sue Wirth, IBCLC

This popular private practice group of certified lactation consultants is available for in-home consultations. This group also offers breast pumps for sale and rental and serves Berkeley, El Cerrito, Oakland, and Richmond.

Eden Medical Center
The Women's Center

20103 Lake Chabot Rd.
Castro Valley
510-727-2715 or 510-537-1234

Eden offers postpartum lactation support at its on-site lactation center.

John Muir Lactation Center

1656 N. California Blvd., Ste. 110
Walnut Creek
925-952-2777

PARENT RATING: ☆ ☆ ☆ ☆ ☆

Staffed by board-certified lactation educators, this center offers a full range of lactation support services, including one-on-one consultations, classes, breastfeeding supplies, and breast pump rentals and sales.

Kaiser Permanente

www.kaiserpermanente.org
- Antioch Medical Offices
  Antioch
  3400 Delta Fair Blvd., 925-779-5000

This out-patient clinic offers breast-feeding assistance by appointment with Linda Draper, nurse practitioner.
- Oakland Medical Center
  Oakland
  280 W. MacArthur Blvd.,
  510-752-7557 (After Care Center and Lactation Clinic), 510-752-7613 (Breast Pump Center)

The center offers breastfeeding con-sultations through the After Care Center and Lactation Clinic which is open to Kaiser members only. Ask for Joanne Jasson, RN, IBCLC. They also rent breast pumps through the Breast Pump Center, located at 3372 House St., on the ground floor, and offer "Breastfeeding and the Working Mom," a class on breastfeeding while returning to work. One session is offered monthly.
- Hayward Medical Center
  Hayward
  27400 Hesperian Blvd.,
  510-784-2804 (warm line)

The hospital offers certified lactation consultants for telephone consulta-tions and office appointments for mothers and babies experiencing nursing problems. Ask for Fritzi Drosden. Call the warm line at any time for over-the-phone advice or to schedule an appointment, and a con-sultant will return your call within twenty-four hours.
- Pleasanton Medical Center
  Pleasanton
  7601 Stoneridge Dr., 925-847-5172 (health education)

This hospital offers lactation consul-tations with Karin Gee, RN, CLC, as well as a class on breastfeeding and returning to work called, "Breastfeeding and Managing Schedule Changes."
- Walnut Creek Medical Center
  Walnut Creek
  1425 S. Main St., 925-295-4368,
  Pat Ross, RN, IBCLC

They offer out-patient lactation con-sultations by appointment through Pat Ross.

La Leche League

510-496-6009 (East Bay referral line)
See under Entire Bay Area.

The Nurture Center

3399 Mount Diablo Blvd.
Lafayette
925-283-1346

This community resource center for pregnant women and new parents offers a Nursing Moms' Group. Topics discussed include sore nipples, engorgement, nursing in public, sex and breastfeeding, deciding when to wean, and other topics of interest to nursing moms. Kay Goodyear, IBCLC, facilitates the discussion. They also offer breast pump rentals and sales and nursing apparel.

The Mother's Milk Bank

Valley Medical Center, San Jose, 408-998-4550

One of five milk banks in the United States and the only one in California, the Mothers Milk Bank provides milk for special needs infants, including premature infants whose mothers cannot breast-feed. Donors are screened for HIV, HTLV, hepatitis B and C, rubella, TB, and syphilis. They pump their milk into provided freezer bags or sterilized glass bottles. Donors may deliver milk in a cooler to the bank or may arrange for pickup. If you have milk to spare and wish to be a donor, contact the bank at the above number.

San Ramon Regional Medical Center
The Breastfeeding Resource Center

6001 Norris Canyon Rd.
San Ramon
925-275-8459 (general information and appointments)
925-275-8447 (warm line)
www.sanramonmedctr.com

Certified lactation consultants offer education and support. The resource center also offers breastfeeding apparel and breast pumps for rental and sale.

Sutter Delta Medical Center

3901 Lonetree Way
Antioch
925-779-7230

This center has a single lactation consultant who leads a bimonthly breast feeding support group. Babies and second- and third-time moms are welcome! Ask for Kimberly Chilcote, RN, IBCLC, and childbirth educator.

South Bay

Breastfeeding Care Center

32 W. 25th Ave.
San Mateo
800-205-0333 (WIC breastfeeding telephone help line)

Sponsored by a federally funded program, this center offers lactation consultation by appointment and lends breast pumps to women eligible under the Supplemental Nutrition Program for Woman, Infants, and Children known as the WIC program. They also run a breastfeeding telephone helpline and offer all services in English and Spanish. Based in San Mateo, they also have sites in Daly City, South San Francisco, Redwood City, Palo Alto, and Half Moon Bay.

Community Hospital of Los Gatos

815 Pollard Rd.
Los Gatos
408-378-6131

PARENT RATING: ☆ ☆ ☆ ☆ ☆

This hospital offers a breastfeeding support group.

El Camino Hospital

Maternal Connections Lactation Center
La Casa Real
2400 Hospital Dr., Ste. 1B
Mountain View
650-988-8287

PARENT RATING: ☆ ☆ ☆ ☆ ☆

Staffed by IBCLC registered nurses, Maternal Connections is a full-service lactation center offering lactation consultations, sales and rentals of breast pumps and supplies, videos, books, other educational materials on breastfeeding, and nursing apparel. You need not have delivered your baby there to use their services. A drop in breastfeeding support group is also offered.

Good Samaritan of Santa Clara Valley

2425 Samaritan Dr.
San Jose
408-559-BABY

Good Samaritan's parenting and breastfeeding services offer over-the-phone advice and one-on-one consultations with board-certified lactation consultants. They also offer a breastfeeding support group.

Healthy Horizons Breastfeeding Center

720 Howard Ave.
Burlingame
650-579-2726 (appointments)
650-553-0115 (non-urgent breastfeeding question line)

This center offers private lactation consultations as well as rental and sales of breast pumps and nursing supplies for which home delivery is available. They have hospital contracts with Seton Hospital and Mills Peninsula and staff the latter's breastfeeding question line. They also host a free support group for new breastfeeding mothers.

Kaiser Redwood City Breastfeeding Center

610 Walnut St. (in the pediatric clinic)
Redwood City
650-299-2692
www.kaiserpermanente.org

The center offers a full range of post-partum breastfeeding support.

La Leche League

See under Entire Bay Area.

Menlo Park/Palo Alto chapter
650-365-2070

They offer evening meetings, especially for mothers employed outside of the home.

San Jose/Almaden chapter
408-323-1269

Santa Clara County chapter
408-264-0994

Sunnyvale chapter
408-749-1594

Best Places to Nurse and Change Baby when Out and About

When out with baby, it always helps to know where you might change his diaper, or where you might stop to nurse her. Here are some Bay Area parents' favorite spots:

◆ Nordstrom (Among mothers, Nordstrom is known for having a semi-private room for nursing and clean changing facilities in its women's lounge.)

◆ Baby and children's stores (The Right Start, Kids, Gymboree, as well as the larger baby gear retailers, have changing tables and have seen a nursing mother before!)

◆ Parent resource centers (Day One, Natural Resources, Bananas, Blossom Birth, Maternity of Marin, etc. are here to support new parents!)

◆ Coffee shops and bookstores, or any store that has chairs scattered about and don't mind people lingering, offer a place to sit and nurse, albeit not a private one.

Lucile Packard Children's Hospital
Stanford University Medical Center-Lactation Center
725 Welch Rd.
Palo Alto
650-725-8767
Phone consultations and one-on-one breastfeeding consultations are offered for mothers who delivered at Lucile Packard Children's Hospital. One mom recommended Melanie Ashworth, IBCLC. They also offer breast pump rentals.

Peninsula Medical Center (Mills-Peninsula Health Services)
1783 El Camino Real
Burlingame
650-696-5600 (The Wellness Center and Community Education)
650-553-0115 (non-urgent breastfeeding question line)
www.mills-peninsula.org
The Wellness Center and Community Education department offers a class on breastfeeding and the working mom. Mills Health Center (1000 S. San Mateo Dr., San Mateo) hosts the Nursing Mothers Council. This drop in breastfeeding support group meets weekly.

Nursing Mothers Council
See under San Francisco.
Santa Clara County
408-272-1448
San Mateo County
650-327-6455
Santa Cruz County
408-688-3954

O'Connor Hospital
2105 Forest Ave.
San Jose
408-947-2743

This hospital has a lactation consultant who offers private consultations. It also offers a weekly Nursing Mothers' Circle.

Palo Alto Medical Foundation
795 Camino Real
Palo Alto
650-967-8715
This group offers lactation consultations through Joanna Koch, IBCLC.

Other Resources for Breastfeeding

◆ www.breastfeeding.com

This website contains helpful breastfeeding information, support, humor, and links.

◆ www.breastfeedingbasics.com

This site offers answers to commonly asked questions about breastfeeding, as well as practical solutions to breastfeeding issues.

◆ www.aap.org/family/brstguid.htm

This website contains the book, *A Woman's Guide to Breastfeeding*, from the American Academy of Pediatrics.

◆ www.askdrsears.com

This website includes all you would ever want to know about breastfeeding, including about taking medications while nursing.

◆ www.babycenter.com

This parenting site includes a lot of helpful tips and information about breastfeeding.

◆ *The Complete Book of Breastfeeding,* by Marvin S. Eiger, MD

◆ *The Nursing Mother's Companion,* by Kathleen Huggins, RNMS

◆ *Nursing Mother, Working Mother,* by Gale Pryor

◆ *The Nursing Mother's Problem Solver,* by Claire Martin (editor), et. al.

◆ *The Breastfeeding Book,* by Martha Sears, RN, and William Sears, MD

◆ *The Ultimate Breastfeeding Book,* by Jack Newman and Teresa Pitman

Regional Medical Center of San Jose
225 N. Jackson Ave.
San Jose
408-259-5000
This center offers a breastfeeding clinic for postpartum mothers.

St. Louise Regional Hospital
9400 No Name Uno
Gilroy
408-848-8663
Call Jana Toma for details regarding breast pump rentals and a weekly breastfeeding support group.

Sequoia Hospital
The Lactation Education Center
702 Marshall St.
Redwood City
650-367-5597 (calm line)
www.chwbay.org/sequoia

Kay McNab offers lactation consultations by appointment and breast pump rentals and supplies, as well as personalized instruction of use of equipment. In addition, the above number is a calm line, where lactation educators are available by phone daily.

Seton Medical Center
The Breastfeeding Center
1900 Sullivan Ave.
Daly City
650-301-8885
www.chwbay.org/seton
The Breastfeeding Center is located on the third floor of the hospital, across from the nursery, and offers in-person consultations by appointment, breast pump rentals and sales, nursing bras, and pillows. Join other new moms and lactation educators at a free weekly breastfeeding support group.

Individual Lactation Consultants

San Francisco

Patti Neely, RN, CLE
415-296-7122

East Bay

Joanne Bergeson, RN, IBCLC
510-881-8269

Janaki Costello, IBCLC, ICCE
510-525-1155

Joan Gress, RN, IBCLC
510-654-8504

Miriam Levitt, IBCLC
510-849-1271

Sue Wirth, IBCLC
510-524-6917

Michelle Larager, RN, IBCLC
510-843-6497

South Bay

Marcie Bertram, IBLC
San Carlos
650-591-5447

Janice Curry, RN, IBCLC
San Jose
408-223-1134

Ellen Hamilton, MPH, CLE
650-322-2717

Sheila Janakos, MPH, IBCLC
650-579-2726

Carol Knight, MD, CM, CLE
650-725-8767

Joanna Koch, IBCLC
Los Altos
650-967-8715

Susan McCabe, IBCLC
San Mateo
650-991-6680 or 650-579-2726

Beverly Morgan, IBCLC, CLE
San Jose
408-629-6455

Laurie Schmiesing, RN, BSN, ICBLC
Mountain View
650-969-1017

Cora Williams, CLE
Half Moon Bay
650-740-0039

Resources for Dealing with Postpartum Depression

Postpartum depression (PPD) is a combination of symptoms that may occur any time during the first year following the birth of a baby. Symptoms in a new mother range from mild sadness or crying to a complete inability to care for herself or her baby. If you are a new mom and suspect that you are experiencing postpartum depression, contact your lactation consultant, obstetrician, pediatrician, or one of the many resources listed below. In addition, many medical centers in the Bay Area offer support groups for new parents, including groups that focus on postpartum depression. If you don't see your hospital listed here, call and ask whether they currently offer a support group. Also, for more information about postpartum depression, see *Beyond the Blues: Prenatal and Postpartum Depression—A Treatment Manual* by Dr. Shoshanna Bennett and Dr. Peck Indeman, two of the Bay Area's best known professionals in the field, see below. Remember, you are not alone, and PPD is very treatable.

San Francisco and North Bay

California Pacific Medical Center Newborn Connections
3698 California St., 1st Fl.
San Francisco
415-600-BABY (2229)

This center offers a free Postpartum Depression Support Group for postpartum women experiencing emotional challenges. They offer help, understanding, and coping skills to reduce anxiety and develop realistic expectations. Joanne Foote, who is a doctoral candidate in clinical psychology, facilitates the group.

Day One
See under "Baby Nurses and Postpartum Doulas"—San Francisco and North Bay.

Day One offers a weekly drop in support group called The Fourth Trimester, that focuses on the emotional adjustments and needs of parenting.

Elizabeth Greason, LCSW

1036 Sir Francis Drake Blvd.
Kentfield
415-454-2636

She runs PPD support groups and offers individual counseling. She specializes in working with women who are having difficulty adjusting to having a child.

Deborah Miller, RN and MFT Intern

3972 24th St.
San Francisco
415-364-3063

Deborah is an OB labor and delivery nurse who is currently a marriage and family therapist intern specializing in women's anxieties, including postpartum anxiety and depression. She offers one-on-one counseling and postpartum depression support groups that deal with the grief, anger, and confusion of postpartum depression and pregnancy loss in a supportive environment.

Galina Gorodetski, MD

San Francisco
415-563-8170

Dr. Gorodetski is a board-certified psychiatrist who offers one-on-one counseling for mothers dealing with postpartum depression.

East Bay

Elizabeth Gayner, Psy.D

2820 Adeline St.
Berkeley
510-390-3060

Elizabeth is a licensed clinical psychologist, offering a postpartum support group for mothers, as well as individual counseling.

Alisa Genovese, MFT

510-286-7599

Alisa is a marriage and family therapist who among other services, offers one-on-one counseling for mothers dealing with postpartum depression.

Birthways

See under "Baby Nurses and Postpartum Doulas"—East Bay.

A nonprofit, volunteer organization, Birthways offers a class entitled Prenatal and Postpartum Realities which addresses risk factors for pre- and postpartum depression and anxiety, warning signs, when to seek help, and steps to healing. Screening and resources are available.

Kaiser Richmond

901 Nevin Ave.
Richmond
510-307-2539

This hospital offers a postpartum support group to new mothers.

John Muir Medical Center

1601 Ygnacio Valley Rd.
Walnut Creek
510-889-6017
www.johnmuirmtdiablo.com

JMMC offers a free Perinatal and Postnatal Stress Support Group.

The Nurture Center

See under "Baby Nurses and Postpartum Doulas"—East Bay.

Dr. Shoshanna Bennett of PAM, see below, facilitates a bimonthly postpartum support group here. These groups give mothers an opportunity to share their challenges, be listened to, obtain support, and discuss coping mechanisms with other moms experiencing similar issues.

Dr. Shoshanna Bennett
Postpartum Assistance for Mothers (PAM)
Castro Valley
510-889-6017
One of the first Bay Area counselors to specialize in helping women with postpartum depression, psychotherapist Dr. Shoshanna Bennett founded Postpartum Assistance for Mothers (PAM) in 1987. PAM offers support groups where women can share experiences, coping techniques, and parenting anxieties in a safe environment in the East Bay, South Bay, and South San Francisco. Dr. Bennett also counsels clients individually, providing a concrete strategy for recovery. She makes home visits when necessary and offers telephone support for women all over the country. Dr. Bennett is also the president of the Postpartum Health Alliance, a statewide organization.

South Bay

Dr. Pec Indman, Ed.D., MFT
San Jose
408-252-5552
She runs support groups for PPD and offers individual counseling.

Dr. Anna Kieken, Ph.D.
885 Oak Grove Ave., Ste. 301
Menlo Park
650-322-7600
Based in Menlo Park, Dr. Kiekan is a clinical psychologist specializing in providing postpartum counseling and support for mothers with young children via support groups and individual and couples counseling. Her ongoing support group meets weekly and requires a 10-week commitment from participants.

Hotlines, Warm Lines and Stress Lines

Being a parent is an awesome responsibility—we all know that it comes with its share of challenges. When a new parent feels out of control, or needs a good listener and some reassurance, a hotline, warm line, or stress line can be of great assistance. It's nice to know that people are out there waiting to listen and wanting to help!

CRISIS LINES

Childhelp Hotline
800-4-A-CHILD
The focus of this hotline is the prevention and treatment of child abuse.

Child Abuse Reporting Hotline
415-558-2650

PARENTING AND CHILD DEVELOPMENT ADVICE, WARM LINES, AND HOTLINES

San Francisco

Parents Place
415-931-WARM (9276) 8:30 a.m.-5 p.m.
PARENT RATING: ☆ ☆ ☆ ☆ ☆

This is an advice line for parents with young children. Comments: "Great advice, great therapists."

TALK Line—Family Support Center
1757 Waller St.
415-441-KIDS (5437)
Located in the Haight, TALK Line is a nonprofit organization that offers Bay Area parents a place to talk about parenting challenges and other issues. They are best known for their twenty-four-hour hotline that provides parents with a trained volunteer to consult with in times of need. Drop ins are welcome. Counseling is priced on a sliding scale.

East Bay

Alameda County Child Protective Services
510-259-1800
This agency investigates reports of child abuse.

Children's Hospital Oakland Child Health Resource Line
800-400-PEDS

Bananas
522 Claremont Ave.
Oakland
510-658-6046
www.bananasinc.com
They provide advice for parents and child care providers.

Parental Stress Service
510-893-5444 (twenty-four-hour hotline in the East Bay)
This group offers supportive services to parents, caregivers, and children such as counseling and crisis intervention. They also offer referrals to Alameda County resources.

Bay Area Postpartum Hot Line
888-773-7090
This hotline is staffed seven days a week from 9 a.m.-9 p.m. by volunteers from The Northern California Chapter of the Postpartum Health Alliance. All volunteers are survivors of PPD, and some speak Spanish. Leave a message, and your call will be promptly returned.

South Bay

Contact Care
408-279-8228
They provide twenty-four-hour help and reassurance and provide crisis intervention to parents in Santa Clara County.

Family Stress Center
925-827-0212

Family Stress Service
650-368-6655 (Daly City to San Mateo)
650-692-6655 (Belmont to Menlo Park)
650-726-6655 (on the San Mateo coast)

Parent Information and Referral Center—Lucile Packard Children's Hospital at Stanford
650-498-KIDS (5437) or 800-690-2282
This center answers questions concerning your child's health, behavior, development, and safety. Hours are 7 a.m.-11 p.m.

Parent Support Sequoia Hospital
650-368-2229

Parents Helping Parents
408-727-5775

Meal Preparation and Delivery

Forget about cooking in those early weeks of parenthood and enlist a friend or family member to prepare some meals for you. Alternatively, the Bay Area has a tremendous number of reasonably-priced restaurants and services that offer take-out and meal delivery, as well as personal in-home chefs. Here are a few favorite meal preparation and delivery services of Bay Area parents:

Entire Bay Area

Jessie et Laurent (meal preparation and delivery)
415-485-1122 or 800-MEAL-TO-YOU
www.jessieetlaurent.com

Pickles on Request (meal preparation and delivery)
Belmont
650-610-0208
www.picklesonrequest.com

San Francisco and North Bay

Girlfriend's Kitchen (grocery shopping and in-house meal preparation)
510-681-3186 or 925-685-5341
www.girlfriendskitchen.com

Home on the Range (meal preparation and delivery)
510-251-8030

Jane Peal Cuisine (vegetarian meal preparation and delivery)
415-826-2133
www.pealcuisine.com
PARENT RATING: ☆ ☆ ☆ ☆ ☆

Mitchell and Gilbert (gourmet meal preparation and delivery)
415-831-3497
www.mitchellandgilbert.com

Room Service of Marin (meal preparation and delivery)
415-389-8871

Waiters on Wheels (restaurant meals delivery)
San Francisco
415-452-6600
www.waitersonwheels.com

East Bay

Girlfriend's Kitchen (grocery shopping and in-house meal preparation)
See under San Francisco and North Bay.

Home on the Range (meal preparation and delivery)
See under San Francisco and North Bay.

Best Interest at Heart
Mary Anne Simmons (meal preparation and delivery)
510-845-3161

Nancye Benson ("Ms. Dish") (in-home meal preparation, specializing in vegan and organic meals)
510-459-7480
www.nancye@msdish.com

Total Chef (meal preparation and delivery)
Sharon Katz
510-339-0503
totalchef@aol.com

Adrienne's Gourmet Cuisine (grocery shopping and out of or in-home meal preparation and delivery)
650-593-4003
www.theladychef.com

To Go! (restaurant meals delivery)
650-692-4200
www.mealstogo.com

Your Secret Ingredient (grocery shopping and in-home meal preparation)
650-322-5104

Waiters on Wheels (restaurant meals delivery)
See under San Francisco and North Bay.

Grocery Delivery

At the time that this book goes to press, we understand that Safeway now offers on-line grocery ordering and delivery at www.safeway.com, and that Albertson's is making its plans for on-line delivery as well. In addition, some grocery stores deliver for free, provided that you go to the store and do the shopping yourself. Other stores listed here will do your shopping as well as deliver for a fee.

Real Foods
2140 Polk St.
415-673-7420
They charge $5 for orders that are called in for delivery to surrounding neighborhoods.

Whole Foods
1765 California St.
415-674-0500
Whole Foods has an arrangement with a personal shopper and delivery service person (Chris, 415-933-9041) who, for $15.95, will do your leg work for you. He serves most of the San Francisco metro area and Walnut Creek. Another service also delivers from Whole Foods called Store to Door.

They offer same-day delivery if you call 800-529-5761 or fax your order to 972-774-0865. You may also e-mail your order at ISCOM@aol.com.

Marin Milkman
888-USE-MILK
PARENT RATING: ☆ ☆ ☆ ☆ ☆
They offer home delivery of organic milk and other dairy products.

Planet Organics
915 Cole St., Ste. 3172
415-522-0526
www.planetrorganics.com
PARENT RATING: ☆ ☆ ☆ ☆
Serving Marin and San Francisco, this organic produce and grocery service will deliver to your home your pick of organic delicacies,

217

including fruits and vegetables and other organic groceries such as cereal and peanut butter, weekly or biweekly. They offer a user-friendly custom-order form on their website.

The BOX (Bay Area Organic Express)

415-695-9688

www.organicbox.com

PARENT RATING: ☆ ☆ ☆ ☆ ☆

Have a box of fourteen to sixteen different organic veggies and fruits delivered to your doorstep every week or every other week! Delivery is available throughout most of the Bay Area from Los Gatos to San Rafael.

The Milkman

925-376-3385 or 800-464-6455

www.bayareamilkman.com

Serving most of the Bay Area, The Milkman offers home delivery of almost any dairy product (including yogurt, ice cream, and cheese) and a limited number of groceries. They also deliver fully cooked frozen meals such as lasagna, enchiladas, chili, macaroni and cheese, burritos, and chicken nuggets for kids. The Milkman's real specialty is a variety of gourmet soups that are made in small batches without preservatives, available in frozen 40 ounce pouches. Call for an order form and to arrange weekly delivery.

Cal-Mart

3585 California St.

415-751-3516

415-751-2744 (fax)

They deliver faxed orders received before 12 p.m. on Monday, Tuesday, Thursday, and Friday to surrounding neighborhoods. The fee is $10. Otherwise, do your own shopping before 2 p.m. and they'll deliver for free!

Diaper Services

The jury is still out as to whether cloth or disposable diapers are more environmentally friendly. Cloth diapers use energy and water to launder, while disposable diapers often go to a landfill. The costs are about the same. If you decide on cloth diapers, you'll probably want to hire a diaper service that will pick up soiled diapers and deliver freshly laundered ones to your door. Here are the major diaper services that the Bay Area has to offer:

San Francisco and South Bay

Tiny Tots

200 E. Campbell Ave.

Campbell

408-866-2900 or 800-794-5437

www.tinytots.com

PARENT RATING: ☆ ☆ ☆ ☆

For the most part, we've heard good things about Tiny Tots: "very convenient...helpful and knowledgeable staff...the newsletter is invaluable!" "Their delivery is always on time, and diaper counts are accurate." "Staff is friendly, capable, and very service oriented." "Their billing is efficient and a no-brainer." "Service is top-notch." "On the rare occasion of a mistake in the diaper count, they have overnight delivered the remaining diapers at no additional cost." Serving San Francisco and San Mateo County, Tiny Tots delivers and picks up diapers once a week. In addition to home delivery of diapers, they also have a store that sells diaper covers and accessories for the nursing mother. If you'd like a lesson in using cloth diapers, they'll send a representative to your home free of charge.

North Bay

Tidee Diddee

800-892-8080

PARENT RATING: ☆ ☆ ☆ ☆

Serving San Rafael, Novato, Corte Madera and Mill Valley, Tidee Diddee will deliver eighty diapers weekly and pick up dirty ones. They sell and rent diaper covers. There is a minimum four-week commitment.

East Bay

ABC Diaper Service

800-286-4222

PARENT RATING: ☆ ☆ ☆ ☆

We've heard mixed reviews about ABC: "ABC's prices compare favorably to other diaper services." "No complaints...very accommodating when we've called to change our order." "Problems with the diaper count and missing pickup days." Serving Alameda, Contra Costa, and Solano Counties, ABC will deliver eighty diapers weekly and pick up soiled ones. They sell diaper covers. There is a minimum four-week commitment.

On-line Disposable Diaper Delivery

If you chose to go with disposable diapers, youmay find it more convenient to order them on-line and have them sent to your door via the mail. To follow are a few websites that offer this service:

www.diapersite.com

www.drugstore.com

www.drugemporium.com

www.target.com

www.walmart.com

www.walgreens.com

CHAPTER 6

KEEPING YOUR SANITY:
Join a Parents' Group

Joining a group of new mothers or parents is probably one of the most beneficial things that a new parent can do for her or himself during the postpartum period. These groups are often the source of long-lasting bonds between parents, as well as play groups and strong friendships for their children. For example, if you are a new mom and ready to venture out of the house—any time from when your baby is a few weeks to a couple of months old—you'll enjoy getting out to share baby stories with other new mothers and gain advice from experts on how to care for your infant.

Besides companionship and empathy, such groups also offer exposure to a variety of parenting styles (to help define your own style), provide emotional support with the transition to parenthood, and serve as a source of advice on all sorts of parenting issues. Mothers' and parents' groups offer socialization for babies too. In short, there is much to be gained by connecting with other new parents and learning from one another's experiences.

There are numerous types of parents' groups to chose from, and in this chapter we will answer the following questions:
- What is a new parents' group or a "Mommy and Me" class and where can I go to join one?
- What are the benefits of joining a mothers' group and how can I find out about joining one?

- What are parenting classes and where do I go to take them?
- What kinds of special support groups exist for parents and how do I join one?

New Parents' Classes

Often the first type of group that new parents join with their babies, new parents' classes are most often offered by hospitals, parenting centers, or other professional facilitators. The atmosphere is casual— parents (mostly mothers) and babies sit in comfortable chairs or on mats on the floor, and a speaker or facilitator leads a discussion on a specific topic, such as sleeping through the night, breastfeeding, coping with depression, or adjusting to motherhood. It's a comfortable place to breastfeed or deal with a crying infant, as everyone there is in the same situation! These classes tend to focus on infants ages newborn up to eight or nine months, when the crawling and discovering stage makes it more challenging to bring your baby.

The hospitals and parenting resource centers listed below offer new mother and/or new parent classes and groups. If you don't see your hospital listed here, be sure to inquire there about a new parents' support group. Most of the hospital groups are free and open to all on a drop in basis, except where indicated. Some hospitals charge a nominal fee if you didn't deliver there. The groups run by parenting resource centers typically charge a fee for a series or by individual session.

San Francisco

California Pacific Medical Center (CPMC)
Newborn Connections
3698 California St.
415-600-BABY (2229)
www.cpmc.org
PARENT RATING: ☆ ☆ ☆ ☆ ☆

CPMC's pioneering perinatal center offers two support groups where new parents and babies interact with one another, with one group for parents with babies newborn to 8 months and another group for parents that focuses on the first 8 weeks of your newborn's life. The new parents' group covers topics including child-proofing your home, exercise for new mothers, how to properly install a car seat, infant massage, and the decision to return to work. The "first 8 weeks" group focuses on topics such as what to keep in your medicine cabinet, postpartum adjustments, partners as parents, and coping with a crying baby. Both groups meet one morning per week and are free if you delivered at CPMC. Comments: "The CPMC groups were all great, very helpful, and a tremendous source of information for new and struggling parents." "CPMC was a significant influence in who I became as a mom. A great place for encouragement and friendship—I met my best friend there!" "It is a great way to meet people and not feel like you are the only one out there going through all the things you're going through." "A great variety of topics." "A little on the crowded side at times, but still worth it."

California Pacific Medical Center The Community Health Resource Center

2100 Webster St.
415-923-3155
www.chrc.citysearch.com.

The CPMC Perinatal Center teams up with the Community Health Resource Center to present free monthly educational lectures for new and expectant parents. Topics include helping your baby sleep, nutrition before and after the baby, immunizations, caring for multiples, holistic parenting, and common illnesses in infancy. Lectures are often held at CPMC's California Campus (3700 California St.) in the cafeteria.

Calvery Presbyterian Church

2515 Fillmore St.
415-346-3832
This group of mothers, babies, and toddlers meets one morning a week.

Day One

3490 California St., 2nd Fl., Ste. 203
415-440-Day1 (3291)
PARENT RATING: ☆ ☆ ☆ ☆ ☆

Day One, a privately run center for new and expectant parents, is truly a unique resource in a very inviting atmosphere. Among their various parenting classes, they offer a New Moms' Group for moms and babies ages newborn to 12 weeks, a Movers and Shakers group for moms and babies ages 3 months and up, and Creepers and Crawlers for moms and babies ages 5 months and up. They also offer "The Fourth Trimester," which focuses on emotional postpartum adjustments. In addition they offer a breastfeeding support group, see chapter 5. There is a $7 fee for each session, or $25 prepaid for four sessions. Groups are usually facilitated by registered pediatric nurses with extensive experience in childbirth education, lactation support, and postpartum issues. Moms are encouraged to stay after the group's meeting to enjoy each other's company. Drop ins are welcome on a space available basis.

Kaiser Permanente San Francisco Medical Center

4131 Geary St., Ste. 435
415-883-4120
The center offers several postpartum support groups, including a positive parenting group that focuses on baby care and development through the first year.

Natural Resources

1307 Castro St.

415-550-2611

PARENT RATING: ☆ ☆ ☆ ☆ ☆

Many new mothers in the Noe Valley neighborhood couldn't imagine life without this community-based center that focuses on pregnancy, childbirth, and early parenting. This center is known to place some emphasis on natural and alternative methods of childbirth and childrearing, but offers a friendly welcome to all mothers, whether or not they opted for a natural childbirth! Natural Resources offers an ongoing drop in group for mothers and babies up to 6 months old to interact with other mothers and newborns and share their experiences of emotional and physical recovery after birth. Facilitated by Lucia Maya, a doula and mother; the fee is $50 for six sessions or $10 per session. This very popular mothers' group is known for spinning off play groups.

Parents Place

1700 Scott St.

415-359-2454

www.jfcs.org/index.html

PARENT RATING: ☆ ☆ ☆ ☆

Parents Place began as a mother-infant support group in 1975 and has grown into a nationally recognized full-service family resource center for families with children of all ages. Among a large offering of parents' resources including parent workshops, play groups, support groups, and child care resource and referral services, Parents Place offers a New Mother/New Baby Group. The group meets once a week for eight sessions, focusing on issues pertinent to new parents with infants up to 6 months old. The cost is $120 for the eight-week session, which is offered throughout the year. Pre-registration is required. Parents Place is a Jewish and Family Children's Services program and welcomes parents of all faiths. Comment: "May be the best parenting resource in town."

Parents' Support Network (PSN) of San Francisco

1546 Fulton St.

415-307-9526

Parents' Support Network is a sister organization of Mothers' Support network, a nine-year-old nonprofit organization based in Sacramento. Their purpose is to nurture parents in a manner that empowers, educates, and supports their needs to love and protect their children. They offer a quarterly publication, *Wellspring*, as well as lectures, workshops, networking, and community-building activities that support the parenting process. Membership fee is $25-50 (on a sliding scale). They also offer network community dialogues for parents of babies to share their experiences and questions with other parents in San Francisco. They meet at the Presidio Alliance Community center, located at Lombard St., the first building on the left inside the Lombard St. Gate. The drop in fee is $4 for members and $6 for nonmembers. Drop ins are welcome. Each session focuses on a different aspect of parenting and child development and is facilitated by Heather Lanier, mother of two and a Waldorf early childhood educator who also leads classes in parenting at the San Francisco Waldorf School.

Temple Emanu-El Building Blocks

2 Lake St.

415-751-2535

This popular Mommy and Me group is for mothers and babies 3-18 months old and is open to temple members and non-members. They meet one morning a week. Registration is required.

North Bay

Bug a Boo

14 Bolinas Ave.

Fairfax

415-457-2884

PARENT RATING: ☆ ☆ ☆ ☆

This children's store offers a New Mothers' Group that is facilitated by the executive director of the A.P.P.L.E. Family Center in San Rafael. The fee is $60 for a five-week session, or $15 drop in. The group draws mothers from San Anselmo, Fairfax, Woodacre, San Rafael, and West Marin. Mothers bring their infants and discuss issues relating to infants and first-time parents. Advance registration is recommended.

Center for Creative Parenting

Pacheco Plaza Shopping Center

446A Ignacio Blvd.

Novato

415-883-4442

www.creativeparenting.com

PARENT RATING: ☆ ☆ ☆ ☆

The Center for Creative Parenting offers several different early parenting education classes to chose from, including a weekly group for mothers with infants up to 3 months old, and another for mothers with infants ages 3-6 months. A nice way to get to know other mothers in Marin with babies of a similar age, these groups meet for four weeks, for one-and-a-half-hours each week. Discussion topics include child development, safety, nutrition, play, and child care. The groups allow ample time for questions and sharing information. Enrollment is limited to eight mother-baby couples. Each four-week session begins at the start of the month, and mothers are welcome to continue attending on a month-to-month basis for as long as they want. The cost is $44 for four weeks. Advance registration is recommended. Comments: "Good information, personal attention, and bonding with other new moms." "Great resource for the first six months!"

MOM (Maternity of Marin)

874 4th St.

San Rafael

415-457-4955

PARENT RATING: ☆ ☆ ☆

MOM offers two five-week support groups that focus on the many changes new mothers commonly experience. One group focuses on issues related to babies up to 6 months and the other group is geared toward mothers with babies ages 6 months to one year. Facilitated by a registered nurse and mother, discussion topics include adapting to parenthood—changing roles and sharing responsibilities, how to comfort a crying baby, sleeping and feeding schedules, infant health care, returning to work and child care options, breast and/or bottle feeding, and sexuality. The cost is $50 for five weeks. Advance registration is recommended.

Parents Place Marin
600 5th Ave.
San Rafael
415-491-7959
www.jfcs.org/index.html
Parent's Place offers a New Mother/New Baby series for new mothers with babies up to 6 months old, providing information, discussion, and support. Call in advance to register. See under "New Parents' Classes"—San Francisco.

Parents Place Sonoma
1360 N. Dutton Ave.
Santa Rosa
707-571-8131
www.jfcs.org/index.html
This parenting center offers a new Mother/New Baby group. Advanced registration is required. See under "New Parents' Classes"—San Francisco.

Pregnancy to Parenthood Family Center
555 N. Gate Dr.
San Rafael
415-456-6466
A program of Family Services Agency of Marin, this private non-profit parenting center specializes in providing counseling to parents with children under 3 years old. They also offer a Baby's First Year, Mother Support, and Therapy Group that focuses on the care of babies up to one year old, infant development, postpartum depression, nurturing oneself, play between mothers and

babies, developing a support system, and adjusting to parenthood. Fees are determined on a sliding scale. Drop ins are welcome.

St. Helena Hospital and Health Center
The Woman's Resource Center
650 Sanitarium Rd.
Deer Park
707-963-1912
At the time this book goes to press, St. Helena is reviving its new parent support group. The group will be meeting at The Woman's Resource Center, located at 1299 Pine St. in St. Helena. Call the Center for details.

East Bay

Alta Bates Medical Center Perinatal Center
5730 Telegraph Ave.
Berkeley
510-204-1507
www.altabates.com
PARENT RATING: ☆ ☆ ☆
Alta Bates offers a weekly New Mother/New Baby support group.

Birthways
478 Santa Clara Ave., 3rd Fl.
Berkeley
510-869-2797
www.birthways.com
This resource center for new and expectant mothers offers an ongoing drop in New Mom's Support Group for mothers and infants up to 6 months old. Issues include sleep, breastfeeding, returning to work, and relationships. Sessions are facilitated by Lucia Maya, a postpartum doula.

Birth and Bonding Family Center

1126 Solano Ave.

Albany

510-527-2121

www.birthbonding.org

This center offers a First Time Mothers and Babies Support Circle for new mothers of infants up to 5 months old. This ten-week series provides a caring and supportive setting to address the many changes commonly experienced by new mothers. Topics for baby care include bonding with baby, schedules, health care for babies, crying babies, the developmental process, child care, and nursing/bottle feeding. Topics for mother care include organizational skills, making time for yourself, body image, sexuality, relationship with your partner, and returning or not returning to work. Advance registration is recommended.

Hayward Adult School Parent Education

22100 Princeton St.

Hayward

510-293-8599

This center offers a class for new parents called Parenting the Infant. Advance registration is required.

John Muir Women's Health Center

1601 Ygnacio Valley Rd.

Walnut Creek

925-941-7901

cindy.tetzloff@jmmdhs.com.

PARENT RATING: ☆ ☆ ☆

The center offers a drop in new mothers' group facilitated by Cindy Tetzloff.

Kaiser Permanente

Hayward Medical Center

27400 Hesperian Blvd.

Hayward

510-784-4000 (ask for Health Ed)

www.haykaiser.org

This hospital offers a Baby and Me group for new mothers.

Richmond Medical Center

901 Nevin Ave.

Richmond

510-307-2539

This hospital offers a support group for moms and babies up to one year old.

Walnut Creek Medical Center

1425 S. Main St.

Walnut Creek

925-295-4484

Kaiser Walnut Creek's Mom/Baby Pump Station offers a New Mother/New Baby support group.

Krista Kell's Mothers' Groups

925-254-1844

PARENT RATING: ☆ ☆ ☆ ☆ ☆

Krista Kell, RN facilitates first-time mothers' groups primarily from the Contra Costa area. She offers a five-week class for $100 that focuses on issues pertaining to newborns and first-time mothers; the group itself largely selects the topics. She then helps the group continue to meet by forming play groups and organizing other activities. She prides herself on enabling new mothers to bond and form lasting friendships. Krista is a registered nurse and Assistant Dean of Women at St. Mary's College.

Noll Adult School

Parent Education
39600 Sundale Dr.
Fremont
510-651-9030
www.fasce.com/pe-general.htm

The school offers a class for parents of babies, ages 6-12 months. Parents receive support, encouragement, and training. Advance registration is required.

The Nurture Center

3399 Mt. Diablo Blvd.
Lafayette
925-283-1346
nurturecenter@earthlink.net

PARENT RATING: ☆ ☆ ☆ ☆ ☆

Started by two local moms, this parent resource center and store offers great parent education and support groups, including an ongoing new parent/baby support group where parents discuss topics of interest and network with other new parents. The group is facilitated by Beth Hammond, an experienced birth and postpartum doula. The fee is $9 a session, or four for $32. Drop ins are welcome. The Nurture Center also offers infant massage, postpartum stress support groups, a nursing moms' group, and a sibling preparation class. Their quarterly newsletter is free for East Bay residents. Comments: "There is nothing else like this for new parents in Contra Costa!" "A definite must!"

Sherry Reinhardt's Support Groups for Mothers

510-524-0821
www.supportgroupformothers.com

PARENT RATING: ☆ ☆ ☆ ☆ ☆

Coordinated and facilitated by Sherry Reinhardt, RN, MPH, MOM, Sherry has been organizing and facilitating mothers' groups for over twenty years and has helped launch over five hundred First-Time Groups, primarily from the Berkeley/Alameda area. First-Time Moms' Groups are constantly forming and are organized by geography and age of baby. She also organizes groups for second- and third-time mothers and is available for individual consultations. Comments: "It was a huge relief to hear that other first-time moms were experiencing the same struggles as I was and that our babies and husbands had similar habits!" "Sherry does a great job of creating a relaxed and inviting atmosphere that is conducive to deep bonding between the moms in her group."

Valleycare Medical Center

5555 W. Las Positas Blvd.
Pleasanton
925-847-3000
www.valleycare.com

The center offers a Thank God It's Wednesday support group for new mothers. It's open only to those who have delivered here.

Washington Hospital
Childbirth and Family Education Department

2000 Mowry Ave.
Fremont
510-791-3423
www.whhs.com

This hospital offers a weekly New Mother/New Baby support group.

Blossom Birth Services

1000 Elwell Ct.
Palo Alto
650-964-7380
www.blossombirth.com

This center offers myriad new parents groups and classes, including a mother-baby gathering and tea, where new mothers meet over tea and discuss changes in their relationship with their partners; interrupted sleep and how to cope; ways to nurture yourself; balancing work, home, and relationships, self and baby; and your role as a mother. Advance registration is recommended.

The Children's Health Council Parenting Education

650 Clark Way
Palo Alto
650-688-3608
www.chconline.org

This center offers a seven-session class entitled Your Young Baby for parents and babies up to 6 months old, as well as Parenting Older Babies, ages 7-14 months. This series includes mini-lectures and group discussions on bonding, baby's crying, sleep, feeding, play and stimulation, and health issues. Babies welcome! Pre-registration is required.

Community Hospital of Los Gatos

815 Pollard Rd.
Los Gatos
408-378-6131
www.tenethealth.com/losgatos

PARENT RATING: ☆ ☆ ☆ ☆ ☆

This hospital offers a weekly New Mother/New Baby support group.

El Camino Hospital Maternal Connections Lactation Center

2500 Grant Rd.
Mountain View
650-988-8287
www.elcaminohospital.org

The center offers several new mothers' support groups, based on babies' ages.

Good Samaritan Hospital of Santa Clara Valley

2425 Samaritan Dr.
San Jose
408-559-BABY (2229)
www.goodsamsj.org

This hospital offers a New Mother/ New Infant support group.

Kaiser Permanente Redwood City Medical Center Breastfeeding Center

600 Walnut St.
Redwood City
650-299-2692

This center offers a group for mothers and newborns, and a group for mothers with infants 5-9 months old.

Kaiser Permanente Santa Clara Medical Center Birth Center

900 Kiely Blvd.
Santa Clara
408-236-5699
www.kasiersantaclara.org

This center offers a Mommy and Me class for new mothers and their infants one morning a week.

Peninsula Hospital (Mills Peninsula Health Sysem)

1783 El Camino Real
Burlingame
650-696-5872
www.mills-peninsula.org

This hospital offers a new mother-infant support group.

Peninsula Parents Place

410 Sherman Ave.
Palo Alto
650-688-3040
www.jfcs.org/index.html

Peninsula Parents Place offers several new parents' classes. See under "New Parents' Classes"—San Francisco.

Santa Clara Adult Education

1840 Benton St.
Santa Clara
408-423-3500
www.scae.org/infant.htm

Offering a class entitled "Parenting the Infant, 0-12 Months," parents share the joys and challenges of the first few months and discuss health, nutrition, safety, sleep, and development. Babies included! Advance registration is required.

Sequoia Hospital District

170 Alameda de las Pulgas
Redwood City
650-368-BABY
www.chwbay.org/sequoia

They offer several new parents' groups, according to the babies' ages.

Stanford Medical Center Johnson Center for Pregnancy and Newborn Services Perinatal Education

211 Query Rd., Rm. NC
Hoover Pavilion
Stanford University
Palo Alto
650-723-4600
www.med.stanford.edu/lpch/johnsoncenter

PARENT RATING: ☆ ☆ ☆ ☆ ☆

This center offers a popular New Family Program series of classes and support groups that includes Mother-Baby Mornings, Father-Baby Evenings, and a Working Mothers' Group. The Mother-Baby Mornings are designed for mothers and newborns and are led by an experienced postpartum facilitator. Intended to take you through the first nine months of your baby's life, the group meets two mornings a week and is divided into two groups, depending on your baby's age, newborn to 5 months and 6-9 months. Activities include discussion and guest speakers, and the group is ongoing; you may join at anytime. The Father-Baby group meets once a month to discuss issues unique to being a parent or father and includes guest speakers. The Working Mothers' Group is an evening meeting once a month for mothers who work outside the home. Costs for the series are $150 for families of Stanford-delivered babies and $175 for other families. Advance registration is required.

Mothers' and Parents' Groups and Clubs

Mothers' and parents' groups or clubs often are organized by volunteer mothers and provide an opportunity to meet local parents with young children. These groups often offer monthly meetings for mothers, with speakers, play groups, special interest groups, family outings, mom's nights out, baby-sitting co-ops, monthly newsletters, and even meal deliveries to new mothers. Annual dues typically range from $25-75. Getting involved in one is also a nice way to participate in your community, as they often sponsor community service projects. Here are the ones that we heard about—be sure not to miss many of their great websites! Also, if you don't see a club listed that you are looking for, visit the website for the San Francisco Bay Area Association of Mothers' Clubs at www.geocities.com/sfbamc/.

San Francisco

Golden Gate Mothers' Group

415-789-7219
www.ggmg.org
PARENT RATING: ☆ ☆ ☆ ☆ ☆

With over three hundred members, GGMG is the largest organized mothers' group in San Francisco. Offering monthly newsletters, monthly meetings with speakers, mom's nights out, special events for toddlers and preschoolers, special family and holiday events, play groups, community outreach, and a meal delivery service for new mothers, GGMG has become a very popular group for mothers of children from infants through preschoolers. Comment: "A true support system of committed mothers and interesting women!"

Mothers and More

415-641-0416, Julia Pattinson
415-668-2440, Maren Lage
www.mothersandmore.com
PARENT RATING: ☆ ☆ ☆ ☆ ☆

Formerly FEMALE (Formerly Employed Mothers at the Leading Edge), this international nonprofit organization has several active local chapters, including San Francisco, Walnut Creek/East Bay, and the Silicon Valley. Geared specifically to women who have interrupted their careers to have children, Mothers and More has over 180 chapters and nearly eight thousand members worldwide. The group includes full-time mothers as well as those who work outside the home. Mothers and More dubs itself as "the network for sequencing women," borrowing a term coined by Arlene Rossen Cardozo's 1986 book, *Sequencing: Having It All But Not All At Once—A New Solution for Women Who Want Marriage, Career, and Family*. The group offers myriad activities, including monthly meetings, playgroups, and mom's nights out.

Noe Strolls
www.noestrolls@yahoo.com
San Francisco's play group on wheels, new moms and their babies and toddlers take stroller walks, jogs, trips to local museums, and much more at 1 p.m. the first Tuesday of every month. See chapter 2 under San Francisco walks for more information.

North Bay

Corte Madera and Larkspur Mothers' Club
415-451-7234

MOMS of San Rafael (Mothers Offering Mothers Support)
415-457-4955
www.momsclub.org (general information)
This is a local chapter of a national, non-profit group supporting the choice of at-home mothers to stay home to raise their children.

Novato Mother's Club
415-458-3203
www.novatomothersclub.com
PARENT RATING: ☆ ☆ ☆ ☆ ☆
Over two hundred members participate in this club's offerings, including weekly playgroups, children's outings, family events, guest speakers, and a monthly newsletter. Comments: "Excellent way to meet other mothers." "A great place to find a playgroup and get connected with other new moms." "I especially enjoy the hiking with moms and babies!"

Petaluma Mothers' Club
707-778-6494

Ross Valley Mothers' Club
415-721-4576
PARENT RATING: ☆ ☆ ☆ ☆ ☆
This very active club serves Greenbrae, Kentfield, Ross, San Anselmo, and surrounding areas.

San Rafael Mothers' Club
415-451-7355
www.srmoms.org
PARENT RATING: ☆ ☆ ☆ ☆ ☆
The club serves San Rafael, San Anselmo, Fairfax, Sleepy Hollow, Terra Linda, Santa Venetia, and Marinwood. Comments: "San Rafael Mothers' Club was a real lifesaver and continues to be the best source of support that I have!" "Very active and well organized."

Santa Rosa Mother's Club
707-525-5902
SRMothersClub@yahoo.com
(membership information)

Sonoma Valley Mothers' Club
707-996-9890
svmc@vo.com
Includes mothers in Sonoma Valley, Sonoma to Kenwood.

Southern Marin Mothers' Group

415-273-5366

www.southernmarin.com

PARENT RATING: ☆ ☆ ☆ ☆ ☆

Serves Sausalito, Marin City, Mill Valley, Tiburon, and Belvedere. Comment: "Excellent source of support!"

Spring Marin Moms

debspn@aol.com (membership information)

This group is for moms of children born in the spring of 1999.

East Bay

Amador Mothers' Club

925-927-2444 (membership and referral line for the Tri-Valley Mothers' Clubs)

www.amadormothersclub.com

Serves Dublin, Livermore, Pleasanton, and surrounding areas. The focus is on infants and children up to age 5. They offer many play groups, activities, outings, and parties that can provide a great social and support network.

Castro Valley Mothers' Club

510-475-6864 (membership and referral line for the East Bay Mothers' Clubs)

This group serves Castro Valley, Hayward, San Leandro, and surrounding areas.

Concord/Clayton Newcomers' Club

925-946-2539

This club offers family activities, including Mom or Dad and Tot mornings.

Contra Costa Mothers' Club

925-988-3383

www.homestead.com/ccmc

Serving the Central Contra Costa County communities of Antioch, Bay Point, Clayton, Concord, Martinez, Pacheco, Pittsburg, Pleasant Hill, and Walnut Creek, the Contra Costa Mothers' Club offers social and support opportunities for pregnant women and mothers of infants and children up to age 5, including moms-only meetings, play groups, family activities, outings, baby-sitting co-op, and newsletters. They welcome newcomers to general meetings.

East Bay Moms

510-653-7867

www.eastbaymoms.com

PARENT RATING: ☆ ☆ ☆ ☆ ☆

Based in the North Oakland area, focus is on outdoor activities with infants, toddlers, and preschoolers. Activities include scheduled hikes, stroller walks, a monthly Moms' Night Out, and a resourceful monthly newsletter. Comment: "I don't know what I would do without this incredibly active and well organized group of fun moms!"

East County Mothers' Club

925-988-3383

www.eastcountymothersclub.org (general information)

eastcountymoms@yahoo.com (membership information)

ECMC serves the East Contra Costa County communities of Bay Point, Pittsburg, Antioch, Oakley, Bethel Island, Knightsen, Brentwood, Byron, and Discovery Bay. ECMC is a non-profit organization of families with children up to age 5 offering play groups, outings, and baby-sitting co-ops. ECMC welcomes mothers who work outside the home full-time, those who work part-time, those with home-based businesses, and those who stay at home full-time.

Fremont, Union City, Newark (FUN) Mothers' Club
510-475-6864
www.funmothersclub.org
This club serves mothers of children up to pre-kindergarten-age in Fremont, Union City, and Newark. They organize activities for moms and kids, such as play groups, nights out, children's outings, and other social events.

Hayward Mothers' Club
510-475-6864
This club is for expectant mothers and mothers of children up to 6 years old, and includes mothers from Hayward and San Lorenzo.

Iron Horse Mothers' Club
925-927-2444 (membership and referral line for the Tri-Valley Mothers' Clubs)
www.ironhorsemothersclub.com (general information)
ironhorsemothersclub@yahoo.com (membership information)
PARENT RATING: ☆ ☆ ☆ ☆ ☆
This club serves Dublin, Danville, and San Ramon.

Lamorinda Mothers' Club
925-941-4714
www.lamorindamomsclub.org
PARENT RATING: ☆ ☆ ☆ ☆
This club serves Lafayette, Moraga, and Orinda. Comment: "Has many different special interest groups."

MOMS Clubs
See under North Bay.

Antioch/Oakley/Brentwood
925-776-7780
www.momsclubantiochca.home-stead.com (general information)
mommie2mommie@aol.com (membership information)

Discovery Bay
momsclubdb@aol.com (membership information)
dbmoms@jps.net (membership information)

Moms, Dads, and Munchkins
510-799-2044, Dean Becker
This group offers support/play groups for parents with infants and preschoolers in the West Contra Costa County area (Richmond, Hercules, and Pinole). Play groups meet at neighborhood parks and other venues.

MOPS (Mothers of Preschoolers)
925-283-3989, Jennifer Engstrom (membership information)
www.mops.org
MOPS is a nonprofit Christian organization that works with local churches in bringing together mothers and children, from babies to preschoolers.

Walnut Creek
925-934-1110, Hillside Covenant Church (general information)
925-935-1574, Walnut Creek Presbyterian Church (general information)
This organization has two groups for mothers of children up to 5 years old.

Alamo

925-820-9031, Creekside Community Church (general information)

Mothers and More

See under San Francisco. Locate local chapter leaders by visiting their website.

Mount Diablo Mothers' Club

925-927-2424 (membership information)

www.coincide.com/mdmc/ (general information)

This is a social and support group for expectant mothers and mothers with children under age 5 years. They serve Walnut Creek, Pleasant Hill, Concord, Clayton, and surrounding areas and welcome working mothers, at-home mothers, single, and adoptive mothers.

Neighborhood Parents' Network (NPN) (formerly Neighborhood Moms)

510-527-6667 (membership information)

www.parentsnet.org (general information)

PARENT RATING: ☆ ☆ ☆ ☆ ☆

This independent, all-volunteer organization provides an extensive offering of play groups, support groups to support and educate children and their parents about parenting and early childhood, and social activities. NPN has a membership of more than eight hundred families. Members receive a monthly newsletter containing parenting articles, a calendar of events and activities, support group and play group listings, baby-sitting, and classified ads. Definitely one of the best newsletters around! Comments: "An incredibly comprehensive parents' group with offerings of every kind." "Great website!"

Point Richmond Association of Moms (PRAM)

510-273-9959 (membership information)

www.pram.net (general information)

cyndi@vertigosoftware.com (membership information)

This association is a recently formed, volunteer-run organization for mothers in the Point Richmond, Marina Bay, and Brickyard Areas.

Pleasant Hill/Walnut Creek Mothers' Club

925-939-6466 (membership information)

www.mom4mom.org (general information)

4u2join@home.com (membership information)

This club is a network of parents and parents-to-be, encompassing all areas of the East Bay.

Pleasanton Mothers' Club

925-927-2444 (membership and referral line for the Tri-Valley Mothers' Clubs)

www.pleasantonmothersclub.homestead.com/PMC.html (general information)

PARENT RATING: ☆ ☆ ☆ ☆ ☆

This club offers many activities, outings, and events for mothers and their families in Pleasanton.

San Ramon Valley (Mothers' Club of)

925-927-2444 (membership and referral line for Tri-Valley Mothers' Clubs)

www.mcsrv.homestead.com/mcsr.html

PARENT RATING: ☆ ☆ ☆ ☆ ☆

This is a social and support group for mothers with infants and children up to 5 years old in Alamo, Danville, San Ramon, and surrounding areas.

South Bay

Burlingame Mothers' Club

650-635-6777 (membership information)

www.burlingamemothers.org (general information)

PARENT RATING: ☆ ☆ ☆ ☆ ☆

This club of three hundred members is for mothers with infants and children up to 5 years old. They offer speakers, play groups, a baby-sitting co-op, a newsletter, and outings.

Coastside Mothers' Club

650-728-5038, Kate Meyer (membership information)

www.armadillosoft.com/cmc (general information and membership)

Serving Half Moon Bay, El Granada, Moss Beach, and Montara, this 150-member club supports mothers of children not yet in school. Check their website for membership forms.

Daly City Mothers' Club

650-520-3420, Denise (membership information)

dalycitymoms@yahoo.com (membership information)

This club is for mothers from Daly City, San Francisco, and surrounding areas.

Foster City Mothers' Club

650-634-9767 (membership and general information)

www.fostercitymothersclub.org

Jewish Community Federation Womens' Alliance Mothers' Group

Palo Alto

650-494-8444

Las Madres Neighborhood Play Groups (LMNP)

650-390-9505 or 408-806-6437

www.lasmadres.org

Serving Santa Clara county, Las Madres is a large network of neighborhood play groups for children born in the same year, with special interest groups for adoptive, single, and older mothers, and those with three or more children. Begun in 1953, it's one of the Bay Area's oldest mothers' groups. Through LMNP, members find friendship, support, and new things to do, as well as an opportunity for their children to learn socialization skills.

MOPs (Mothers of Preschoolers)

See under East Bay.

San Jose

408-252-3700, West Gate Community Bible (general information)

Los Gatos

408-356-5126, Calvary Baptist Church (general information)

Mothers and More

www.mothersandmoresv.homestead.com (general information and membership)

The Silicon Valley chapter supports mothers south of Palo Alto to San Jose. Visit their website to locate local chapter leaders. See under San Francisco.

Mothers Offering Mothers Support (MOMS)

Pacifica/Coastside chapter

650-738-0717 Julie (membership information)

See under North Bay.

San Jose chapter

408-227-2157

www.bayareamoms.org

See under North Bay.

Sunnyvale chapter

(serving San Jose, Campbell, and Los Gatos)

www.dmflemming1@attbi.com

See under North Bay.

Palo Alto/Menlo Park Mothers' Club

650-306-8182

www.batnet.com/momsclub/

PARENT RATING: ☆ ☆ ☆ ☆ ☆

This club describes itself as the largest mothers' club on the peninsula, serving Palo Alto, Menlo Park, Los Altos, Mountain View, and Atherton. It provides a supportive community for mothers (and dads) and their young children. Most activities take place in the Palo Alto/Menlo Park area, but anyone on the Peninsula with a child under 5 is welcome to join.

Play groups and special interest groups include adoptive, over-40, single and working moms, and stay-at-home and working dads. They also offer a baby-sitting co-op and opportunities for community service.

Redwood City Mothers' Club

650-654-5244 (membership information)

www.rwcmc.org (general information that includes a membership form)

This club is for mothers of infants and children under the age of 5 years in Redwood City and surrounding areas.

San Bruno Mothers' Club

650-871-8096

www.geocities.com/sanbrunomoms

sanbrunomothersclub@aol.com

This club serves San Bruno, South San Francisco, Daly City, Millbrae, San Mateo, Pacifica, and Hillsborough.

San Carlos/Belmont Mothers' Club

650-654-0349

http://belmont.gov/orgs/mc

San Mateo Mothers' Club

650-286-3404

www.geocities.com/sanmateomothersclub/

For mothers of children up to 5 years old (and moms-to-be) in the San Mateo, Palo Alto, and Menlo Park areas.

South San Francisco Mothers' Club

650-615-0719, Maria Collins

How to Find or Start a Play Group

For babies and toddlers who aren't in day care or preschool yet, a play group is a great way for them to learn socialization skills and have fun. It's also a great way for new parents to network, share parenting stories, and form great friendships! Almost all of the mothers' clubs listed above offer play groups for many different ages of children. However, you can also start your own play group with the following tips:

◆ Decide who you'd like to invite to join the play group. You can meet new moms at parks and playgrounds, new parenting classes, and other activities for moms and babies or toddlers. You can also distribute flyers at your pediatrician's office, the library, church, or other places frequented by parents of young children.

◆ Decide the age of the children you want in the play group. Children should be roughly the same age—especially when they are babies—we suggest within a 3-4-month span of each other.

◆ Decide whether you want a children's play group, a mother's group, or a combination. Some groups work as a baby-sitting co-op, where a few moms leave their children with other moms and have some time off, and then swap duties. Other groups gather with both parents and children so moms have a regular meeting time to socialize with their babies and one another.

◆ Consider the size of your play group—anything over ten can be overwhelming, especially if you meet inside one another's homes when the weather isn't nice. For toddlers, a smaller group is even better; once they start walking, it's a different kind of a play group!

◆ Choose a day and time that works best for everyone in the play group. Keep in mind that young children are most active in the morning, before they need a nap. Most play groups meet once a week, but sometimes meet more frequently.

◆ Have an initial organizational meeting, where you decide on scheduling and share names, addresses, phone numbers, and e-mails.

◆ Select a coordinator or leader for your play group. This person will coordinate requests, such as the need to change the time based on nap schedules or preschool.

♦ We suggest rotating your meeting venues, giving each mom a chance to organize or host the play group. The parent who is responsible for that week decides where to meet and makes reminder calls or e-mails.

♦ Keep things interesting by planning outings appropriate for the season, such as a trip to a pumpkin patch, a visit to Santa at the mall, a Valentine's Day party where older toddlers can help make valentines with their moms, and other holiday events and crafts.

Other Groups

In addition to mothers' groups, there are many other groups for parents with babies and young children. These groups focus on a particular aspect or way of parenting:

ATTACHMENT PARENTING

Attachment Parenting International
- San Francisco
  415-820-9666
  www.attachmentparenting.org
  (general information)
- Concord/Walnut Creek
  www.babyknowsbest.com
- Peninsula
  easearles@prodigy.net

This group provides emotional, educational, and practical support to parents who practice or wish to learn about attachment parenting, which includes "wearing" your baby, breastfeeding, and co-sleeping.

SECOND- AND THIRD-TIME MOMS' GROUPS

North Bay

Support Group for Moms with Two or More Babies
Center for Creative Parenting
See under "New Parents Classes"—North Bay.

This group is for second- and third-time mothers who are adjusting to balancing the demands of a newborn with other children.

East Bay

Moms with Three or More Children
510-526-7999, Ellen

This group meets one evening a month to share their joys and challenges as mothers of larger families. Infants are welcome.

The Parenting Center
Berkeley-Richmond Jewish Community Center
1414 Walnut St.
Berkeley
510-704-7475

The JCC offers a Mothers with Older Children and New Baby support group.

PARENTS OF MULTIPLES' GROUPS

San Francisco

San Francisco Mothers of Twins
415-440-TWIN
www.nomotc.org
(general information)
www.members.aol.com/sfmotc/
(San Francisco chapter)
SFMOTC@aol.com
(membership inquiries)

PARENT RATING: ☆ ☆ ☆ ☆ ☆

This group offers support and encouragement to mothers of multiples through monthly meetings, a monthly newsletter, semimonthly new moms' group support meetings, play dates, garage sales, social events, and membership in the National Mothers of Twins' Club. Comment: "This group is great for meeting people who are coping with similar issues, particularly during those trying early months."

North Bay

Marin Mothers of Multiples
415-460-9049
Providing educational and emotional support, MMOM is for all expecting moms and moms of multiples. Monthly meetings include support groups for each stage of multiples' development as well as speakers on pertinent issues. Membership also includes a monthly newsletter, a big sister program that teams new moms with experienced ones, moms' nights out, community outreach, and annual holiday parties.

Redwood Empire Parents of Multiples Santa Rosa
twins2tnt@aol.com

Sonoma County Mothers of Multiples
P.O. Box 9459
Santa Rosa
www.sonic.net/alp/
Alp@sonic.net (membership inquiries)
This group meets monthly for a new mom discussion and general meeting.

East Bay

Alameda Parents of Twins
510-522-0821

Contra Costa Mothers of Multiples
925-431-8355

Diablo Valley Mothers of Multiples
800-676-6010

East Bay Mothers of Twins' Club
510-278-6209

Tri-City Mothers of Multiples
510-888-4444
www.tricitymoms.homestead.com
This group serves Fremont, Union City, and Newark.

Triplet Connection
P.O. Box 99571
Stockton
209-474-0885
www.tripletconnection.org
This is the headquarters of this international group that offers support and information, including a medical database, newsletter, and referrals for expectant parents and parents of triplets, quadruplets, and quintuplets. They do not officially sponsor local support groups.

Twins By the Bay
510-655-4139
This group meets monthly at Alta Bates Hospital in Berkeley.

Twin Valley Mothers of Twins' Club
925-948-0004
www.homestead.com/twinsbythe
bay/index.html
twinsbythebay@yahoo.com
This group serves Pleasanton.

Coastside Mothers of Twins' Club

www.cmotc.homestead.com/
cmotc.html
Jmcca54324@aol.com, Julie McCarron
(membership information)

This club serves Pacifica, Millbrae, San Mateo, Foster City, and Burlingame.

Gemini Crickets Parents of Multiples

408-536-0811
webmaster@geminicrickets.org
(membership inquiries)

This group serves San Jose and the Silicon Valley.

Mid-Peninsula Parents of Multiples

650-599-2022
www.mppm.org

Redwood Empire Parents of Multiples' Club

twins2tnt@aol.com

Santa Clara County Mothers of Twins

www.sccmotc.com (general information and membership)

GAY PARENTS' GROUPS

Non-birth Moms' Group

510-528-3481

This group is for non-birth moms of lesbian couples.

Our Family, The Bay Area Gay & Lesbian Family Group

P.O. Box 13505
Berkeley
415-681-1960 or 415-865-5615
www.ourfamily.org

This group includes more than two hundred families throughout the Bay Area. They plan social and educational events each month where families can enjoy potlucks at the beach, visit museums, parks, and the zoo. Every two months, members who want to help plan events meet and schedule upcoming events. Offering a bimonthly newsletter, a weekly e-mail update, and a website listing many family resources, this group's goal is to create a more positive and nurturing world for gay and lesbian families.

DADS' GROUPS

San Francisco

California Pacific Medical Center

See under "New Parents' Classes"—San Francisco.

CPMC offers an eight-week structured new father support group for fathers with infants up to 2 years old. The group focuses on such topics as parenting skills, the relationship with his partner, time management, and activities for children.

Day One

See under "New Parents' Classes"—San Francisco.

This new and top-notch center for new and expectant parents offers The Dad's Forum twice a month. This is an hour-long session for dad and baby to learn together while getting to know some of the dads in the neighborhood.

Parents Place

See under "New Parents' Classes"—San Francisco.
www.jfcs.org/ppl/sfinfantclass.html

Dads meet monthly with other dads at the Dads' Connection and discuss the role of the father, life-style changes, and the joys and challenges of fatherhood.

North Bay

The California Parenting Institute

3650 Standish Ave.
Santa Rosa
707-585-6108, Bill Haigwood

The Dads' Connection is a free forum where low-income fathers of all ages can meet to discuss their role as parents. Recent topics included the legal rights and responsibilities of fathers under California family law, the rewards of raising a child with a partner or ex-partner, and finding where work fits in family life. Dads' Connection sessions are scheduled about every four to six weeks on a weeknight.

Parents Place Marin

See under "New Parents' Classes"—North Bay.

Fathers meet with other fathers of infants and children up to 6 years old to discuss parental aspirations, issues of co-parenting, doing things the same or differently from their fathers, and balancing the demands of home and career.

East Bay

At-Home Dads' Group

510-524-3724, Richard Thomason

This group of at-home dads meets Monday mornings with their kids either in Berkeley or Oakland. Depending on the weather, they hike, have a play group, or go on some other kind of outing.

Boot Camp for New Dads

drlinton@best.com

Bruce Linton offers support groups and workshops for new fathers in the East Bay.

East Bay Fathers' Walking Group

510-524-3724, Richard Thomas (general information)
hgoldstein@winstar.com
510- 530-8334, Ryna Young (general information)
bredt19-2@idt.net

New Dads' Support Groups

925-930-9350

Marti Sochet organizes support groups for new dads in the East Bay.

South Bay

The Children's Health Council

See under "New Parents' Classes"—South Bay.

This group offers a Breakfast Club for Dads where dads drop in to meet other dads and talk about their children. A parent educator is on hand to answer questions and facilitate discussion. Different age groups are addressed each week. CHC also offers a Book Club for Dads, where a child development book is selected for reading and dads meet on five consecutive Fridays to discuss it.

Peninsula Parents Place

See under "New Parents Classes"—South Bay.

Peninsula Parents Place offers a group for dads and their babies up to one year old.

Stanford Medical Center
Johnson Center for Pregnancy
and Newborn Services
Perinatal Education

See under "New Parents' Classes"—
South Bay.

STAYING-AT-HOME OR WORK ISSUES

Career Transitions Group

510-547-3704, Janet Keller (general information)
atcallbackcom@earthlink.net

If you are contemplating a return to work or considering a career transition, you may want to join this group for support, brainstorming, and encouragement.

Parents Place
Balancing Work and Family

See under "New Parents' Classes"—
San Francisco.

This workshop for mothers addresses topics such as going back to work, balancing career and family, and child care.

Center for Creative Parenting
Working Moms' Support Group

See under "New Parents' Classes"—
North Bay.

This ongoing group explores the challenges of balancing home, work, and relationships.

Stanford Medical Center
Johnson Center for Pregnancy
and Newborn Services
Perinatal Education
Working Mothers' Group

See under "New Parents' Classes"—
South Bay.

ETHNIC AND INTERNATIONAL GROUPS

African-American Moms' Support Group

510-382-9162, Alai Toure

This group of supportive women shares food and ideas on marriage, family, careers, education, and more with other African-American moms from all over the Bay Area. Children are welcome.

Our Colors

510-655-8264, Nadine
whatareyou2000@ivillage.com

This group is an interracial family forum for parents who are raising biracial, multicultural, transracial, or intercultural children.

Parliamo Italiano!

510-262-0629 (before 7 p.m.)
ios_lrh@yahoo.com

This Italian conversation group meets once a week at a private home that is a five-minute walk from the North Berkeley BART station. Children are welcome.

Swiss Families

510-601-5512, Andrea

Swiss Families gets together socially once or twice a month with the goals of teaching their children the German language and introducing them to Swiss culture. Children are welcome.

SPECIAL NEEDS SUPPORT GROUPS

The Bay Area offers several discussion and support groups for parents with special needs, including those related to issues of adoption, premature infants, and babies with disabilities. See chapter 1 for more references.

Alta Bates Parent Share Group

Redwood City

925-935-9240, Linda Cole

This free support group is for parents of premature or sick babies.

Autism Society Support Groups

* Livermore
  Louise Glueck, 925-373-6468,
* Pleasant Hill/Walnut Creek
  Vicky Smith, 925-930-7639

These groups welcome families of children with autism, Pervasive Developmental Disorder (PDD), or Asperger's Syndrome.

Down Syndrome Connection

117A Town and Country Dr.

Danville

925-362-8660, Martha Hogan (general information)

This organization offers support groups, workshops, and more for families with Down Syndrome children.

Early Start Program

415-546-9222

www.cahwnet.gov/earlystart/main/ESHome.cfm

This is a nationally and state-supported program for families of young children (newborn to age 3) with, or at risk of, developmental delay. Among other services, they offer a multitude of support groups through their Family Resource Centers located in each county.

The Family Resource Network

5232 Claremont Ave.

Oakland

510-547-7322

Staffed by parents of children with disabilities, this group provides support and resources to families of children with special needs. Services include a resource library, a quarterly newsletter, and support groups including A Father's Perspective: Part of the Team, a group for dads of kids with special needs.

Non-verbal Learning Disorders Support Group

831-624-3542 (hotline)

www.NLDline.com

This nonprofit volunteer organization provides support to parents of children with nonverbal learning disorders and other neurocognitive and neurobiological disorders. It offers monthly support groups, newsletters, a resource library, and parenting classes.

Parents Helping Parents

- Hayward
677 Paradise Blvd., 510-276-9479
- San Francisco
594 Monterey Blvd., 415-841-8820

A parent-directed family resource center for children with special needs, this group sponsors workshops, parent support groups, a quarterly newsletter, and does referrals.

Parents of Kids with Special Needs

Epworth United Methodist Church
1953 Hopkins St.
Berkeley
510-524-2921

This group is for parents of children with special medical and/or developmental and educational needs. Parents only.

Support for Families of Children with Disabilities

415-469-4518 (resource line)
- San Francisco
2601 Mission St., Ste. 804 (headquarters)
415-282-7494, Audrey de Chadenedes (general information)
- San Francisco
300 Seneca Ave. (family resource center)

This parent-run organization provides support groups and emotional support to families of children with disabilities.

Through the Looking Glass

2198 6th St., #100
Berkeley
510-848-1112, ext. 107
www.lookingglass.org

This national organization provides services for parents with disabilities, including free, in-home occupational therapy and adaptive baby care equipment.

SUPPORT GROUPS FOR GRIEVING PARENTS

Helping After Neonatal Death (HAND)
HAND of the Peninsula

- San Mateo
650-367-6993
- Santa Cruz
650-367-6993
- Santa Clara County
408-995-6102

24-Hour Telephone Crisis Line (staffed by the Family Stress Service of San Mateo)
650-692-6655, Daly City to San Mateo
650-368-6655, Belmont to Menlo Park
650-726-6655, San Mateo Coast
www.handsupport.org (general information)
www.h-a-n-d.org (resources and support groups)

HAND is a volunteer group of parents who have experienced the loss of a baby before, during, or after birth. HAND originated in Marin

County in 1979. Their experience inspired a desire to offer support to parents, their relatives, and friends during the normal mourning following miscarriage, genetic abortion, stillbirth, or newborn death of their babies. HAND volunteers are not professional psychotherapists. However, they may make referrals to professional counselors. They offer support groups for grieving parents and family members and 24-hour telephone crisis support. Their website includes a lot of helpful information, including several books and links on pregnancy and infant loss.

John Muir Women's Health Center

See under "New Parents' Classes"—East Bay.

The center offers a miscarriage support group, perinatal grief support group, and perinatal and postpartum stress support groups.

www.penparents.org

This is a network of grieving parents who have experienced pregnancy loss or the death of a child. It provides an opportunity for bereaved parents to connect with one another and discuss their loss.

Support After Neonatal Death (SAND)

- San Francisco
  415-282-7330
- East Bay
  510-204-1571 (Alta Bates Hospital)

SAND is a support group for parents who have lost a baby through miscarriage, stillbirth, or during or after birth.

ADOPTION SUPPORT RESOURCES

See chapter 1 for additional resources.

SINGLE PARENTS' GROUPS

San Francisco and North Bay

A.P.P.L.E. FamilyWorks

(Advancing Principles & Practices for Life Enrichment)
4 Joseph Ct.
San Rafael
415-492-0720
www.familyworks.org/parent.html

This organization offers a Single Parents' Support Group. Sessions run six evenings with separate child activities available in an adjacent classroom.

Bay Area Children First

415-751-1086

This nonprofit offers counseling services to parents, including focusing on issues pertinent to the single parent.

Parents Without Partners of San Francisco and San Mateo County

415-905-4145

All single parents are invited to attend general meetings on the first and third Sunday of each month; child care is available.

Parents Place San Francisco Single Mothers' Support Group

See under "New Parents' Classes"—San Francisco.

This is a support group for pregnant single women and single mothers of children up to 6 years old. Advance registration is required.

Parents Place Marin
Single Mothers' Group

See under "New Parents' Classes"—North Bay.

This support group is for single mothers, pregnant single women, single mothers by choice, single adoptive mothers, or mothers ending a relationship. Advance registration is required.

East Bay

Neighborhood Parents Network
(formerly Neighborhood Moms)

510-527-MOMS
www.parentsnet.org

This is an extensive parents' organization with several special interest support groups, including one for single mothers.

Parents Without Partners

www.parentswithoutpartners.org

This national organization for single parents of any age offers orientations in the Alameda/Oakland area twice a month.

Single Mothers by Choice

510-428-2631, Beverly Kraut
www.singlemothers.org

This is the Bay Area chapter of the national organization.

Single Parent Support Group

510-483-6715

This group is sponsored by the San Leandro Unified School District and Family Service Counseling Center. Free child care is provided.

Single Parents' Support Group

510-528-2797, Ellen Freed
ebfreed@aol.com

This group includes both single moms and dads whose main interest is having fun and offering support to one another. Children's ages range from infants to pre-teens. They meet for social outings every two weeks. Children are welcome.

Support Group for Single Parents

925-855-1745, ext. 2, Liz Hannigan (general information)
925-258-9759 , Milton Kalish (general information)

Drop ins are welcome. Free child care is provided. They also offer a children's support group for ages 3-7.

South Bay

Peninsula Parents Place

410 Sherman Ave.
Palo Alto
650-688-3040

This parenting center offers a support group for single parents.

Single Parent Services
Family and Childrens' Services

375 Cambridge Ave.
Palo Alto
650-326-6576

This center offers a support group for single parents, including both men and women.

RESOURCES FOR STEPFAMILIES

Bananas
East Bay Stepfamilies

5232 Claremont Ave.
Oakland
510-653-6344

This stepfamily drop in support group meets once a month to share experiences and helpful information.

Contra Costa Stepfamilies
Lafayette-Orinda Presbyterian Church
49 Knox Dr.
Lafayette
925-254-6211

RESOURCES FOR DIVORCING FAMILIES

A.P.P.L.E. FamilyWorks

See under Single Parents' Groups—San Francisco and North Bay.

This organization offers Parenting Apart classes that includes a free workshop on Divorce Realities, a Single Parents Support Group, Consider the Children seminar, and a Just for Kids group that focuses on support for children whose parents are divorcing.

Bay Area Children First

340 Spruce St.
San Francisco
415-751-1086 or 415-643-4863
They offer support groups for divorcing parents who are interested in creating a healthy coparenting plan and relationship.

Kaiser Permanente Oakland Psychiatric Department Kids Divorce Support Group

3900 Broadway
Oakland
510-752-1000
Dr. Mary Haake leads this group, which is a safe place for young children to discuss with their peers the weighty issues of divorce. Groups are divided by age.

Kids Turn

1242 Market St., 4th Fl.
San Francisco
415-437-0700 or 510-835-8445
www.kidsturn.org
PARENT RATING: ☆ ☆ ☆ ☆ ☆

Kids' Turn is a nonprofit organization that helps children and parents through divorce. Parents think that their six-week workshops (meeting once per week) are very helpful. Kids and parents attend different workshops that meet simultaneously, with the kids' groups divided by age, the youngest group being 4 years old. There is also a special workshop for parents of children under 3.

Lafayette Orinda Presbyterian Church (LOPC)

49 Knox Dr.
Lafayette
925-299-0924
PARENT RATING: ☆ ☆ ☆ ☆ ☆

Parents rave about LOPC support groups, especially the Transition Group, led by Milton Kalish, LCSW, for people dealing with some aspect of divorce. LOPC also offers a group for children of divorce. No religious affiliation is required.

Parents Place of Marin Beyond Divorce

See under "New Parents' Classes"—North Bay.

Move beyond the pain of divorce with the help of this ongoing support group. Discussion topics include loss and grief, building support systems, parenting yourself and your children, and moving on with your life. Advance registration is required.

Touchstone Counseling Services
140 Mayahew Dr.
Pleasant Hill
925-932-0150

This service offers support groups for divorced parents and children of divorced parents.

PARENTING EDUCATION

As your baby grows (and you both outgrow new parents' groups), you may want to take a few parenting classes. We are fortunate in the Bay Area to have a plethora of resources to choose among in this regard. They cover everything from parenting the toddler, to dealing with discipline, managing anger, toilet training, and preparing your child for a sibling. Here is a sampling of parenting education programs offered locally:

San Francisco

California Pacific Medical Center Community Health Resource Center

See under "New Parents' Classes"—San Francisco.

CPMC and the Community Health Resource Center jointly offer free parenting classes for parents of young children, including monthly lectures for new parents co-hosted by CPMC's Perinatal Lactation Program. Topics have included choosing a pediatrician, finding parenting advice on the Internet, stimulating your infant, and nutrition while breastfeeding. CPMC also offers occasional lectures on toddler topics.

City College of San Francisco Parent Education Program
1860 Hayes St., Rm. 139
415-561-1920

This program offers infant development classes relating to children up to 5 years old.

Day One

See under "New Parents' Classes"—San Francisco.

This full-service, privately run center for new and expectant parents offers a unique selection of parenting classes and workshops, focusing on topics such as The Art and Science of Child's Play, Signing with Baby, Financial Planning for Children, and Choosing Childcare.

Parents Place

See under "New Parents' Classes"—
San Francisco.

This center offers a large range of
parenting classes and workshops,
including How to Take Care of Your
Newborn, Raising Boys, Your One-
Year-Old, Toilet Training, and
Discipline Issues. Most are held in
the evening with a nominal fee.

San Francisco Waldorf School

2938 Washington St.
415-931-2750
www.sfwaldorf.org

This school offers The Parent-Infant
and Parent-Toddler Program for
expectant parents and parents of
children up to 3 years old to explore
the healthy physical and emotional
unfolding of the very young child.

North Bay

A.P.P.L.E. FamilyWorks

See under Single Parents' Groups—
San Francisco and North Bay.

They offer workshops and services
that focus on confident parenting,
parenting a spirited child, and dealing with other temperament issues.

California Parenting Institute

See under Dad's Groups.

This parenting center offers classes
that focus on parenting infants and
older babies. They also offer video-
taping services, where they tape you
and your baby playing and provide
insight and advice on your parenting
style.

Center for Creative Parenting

See under "New Parents' Classes"—
North Bay.

This center offers several parenting
classes, including healthy eating for
babies, toilet training, and discipline
and temperament issues.

Parents Place Marin

See under "New Parents' Classes"—
North Bay.

Parents Place Sonoma

See under "New Parents' Classes"—
North Bay.

East Bay

Bananas

See under Resources for Step
Families.

Bananas offers many different free
parenting workshops, from Living
with Ones and Twos, to Raising a
Spirited Child. Child care is available
at some workshops.

Birthways

See under "New Parents' Classes"—
East Bay.

They offer a class called "As the
Twig is Bent—the Path to Successful
Childrearing."

Child and Family Forum

510-528-0200

This center offers parent training on
a preventive approach to problems in
early and middle childhood.

Family Stress Center

2086 Commerce Ave.
Concord
925-827-0212
This center offers parenting education and counseling.

Habitot Children's Museum

2065 Kittredge St.
Berkeley
510-647-1112
The museum offers parenting classes and workshops given by professionals. Topics include sleeping and eating, choosing a preschool, positive parenting, terrific twos, discipline, fostering artistic development, and child safety. Class fees are determined on a sliding scale. Free child care is available for parents attending classes, if registered in advance.

Hayward Adult School

22100 Princeton St.
Hayward
510-293-8595
Hayward Adult School offers parent education classes.

Noll Adult School

See under "New Parents' Classes"—East Bay.
Run by the Fremont Unified School District, the Noll Adult School offers several classes for parents of babies and toddlers that are organized according to your child's age from newborn up to 5 years old.

Tri-City Health Center

39500 Liberty St.
Fremont
510-770-8133, ext. 129
This center offers free parenting classes that focus on children under 6.

South Bay

Fremont Union High School Adult Education

589 W. Fremont Ave.
Sunnyvale/Cupertino
408-522-2710

Palo Alto Medical Clinic, Education Department

795 El Camino Real
Palo Alto
650-853-2960
This clinic offers parenting classes and support groups.

Parents Leadership Institute

P.O. Box 50492
Palo Alto
650-322-5323
www.parentleaders.org

Peninsula Parents Place

See under Single Parents' Groups.
This parenting center offers a vast array of parenting classes on topics ranging from helping children with aggression to toilet training.

Santa Clara Unified School District Adult Education

1840 Benton St.
Santa Clara
408-423-3500
www.scae.org/infant.htm
This organization offers classes for parenting babies and toddlers.

Sequoia District Adult School

3247 Middlefield Rd.
Menlo Park
650-306-8866
www.adultschool.seq.org

The Children's Health Council

See under "New Parents' Classes"—South Bay.

Serving the developmental needs of families and children for more than fifty years, the CHC was founded in 1953 by Dr. Esther Clark, Palo Alto's first pediatrician. They offer a wide variety of parenting classes and services.

YWCA

275 S. 3rd St.
San Jose
408-295-4011

The YWCA offers a three-evening class series on parenting the young child, ages one to 5 years. They focus on encouraging cooperation and good parent-child relationships, including reducing tantrums, stress, and conflicts. They also offer classes on developing parenting skills for single and divorced parents, lesbian and gay parents, and parenting the child with challenging behavior.

PARENTING E-MAIL DISCUSSION GROUPS

The Virtual Village

www.virtualvillage@parentsnet.org

This e-mail discussion group is for Neighborhood Parents Network (NPN) members (an East Bay based parents' group), with nearly 400 members participating in this valuable information exchange. Members receive mail once a week, including requests for information or advice, baby-sitting, and announcements.

UCB Parents Network Mailing

List-parents@parents.berkeley.edu

This is a parent-run e-mail exchange for parents in the Berkeley area. With immediate access to local parents' experience and advice, this is the best of its kind! At the time of press, UCB is merging with Neighborhood Parents Network, see above listing. By the end of 2002, this website will be accessed and replaced by www.parentsnet.org.

ADDITIONAL PARENTING ORGANIZATIONS AND WEBSITES

www.geocities.com/sfbamc

www.parentsnet.org/npn-parent org.html

www.parentspress.com

These sites provide a complete listing of Bay Area mothers' clubs.

www.plumsite.com/bayareamoms

This site provides resources from local parenting experts and moms. You can also meet other moms, form play groups, and more.

www.parentsoup.com

This website contains an extensive guide to many national parenting organizations for dads, moms who work outside the home, adoptive parents, and others.

www.athomemothers.com

This is the National Association of At-Home Mothers' website. Join this group and receive the *At-Home Mother* magazine. Their website includes lots of tips and opinion polls.

www.mah.org

This site features parenting advice, healthy recipes, product reviews, and more. Subscribe to their newsletter *Welcome Home,* and check the website for articles and advice.

www.preemieparenting.com

This helpful website focuses on parenting and caring for preemies.

www.slowlane.com

This is a searchable on-line resource and network for Stay At Home Dads (SAHD) featuring articles, media clips, and many links to sites on fathering issues.

CHAPTER 7

GETTING OUT:
Classes for Kids

No one wants to pressure a child to become a superkid. On the other hand, too many days at home watching Barney on television can get very old. On the theory that exposing your offspring to sports or the arts can be fun for both you and your children, we offer the following selection of Bay Area classes for kids.

In this chapter, we present classes appropriate for infants, toddlers, and preschoolers (through age five), and tell you which classes are best for which ages. Typically, parents accompany children to classes if they are under three years old. Beginning around three, children often go by themselves to short "drop off" programs. We've divided the classes by subject matter, so you can easily jump to a topic—whether it's gym, swimming, music, art, or dance—that interests you. If an organization offers multiple classes in different subject areas, we've included a complete listing the first time it is mentioned, and just the name under subsequent listings, so refer to the first listing for complete details.

Be sure to check current class offerings, schedules, and prices. And keep in mind, as parents reiterated to us, that the value of these classes is highly dependent on individual teachers. It's best to preview a class before you commit time and money to weeks and weeks of it, particularly since fees range from $10-25 per class for most classes. Most good programs offer free preview classes. You may also want to check the make-up class policy, as kids often get sick. Select a class that is not so large as to overwhelm your young child, who may be happier in a smaller group. Keep in mind that many of these locations, particularly gyms and art studios, offer wonderful children's birthday parties. Finally, check the museums section of the next chapter for more fun classes and workshops.

This chapter will answer the following questions and more:
- Where are the local classes, and which are parents' favorites?
- If we have only time for one class, which type should it be?
- What types of swimming lessons are offered, and which facilities are appropriate for my child?
- What approaches do different types of music classes teach?
- Which classes are appropriate for which ages?

Recreation Departments

Many municipal parks and recreation departments are a general resource for activities and offer low-cost classes for kids, running the gamut from swimming to gymnastics to music. If you don't find what you need in the listings below, be sure to check with your own city. Here are some parent favorites (**PARENT RATING:** ☆ ☆ ☆ ☆ ☆):

San Francisco

San Francisco Recreation and Park Department Tiny Tots Program
415-666-7079
http://parks.sfgov.org
The city's recreation department sponsors low-cost, weekly child development and play classes at recreation centers and playgrounds all over the city. The program is fairly free-form and includes creative arts and crafts, nature and science, games, books, large motor skills activities (running, driving tot vehicles, climbing, and so on), and

music. Ages vary by location and start as young as 9 months. The new Richmond Recreation Center (415-666-7020) is a parent favorite. Parents especially recommended the programs at the Cow Hollow Playground (415-292-2003), Presidio Heights Playground (415-292-2005), Upper Noe Valley Recreation Center (415-695-5011), and Moscone Recreation Center (415-292-2006). About the last one, a parent commented: "A bit chaotic at times but has all the toys I can't fit in my house...Good for kids older than 18 months."

San Francisco Recreation and Park Department Aquatics Programs
http://parks.sfgov.org
Some of the city's many public pools offer swim lessons for preschool-age children with parent participation. The following pools offer classes indoors and are heated to 80 degrees: Balboa (415-337-4701, 51 Havelock St.), Coffman (415-337-4702, 1700 Visitacion St.), Garfield (415-695-5001, 26th St. at Harrison St.), Rossi (415-666-7014, 600 Arguello Blvd.), Sava (415-753-7000, 19th Ave. at Wawona St.).

North Bay

Corte Madera Parks and Recreation
498 Tamalpais Dr.
Corte Madera
415-927-5072
www.ci.corte-madera.ca.us

Mill Valley Parks and Recreation Community Center
180 Camino Alto
Mill Valley
415-383-1370

Novato Parks, Recreation and Community Services Department
917 Sherman Ave.
Novato
415-897-4323
www.ci.novato.ca.us

Ross Recreation
P.O. Box 117
Ross
415-453-6020
www.rossrecreation.org

San Anselmo Recreation
1000 Sir Francis Drake Blvd.
San Anselmo
415-258-4640
www.townofsananselmo.org/recreation/

San Rafael Community Services
618 B St.
San Rafael
415-485-3333
www.cityofsanrafael.org/cs

Strawberry Recreation District
118 E. Strawberry Dr.
Mill Valley
415-383-6494
http://strawberry.marin.org

East Bay

City of Berkeley Recreation Division, King Swim Center
1700 Hopkins
Berkeley
510-644-8518
www.ci.berkeley.ca.us/recreation/aquatics.html

Livermore Area Recreation and Park District
71 Trevarno Rd.
Livermore
925-373-5700
www.larpd.dst.ca.us

Pleasanton Parks and Community Services
• Pleasanton
  200 Old Bernal Ave., 925-931-5340
  www.ci.pleasanton.ca.us/parks.html
• Pleasanton
  Dolores Bengston Aquatic Center
  4455 Black Ave., 925-931-3420

San Ramon Community Center
- San Ramon
  12501 Alcosta Blvd.
  925-973-3200
  www.ci.san-ramon.ca.us
- San Ramon
  San Ramon Olympic Pool and
  Aquatic Park
  99007 Broadmoor Dr.
  925-973-3240

Don't miss this beautiful new facility
with a wonderful indoor pool.
Swimming lessons and gymnastic
classes fill quickly.

South Bay

Belmont Parks and Recreation Department
1225 Ralston Ave.
Belmont
650-595-7441
www.belmont.gov

Burlingame Parks and Recreation Department
850 Burlingame Ave.
Burlingame
650-558-7300
www.burlingame.org

Menlo Parks and Community Services
501 Laurel St.
Menlo Park
650-858-3470
www.ci.menlo-park.ca.us/comres.htm

Palo Alto "Enjoy" Program
Department of Community Services
Lucie Stern Community Center
1305 Middlefield Rd.
Palo Alto
650-463-4900
www.paEnjoy.org or www.city.
palo-alto.ca.us

Gyms and Play Programs

These programs are the staples of kids' classes. If you do nothing
else, try a play-based program, which often includes music and
movement as well as development of large motor skills. We found that
the drop in programs offer flexibility and convenience, as you are not
committed to one particular time slot in case you need to miss a
class. If you want to meet other parents on a consistent basis, however, a regular class is probably best. Some facilities express age eligibility for their classes and programs in a decimal form: For instance,
age 2.9 years means two years, nine months old. When checking out
a class, consider whether the equipment is appropriate for the age of
the children in the class. Large gymnastics equipment should be
scaled down to toddler size. For example, a balance beam should be
inches, rather than feet, off the ground.

Acrosports

639 Frederick St.
415-665-ACRO (2276)
www.acrosports.org

PARENT RATING: ☆ ☆ ☆ ☆

These popular movement and gymnastics classes include parent participation programs for ages 18-36 months, and drop off classes for older children. Comments: "Great if you have a good instructor." "Very fun."

American Gymnastics Club

2520 Judah St.
415-731-1400

PARENT RATING: ☆ ☆ ☆ ☆

Designed for children of all ages, this gymnastics program bills itself as "more than just gymnastics," and aims to teach motor development, listening skills, teamwork, self esteem, and discipline. The club offers classes at all levels, beginning with the tot program for ages 2-5 and progressing to competitive gymnastics. The youngest children (ages 2-3) attend parent participation classes.

City College of San Francisco Child Observation Classes

1860 Hayes St., Rm. 139 (office)
415-561-1922
www.ccsf.cc.ca.us

PARENT RATING: ☆ ☆ ☆ ☆ ☆

City College child development students run free parents' and infants' groups (newborn to 14 months) and child observation classes (15 months to 5 years) at local churches and playgrounds throughout the city. College students learn by observing and teaching the parents and children. Classes include free play, circle time, snacks, and cleanup. Comments: "Basic socialization... Good program that offers play, art, water projects, Play-Doh, and sorting."

Congregation Sherith Israel Parent-Baby Playgroups

2266 California St.
415-346-1720, ext. 32
www.sherithisrael.org

PARENT RATING: ☆ ☆ ☆ ☆ ☆

In a large, clean, carpeted room with lots of well-maintained equipment and toys, the Temple offers weekday drop in play programs for children from newborn to age 3. The classes include free play, circle and music time, puppets, parachute time, and snacks. Friday and Saturday groups celebrate Shabbat. Comments: "Lots of great indoor toys in a big open space but can get crowded." "Drop in pass is a good feature, huge play area, less frantic than Gymboree." "Great rainy day activity!"

Gymboree

www.gymboree.com (for Bay Area locations)

PARENT RATING: ☆ ☆ ☆

These developmental play and music classes (franchised all over the country) are divided by age, from newborn to 4 years. Classes received mixed reviews, from "very good program" and "good for younger kids" to "teachers are not great" and "we got sick every time we went" to "well organized but often too campy." The consensus was that "the value is completely dependent on the teacher." (Personally, we had a wonderful teacher for our Gymbabies class and loved it, mainly because it enabled us to meet other moms with new babies.) Others said that the classes are more worthwhile "once babies are really moving." The padded equipment and mats are great for crawlers and toddlers learning mobility, and Gymboree is one of the few programs for very young babies in the city. The make-up policy is fairly flexible, which is nice when kids inevitably get sick!

Jewish Community Center of San Francisco

3200 California St.
(temporarily located at 1808 Wedemeyer Way in The Presidio, 2001-2003)
415-346-6040
www.jccsf.org
PARENT RATING: ☆ ☆ ☆ ☆

A great resource for families in the city, the JCC offers many different classes for young children. The Kindergym weekday drop in play program for crawlers through age 2 is held in a large gym and is always crowded, but it features slides, tunnels, climbing apparatus, vehicles, and parachute time. Gym Buddies, for ages 2-3 with a parent, introduces tumbling and equipment and includes play with tricycles, cars, and balls. Gymnastics skills begin in Tiny Tumblers (ages 2.6-3.6) and preschool gymnastics (ages 3-5). Music and dance classes begin at age 3 with ballet, tap, and creative movement. Children can also explore art classes for ages 3 and up, with or without parents. Swim classes will resume when the California Street facility reopens. Classes are open to the public.

Parents Place

1710 Scott St.
415-359-2454
www.parentsplaceonline.org
PARENT RATING: ☆ ☆ ☆ ☆ ☆

This offshoot of Jewish Family and Children's Services provides a variety of great play and parenting classes for children and their parents. Selections include age-appropriate play classes or music classes from 6 months and up, art for ages 2-3 years old, and many other parenting workshops. The drop in play center is open many afternoons if you just need to get out of the house. Classes are open to the public. Comment: "An incredible resource...my kids loved it."

Presidio YMCA

Lincoln Way at Funston (Building 63)
415-447-9622
www.presidioymca.org
PARENT RATING: ☆ ☆ ☆ ☆

Formerly a military base gym, this renovated facility offers an assortment of programs for preschoolers, including Biddy Sports for ages 3-5. Soccer, t-ball, basketball, and tumbling are some of the options in the Biddy program. In addition, junior tennis classes start for children as young as 4 years old. Membership is inexpensive and recommended, as you can get your own workout while your children are in classes or the "childwatch" facility!

UCSF Millberry Recreation and Fitness Center

500 Parnassus Ave.

415-476-0334

www.cas.ucsf.edu/MPS/membership/

PARENT RATING: ☆ ☆ ☆ ☆ ☆

Millberry Union offers Kindergymusic classes (movement, gymnastics, and music) for parents and children ages 18 months to 3 years, as well as private, semiprivate, and group swim lessons for children ages 6 months to 3 years. These popular classes fill quickly.

North Bay

Center for Creative Parenting

446A Ignacio Blvd.

Novato

415-883-4442

PARENT RATING: ☆ ☆ ☆ ☆ ☆

This resource center's drop in play program for children up to age 3 features great toddler-size equipment and toys in an enclosed area. There are also several facilitated play groups featuring music, bubbles, and play beginning at age 6 months.

Gymboree

See listing under San Francisco.

Gymworld

555 E. Francisco Blvd., Ste. 19

San Rafael

415-482-8580

PARENT RATING: ☆ ☆ ☆ ☆ ☆

These gymnastics classes begin with parent participation classes for ages 18 months to 2 years. Mom or Dad can drop off children ages 3 and up. Private and semiprivate instruction is also available. Comment: "Great for birthday parties."

Jumping Jacks

- Mill Valley
  Strawberry Recreation District Center, 118 E. Strawberry Dr., 415-383-6494
- San Rafael
  San Rafael Community Center, 618 B St., 415-485-3333

PARENT RATING: ☆ ☆ ☆ ☆ ☆

Jumping Jacks offers an indoor gym with mats, obstacle courses, play structures, slides, songs, parachutes, games, bubbles, and more—all designed to build social and motor skills. Classes are divided by age, with one class for crawlers to 22 months, and another for 23 months to 3 years. You can drop in on a class or buy a series and create your own schedule. Comments: "Excellent...Very fun on a rainy day... Kind of like taking your kid to a dog park—chaos but they love it."

Marin Elite Gymnastics Academy (MEGA)

72 Woodland Ave.

San Rafael

415-257-6342

www.megagymnastics.com

PARENT RATING: ☆ ☆ ☆ ☆ ☆

This fully-equipped gym offers gymnastics classes for ages 2 and up, grouped by age and ability level. Preschool programs with age-appropriate equipment aim to build basic strength and coordination, as well as gymnastics skills. Parents attend classes with children under age 3.

Novato Parents Nursery School Toddler Time Program

1473 S. Novato Blvd.
Novato
415-897-4498
www.ccppns.org/npns/

PARENT RATING: ☆ ☆ ☆ ☆ ☆

These parent-child participation classes for ages 18 months and up received rave reviews.

Osher Marin Jewish Community Center

200 N. San Pedro Rd.
San Rafael
415-444-8000
www.marinjcc.org

PARENT RATING: ☆ ☆ ☆ ☆ ☆

The JCC's extensive children's programming, open to the public, includes the ever-popular Side-by-Side class (art, music, and play with parents for pre-preschoolers ages 18 months to 3 years), Music Together classes (ages 3 months to 4 years), movement and dance classes (ages 3 and up), and gymnastics classes (ages 2 and up). There are also both parent-tot swimming and learn-to-swim classes in indoor and outdoor pools.

Parents Place Marin

600 5th Ave.
San Rafael
415-491-7959
www.parentsplaceonline.org

Parents Place has a new facility in Marin with a drop in play center for families, as well as many wonderful age-appropriate play groups and parenting classes. See the San Francisco listing for more details.

YMCA—Marin

1500 Los Gamos Dr.
San Rafael
415-492-9622
www.ymcasf.org/marin/

PARENT RATING: ☆ ☆ ☆

Try the mini-sports program for children ages 3-5 years. The Y also offers swim lessons in an indoor pool, beginning with parent-child water adjustment lessons for children 6-36 months, and progressing to learn-to-swim lessons for preschoolers ages 3-5 years.

East Bay

Bay Island Gymnastics

2317 Central Ave.
Alameda
510-521-1343

This gymnastics program for children ages 2 and up begins with parent-child classes and progresses to drop off classes. The classes include listening skills, obstacle courses, a trampoline, and a foam pit.

Diablo Gymnastics

2411J Old Crow Canyon Rd.
San Ramon
925-820-6885
www.diablogym.com

PARENT RATING: ☆ ☆ ☆

This thirty-four-year-old program offers Kindergym classes for children ages 2-5 years. Kids can attend classes on their own beginning at age 3. Classes involve slides, climbing equipment, parachutes, and songs. Comment: "It draws from the local community—less equipment than Gymboree but fun."

261

Golden Bear Gymnastics

UC Berkeley Department of
Intercollegiate Athletics and
Recreational Sports
Golden Bear Recreation Center,
25 Sports Ln.
Berkeley
510-642-9821 (registration)
510-643-1133 (program information)
www.oski.org

PARENT RATING: ☆ ☆ ☆ ☆

These popular gymnastics classes for
children ages 18 months and up are
taught by professionals and college
students and are divided by age.
Parent participation is required for
the youngest Bear Cubs classes
(under age 3), which focus on play
and movement. At age 3, kids start
learning fundamental gymnastics
skills without their parents.

Gymboree

See listing under San Francisco

Gym Rompers Gymnastics

1601B 63rd St.
Emeryville
510-428-2052

This gym offers recreational gymnastics classes for children ages 18
months and up in a noncompetitive
environment. Children learn tumbling,
use balls and hoops, and may try
trampolines, bars, beams, and a gymnastics horse. Classes for kids under
age 4 require parent participation.

Gymtastic!

1401 Camino Ramon, Ste. D
Danville
925-277-1881

PARENT RATING: ☆ ☆ ☆ ☆ This
noncompetitive, recreational program
offers classes in gymnastics, tumbling,
and sports skills development. The
program encourages children to learn
at their own pace. Children attend
classes with parents until age 3.

Head over Heels Gymnastics

1250 45th St., Ste. E
Emeryville
510-655-1265
www.mindspring.com/
~hohgymnastics/

This nonprofit gymnastics school has
a noncompetitive philosophy for its
toddler and recreational gymnastics
classes. Children begin at 2.6 years
in parent-participation classes, and
they may attend classes solo beginning at age 4.

Kids in Motion Gymnastics

4137 Piedmont Ave.
Oakland
510-601-8424

PARENT RATING: ☆ ☆ ☆ ☆

This program offers noncompetitive
gymnastics classes with an emphasis
on play. Parent participation is
required in classes for children under
age 3.

University Village Recreation Program

1125 Jackson St.
Albany
510-524-4926

PARENT RATING: ☆ ☆ ☆ ☆ ☆

This ever-popular UC-Berkeley program offers gymnastics (for ages 18
months and up), creative movement
and dance (ages 3-5), and art (ages
2 and up) classes to the public and

university communities. Gymnastics classes require parent participation with children up to age 3. Parents rave about these classes as fun and inexpensive.

Windmill Gymnastics

5221 Central Ave., #2
Richmond
510-527-0570
www.windmillgymnastics.com

PARENT RATING: ☆ ☆ ☆ ☆

This 12,000-square foot gym is packed with equipment and offers gymnastics and dance classes for ages 2 and up. Parents participate with children under age 4. Parents can watch children from the lobby through the windows, and there is a play area for younger siblings.

YMCA—Downtown Berkeley

2001 Allston Way
Berkeley
510-848-9622
www.baymca.org

PARENT RATING: ☆ ☆ ☆ ☆ ☆

The largest YMCA in the East Bay offers open gym drop in classes, kindergym gymnastics, little sportsters soccer classes (ages 3-6), swimming (6 months and up), art, and dance classes. Swimming lessons are very popular, inexpensive, and held in a small, shallow, very warm indoor pool for the youngest children, and progressing to a larger pool for older children.

YMCA of the East Bay

(Branches in Oakland, Hayward, Fremont, Livermore, and Richmond)
510-451-8039
www.ymcaeastbay.org

With nine East Bay branches, this full-service YMCA offers many different programs for young children. Choose from kindergym, preschool sports, parent-tot (6-36 months) swim classes, or learn-to-swim classes for ages 3-5 using flotation devices.

YMCA—Mt. Diablo Region

(Branches in Oakley, Walnut Creek, Pleasant Hill, and Danville)
925-609-9622
www.mdrymca.org

PARENT RATING: ☆ ☆ ☆ ☆

This YMCA has four large branches in Contra Costa and eastern Alameda counties, each offering preschool sports and swim classes.

Aerial Tumbling and Acrobatics, Inc.

422 Blossom Hill Rd.
San Jose
408-224-5437

This 7,000-square-foot gym offers recreational gymnastics classes for children ages 18 months and up. Classes for children under age 3 require parent participation. The gym features a Tumbl-Trak with a springy surface to introduce tumbling skills.

Airborne Gymnastics

2250 Martin Ave.
Santa Clara
408-986-8226
www.airborne-gymnastics.com

This 18,000-square foot facility offers gymnastics classes for walkers and up. The beginning classes (for children under age 3) require parent participation.

263

California Sports Center

www.calsportscenter.com
- San Jose
  336 Race St., 408-280-KIDS
- San Jose
  832 Malone Rd., 408-269-KIDS

A Junior Olympic sports training facility, CSC offers gymnastics, swimming, and dance classes in two Willow Glen locations. The GymKids program (ages 18 months to 6 years) requires parent participation up to age 3 and focuses on basic motor skills, gymnastics, and hand-eye coordination. Dancing Tots (ages 2-4) and Dance and Gym (ages 3 and up) emphasize dance as a method to improve grace in gymnastics. The swimming program (scheduled to open in May 2002) will include parent-child classes for kids under age 3, and Red Cross learn-to-swim lessons for children ages 3 and up.

Gymboree

See listing under San Francisco

The Junior Gym

101 South B St.
San Mateo
650-548-9901
www.juniorgym.com

This program is designed to boost self-confidence in children through motor development, music, and movement. Terrific Tots is a motor development program for preschoolers (ages 2.9-5), incorporating arts and crafts, stories, and snacks in a preschool morning format. Gymnastics classes (ages 4 months and up) are divided by age.

Palo Alto Jewish Community Center

655 Arastradero Rd.
Palo Alto
650-493-9400
www.paloaltojcc.org

PARENT RATING: ☆ ☆ ☆ ☆ ☆ The JCC offers many different classes for children through its International Children's Academy, including pre-gymnastics, sing and play, music, science, and art. Children ages 3 years and up may also take private and semiprivate swim lessons at the Fitness Center. Classes are open to the public.

Peninsula Parents Place

410 Sherman Ave.
Palo Alto
650-688-3040
www.parentsplaceonline.org

PARENT RATING: ☆ ☆ ☆ ☆ ☆

This center offers a multitude of classes and resources for parents and children, and all are open to the public. Classes for kids include age-appropriate play groups, music for children ages 1-5, and art for ages 18 months and up. A great drop in play center is open many weekdays, and there are parenting classes on almost every topic imaginable.

Peninsula Gymnastics

1740 Leslie St.
San Mateo
650-571-7555
www.peninsulagym.com

This 15,000-square foot facility offers preschool gymnastics classes for children ages 2 and up.

264

Peninsula Jewish Community Center Playgroups

2440 Carlmont Dr.
Belmont
650-591-4438
www.pjcc.org

The JCC's age-appropriate play programs for children ages 18 months and up offer basic socialization, music, art, and physical activity for the pre-preschool crowd. Classes are open to the public.

A Place 2 Play Fun Fitness

476 San Mateo Ave.
San Bruno
650-875-1001
www.aplace2play.com

This for-profit indoor playground offers physical education and movement classes for children ages one year and up. Classes are loosely structured, divided by age, and focus on locomotor skills: jumping, landing, throwing, catching, striking, kicking, balance, body part awareness, rhythm, and small-motor skills. Drop in times are also available.

San Mateo Gymnastics

1306 Elmer St.
Belmont
650-591-8734
www.smgym.com

Billed as "the largest gymnastic facility in the Bay Area," this gym offers a Munchkins program for children ages 2-6. Parents participate until children reach age 3. Teachers include former Olympians.

Santa Clara Unified School District Adult Education

1840 Benton St.
Santa Clara
408-984-6220 or 408-423-3500
www.scae.org

SCAE offers parenting and play classes for parents and children, newborn to 30 months, divided by age. Parents discuss developmental issues, and babies experience play, socialization, songs, games, and art.

Twisters Gym

2639 Terminal Blvd.
Mountain View
650-967-5581
www.twistersgym.com

This climbing gym's classes feature gymnastics, movement, and music for children ages 18 months and up. Parent participation is required in classes for children under age 3.

West Valley Gymnastics

1190 Dell Ave., Unit I
Campbell
408-374-8692
www.wvgs.com

This competitive gym offers preschool and recreational classes in addition to its team program. Parents participate in classes until children reach age 3.

YMCA of the Mid-Peninsula
(Branches in Palo Alto, E. Palo
Alto, Mountain View, and Redwood
City)
3412 Ross Rd.
Palo Alto
650-856-9622
www.ymcamidpen.org
PARENT RATING: ☆ ☆ ☆ ☆ ☆
With five Peninsula locations, this
YMCA offers a multitude of classes
for young children, including gymnastics, sports (hockey, soccer, and
basketball), parent-tot swim classes
for ages 6 months to 3 years, and
learn-to-swim classes for ages 3-5.
A parent comments that gym classes
are "short ... but inexpensive and
well-run." Some complain that the
pool temperature is not warm
enough for babies under age 2.

Swimming

Swimming lessons generally come in two flavors: parent-child
classes, which focus on getting young babies and toddlers accustomed
to the water, and formal swimming lessons, which actually teach older
children to swim. Most swimming classes require an adult to accompany each child under age 3 in the pool! The American Academy of
Pediatrics recommends delaying formal swimming lessons until after
the child reaches age 4, when he or she is developmentally ready. The
Mommy and Me types of classes can be fun but won't teach survival
skills in the water. Some places do offer more formal survival classes
for younger children, but pediatricians say that they will not ensure a
child's safety in the water. A swim tip: Make sure that the pool you
choose for baby and toddler classes is kept very warm. Parents
responding to our surveys complained that some of the adult pools
offering children's classes weren't warm enough for babies and young
children. Also, see above under the "Recreation Departments" section.
If so, try one of the swim schools specializing in instructing children.

Many local recreation departments, community centers, and private clubs offer low-cost swim lessons. The following pools stood out
as parent favorites:

San Francisco

**Golden Gateway Tennis and
Swim Club**
370 Drumm St.
415-616-8800
www.ggtsc.com

PARENT RATING: ☆ ☆ ☆ ☆ This
private club offers private swim lessons to the public for all ages, as
well as a parent-tot class for babies.
The pools are beautiful, and if there
is anywhere warm in San Francisco,

this is it! But parents do complain that it can be chilly on colder days.

Jewish Community Center of San Francisco

See listing under "Gyms and Play Programs" section—San Francisco.

Recreation Center for the Handicapped

Herbst Pool
207 Skyline Blvd.
415-665-4100, ext. 5601
www.rchinc.com

PARENT RATING: ☆ ☆ ☆ ☆ This private, nonprofit organization has long been offering Mommy and Me type swim lessons to the public for ages 6 months to 5 years in its warm, therapeutic indoor pool. The pool's depth (two to six feet) and temperature (92-94 degrees) are perfect for babies, and the classes are relatively inexpensive. Some complain that the changing room is not terribly fancy, but this is the only game in town if you want a truly warm indoor pool.

UCSF Millberry Recreation and Fitness Center

See listing under "Gyms and Play Programs" section—San Francisco.

USF Koret Health and Recreation Center

Parker and Turk Sts.
415-422-6697

PARENT RATING: ☆ ☆ ☆ ☆ The University of San Francisco's fitness center is a sparkling, newer facility with an Olympic-size indoor pool. Parent-child group swim lessons for ages 9 months to 5 years are open to nonmembers and focus on water adjustment and beginning swimming skills. Private and semiprivate lessons are also available. However, the water is kept at adult temperatures, so it may be too cool for young children, particularly babies.

Presidio Community YMCA

Letterman Pool
1151 Gorgas
415-447-9686
www.presidioymca.org

PARENT RATING: ☆ ☆ ☆ ☆ Skippers Program swim classes for children ages 6 months to 5 years begin with parents working with children on water adjustment (up to age 3) and progress to children learning swimming skills. The classes themselves received positive reviews, but many complained of the "variable" or "chilly" pool temperatures. Even so, these classes fill up fast.

North Bay

Ann Curtis School of Swimming, Inc.

25 Golden Hinde Blvd.
San Rafael
415-479-9131

PARENT RATING: ☆ ☆ ☆ ☆ ☆ Founder Ann Curtis was an Olympic swim star during the 1940s. Swim lessons are held May through August in an outdoor, heated pool (85-87 degrees) for children ages 4 and up. The school is open to nonmembers, but members receive preference in scheduling lessons.

Marinwood Community Center Pool

775 Miller Creek Rd.
San Rafael
415-479-0775
www.marinwood.org/recprog.html

PARENT RATING: ☆ ☆ ☆ ☆ Open only during the summer season, this public pool offers a parent-tot class for children ages 18-36 months, as well as private or group lessons for ages 3 and up. The pool is outdoors and heated to 82 degrees.

Mt. Tam Racquet Club

Magnolia Ave. and Doherty Dr.
Larkspur
415-924-6226
www.mttamrc.com

PARENT RATING: ☆ ☆ ☆ This club features both indoor and outdoor heated pools, so classes are held year-round. American Red Cross-based parent-child swim classes for children ages 6 months to 3 years, as well as learn-to-swim group lessons for ages 4-8, are open to nonmembers. Private and semiprivate lessons are also available.

Nancy's Mommy and Me Swim School

San Rafael
415-459-5145

PARENT RATING: ☆ ☆ ☆ ☆ Nancy's approach is to teach babies and toddlers life-saving water techniques (e.g., holding their breath underwater, getting their heads above water, and swimming to the side of the pool). Parent participation classes begin in a hot tub and progress to a small round covered pool heated to 90 degrees. She teaches babies as young as 3 months old, and mixes ages and abilities in classes.

Osher Marin Jewish Community Center

See listing under "Gyms and Play Programs" section—North Bay.

Rafael Racquet and Swim Club

95 Racquet Club Dr.
San Rafael
415-456-1153

This club offers group learn-to-swim lessons for children ages 4 and up, and private lessons for ages 3 and up, during the summer season. The pool is well-maintained, outdoors, and heated to 81-83 degrees. Classes are open to nonmembers.

Rolling Hills Club

351 San Andreas Dr.
Novato
415-897-2185
www.rollinghillsclub.com

PARENT RATING: ☆ ☆ ☆ ☆ ☆

Parent-tot classes, for children ages 6 months to 3 years, are held only in the summer. Group and private lessons for ages 4 and up are held year-round, as one of the club's two outdoor twenty-five-yard pools is covered in winter and heated to 81-83 degrees. Classes are open to nonmembers. Comment: "Very professional and effective."

Ross Valley Swim and Tennis Club

235 Bon Air Rd.
Kentfield
415-461-5431

PARENT RATING: ☆ ☆ ☆ ☆

This private club offers group lessons for children ages 4 and up, and private lessons for all ages, in an outdoor, heated pool (81-83 degrees) during the summer season. Classes are open to nonmembers.

Sleepy Hollow Homes Association

1317 Butterfield Rd.
San Anselmo
415-455-5952
www.shha.org

This private pool offers private and group learn-to-swim lessons to the public in an outdoor pool heated to 83 degrees during the summer season. Children must be 3 years old to participate, and there are no parent-tot classes.

Tiburon Peninsula Club

1600 Mar West
Tiburon
415-435-2169
www.tiburonpc.org

This private club offers private lessons to the public for children ages 3 and up in an outdoor heated pool during the summer season.

YMCA

See listing under "Gyms and Play Programs" section—North Bay.

East Bay

Albany Community Pool

1311 Portland Ave.
Albany
510-559-6640
PARENT RATING: ☆ ☆ ☆ ☆

This heated (up to 84 degrees) indoor public swimming pool offers parent-tot classes for children ages 6 months to 4 years, and learn-to-swim classes for children ages 4 and up.

Canyon Swim School

21 Campbell Ln.
El Sobrante
510-223-4600
PARENT RATING: ☆ ☆ ☆ ☆ ☆

This school offers both a parent-baby class and learn-to-swim classes during the summer season. Comment: "A very warm outdoor pool, lots of personal attention, and great teachers."

ClubSport Pleasanton

7090 Johnson Dr.
Pleasanton
925-463-2822
www.clubsports.com
PARENT RATING: ☆ ☆ ☆ ☆

This private club offers parent-infant water awareness classes (for any age), as well as learn-to-swim group lessons for children ages 3 and up, to the public during the summer season. The pool is outdoors and heated to 82-86 degrees. Comment: "A very good ratio (four children to one instructor)."

Contra Costa Jewish Community Center

2071 Tice Valley Blvd.
Walnut Creek
925-938-7800
www.ccjcc.org

This community center offers both private (for all ages) and group (for ages 3 and up) swim lessons to the public in an outdoor pool heated to 78-81 degrees during the summer season.

Fremont Swim School

www.fremontswimschool.com
• Fremont
   42400 Blacow Rd., 510-657-SWIM

- Newark
  37400 Cedar Blvd., 510-794-SWIM
- Livermore
  2821 Old First St., 925-373-SWIM

PARENT RATING: ☆ ☆ ☆ ☆ ☆

Classes are held year-round in indoor pools heated to 92 degrees. Tiny tot classes (for ages 10 months to 3 years) require parent participation and teach water adaptation, while preschool classes for ages 3 and up focus on water safety, and children attend on their own.

Piedmont Swim Club

777 Magnolia Ave.
Piedmont
510-655-5163

PARENT RATING: ☆ ☆ ☆ ☆

This private club opens its swim lessons to the public during the summer. Kids as young as 3 years old may begin lessons in the club's 90-degree outdoor pool.

Strawberry Canyon Recreation Area Pool

Centennial Dr.
Berkeley
510-643-7470
www.oski.org

PARENT RATING: ☆ ☆ ☆ ☆ ☆

This university outdoor pool, open to the public, offers private, semiprivate, and group lessons for children ages 6 months and up during the season, following the American Red Cross methods. Classes for children up to age 3 require parent participation. Parents rave about the quality of the instruction. The pool water is kept warm, but it can be cool on the deck.

YMCA

See listing under "Gyms and Play Programs" section—East Bay.

South Bay

Aitken's Peninsula Swim School

1602 Stafford St.
Redwood City
650-366-9211
www.peninsulaswim.com

PARENT RATING: ☆ ☆ ☆ ☆

For thirty-five years this swim school has been offering classes for children ages 6 weeks and up, in an indoor/outdoor pool heated to 91 degrees.

Almaden Valley Athletic Club (AVAC) Swim School

5400 Camden Ave.
San Jose
408-267-4032
www.almadenvalleyathletic.com

This club offers group classes for children ages 6 months and up in a shallow indoor pool heated to 90 degrees. Student-teacher ratios are kept at four to five students per teacher.

Betty Wright Swim Center at the Community Association for Rehabilitation (C.A.R.)

3864 Middlefield Rd.
Palo Alto
650-494-1480

PARENT RATING: ☆ ☆ ☆ ☆

This rehabilitation center offers year-round swim classes to the public in its warm indoor pool. Choose from parent-child classes for children ages 3 months to 3 years, or learn-to-swim classes for ages 3-5.

Comments: "The water is 90-91 degrees—perfect." "Warm water—great teacher."

California Sports Center

See listing under "Gyms and Play Programs" section—South Bay.

DACA (DeAnza Cupertino Aquatics) Swim School

21111 Stevens Creek Blvd.
Cupertino
408-446-5600
www.daca.org

PARENT RATING: ☆ ☆ ☆ ☆ ☆

Specializing in teaching preschoolers, this school offers weekly private, semiprivate, and group classes in a 90 degree indoor pool. Parent-tot classes begin at 3 months, and learn-to-swim classes begin at 3 years.

La Petite Baleen Swim Schools

- San Bruno
  434 San Mateo Ave., 650-588-7665
- Half Moon Bay
  775 Main St., 650-726-3676

PARENT RATING: ☆ ☆ ☆ ☆ ☆

The indoor pools at this children's swim school—a favorite of city and Peninsula parents—are very warm (90 degrees) and great even for young babies. Parent-tot classes, from ages 2-36 months, focus on water adjustment and play. Once a child reaches 30 months and demonstrates certain skills, he or she may enter a learn-to-swim class without a parent. Comments: "The classes are small and focus on technique." "Love it." "Great teachers."

Los Gatos Swim and Racquet Club

14700 Oka Rd.
Los Gatos
408-356-2136
www.lgsrc.com

PARENT RATING: ☆ ☆ ☆ ☆ ☆

Lessons are open to the public and are taught in an outdoor pool heated to 84 degrees. Parent-tot classes for children ages 6-36 months teach water adjustment, and learn-to-swim group and private lessons begin at age 3.

Palo Alto Jewish Community Center

See listing under "Gyms and Play Programs" section—South Bay.

Peninsula Covenant Community Center

1315 Madison Ave.
Redwood City
650-780-7296
www.peninsulacovenant.com

PARENT RATING: ☆ ☆ ☆ ☆

Learn-to-swim classes are held in a covered pool heated to 82 degrees for children ages 3 and up. In the summer the center also hosts parent-tot classes for ages 6 months and up.

Peninsula Jewish Community Center Aquatics Program

2440 Carlmont Dr.
Belmont
650-591-2845
www.pjcc.org

This year-round, indoor/outdoor pool heated to 84 degrees offers parent-child group classes for ages 9 months to 3 years, learn-to-swim classes beginning at age 3, and private and semiprivate lessons for all ages. Classes are open to the public.

Taft Swim School
57 E. 40th Ave.
San Mateo
650-349-SWIM
This school has been teaching children to swim since 1955 in its indoor pool heated to 88 degrees. Parent-tot classes teach water safety habits. Small group lessons for children ages 4 and up teach children to swim.

YMCA of the Mid-Peninsula
See listing under "Gyms and Play Programs" section—South Bay.

Music

There are several major schools or music instruction franchises for young children, and you may want to familiarize yourself with each of their approaches before deciding on a class for your child.

◆ **Kindermusik International**
(www.kindermusik.com or 800-628-5687) is a series of classes designed for children ages newborn to 7 years. Classes are divided by age, and within each age range there are four to six different semesters of classes, each with a different theme. Generally class tuition includes a CD of the semester's music and home materials incorporating the theme. In the Kindermusik philosophy, "Every child is musical, and every parent is the child's most important teacher." Kindermusik is a national program; classes are taught by individual licensed instructors at various locations locally. Log onto the website to find a licensed educator near you.
PARENT RATING: ☆ ☆ ☆ ☆ ☆
Comments: "Excellent, but depends highly on the teacher." We took these classes when our children were babies and loved them.

◆ **Music Together** (www.musictogether.com or 800-728-2692) is a research-based, developmentally appropriate national program of musical instruction for infants, toddlers, preschoolers, and kindergarteners. It focuses on "encouraging the actual experiencing of music rather than the learning of concepts or information about music." Classes are mixed age so siblings may attend together. The program is taught internationally by independent certified teachers. Tuition includes a CD, a cassette, a songbook, and a book for parents about music education. Log onto the website to find a licensed educator near you.
PARENT RATING: ☆ ☆ ☆ ☆ ☆
Again, your experience will depend on your instructor, but we took these classes with our toddlers and loved them. Comment: "The CDs are lifesavers in the car."

◆ **Orff-Schulwerk** (www.aosa.org), based on the philosophy of American composer Carl Orff, is a method of teaching music emphasizing singing, chanting rhymes, clapping, and keeping a beat with instruments like drums, xylophones, and glockenspiels. Log onto the website for more details. Certain of the classes listed below incorporate this teaching method, but the method is not franchised.

In addition to the Kindermusik and Music Together classes listed above, the following music classes stood out as parent favorites:

Music Time of San Francisco
4150 Balboa St. (classes)
415-750-1166
www.musictime.org
This Sunset area music studio has been offering music classes to children for eighteen years. Children are grouped by age, from 18 months to 5 years. Classes include songs, finger plays, rhythm and movement, learning musical notes, and playing instruments. Students play in their own orchestra; teachers sing and play piano and guitar.

Natural Resources' Music Classes
1307 Castro St.
415-550-2611
www.naturalresourcesonline.com
PARENT RATING: ☆ ☆ ☆ ☆
Parents highly recommended these music classes with a professional cellist. Try a series, Rhythm Kids, for ages 18 months to 3 years, or a Mother/Baby Music Workshop for infants to 14 months.

Parents Place
See listing under "Gyms and Play Programs" section—San Francisco.

Playsongs Music and Movement
25 Lake St. (classes)
415-567-7838
www.sfplaysongs.com
PARENT RATING: ☆ ☆ ☆ ☆ This program offers Kindermusik classes from newborn through three years, as well as Orff-inspired Playsongs class-

es for ages 2-5. Parents raved about the former director of this music school; the school has since been taken over by two new teachers and we do not yet have ratings for them.

San Francisco Conservatory of Music, Preparatory Division
1201 Ortega St.
415-759-3429
www.sfcm.edu
The conservatory's early childhood education department offers classes in several different musical theories, including Orff-Schulwerk, for children ages 4 and up. Students are asked to commit to classes for an entire academic year.

Mary Ann Hall's Music for Children
415-435-2180
www.musicforchildrenca.com
PARENT RATING: ☆ ☆ ☆ ☆ ☆
These sequential music classes for toddlers through age 6, with hands-on instruments, are held in locations throughout Marin. The curriculum is twenty-eight weeks in duration and extends throughout the school year. Beginning at age 4, children attend class on their own and receive piano lessons each week. Music for Children is a national program involving live and recorded music, singing, movement, hands-on instrument play, rhythm training, and a different theme every week.

Music Makers
240 Tiburon Blvd. (classes)
Tiburon
415-461-1066
www.music-makers.org

PARENT RATING: ☆ ☆ ☆ ☆ ☆

These age-appropriate music classes for ages 18 months to 6 years include songs, finger plays, instruments, rhythm and movement, ear training, live music, music theory, and cassette tapes to take home. Each week focuses on a different instrument and theme, and children are taught about note values, beats, and so on. Parents say the format is more "structured" than other more free-form music classes. The benefits are that children seem to "pay close attention" and even 2-year-olds can "recognize clefs and notes."

East Bay

The Crowden Center for Music in the Community
1475 Rose St.
Berkeley
510-559-6910
www.thecrowdenschool.org

This classical music school offers Orff-Schulwerk-based preinstrument training for children ages 3-6, Music Together classes for newborns to age 4, and creative art classes for ages 3 and up.

Music Time of the East Bay
2727 College Ave.
Berkeley
415-750-1166
www.musictime.org
See listing under San Francisco.

South Bay

Almaden School of Music, Art and Dance
5353 Almaden Expwy., Ste. 12

San Jose
408-267-3651

This studio offers private instrumental lessons, group music and movement classes (for children ages 18 months to 5 years), preballet and tap classes for ages 3-5, and art lessons for ages 4 and up.

Community School of Music and Arts
253 Martens Ave.
Mountain View
650-961-0342
www.arts4all.org

This nonprofit community organization offers an early childhood music program (for ages 18 months to 6 years), with singing, dancing, and instruments. You can also enroll children in private voice or instrumental music lessons.

Lessons on "B"
25 North B St.
San Mateo
650-343-1579

This studio offers early childhood music classes for infants and up.

The Music Place, Fine Arts for Children!
1617 Willowhurst Ave.
San Jose
408-445-ARTS
www.musicplace.com

This private school offers music and fine arts classes for young children. Choose from early music awareness classes (for ages 2 and up), instrument readiness or performance classes (for ages 4 and up), or private music lessons.

Peninsula Parents Place

See listing under "Gyms and Play Programs" section—South Bay.

Strings of Art Performing Art Center

First Baptist Church
1430 Palm Dr.
Burlingame
650-342-0202
www.stringsofart.com

This studio offers group and private instrumental music lessons for children ages 4 and up. The drama and dance program begins with creative movement classes and "little plays" classes for ages 4 and up.

Tunes for Tots

First Baptist Church
1430 Palm Dr.
Burlingame
650-340-1729

These Orff-based classes involve singing, rhythm, movement, dancing, and playing instruments. Group classes are divided by age from 1-5 years. Parents participate in the classes for children under age 2.

Art

We found it best to delay formal art classes until our children were almost two years old, when they had sufficient hand-eye control and coordination to draw, paint, and learn to use scissors. Before that time, we introduced them to art by coloring at home and attending drop in classes at the Bay Area Discovery and Habitot museums, see chapter 8.

San Francisco

Jewish Community Center

See listing under "Gyms and Play Programs" section—San Francisco.

KidsArt

360A&D West Portal Ave.
415-759-5757

This studio offers drop off art classes for ages 4 and up. Each student works individually at his or her own pace, progressing from basic drawing to three-dimensional drawing to forms and shapes to painting in different media.

Parents Place

See listing under "Gyms and Play Programs" section—San Francisco.

Precita Eyes Mural Arts Center

348 Precita Ave.
415-285-2311
www.precitaeyes.org

PARENT RATING: ☆ ☆ ☆ ☆

This community mural organization offers wonderful drop in workshops using mixed media for children ages 18 months to 5 years. Comment: "It can be chaotic, but the materials and ideas are usually great fun."

Purple Crayon Art Studio

301 Cornwall St.
415-831-0693
www.purplecrayon.com

PARENT RATING: ☆ ☆ ☆ ☆ ☆

For the 2- and 3-year-olds, the format of these art classes is a set process-oriented project designed to encourage hand-eye coordination, followed by free time for open-ended drawing painting. Older children can progress to sculpture, mobiles, masks, and dioramas. Comments: "Expensive, but good supplies and the teacher is very prepared." "Great birthday parties." Our 2-year-olds enjoyed these classes very much!

San Francisco Children's Art Center

692 Fort Mason Center (Building C)
415-771-0292
www.childrensartcenter.org
PARENT RATING: ☆ ☆ ☆ ☆ ☆

A great feature of this center is that you can drop off your child, age 27 months and up, for a series of art classes. Classes are divided by age and feature painting, drawing, sculpture, print-making, and collage. Kids get to choose their own materials and create what they want (as opposed to a fixed project).

North Bay

Art Start

1407 4th St.
San Rafael
415-454-8332
PARENT RATING: ☆ ☆ ☆ ☆ ☆

This studio offers six-week sessions or drop in classes for children ages 2 and up. Younger children focus on painting and drawing, while older children engage in mixed media (including ceramics and sculpture) and make crowns and masks. Parents rave about the excellent materials, involved teachers, and great drop off policy so kids can explore art on their own. We took these classes and can't say enough good things about them. Our 3-year-olds came home with bags full of their wonderful creations!

Doodlebug

641 San Anselmo Ave.
San Anselmo
415-456-5989

This ceramics studio offers art workshops in mixed media for preschoolers.

Falkirk Cultural Center

1408 Mission Ave.
San Rafael
415-485-3328 or 415-453-8518
www.falkirkculturalcenter.org
PARENT RATING: ☆ ☆ ☆ ☆ ☆

This center offers art classes with mixed media, painting, and clay to children ages 3 and up.

East Bay

The Crowden Center for Music in the Community

See listing under "Music" section—East Bay.

University Village Recreation Program

See listing under "Gyms and Play Programs" section—East Bay.

YMCA

See listing under "Gyms and Play Programs" section—East Bay.

Almaden School of Music, Art and Dance

See listing under "Music" section—South Bay.

DeColores Fine Arts School

49 N. San Mateo Dr.
San Mateo
650-347-0267
www.decolores-art.org

Encouraging "diversity through the arts," this school offers classes incorporating art history and theory with creative art projects. Students begin with Tiny Tot Art for ages 2-3 years and progress to painting and mixed media classes.

Kollage (Community School for the Arts)

801 Granada St.
Belmont
650-592-8842
www.kollage.org

With a mission to provide art education for everyone in San Mateo County, this nonprofit school offers classes in visual arts, ceramics, drawing, and mixed media for children ages 2 and up. The school also offers music and movement classes for preschoolers.

Peninsula Parents Place

See listing under "Gyms and Play Programs" section—South Bay.

San Bruno Art Center

721 Camino Plaza
San Bruno
650-875-0207

This center's classes for children ages 3-6 feature mixed media, including drawing, painting, paper mache, collage, and clay.

Dance and Drama

Ballet with Miss Tilly

3119 California St. (office)
5499 California St. (school)
415-923-9965

PARENT RATING: ☆ ☆ ☆ ☆ ☆

This very popular Richmond neighborhood program has a long wait list, so sign your child up early to ensure enrollment. Children must be 3 years old to begin ballet.

Jewish Community Center

See listing under "Gyms and Play Programs" section—San Francisco.

Sunset Movement Arts

1647 Taraval St.
415-665-6444

This school offers preballet classes for preschoolers ages 3-5.

Westlake School for the Performing Arts

200 Northgate Ave. #4
Daly City
650-757-1244

Children ages 3-6 begin with a ballet and tap combination class.

Young Performers Theatre, Theatre Arts Academy

Fort Mason Center (Building C), Fl. 3
415-346-5550
www.ypt.org

This youth drama organization offers classes for children ages 3 and up, including Let's Pretend for ages 3-5, with puppetry, storytelling, music, and dramatization (including the use of costumes and props!).

Happy Feet Dance Studio
15 Montford Ave.
Mill Valley
415-381-0811
PARENT RATING: ☆ ☆ ☆ ☆ ☆
Instruction at this popular Marin studio begins with Tiny Toes, a parent participation dance and movement class for children ages 2-3. Children ages 3 and up may take tap and jazz classes. Get on the waiting list early as these classes fill very quickly.

Luna Kids Dance
510-525-4339
www.lunakidsdance.com
These dance classes held in Marin and San Francisco emphasize creativity, improvisation, and games to teach dance fundamentals. Classes are open to children ages 3 and up.

Marin Ballet
100 Elm St.
San Rafael
415-453-6705
www.marinballet.org
This classical ballet school and regional company offers classes for ages 3 and up, beginning with creative movement for 3- and 4-year-olds and preballet for 5- and 6-year-olds.

Osher Marin Jewish Community Center
See listing under "Gyms and Play Programs" section—North Bay.

Roco Dance and Fitness
237 Shoreline Hwy.
Mill Valley
415-388-6786
www.rocodance.com
This contemporary dance program and gym offers hip-hop, preballet, jazz, and creative movement classes for children ages 3 and up.

Stapleton School of the Performing Arts
118 Greenfield Ave.
San Anselmo
415-454-5759
PARENT RATING: ☆ ☆ ☆ ☆ ☆
Age-appropriate classes at this long-time San Anselmo favorite include Rhythm and Dance for 3-year-olds, Intro to Dance for 4-year-olds, and preballet for 5-year-olds.

Berkeley Ballet Theater School
2640 College Ave.
Berkeley
510-843-4687
www.berkeleyballet.org
This classical ballet school offers year-long classes, including a preballet program for children ages 3.6-6 years.

Berkeley City Ballet
1800 Dwight Way
Berkeley
510-841-8913
This dance troupe offers preballet classes for children beginning at age 4. The classes focus on creative movement and some beginning technique.

Danspace
473 Hudson St.
Oakland
510-420-0920

PARENT RATING: ☆ ☆ ☆ ☆ ☆
This studio's dance program for children begins at age 3.6 with creative movement classes. These classes focus on basic motor skills, coordination, and self-expression rather than technical positions.

Davlin Dance and Music School
2311 Stuart St.
Berkeley
510-843-9740
Classes for the youngest students begin at age 2, with an introduction to dance, floor exercises, balls, tambourines, and nursery rhymes. Classes for older students progressively introduce more formal dance elements.

East Bay Dance Center
3501 Grand Ave.
Oakland
510-465-6678
PARENT RATING: ☆ ☆ ☆ ☆ The official school of the nonprofit Move Dance Theatre, this center features an introductory dance class for children ages 3-5.

Ha Ha This A-Way
2525 8th St.
Berkeley
510-644-1788
PARENT RATING: ☆ ☆ ☆ ☆ ☆
These popular Creative Movement/Theatre Arts classes for children beginning at age 3 are divided by age and include a blend of dance, drama, clowning, yoga, puppetry, music, tumbling and storytelling, with improvisation encouraged.

Julia Morgan Center for the Arts
2640 College Ave.
Berkeley
510-845-8542
www.juliamorgan.org
The Kaleidoscope program for children ages 4 and up provides creative dance and drama classes and camps. The emphasis is on creativity; children get to use props and costumes to invent their own characters and stories.

University Village Recreation Program
See listing under "Gyms and Play Programs" section—East Bay.

YMCA
See listing under "Gyms and Play Programs" section—East Bay.

South Bay

Almaden School of Music, Art and Dance
See listing under "Music" section—South Bay.

California Sports Center
See listing under "Gyms and Play Programs" section—South Bay.

Conservatory of Performing Arts
1401 Parkmoor Ave.
San Jose
408-288-5437, ext. 22
www.sjcmt.com
This offshoot of the San Jose Children's Musical Theater offers classes in acting, dance, voice and production for ages 4 and up.

Dance Academy USA
21269 Stevens Creek Blvd., Ste. 600
Cupertino
408-257-3211

DAU's Creative Dance introductory classes for children ages 2-5 explore tap, ballet, tumbling, and group work.

Dance Dynamics
764 Polhemus Rd.
San Mateo
650-573-9522
Children begin at age 3 in combination classes incorporating tap, tumbling, and ballet.

Kirkpatricks School of Dance
309 8th Ave.
San Mateo
650-342-3315
Preschoolers' classes (for ages 3-5) consist of ballet, tap, and tumbling.

Kollage
See listing under "Art" section—South Bay.

Miss Teri Dance Studio
650-342-3514
• San Mateo
  38 South B St., Ste. 205
• Foster City
  1463 Beach Park Blvd.
This studio offers ballet and tap combination lessons for children ages 3 and up.

Professional Ballet School
425 Harbor Blvd., #3
Belmont
650-598-0796
www.yabt.org
An offshoot of a semiprofessional ballet theater, this school offers preballet classes for children ages 4-6.

Strings of Art Performing Art Center
See listing under "Music" section—South Bay.

More Classes

Adventures with Toddlers
Mill Valley (office)
72 Lovell Ave.
415-331-8882, Loni Greenfield
PARENT RATING: ☆ ☆ ☆ ☆ ☆
Is your child too old for a backpack but too young for strenuous hiking? Try these nature walks for children ages 18 months to 5 years. Parents call them "a good speed" for toddlers and say they "learned about new, off-the-beaten-track places to go with kids." Classes are offered through various Marin recreation departments.

Alphabet Soup
Marin Art and Garden Center
Ross
415-460-0614
www.maagc.org
PARENT RATING: ☆ ☆ ☆ Cooking, art, and gardening are among the activities offered in this multifaceted class, with weekly themes centering around local or world cultures, current events, or holidays. Classes are divided by age and begin at age 18 months, but parents recommended waiting until children are over age 3.

Tot Drop
925-284-3999 or 888-868-3767
With locations throughout the East Bay, these drop in classes for walking babies to preschoolers feature art, music, play, and socialization. You design your own schedule to a maximum of twelve hours per week; you pay by the hour and may drop off your children.

CHAPTER 8

GETTING OUT:
Parks, Museums, Animals, Stories, and Other Adventures

You are going to need to get out of the house sometime after you have your baby—and the sooner the better, in our opinion. Fortunately, the Bay Area is home to many great kid-friendly places to visit—indoor and outdoor, natural and man-made. Not all of these locales are appropriate for children under age five, however. Hence, this chapter. We've selected age-appropriate activities, and divided them topically. From parks and playgrounds, to beaches and pools, museums, zoos and farms, libraries, transportation of all sorts, amusement parks, and special events—check them all out. We'll also tell you the best parent-tested family restaurants and vacation spots. Have fun!

Wherever you go with kids in tow, we recommend packing a few essentials: snacks, drinks, diapers, sunscreen, an extra outfit for each kid, and sweatshirts and hats for everyone. You may find it helpful, as we do, to keep a bag in the car at all times with all of these items and replenish as necessary.

Always call ahead, as programs, hours, and admission prices may change. We've found that going on-line beforehand can be very useful;

each organization's website, listed below, usually features helpful directions, maps, and parking or public transit information.

This chapter will answer the following questions and more:

♦ Which are the best parks in my neighborhood for kids?

♦ What can I do with my kids on a rainy day?

♦ Which museums are worth visiting?

♦ Where can I find a free story-telling hour?

♦ Are there kid-friendly restaurants in my neighborhood?

♦ Where do Bay Area families recommend going for easy vacations?

♦ Where can I find great entertainment or help for my child's birthday?

Parks and Playgrounds

As a new parent, you may find yourself spending more time at your local park than at home. In that spirit, we've put this topic first. We'd love to cover every park and playground in the Bay Area, but space limitations have forced us to confine ourselves to those rated as "favorites" by local parents who completed our surveys. For more comprehensive directories of parks and recreation areas, check out the regional park websites listed below or your local Parks and Recreation Department's website (many of which are also listed below). In addition, you can find all sorts of information about California's many wonderful state parks on www.cal-parks.ca.gov. On a related topic, see chapter 2 under the "Favorite Walks and Hikes" section for fun, family exercise.

San Francisco

San Francisco Parks and Recreation Department

www.parks.sfgov.org

This website features a directory of facilities.

Alta Plaza Park

Jackson St. between Steiner and Scott Sts.

PARENT RATING: ☆☆☆☆☆

You get great views of the city from this Pacific Heights hilltop park and enclosed playground, where you can "bask in the sunshine" (but watch for the high winds!). The self-propelled miniature merry-go-round is always a hit.

Bernal Heights Playground and Recreation Center

Cortland and Moultrie Sts.

The upper level of this two-level park has a nice, sandy playground, and the lower level contains a recreation center and library.

Cow Hollow Playground

Off Miley St. (an alley off Baker St. between Greenwich and Filbert Sts.)

PARENT RATING: ☆ ☆ ☆ ☆ ☆

A perennial favorite, this playground is completely enclosed, very sheltered, and has all sorts of fun equipment, including a miniature cable car for climbing. Parents love it because the park is limited to ages 5 and under.

Douglass Playground

Douglass St. between Clipper and 27th Sts.

PARENT RATING: ☆ ☆ ☆ ☆ ☆

This enclosed playground and recreation center is a huge favorite among Noe Valley parents.

Glen Park Recreation Center and Playground

Bosworth St. and O'Shaughnessy Blvd.

This park features an enclosed playground, a recreation center, a canyon with a stream, and hiking.

Golden Gate Park

Between Stanyan St. and the Great Hwy.

415-831-2745

www.parks.sfgov.org

PARENT RATING: ☆ ☆ ☆ ☆ ☆

The city's largest park, it has over 1,000 acres of meadows, forest, and gardens built on a former sand dune. Parents especially lauded the Children's Playground and Carousel, but recommended that parents "supervise children closely" and "go during the week to avoid crowds." Kid-friendly activities include:

- ◆ **Carousel.** This is an antique 1912 Hirschel-Spillman merry-go-round on Kezar Dr.
- ◆ **Children's Playground.** This is locatated at Kezar Dr. next to the Carousel.
- ◆ **Japanese Tea Garden** (415-752-4227). This is best for walks with babies in carriers.
- ◆ **Model Yacht Sailing.** Most weekends you can watch people sailing model boats on Spreckels Lake opposite 36th Ave.
- ◆ **Picnic** in the park (415-831-5500 for group reservations) or visit the **Beach Chalet** at the Great Hwy. for brew pub food, ocean views, and a look at the restored WPA murals (415-386-8439).
- ◆ **Stow Lake.** Opposite 17th Ave. (415-752-0347). Rent a paddle-boat or picnic along the banks.
- ◆ **Strybing Arboretum and Botanical Gardens.** 9th Ave. at Lincoln Way. (415-661-1316, www.strybing.org.) The beautiful botanical gardens are a great place for a stroller walk and parents say it's "fun for exploring in a contained area."
- ◆ **Walking Tours.** Golden Gate Park Guides offer free historical walking tours of the park. Call 415-263-0991 for a reservation.

Grattan Playground

Stanyan St. at Alma St.
Cole Valley

PARENT RATING: ☆ ☆ ☆ ☆

This neighborhood playground covers an entire city block, with an adjacent recreation center.

Julius Kahn Playground

The Presidio, W. Pacific Ave. and Spruce St.

PARENT RATING: ☆ ☆ ☆ ☆

Many parents felt this park was a great place to meet other moms, but complained that it can be "overrun" with older children from nearby schools. Even so, a nice feature of this park is that it is fenced in and parking is usually easy. The equipment is sized for older kids. Baby swings are located separately from the main playground.

Lafayette Park

Laguna St. at Clay St.

PARENT RATING: ☆ ☆ ☆ ☆ ☆

This park features an enclosed playground and a separate enclosed grassy area for playing ball or spreading a blanket. Comment: "Nice because little ones can't run away."

Michelangelo Playground

Greenwich St. between Leavenworth and Jones Sts.

PARENT RATING: ☆ ☆ ☆ ☆

This great multi-level playground was recently renovated.

Mountain Lake Park

Lake St. at Funston Ave.

PARENT RATING: ☆ ☆ ☆ ☆

Feed the ducks and play in the bi-level playground of this popular park. Caution: the playground is not enclosed, so watch kids carefully, especially on the lower level near the lake.

Noe Valley Courts

24th and Douglass Sts.
Noe Valley

PARENT RATING: ☆ ☆ ☆ ☆

Comment: "My favorite baby park."

West Portal Playground

Lenox St. between Taraval and Ulloa Sts.

There is a large enclosed playground, a recreation center, and a field. Pick up a sandwich or coffee down the street on West Portal Ave.

North Bay

Marin Parks Guide

www.marinweb.com/parks/

This website features a comprehensive directory of Marin County parks by city and facilities. This is a great way to find a new park near you! If you are overwhelmed, try some of our favorite North Bay parks and playgrounds, listed below.

Parks and Recreation in Sonoma County

www.parks.sonoma.net/index.htm

This website describes many Sonoma County parks.

Angel Island State Park

www.angelisland.org

PARENT RATING: ☆ ☆ ☆ ☆ ☆

Thirteen miles of hiking and biking trails, as well as spectacular views of the Bay, await you at Angel Island, the former Ellis Island of the West. To get there, take Blue and Gold Fleet ferries from San Francisco's Pier 41 (415-705-5555, www.blueandgold-fleet.com), the Angel Island ferry from Tiburon (415-435-2131, www.angelislandferry.com), the Alameda-Oakland ferry from Alameda or Oakland (510-522-3300, www.eastbayferry.com), or the Blue

284

& Gold Fleet from Vallejo (707-643-3779, www.baylinkferry.com). Be sure to bring warm clothes. You can eat at the Cove Café (415-897-0715) on the island or bring a picnic lunch.

Belvedere Community Park
San Rafael Ave. next to the Police Dept. and Town Hall
Belvedere

PARENT RATING: ☆ ☆ ☆ ☆ ☆

This park features a nice, not-too-crowded fenced playground for even very young children, with picnic tables nearby. Equipment includes new baby swings and climbing structures, and weather is usually sunny. The large stationary fire truck is a favorite with our boys. You can pick up a decent sandwich at the Tiburon Deli on Ark Row.

Boyle Park
E. Blithedale Ave. near Carmelita Ave.
Mill Valley

PARENT RATING: ☆ ☆ ☆ ☆

This popular playground has been completely rebuilt and has shaded picnic tables nearby. Caveat: it can be quite crowded in the mornings.

Civic Center Park
N. San Pedro Rd. across from the Civic Center
San Rafael

PARENT RATING: ☆ ☆ ☆ ☆

The playground and duck pond will entertain kids. Model sailboat enthusiasts often hold races on weekends.

Corte Madera Town Park
Pixley and Tamalpais Drs.
Corte Madera

PARENT RATING: ☆ ☆ ☆ ☆ ☆

This park was renovated in 2001 and features a fabulous playground with swings, slides, a water and sand play area, a tricycle track, and a special climbing structure for the very young who usually can't navigate larger play structures. The park also offers many seating areas for parents. An insider's tip: the park is so popular that it can be virtually overrun with children and caregivers during mornings. Try the early afternoon hours if you want to avoid the crowds.

Creekside Park
Bon Air Rd. across from Marin General Hospital
Kentfield

PARENT RATING: ☆ ☆ ☆ ☆

This park features a nice sunny playground with an adjacent shady picnic area (perfect for parking infants while the older kids play). It's not enclosed, but it is surrounded by playing fields so it's easy to keep track of wandering kids.

Freitas Park
Montecillo Rd. next to Kaiser Permanente Medical Center
Terra Linda

PARENT RATING: ☆ ☆ ☆ ☆ ☆

Known locally as the "water park," this park features a three-ringed water structure through which kids can run and douse themselves in the summer. Our toddlers had a ball! Bring a beach umbrella as there is only one small pergola structure and no shade.

Gerstle Park

D St.

San Rafael

PARENT RATING: ☆ ☆ ☆ ☆ ☆

There are several playgrounds and shaded benches in this tree-filled neighborhood park.

Hoog Park

Off Marin Oaks in the hills of Ignacio

Novato

PARENT RATING: ☆ ☆ ☆ ☆

Parents say this park has "lots of grassy hills and a contained playground" perfect for younger kids.

Mount Tamalpais State Park

Panoramic Hwy.

Mill Valley

415-388-2070

http://cal-parks.ca.gov/

PARENT RATING: ☆ ☆ ☆ ☆ ☆

Miles of hiking trails and the 2,571-foot peak of Mount Tamalpais, where you can catch wonderful views of the ocean, bay, and city, are some of the attractions in this wonderful park. Bring a jog stroller or backpack, as trails are rocky and sometimes steep.

Muir Woods National Monument

Off Panoramic Hwy.

Mill Valley

415-388-2595

www.visitmuirwoods.com

PARENT RATING: ☆ ☆ ☆ ☆ ☆

This giant old-growth redwood forest features lots of hiking trails and picnic areas. The valley floor is stroller accessible and fairly cool in the summer. A caution: It can be very wet in the rainy season! Weekends can also be crowded with tourists. Lunch in the café; picnics are not allowed.

Peacock Gap Park

Peacock Dr. off San Pedro Rd.

San Rafael

PARENT RATING: ☆ ☆ ☆ ☆ ☆

Two adjacent playground areas make up this park; one is for the toddler crowd, and the other is for older children. Shaded benches and lots of sand for playing are great amenities. The park is not enclosed, but it is surrounded by fields and is very quiet. It can be cool, as it is near the Bay.

Piper Park

Doherty Dr. next to the Police Dept.

Larkspur

PARENT RATING: ☆ ☆ ☆ ☆

An open playground and adjacent picnic tables make this a nice choice for groups. A caution: there is no shade from summer sun in the playground itself.

Pixie Park

Marin Art and Garden Center, Sir Francis Drake Blvd. at Lagunitas Rd.

Ross

www.pixiepark.org

PARENT RATING: ☆ ☆ ☆ ☆ ☆

Pixie is a veritable Marin institution—a members-only cooperative park and a "must join" for Marin families with young children. Parents must contribute a number of hours in park maintenance and fundraising events. Parents appreciate the locked gate, the relative quiet, and the fact that everything is geared toward younger children. Only children ages 6 and under are allowed into the park.

Richardson Bay Lineal Park (aka Blackie's Pasture)

Begins at Blackie's Pasture Rd. at Tiburon and Trestle Glen Blvds. and continues into downtown Tiburon along the Bay

PARENT RATING: ☆ ☆ ☆ ☆ ☆

This park features a great walking path for stroller walks, as well as a fenced playground about halfway down the path to Tiburon. A caution: there is little protection from the sun and wind, so be sure to bring hats and jackets.

San Anselmo Memorial Park

Off San Francisco Blvd. near Sir Francis Drake Blvd.
San Anselmo

PARENT RATING: ☆ ☆ ☆ ☆ ☆

A group of volunteer parents rebuilt the Millennium playground at this park in 2000, creating two great play areas for kids. One area is for toddlers and preschoolers, and one is for ages 6 and up. Innovative structures include castles, a train, a lighthouse, and a water play area.

East Bay

East Bay Regional Park District Website

www.ebparks.org

This website features a useful directory of Alameda and Contra Costa counties regional parks and recreation facilities.

Websites for some popular municipal parks departments include:

Berkeley
www.ci.berkeley.ca.us/parks
Concord
www.ci.concord.ca.us/recreation/parksguide.pdf
Danville
www.ci.danville.ca.us/parks/parkdes.htm
Dublin
www.ci.dublin.ca.us/html/facdir.html
Orinda
www.ci.orinda.ca.us/parkrec.htm
Pleasanton
www.pleasanton.com
San Ramon
www.ci.san-ramon.ca.us
Walnut Creek
www.ci.walnut-creek.ca.us

Adventure Playground

Berkeley Marina
160 University Ave.
Berkeley
510-644-6376
www.ci.berkeley.ca.us/marina/

Older children (ages 7 and up) may hammer, saw, and paint to "build" parts of the playground; younger children will enjoy just playing on what is already built.

Aquatic Park

Bolivar Dr. at the west end of Bancroft Way
Berkeley

Parents rebuilt this playground in 2000, and it offers separate areas for kids under age 5 and for older kids, as well as a very popular dragon slide. Bring a hat as it is very sunny.

Central Park

12501 Alcosta Blvd.
San Ramon

PARENT RATING: ☆ ☆ ☆ ☆ ☆

Home of the San Ramon Community Center and pool, this park features a rose garden, a playground, and picnic areas.

Civic Park

1375 Civic Dr. at N. Broadway
Walnut Creek
925-943-5852

PARENT RATING: ☆ ☆ ☆ ☆ ☆

This ten-acre park offers a children's play area, a picnic area, a community center, a gazebo, and arts studios.

Codornices Park

1201 Euclid Ave. at Eunice St.
Berkeley

PARENT RATING: ☆ ☆ ☆ ☆

This park features two separate play areas—the Tot Lot for younger kids (with a fence and a sandbox) and the older kids' area (with bigger swings, play structures, and slides). Combine the outing with a walk through the Berkeley Rose Garden across the street.

Diablo Vista Park

1000 Tassajara Ranch Dr.
Danville

PARENT RATING: ☆ ☆ ☆ ☆ ☆

Famous for its mosaic water snake winding down the hillside, this twenty-acre park has great play and picnic areas.

Heather Farm Park

301 N. San Carlos Dr.
Walnut Creek
925-943-5858

This 102-acre park features a duck pond, gardens, an equestrian center, swimming, a playground, and picnic areas.

Lafayette Reservoir

3849 Mt. Diablo Blvd.
Lafayette
925-284-9669
www.ebmud.com/info/recreation/ebrec.html

This reservoir, operated by the East Bay Municipal Utility District, offers 925 acres of hiking trails, boating, fishing, and picnicking. There are two children's play areas near the picnic areas, as well as a popular paved trail. Rowboats and pedal boats may be rented.

Lakeside Park

Lakeside Dr. on Lake Merritt
Oakland

PARENT RATING: ☆ ☆ ☆ ☆

This is a great place for a stroll along the lake, with many spots to stop and feed the ducks. Don't miss the Kids' Kingdom Playground (Bellevue Ave. between Elita and Perkins Sts.).

Live Oak Park

Berryman St. between Shattuck Ave. and Walnut St.
Berkeley

PARENT RATING: ☆ ☆ ☆ ☆

Parents appreciate the fenced playground; kids like the swings, toddler-sized climbing area, and ride-on animals.

Mission Hills Park

Independence Dr. and Junipero St.
Pleasanton

PARENT RATING: ☆ ☆ ☆ ☆ ☆

This is a popular park because of the creek (with frog-filled lagoon and island) and the fifty-foot slide built into the hill.

Moraga Commons

St. Mary's Rd. off Moraga Rd.
Moraga
PARENT RATING: ☆ ☆ ☆ ☆ ☆

This ever-popular park "for younger kids" features the Moraga Cooler water structure through which kids can run and spray themselves.

Oak Hill Park

3005 Stone Valley Rd.
Danville
PARENT RATING: ☆ ☆ ☆ ☆ ☆

Kids love feeding the ducks and geese, and you can stroll around the lake on level paths. There is also a playground and more adventurous hiking terrain.

Old Ranch Park

1000 Vista Monte Dr.
San Ramon
PARENT RATING: ☆ ☆ ☆ ☆ ☆

This park offers a revamped playground with new equipment and picnic areas.

Orinda Park

26 Orinda Way
Orinda
PARENT RATING: ☆ ☆ ☆ ☆ ☆

Remodeled several years ago, this park in the center of Orinda is hugely popular. There are separate big kids' and little kids' areas, a gazebo, a community center, and a paved bike path.

Osage Station Park

816 Brookside Dr.
Danville

PARENT RATING: ☆ ☆ ☆ ☆ ☆

Stroll through the lovely rose garden or visit the playground, which features a train station, water play, and picnic areas.

Pleasanton Sports Park

5800 Parkside Dr.
Pleasanton
925-484-8160
PARENT RATING: ☆ ☆ ☆ ☆ ☆

This park has over one hundred acres of sports facilities, including several children's play areas.

Shannon Park

11600 Shannon Ave.
Dublin
925-833-6645
The water play area makes this an extremely popular park for kids.

Terrace Park

Terrace Dr. and Tevlin St.
Albany
PARENT RATING: ☆ ☆ ☆ ☆

This park features shaded picnic tables, wide fields, "good equipment" (swings, slides, climbing equipment), and "separate sides for older and younger kids."

Tilden Park

Entrances off Wildcat Canyon Rd.
and Grizzly Peak Blvd.
Berkeley
510-562-PARK
www.ebparks.org
PARENT RATING: ☆ ☆ ☆ ☆ ☆

There are over two thousand acres in this East Bay treasure, with spectacular hiking and views of the bay, including the following fun attractions for kids:

- **Reservable picnic areas** (510-636-1684).
- **Swimming at Lake Anza** (510-843-2137). Visit the sandy beach during the season. Comment: "Best non-pool swimming!"
- **Little Train** (510-548-6100). A miniature steam passenger railway, a huge hit with kids, travels through stunning eucalyptus groves and offers views of the Bay.
- **Botanic Garden** (510-841-8732). This garden features beautiful native California plants from twelve geographic ranges; it's a good place for a leisurely walk.
- **Merry-Go-Round** (510-524-6773). This antique carousel has an organ and adjacent snack bar with "amusement park" fare.
- **Pony Rides** (510-527-0421). Kids love them!
- **Little Farm and Environmental Education Center** in Tilden Nature Study Area (510-525-2233). The EEC features interactive displays where kids can use microscopes to see pond life. Feed the animals at the farm! Naturalists lead nature walks by the ponds and through the hills and meadows. The adjacent picnic area and playground will also entertain kids.

Totland Playground
McGee Ave. and Virginia St.
Berkeley
PARENT RATING: ☆ ☆ ☆ ☆

This fenced playground was renovated recently and is very popular for families with young children. The sand and water play area is a huge hit.

Village Green Park
9540 Village Pky.
San Ramon
PARENT RATING: ☆ ☆ ☆ ☆ ☆

This is a popular playground and picnic area.

South Bay

Santa Clara County Parks and Recreation Department
www.parkhere.org

San Mateo County Parks and Recreation Division
www.eparks.net

Websites for some popular municipal parks departments include:
Burlingame
www.burlingame.org/p_r/parks/parks.htm
Campbell
www.ci.campbell.ca.us/communityandarts/parks.htm
Los Gatos
www.los-gatos.org/main/parks.html
Menlo Park
www.ci.menlo-park.ca.us
Mountain View
www.ci.mtnview.ca.us/citydepts/cs/parks.htm
Palo Alto
www.city.palo-alto.ca.us/parks/
Redwood City
www.redwoodcity.org/parks/
San Jose
www.sanjoseparks.org
San Mateo
www.ci.sanmateo.ca.us/dept/parks/
Sunnyvale
www.ci.sunnyvale.ca.us/parks-and-rec/

Bowden Park

Alma and N. California Sts.
Palo Alto

PARENT RATING: ☆ ☆ ☆ ☆ ☆

This park is great for the youngest children, with a large children's play area full of equipment, such as a climbing gym and a brick wall maze. There are also attractive gardens, a small picnic area, and a redwood grove.

Briones Park

Arastradero Rd. between Foothill Expwy. and El Camino Real
Palo Alto

PARENT RATING: ☆ ☆ ☆ ☆

This park has a playground, a picnic area, and a tot area with a stationary locomotive.

Burgess Park

701 Laurel St.
Menlo Park

PARENT RATING: ☆ ☆ ☆ ☆

This is Menlo Park's main recreation area, with playing fields, a playground, a swimming pool, and a gymnasium.

Central Park

5th Ave. and El Camino Real
San Mateo

A miniature train for kids, play structures, and a Japanese Tea Garden grace this park.

DeAnza Park

1150 Lime Dr.
Sunnyvale

You can find a playground, horseshoe pits, picnic areas, a skating rink, and more at this park.

Jack Fischer Park

Abbott Ave. and Pollard Rd.
Campbell

PARENT RATING: ☆ ☆ ☆ ☆ ☆

This park features play equipment for both toddlers and older children, including a stream that kids can activate on demand, and picnic areas.

Greer Park

1098 Amarillo Ave.
Palo Alto

PARENT RATING: ☆ ☆ ☆ ☆

This park offers a tiny tot area with a nautical theme, as well as traditional play structures and picnic areas.

Hoover Park

2901 Cowper St.
Palo Alto

PARENT RATING: ☆ ☆ ☆ ☆

This park features a nice tiny tot area with a merry-go-round, crawling and climbing structures, swings, slides, and sand. A play area for bigger kids has a geodesic climbing dome to ascend, swings, and a roller-coaster slide.

Johnson Park

Waverly and Everett Sts.
Palo Alto

PARENT RATING: ☆ ☆ ☆ ☆

The big concrete slide here is a huge hit with kids.

Las Palmas Park

850 Russet Dr.
Sunnyvale

This park has a newer play structure, a spray pool, and a picnic area on an "island" in the lake.

Mitchell Park
East Meadow and Middlefield Rds.
Palo Alto

The tiny tot area has six gopher holes, slides and swings, bears in the sandpit to climb on, a shady wading pool with two green frogs, and a birthday party area.

John Morgan Park
540 W. Rincon Ave.
Campbell

PARENT RATING: ☆ ☆ ☆ ☆ ☆

There are two playgrounds (one with a water spiral play area), picnic areas, and sports fields.

Nealon Park
800 Middle Ave.
Menlo Park

PARENT RATING: ☆ ☆ ☆ ☆ ☆

Parents call this newly renovated playground "great."

Oak Meadow Park
University Ave. and Blossom Hill Rd.
Los Gatos

There are separate areas for toddlers and older children, with a stationary toy train and model airplane to entertain.

Eleanor Pardee Park
851 Center Dr.
Palo Alto

PARENT RATING: ☆ ☆ ☆ ☆

This park features a tiny tot area, an apparatus play area, sheltered picnic tables and benches, and a stage.

Peers Park
1899 Park Blvd.
Palo Alto

PARENT RATING: ☆ ☆ ☆ ☆

There are picnic areas, a wooden play structure, and a tiny tot area in this park.

Ramos Park
800 E. Meadow
Palo Alto

PARENT RATING: ☆ ☆ ☆ ☆ ☆

Parents say this park, with lots of open space, is a "great place to fly kites." The toddler play area has a sculpture in the sandpit and a climbing structure in the shape of a train.

Rinconada Park
777 Embarcadero Rd.
Palo Alto

PARENT RATING: ☆ ☆ ☆ ☆ ☆

Palo Alto's central park features two playgrounds and pools.

Seminary Oaks Park
Seminary Dr. and Santa Monica Ave.
Menlo Park

PARENT RATING: ☆ ☆ ☆ ☆ ☆

This sunny, new playground offers three age-specific playground areas, as well as a "relaxation garden" for adults.

Serra Park
730 The Dalles
Sunnyvale

There are picnic areas, a playground, and a spray pool in this park.

Shoreline at Mountain View Park

2600 N. Shoreline Blvd.
Mountain View
650-903-6392

PARENT RATING: ☆ ☆ ☆ ☆ ☆

There is a large lake for boating, and the paths are great for strollers or bikes. Comment: "Great place to fly a kite."

Shoup Park

400 University Ave.
Los Altos

PARENT RATING: ☆ ☆ ☆ ☆

This park has a lovely creek.

Stafford Park

Hopkins Ave. and King St.
Redwood City

PARENT RATING: ☆ ☆ ☆ ☆ ☆

The water play area is "the best," say parents. This newly renovated park features two adjacent play areas, one for big kids and one for toddlers.

Sunnyvale Baylands Park

999 E. Caribbean Dr.
Sunnyvale
408-730-7709

Set in open space and baylands, this park has a great Discovery Play Area with climbing structures, a see-saw snake, spring toys, sand terraces, talk tubes, and fossil imprints. There are also miles of trails for stroller walking.

Vasona Lake County Park

333 Blossom Hill Rd.
Los Gatos
408-356-2729

PARENT RATING: ☆ ☆ ☆ ☆ ☆

Wide lawns for play, picnic areas, and a new waterfront theme playground make this a very popular facility for families. There is also a lake for paddle boating, row boating, or fishing.

Washington Park

850 Burlingame Ave.
Burlingame

Located in the heart of Burlingame, this is a popular park with a large playground and a recreation center.

Washington Park

840 W. Washington Ave.
Sunnyvale

PARENT RATING: ☆ ☆ ☆ ☆ ☆

This park offers innovative play structures, picnic areas, a pool, tennis courts, and horseshoe pits.

Indoor Playgrounds

A common lament of local parents is the lack of indoor play areas for kids. The price of Bay Area real estate being what it is, we may not all have dedicated play rooms at home. Try these indoor playgrounds, and don't forget the drop in play programs listed in chapter 7 (e.g., the JCC and Temple Sherith Israel in San Francisco, the Center for Creative Parenting and Jumping Jacks in Marin, the Berkeley YMCA in the East Bay, and Peninsula Parents Place).

Bamboola

5401 Camden Ave.
San Jose
408-448-4386
www.bamboola.com

PARENT RATING: ☆ ☆ ☆ ☆

This thirty-thousand-square-foot indoor play area has an outdoor garden and sand box, art projects, live performances, water play, a separate toddler area (for kids under age 3), and a café.

Chuck-E-Cheese

www.chuckecheese.com

PARENT RATING: ☆ ☆ ☆

Games, rides, and pizza for kids center around "Chuck-E-Cheese," a giant rat! Kids love it; parents don't. Check the website for locations throughout the Bay Area.

The Jungle Fun and Adventure

www.junglefunandadventure.com

PARENT RATING: ☆ ☆ ☆

This indoor playground has climbing structures for older kids, an enclosed toddler area, and an adjacent pizza parlor. The Jungle received mixed reviews; as one parent put it, "Every kid I know likes the Jungle, but parents don't." Most parents felt the facilities were "too big and crowded" and appeared "not that clean." Others point out that it is best for kids ages 3 and up or under 18 months, as 2-year-olds are too old for the toddler area and too young for the big kids' area. Check the website for locations throughout the Bay Area.

Merlin's Magic Kingdom

Round Table Pizza
1565 Novato Blvd.
Novato
415-897-2512

PARENT RATING: ☆ ☆ ☆ ☆

This pizza parlor and indoor play area offers tubes, slides, and crawling structures for kids ages 10 and under.

Toob Town

6591 Commerce Blvd.
Rohnert Park
707-588-8100

PARENT RATING: ☆ ☆ ☆ ☆

This indoor playground for kids ages 2 and up features tube play structures, bumper boats, a dinosaur bounce, a toddler play area, and ball pits. Stay for a pizza lunch at the adjoining restaurant.

Favorite Beaches and Public Pools

We are fortunate to live in an area with great beaches and many pools. While Pacific beaches can be cool and foggy during the summer, and many are not safe for swimming (at least for children), kids will still enjoy a day at the beach making sand castles, hunting for shells, and splashing in tide pools. For serious swimming, check out the family-oriented pools and lakes listed below. You'll also find more pools listed under the "Swimming" section in chapter 7.

San Francisco

Baker Beach
Off Lincoln Blvd. near 25th Ave.
PARENT RATING: ☆ ☆ ☆ ☆ ☆

This sandy beach in the Seacliff neighborhood is probably about as sheltered as you will get in San Francisco, but the winds still blow. It offers views of the Golden Gate Bridge when the fog lifts and has picnic tables in a grove of cypress trees. Note: The north end of the beach is sometimes used by nude sunbathers, and parking is very limited on weekends.

Crissy Field and Marina Green
Parking off Marina Blvd. west of Marina Green
PARENT RATING: ☆ ☆ ☆ ☆ ☆

Newly restored Crissy Field is a wonderful place to spend a sunny morning, as it has a sandy beach, walking trails (great for strollers), and beautiful "can't beat it" Golden Gate Bridge views. It is almost always windy, so be sure to bring a sweatshirt and hat. Don't miss the Warming Hut for lunch or snack located at the far end of Chrissy Field, towards the bridge.

Fort Funston and Ocean Beach
Off Skyline Blvd. just south of John Muir Dr.
415-239-2366
PARENT RATING: ☆ ☆ ☆ ☆

This beach features the stroller-friendly Sunset Trail along the cliff. You will have to carry the stroller down the stairs to the beach, however, and watch for fog.

North Bay

China Camp State Park and Beach
N. San Pedro Road, east of Hwy. 101
San Rafael
415-456-0766
www.cal-parks.ca.gov
PARENT RATING: ☆ ☆ ☆ ☆

Parents call this state park a "good day trip." This bay-front beach is rocky but warmer than Pacific beaches. The park features a museum depicting life in the Chinese shrimp-fishing village that thrived on the site in the 1880s.

Drake's Beach
Point Reyes National Seashore, near Olema
www.nps.gov/pore/home.htm
PARENT RATING: ☆ ☆ ☆ ☆

The four-mile beach along Drake's Bay in Point Reyes includes a small café and a visitor's center.

McNear's Beach County Park
San Pedro Rd. at Cantera Way, east of Hwy. 101
San Rafael
415-499-6387
www.co.marin.ca.us
PARENT RATING: ☆ ☆ ☆ ☆

At this popular county park on San Pablo Bay, you can hang out at the sandy beach, picnic, play frisbee on the lawn, fish off the five-hundred-foot pier, swim in the public swimming pool, play tennis, or eat at the snack bar.

Muir Beach
Off Hwy. 1, west of Mill Valley
PARENT RATING: ☆ ☆ ☆ ☆

It's windy, but you'll enjoy the rugged scenery along the Pacific. Leave your stroller at home.

Stinson Beach
Stinson Beach off Hwy. 1
415-868-1922
PARENT RATING: ☆ ☆ ☆ ☆

There are shaded picnic tables in the nearby park. Note: No lifeguard is on duty during the winter, and surf can be dangerous. Get an early start on summer weekends, as traffic can be backed up fifteen miles to Hwy. 101.

Strawberry Recreation District Pool
118 E. Strawberry Dr.
Mill Valley
415-383-1610
http://strawberry.marin.org
PARENT RATING: ☆ ☆ ☆ ☆

It can be a bit crowded on sunny days, but there is a nice wading pool

for toddlers and a big pool for older children.

Tennessee Valley Beach
Off Tennessee Valley Rd.
Mill Valley
PARENT RATING: ☆ ☆ ☆ ☆

It's a two-mile walk to this small Pacific beach; be sure to bring a jog stroller or backpack carrier, as regular strollers won't cut it on the rocky trail. There are fun tide pools in which young children can play. It can be foggy in the summer, so bring warm clothes.

Tomales Bay Beaches (including Heart's Desire Beach)
Inverness
www.cal-parks.ca.gov

This state park's beaches feature "calm water...perfect for young ones."

East Bay

Clarke Swim Center
Heather Farm Park
1750 Heather Dr.
Walnut Creek
925-943-5856
www.ci.walnut-creek.ca.us

There is a large heated public pool and a children's wading pool at this center.

Lake Temescal
6500 Broadway
Oakland
510-652-1155
www.ebparks.org

Enjoy swimming (lifeguards are on duty in summer), a snack bar, fishing, and picnic areas.

Roberts Regional Recreation Area and Pool

Skyline Blvd. at Joaquin Miller Rd.
Oakland
510-482-0971

This one-hundred-acre recreation area set in a lush redwood grove features a popular heated pool that is open in summer.

San Ramon Olympic Pool and Aquatic Park

9900 Broadmoor Dr.
San Ramon
925-973-3240

PARENT RATING: ☆ ☆ ☆ ☆

This state-of-the-art facility offers three pools, including a water play pool for small children. Comment: "A great kids' area."

Shadow Cliffs Regional Recreation Area

2500 Stanley Blvd.
Pleasanton
925-846-9263

This is a huge 250-acre park with an 80-acre lake for swimming and trout fishing, a four-flume waterslide, and picnic areas.

Almaden Lake Park

Almaden Expwy. and Coleman Ave.
San Jose
408-277-5130

This foothill park features a lake for boating or swimming, surrounded by a biking and strolling trail. There is also a playground, with separate areas for toddlers and older children, and picnic areas.

Half Moon Bay State Beach (aka Francis Beach)

Hwy. 1 at Kelley Rd.
Half Moon Bay
650-726-8820

PARENT RATING: ☆ ☆ ☆ ☆ ☆

We've hit some spectacular days at this beach in the early fall when the fog recedes. It offers a long, open sandy beach and picnic areas.

Montara State Beach

Hwy. 1
Montara

PARENT RATING: ☆ ☆ ☆ ☆ ☆

This beach is popular with surfers.

Santa Cruz Beach and Boardwalk

Beach St.
Santa Cruz
831-426-7433
www.beachboardwalk.com

PARENT RATING: ☆ ☆ ☆ ☆ ☆

The boardwalk features rides, arcades, and lots of food stands. Comment: "Toddlers love the boardwalk and beach."

Museums

Before you say, "my kid will never enjoy a museum," check out some of the museums listed below. Many are geared to young children, and some "adult" museums offer special children's programming. Keep in mind that many museums offer wonderful children's birthday parties.

San Francisco

Most San Francisco museums offer free admission on the first Wednesday of the month. While that sounds like a good deal in principle, we recommend steering clear of the free days because the crowds can be overwhelming for younger children (and enough to give even the most patient of parents a migraine!). A money-saving hint: Many museums provide discounts to members of affiliated museums and to KQED or AAA members. Check with individual museums for policies.

California Academy of Sciences
Golden Gate Park
55 Concourse Dr.
415-750-7145
www.calacademy.org
PARENT RATING: ☆ ☆ ☆ ☆ ☆

The Academy includes the Natural History Museum, Steinhart Aquarium, and Morrison Planetarium. Favorite tot spots include the Africa Hall, featuring the Africa Playspace for children ages 5 and under. In the Playspace kids can try on costumes, do puzzles, or read a book, and there may even be a volunteer with musical instruments and puppets. Other hot spots for young children are the giant dinosaur skeleton in the entrance, the Aquarium (particularly the Fish Roundabout and the hands-on exploration of starfish and coral in the Touch Tide Pool), and the courtyard fountain. There is a decent café for lunch. A few parents thought the museum needed some upgrading, but most appreciated the "variety" of exhibits. Comment: "This is a great membership to have, especially for a rainy or foggy day...my kids love it."

California Palace of the Legion of Honor
Lincoln Park
100 34th Ave.
415-863-3330
www.thinker.org

Though the European art and beautiful building may not interest children under age 5, squire them to the Big Kids, Little Kids program for preschoolers on Saturday afternoons. There you can take a child-oriented gallery tour and art class. While visiting, take advantage of the spectacular views of the Bay from Lincoln Park. Dine in the museum's café or picnic in the park.

Exploratorium

3601 Lyon St.

415-EXP-LORE

www.exploratorium.edu

PARENT RATING: ☆ ☆ ☆ ☆ ☆

This highly rated science and discovery museum features hands-on exhibits like the Tactile Dome, where you crawl around in the dark using your sense of touch to guide you. The Tactile Dome is "better for older kids," since it may be too scary for children under age 3. Younger kids will enjoy Play Lab, a special play area for infants, toddlers, and preschoolers. Eat at the café or head to one of the many Chestnut St. eateries nearby.

Randall Museum

199 Museum Way

415-554-9600

www.randallmuseum.org

PARENT RATING: ☆ ☆ ☆ ☆

Run by the San Francisco Recreation and Park Department, this art and science museum sits atop Corona Heights, commanding spectacular views of the city. Though the museum's collection is small, kids will enjoy seeing the live animals (e.g., snakes and turtles) and the model train exhibit. The museum also offers many family classes and special performances, including drop in art and science programs on Saturdays. Picnic and play in the adjacent Corona Heights playground; there are no café facilities.

San Francisco Cable Car Museum

1201 Mason St.

415-474-1887

www.cablecarmuseum.com

This cable car barn and powerhouse museum features several antique cable cars, a film explaining how cable cars work, and lots of historical memorabilia about the cable car system. You can ride the Powell-Mason or Powell-Hyde lines to the museum; parking is very difficult in this Nob Hill neighborhood. It's best for ages 3 and up.

San Francisco Fire Department Museum

655 Presidio Ave.

415-563-4630 (during museum hours) or 415-558-3546 (voice mail)

www.sffiremuseum.org

Kids will enjoy the model fire engines (showing the development from hand pumpers to mechanized fire trucks), the collection of cast iron toys, and the antique fire engines and wagons on display.

San Francisco Museum of Modern Art

151 3rd St.

415-357-4000

www.sfmoma.org

Much of this highly rated modern art museum will be beyond the comprehension of children under age 6, but there are several special family events worth checking out. Family Day, twice a year, features hands-on art projects, docent-led gallery activities, music, and performances. Monthly hands-on Family Studios, directed by guest artists, include drawing, painting, collage, printmaking, and assemblage. Children's art classes for ages 2 and up are sometimes offered. There is a café and a museum store on site.

Bay Area Discovery Museum

E. Fort Baker
557 McReynolds Rd.
Sausalito
415-487-4398
www.badm.org

PARENT RATING: ☆ ☆ ☆ ☆ ☆

Along with many other Bay Area parents, we can't say enough good things about this hands-on museum for children ages 10 and under and their families. Kids as young as one year old will love it. Easily the most popular family destination in the Bay Area, this indoor/outdoor museum's permanent exhibits include the San Francisco Bay Hall, Architecture and Design (including a great wooden train room), Maze of Illusions, Tot Spot (a special indoor play area for kids under age 3), Art Room (drop in art projects and classes), Ceramics Studio (drop in ceramics classes), Media Center, and Science Lab. Other favorites are the boats "moored" in the play yard, an outdoor water play area, and Miss Kitty's musical performances. There is also a changing exhibit every quarter. The café has recently improved its menu, or you may want to bring your own picnic for the tables outside. The Discovery Store offers a range of stimulating toys for young children. Special events and performances occur throughout the year. We recommend joining the museum if you intend to make several visits per year; membership is inexpensive and provides free admission and discounts in the store. Our kids would visit every week if they could! "It can't be overrated...a great place to go on rainy days...lots of activities...a beautiful location...good for a wide age range." "By far the best deal for weekly outings," say parents.

Blackhawk Museum

3700 Blackhawk Plaza Cir.
Danville
925-736-2277
www.blackhawkauto.org

Children will like the Auto Galleries with over one hundred historically significant cars. The Smithsonian Gallery offers rotating exhibitions from the Smithsonian Institution. The Discovery Room with interactive exhibits is also a sure hit.

Chabot Space and Science Center

10000 Skyline Blvd.
Oakland
510-336-7300
www.chabotspace.org

This science museum features a wonderful planetarium, a Mega-Dome Theater with a seventy-foot dome screen for viewing science movies, telescopes for public viewing in the evenings, simulated space missions in the Challenger Learning Center (for older children), and a Discovery Lab with hands-on learning for children ages 2 and up. The museum offers a café for lunch and is located on thirteen acres of East Bay parkland with great views of San Francisco and Oakland.

Golden State Model Railroad Museum

Miller/Knox Regional Shoreline
900 Dornan Dr.
Richmond
510-234-4884 or 510-758-6288
www.gsmrm.org

PARENT RATING: ☆ ☆ ☆ ☆ ☆

Home to a model railway club, this little-known gem boasts ten thousand square feet of working N, HO, and O scale model railroads. Our train-obsessed 2-year-old was completely fascinated by the extensive layouts, with realistic landscaping, buildings, and vehicles. It's best for ages 2 and up.

Hall of Health

2230 Shattuck Ave.
Berkeley
510-549-1564
www.hallofhealth.org

Sponsored by Children's Hospital Oakland, this is a free health-education museum and science center. Interactive exhibits teach older kids how the body works. Younger kids will enjoy the Kids on the Block puppet shows.

Habitot Children's Museum

2065 Kittredge St.
Berkeley
510-647-1111
www.habitot.org

PARENT RATING: ☆ ☆ ☆ ☆ ☆

This wonderfully hands-on, indoor art and discovery museum for children under age 7 is particularly appropriate for toddlers and preschoolers. Favorites include the water play exhibit (be sure to bring extra clothes), dress-up area and stage, wind tunnel, art projects, grocery store, infant-toddler garden for crawlers, and ride-on cars and trucks. There are great multidisciplinary classes for kids, and special family events occur often. Some found it "too crowded and hectic," especially on rainy days, but most appreciated the convenient downtown Berkeley location.

Junior Center of Art and Science

558 Bellevue Ave.
Oakland
510-839-5777

This museum features live animals, aquariums, a pottery studio, and a bird sanctuary. Fun, drop in art activities (e.g., pottery) are offered for children ages 2 and up and their families.

Lawrence Hall of Science

1 Centennial Dr.
Berkeley
510-642-5132
www.lawrencehallofscience.org

PARENT RATING: ☆ ☆ ☆ ☆

A favorite of young children in this science museum is the Young Explorers Area, with puppets, blocks, books, and an insect zoo. Other fun areas are the interactive science exhibits, a biology lab with animals to pet, the Gravity Wall, and the earthquake exhibit. There are many science and nature classes for kids ages 2 and up. There is a café for lunch.

Museum of Children's Art

538 9th St.
Oakland
510-465-8770
www.mocha.org

Younger children may not be interested in looking at the art, but they can *do* art projects in myriad classes and workshops. The Little Studio offers a great drop in art space for children under age 6.

Oakland Museum of California

1000 Oak St.
Oakland
888-625-6873 or 510-238-2200
www.museumca.org

Most kids under age 5 won't be able to appreciate this extensive museum of the art, history, and natural sciences of California. Try taking them to see the dioramas of California wildlife in the Natural Sciences Gallery. If you have older children, the Family Explorations Program offers fun hands-on activities for kids ages 5-12.

Valley Children's Museum

P.O. Box 305
San Ramon
www.valleychildrensmuseum.org

An interactive, hands-on, nonprofit children's museum in the Tri-Valley area was in the planning stages as of spring 2002. Check the website for updates.

Western Aerospace Museum

Oakland Airport, North Field
8260 Boeing St. (Building 621)
Oakland
510-638-7100
www.aerospace.org/wamhome.htm

Located in an authentic hangar, highlights of this indoor/outdoor aviation history museum include the Short Solent 4-engine Flying Boat formerly owned by Howard Hughes, an instrument trainer, and the sister plane to Amelia Earhart's craft. If you have a

group, arrange a "climb-aboard" guided tour for the kids.

South Bay

Children's Discovery Museum of San Jose

180 Woz Way
San Jose
408-298-5437
www.cdm.org

PARENT RATING: ☆ ☆ ☆ ☆ ☆

A fabulous interactive museum for children ages 13 and under, CDM offers exhibits and programs in science, technology, the arts, and the humanities. Older kids will enjoy climbing the multilevel tower and exploring the exhibits on transportation, communications, electricity, banking, the postal service, and so on, but stick to the early childhood center and bubbles exhibit for young children (ages 4 and under). Often you can participate in free parent-child workshops and drop in art, science, and music classes. Eat lunch in the Kids' Café or picnic in nearby Guadalupe River Park.

Hiller Aviation Museum

601 Skyway Rd.
San Carlos
650-654-0200
www.hiller.org

This aviation museum features vintage and futuristic aircraft, prototypes, photographic displays, and models. It's best for older kids, though even 2-year-olds will like seeing the planes and helicopters.

Palo Alto Junior Museum and Zoo

1451 Middlefield Rd.

Palo Alto

650-329-2111

PARENT RATING: ☆ ☆ ☆ ☆ ☆

This ever-popular nature, science, art, and history museum for children features hands-on exhibits, a small zoo, and a playground with a picnic area in the park next to the museum. A favorite is the Play Spot, an interactive play area for kids under age 5. There are art and science classes for kids ages 2 and up. The museum is best for ages one to 5. Comment: "Small but great exhibits and classes."

Rosicrucian Egyptian Museum

Rosicrucian Park

1342 Naglee Ave.

San Jose

408-947-3635

www.rosicrucian.org

With the largest collection of Egyptian artifacts in the western U.S., this museum features some unusual objects, including mummies, jewelry, a pyramid, and a full-scale replica of an Egyptian tomb. It's best for ages 3 and up.

Tech Museum of Innovation

201 S. Market St.

San Jose

408-294-TECH

www.thetech.org

PARENT RATING: ☆ ☆ ☆ ☆ ☆

Who can live in the Bay Area without visiting a museum devoted to Silicon Valley's technology and innovation? Visit a "clean room," take a picture of yourself with a laser scanner, experiment with teleconferencing or movie animation technology, try being weightless like an astronaut, and experience a simulated earthquake. This museum is full of unique hands-on exhibits sure to intrigue parents as much as children, as well as an IMAX dome-screen theater. It's best for ages 3 and up. There is a café for lunch, and the on-site TechStore is guaranteed to empty your wallet.

Best Things to Do on a Rainy Day

We've found the best cure for cabin fever can be simple activities you can do at home, like renting movies, baking cookies, building forts and obstacle courses, creating Play-Doh works, and doing art projects. If you are itching to get out, try one of the museums or indoor playgrounds listed above, a library or story hour listed below, or some of the following ideas to entertain your kids on rainy days:

Bowling

Bowling is perfect for the 3-and-up crowd; younger kids won't be able to hold the balls. Ask for lighter balls and have them put bumpers in the lanes so the kids' balls don't end up in the gutter zone. Kids don't usually need special shoes.

◆ **Country Club Bowl**
88 Vivian Way
San Rafael
415-456-4661
PARENT RATING: ☆ ☆ ☆ ☆ ☆
Pizza restaurant is on site.

◆ **Boulevard Bowl**
1100 Petaluma Blvd. S.
Petaluma
707-762-4581
PARENT RATING: ☆ ☆ ☆ ☆ ☆

◆ **Presidio Bowling Alley**
Corner of Moraga and
Montgomery Sts.
The Presidio
415-561-BOWL
PARENT RATING: ☆ ☆ ☆ ☆ ☆
The grill serves burgers and similar fare.

◆ **Yerba Buena Gardens Bowling Center**
See below under "Other Amusements"—San Francisco.

Ceramic Painting
Pick and paint your own pottery, and the studio will fire and glaze it for you to pick up a week later. Anything with kids' handprints or footprints make great gifts for relatives! Here are some places to try:

◆ **Terra Mia**
1314 Castro St.
San Francisco
415-642-9911

◆ **Doodlebug**
641 San Anselmo Ave.
San Anselmo
415-456-5989

◆ **Hand Made Ceramics Studio**
237 Shoreline Hwy.
Mill Valley
415-388-8668

◆ **Brushstrokes**
745 Page St.
Berkeley
510-528-1360

Grocery Stores and Farmer's Markets
Kids love to wander the produce section and point out different items. The outing is even more fun if the store has those miniature kiddie carts, so the little ones can push their own. Farmer's markets are wonderful if the weather is not too inclement.

Home Depot Stores
www.homedepot.com
Many Home Depot stores offer free Kids' Workshops on weekend afternoons. Theoretically kids must be 6 years old to attend, but we took our 2-year-olds and they loved it. An adult must supervise kids. Kids can make cool projects like mobiles or bird feeders (all out of prefabricated kits) and learn how to use tools.

Miss Kitty
• Sausalito
Bay Area Discovery Museum,
415-487-4398
www.badm.org
• Fairfax
Bug-a-Boo
14 Bolinas Rd., 415-457-2884
www.bug-a-boo.com

- Corte Madera
  Book Passage
  51 Tamal Vista, 415-927-0960
  PARENT RATING: ☆ ☆ ☆ ☆ ☆

Each week at these locations, the ever-popular Miss Kitty entertains children with her lively guitar playing, dancing, and singing. Kids adore her! For all ages, but the 2- to 4-year-olds are especially enamored.

Mrs. Grossman's Sticker Mania

3810 Cypress Dr.
Petaluma
800-429-4549
www.MrsGrossmans.com

Kids are obsessed with these stickers! Call the Consumer Relations Department to arrange a free tour of the plant where the stickers are made. Tours last for forty-five minutes, including watching a video about the company, and kids get free samples at the end.

Pet Stores

Pretend it's a zoo or you'll go home with a menagerie.

Shopping Malls

Pretend the toy stores are museums or you'll come away with an empty wallet. One of the best for kids is the Sony Metreon. See below under "Other Amusements"—San Francisco.

Animals! Zoos, Farms, and Wildlife

We've found that doing anything involving animals—fish, fowl, or mammal—is a surefire way to please a toddler or preschooler. Did you ever think you would spend so many days at the zoo?

San Francisco

San Francisco Zoo

1 Zoo Rd.
415-753-7080
www.sfzoo.org
PARENT RATING: ☆ ☆ ☆

The largest in Northern California, this zoo received mixed reviews from parents. Many thought it a "fun place...very child friendly...great for kids...with something for everyone." Others found it "depressing...poorly maintained...and shabby." Though it's not the size and scope of zoos in San Diego or Chicago, for kids it's still a great outing because of the fun children's areas. Favorites of children at

the zoo include the newly remodeled Children's Zoo (where children can pet and feed domestic animals), the Little Puffer Steam Train, the carousel, the koalas, and the gorillas. Cafés are available for lunch, but we recommend bringing your own picnic. Be sure to bring a jacket and a stroller; the zoo is located near the ocean in one of the foggiest neighborhoods in the city, and exhibits are spread far and wide!

North Bay

Audubon Canyon Ranch

4900 Hwy. 1
Stinson Beach
415-868-9244
www.egret.org

Hike and view great blue herons and great egrets in miles of the Bolinas Lagoon Preserve, with beautiful views of Bolinas Lagoon and Stinson Beach.

Five Brooks Ranch Pony Rides
Hwy. 1
Olema
415-663-1570
www.fivebrooks.com
Take your child on a hand-led pony ride around the Five Brooks pond to view turtles, great blue heron, and quails (ages 3 and up). They also offer hay rides, trail rides (for older children), and riding lessons.

Marine Mammal Center
Marin Headlands
1065 Fort Cronkhite
Sausalito
415-289-SEAL
www.tmmc.org
TMMC is a nonprofit rescue and rehabilitation center for injured and stranded marine mammals (e.g., seals, sea lions, whales, dolphins, and sea otters). Patients vary by season, but kids will enjoy visiting them in the "hospital." The center also offers a variety of educational programs and beach walks.

Safari West Wildlife Preserve and Tent Camp
3115 Porter Creek Rd.
Santa Rosa
707-579-2551
www.safariwest.com
This four-hundred-acre private wildlife preserve focuses on the propagation of endangered species. Home to over four hundred mammals and birds, Safari West's inhabitants include zebras, giraffes, and lemurs, among others. Safari-vehicle tours led by naturalists last for $2^1/_2$ hours, include a walk around the grounds, and are by appointment only. Overnight stays may be arranged.

Slide Ranch
2025 Shoreline Hwy.
Muir Beach
415-381-6155
www.slideranch.org
PARENT RATING: ☆ ☆ ☆ ☆ ☆
A partner of the Golden Gate National Recreation Area, Slide Ranch is "a nonprofit agricultural and environmental education center in a small-farm, coastal wilderness setting" on 134 acres. Slide Ranch focuses on organic food production, resource conservation and recycling, animal husbandry, and open space conservation. Check out the Family Farm Days and Parent-Child Workshops on weekends, and seasonal events in the spring and fall. Children can learn about where food comes from in the organic garden, feed the farm animals, explore the beach and tide pools, do crafts, and enjoy picnic lunches in the garden.

Victoria's Fashion Stables
4193 Adobe Rd.
Petaluma
707-769-8820
Pony rides, pony wagon rides, hay rides, and a petting zoo are available. Prices can be steep for individuals so it's best to go with a group.

WildCare (Terwilliger Nature Education and Wildlife Rehabilitation)

76 Albert Park Ln.
San Rafael
415-453-1000
www.wildcaremarin.org

PARENT RATING: ☆ ☆ ☆ ☆

This rehabilitation center for injured, ill, or orphaned wild animals offers popular nature programs, including tot walks, family walks, and camps.

East Bay

Ardenwood Historic Farm

34600 Ardenwood Blvd.
Fremont
510-562-PARK (7275)
www.ebparks.org

PARENT RATING: ☆ ☆ ☆ ☆

This 205-acre working farm run by the East Bay Regional Park District re-creates nineteenth-century agricultural practices. The farm features live animals, a horse-drawn train and wagon rides, a blacksmith shop, a Native American village, a Victorian house, a milk house, a picnic area, and gardens. Costumed docents give demonstrations of nineteenth-century farming and craft making. The café has the basics, or bring your own picnic lunch. It's best for ages 3 and up. Avoid the winter months, when the grounds are open but there are no special events. "It's a great place to see farm animals," say parents.

Crab Cove Visitor Center

Crown Beach
1252 McKay Ave.
Alameda
510-521-6887
www.ebparks.org

Kids can learn about shoreline wildlife, visit the aquarium or the bay model, learn about Alameda's history, or explore the tidepools at this estuarine marine reserve.

Don Edwards San Francisco Bay National Wildlife Refuge

1 Marshlands Rd.
Newark
510-792-0222
http://desfbay.fws.gov/basic.html

Hike and fish in the miles of bay marshland or enjoy the many family programs.

Hayward Shoreline Interpretive Center

4901 Breakwater Ave.
Hayward
510-670-7270
http://hard.dst.ca.us/hayshore/index.htm

This center features saltwater aquariums with Bay wildlife and rotating exhibits of wildlife, plants, and history. Hike or bike on the Shoreline Trail amidst wetlands, salt marsh, and ponds. Be sure to check the tide before you wander too far.

Lindsay Wildlife Museum

1931 1st Ave.
Walnut Creek
925-935-1978
www.wildlife-museum.org

PARENT RATING: ☆ ☆ ☆ ☆ ☆ This wildlife education and rehabilitation center features fifty kinds of live, nonreleasable native wild animals and a discovery room with hands-on activities for kids under age 12. Preschoolers can take wonderful science and nature classes.

Oakland Zoo

Knowland Park
9777 Golf Links Rd.
Oakland
510-632-9525
www.oaklandzoo.org

PARENT RATING: ☆ ☆ ☆ ☆ ☆ Favorite features include the Children's Zoo where kids can pet and feed domestic animals, the miniature train (a scaled-down replica of a Civil War-era locomotive), the Sky Ride over the bison and elk range (with views of the bay), the antique carousel, and other children's rides. Concession stands are available in the zoo, or picnic in Knowland Park. "Great for kids and the weather is better than at the San Francisco Zoo...nice and compact...good rides...great scale for young kids...small but in a very nice park setting," rave parents.

Old Borges Ranch

1035 Castle Rock Rd.
Walnut Creek
925-943-5860

One of the first ranches in Contra Costa County, this is now a working and demonstration cattle ranch maintained by the park service. Children will enjoy seeing farm animals, a working blacksmith shop, a windmill, antique farm equipment, and assorted farm buildings including the original ranch house. From the ranch you can access many hiking trails in the surrounding hills.

Rotary Nature Center

600 Bellevue Ave.
Oakland
510-238-3739
www.oaklandnet.com/parks/
facilities/centers_rnc.asp

PARENT RATING: ☆ ☆ ☆ ☆ Run by the Oakland Parks and Recreation Department, this interpretive nature center offers an aviary, a small-animal zoo, and many waterfowl to feed. You can watch the resident naturalists feed the birds daily or purchase feed at the center and do it yourself.

Shorebird Nature Center

160 University Ave.
Berkeley
510-644-6376
www.ci.berkeley.ca.us/marina/

The City of Berkeley's center features a one-hundred-gallon saltwater aquarium displaying creatures from San Francisco Bay, a "touch table," and other wildlife exhibits.

Sulphur Creek Nature Center

1801 D St.
Hayward
510-881-6747
http://hard.dst.ca.us

At this wildlife education and rehabilitation facility you can see reptiles, amphibians, fish, and arthropods, as well as birds and mammals. The center also offers lots of nature classes and programs for children and families through the Hayward Area Recreation and Park District. Toddler Times, held once a month for ages one to 3, introduce animals and the natural world and usually involve an art project.

South Bay

Ano Nuevo State Reserve

Hwy. 1
Pescadero
800-444-4445 (reservations)
650-879-0227 (information)
www.cal-parks.ca.gov

PARENT RATING: ☆ ☆ ☆ ☆ ☆

Ano Nuevo features an elephant seal breeding colony—the largest mainland colony in the world—from December to March, though seals generally can be seen year-round. Take a guided three-mile hike down the beach during breeding season; be sure to reserve early as tours fill quickly.

Coyote Point Museum and Park

1651 Coyote Point Dr.
San Mateo
650-342-7755
www.coyoteptmuseum.org

PARENT RATING: ☆ ☆ ☆ ☆

Located in a lovely waterfront park on the bay, Coyote Point focuses on Bay Area habitats and is fun for all ages. The museum features live animals in habitats, an aviary, gardens, hands-on activities, and educational dioramas. The adjacent park offers playgrounds, picnic areas, a beach, and walking and biking trails. Toddler Tuesdays feature nature appreciation, sizes, shapes, and textures.

Deer Hollow Farm

Rancho San Antonio Open Space Preserve
Mountain View
650-903-6430

Run by the City of Mountain View Recreation Department, this working farm features pigs, goats, sheep, chickens, and other farm animals. Children can look at the animals but not feed or pet them. The farm is also an educational center where kids can learn about animal care and explore the surrounding wilderness preserve.

Fitzgerald Marine Reserve

California and N. Lake Sts.
Moss Beach
650-728-3584
http://bonita.mbnms.nos.noaa.gov

PARENT RATING: ☆ ☆ ☆ ☆

This intertidal marine reserve on San Mateo's coast is home to many species of marine life and will fascinate all ages. You can picnic at the beach or take a tide pool walk. It's best to visit at low tide when marine life is exposed in the tide pools, and be sure to bring a sweatshirt as summer days can be foggy and cool.

Happy Hollow Park and Zoo
Kelley Park
1300 Senter Rd.
San Jose
408-277-3000
www.happyhollowparkandzoo.org
PARENT RATING: ☆ ☆ ☆

This park is for children ages 2-10, with a petting zoo (wild and domestic animals), children's rides (such as a carousel and a train), puppet shows, a Kids' Café, and reservable picnic areas. Parents say the park is "older" but "kids like it."

Hidden Villa Farm
26870 Moody Rd.
Los Altos
650-949-8650
www.hiddenvilla.org
PARENT RATING: ☆ ☆ ☆ ☆ ☆

This sixteen-hundred-acre organic farm and wilderness preserve offers domestic animals, many children's programs in environmental education (most for ages 6 and up), and miles of hiking trails for everyone.

Lintt Trout Farm
11750 San Mateo Rd.
Half Moon Bay
650-726-0845

Rent a pole and take your child trout fishing at this farm, where the staff will clean and bag your catch.

Palo Alto Baylands Nature Preserve
Embarcadero Rd. east to the bay
Palo Alto
650-329-2506
www.paloaltoonline.com/paw/paonline/things_do/baylands.shtml

PARENT RATING: ☆ ☆ ☆ ☆ ☆

Walk around the duck pond and feed the ducks, watch airplanes take off and land at the airport, hike through miles of trails along salt marshes and sloughs, walk on the boardwalk, and watch birds. The interpretive center offers nature walks and other educational programs.

Phipps Ranch
2700 Pescadero Rd.
Pescadero
650-879-0787
www.phippscountry.com

Pick all the olallieberries, raspberries, and strawberries you want (in season from summer to early fall), feed the barnyard animals, picnic, and watch the birds in the aviary. While in Pescadero don't miss lunch at Duarte's Tavern (202 Stage Rd., 650-879-0464).

Prusch Farm Park
647 S. King Rd.
San Jose
408-926-5555
www.sanjoseparks.org

Originally a dairy farm, this park features a huge barn with sheep, pigs, steer, ducks, chickens, geese, and rabbits, surrounded by a fruit orchard, gardens, and open grass for picnicking.

Libraries and Storytelling

Many libraries and bookstores host free children's story times and special events, involving stories, fingerplay, songs, children's performers, or a combination of them all. These are great time fillers on rainy days, and besides, they are free! It may help to tell your youngster that a bookstore is a "library" so that you don't ruin your surprise book purchases. The following libraries and bookstores host parents' favorite storytelling hours and special events for children:

San Francisco

Asian Art Museum of San Francisco
415-379-8800
www.asianart.org
They are scheduled to reopen in a new location in the Civic Center in early 2003. Storytelling for families takes place on weekends, when a storyteller weaves Asian myths and legends with objects on display in the museum's galleries.

Books Inc.
2251 Chestnut St.
415-931-3633

Borders Books and Music
Stonestown Galleria
415-731-0665

Helen Crocker Russell Library, Strybing Arboretum and Botanical Gardens.
Golden Gate Park
9th Ave. at Lincoln Way
415-661-1316
www.strybing.org

San Francisco Public Libraries
415-557-4400
http://sfpl.lib.ca.us/

PARENT RATING: ☆ ☆ ☆ ☆ ☆
Free family storytelling hours, as well as films and special events, take place at the Main Library Children's Center and neighborhood branches. The Children's Center is a wonderful place to hang out on a rainy day. Parents rated the story times at West Portal and Presidio branch libraries very highly; they felt the story times were "well structured" and "very inviting."

North Bay

Barnes & Noble Bookstore
2020 Redwood Hwy.
Greenbrae
415-924-1016

Borders Books & Music
588 W. Francisco Blvd.
San Rafael
415-454-1400
In addition to story hours, this store often hosts vocalist Miss Kitty.

Book Passage
52 Tamal Vista Blvd.
Corte Madera
415-927-0960
PARENT RATING: ☆ ☆ ☆ ☆ ☆
Children's story time features the ever-popular Christopher Smith, and Miss Kitty also performs here.

Marin County Free Libraries

http://countylibrary.marin.org

The following libraries belong to this consortium:

- Bolinas
  415-868-1171
- San Rafael Civic Center
  415-507-4048
- Corte Madera
  415-924-4844
- Fairfax
  415-453-8092
- Inverness
  415-669-1288
- Marin City
  415-332-6159
- Novato
  415-897-1143
- Point Reyes Station
  415-663-8375
- San Geronimo Valley
  415-488-0430
- South Novato
  415-446-4555
- Stinson Beach
  415-868-0252

All of these libraries have story times for young children. Parents cited Corte Madera and Novato (**PARENT RATING:** ☆ ☆ ☆ ☆ ☆) as favorites.

Marinet Consortium of Public Libraries

www.marinet.lib.ca.us

The following libraries belong to this on-line card catalog consortium:

- Belvedere-Tiburon
  415-789-2662
  http://bel-tib-lib.org

- Mill Valley
  415-389-4292 ext. 106
  http://millvalleylibrary.org
- San Anselmo
  415-258-4656
  www.townofsananselmo.org/library
- San Rafael
  415-485-3322
  www.cityofsanrafael.org/library
- Sausalito
  415-289-4121
  www.ci.sausalito.ca.us/library

All of these libraries host story times for young children and other special family events. Belvedere-Tiburon's and San Rafael's programs are parent favorites (**PARENT RATING:** ☆ ☆ ☆ ☆ ☆).

East Bay

Alameda County Library

510-745-1591 (Children's Services)
www.aclibrary.org

Branches throughout the county offer preschool story times and toddler times, as well as special events like magicians and puppet shows.

Barnes and Noble Book Stores

- Berkeley
  2352 Shattuck Ave., 510-644-0861
- Oakland
  98 Broadway, 510-272-0120
- Walnut Creek
  1149 S. Main St., 925-947-0373

Berkeley Public Library

510-981-6100
www.infopeople.org/bpl/

The main and branch locations of this library offer baby, toddler, and preschool story times, as well as other family programs.

Borders Books and Music
www.bordersstores.com

Popular children's story hours occur at many branches.

Cody's Books
www.codysbooks.com
- Berkeley
  1730 4th St., 510-559-9500
- Oakland
  2454 Telegraph Ave., 510-845-7852

Contra Costa County Library
1750 Oak Park Blvd.
Pleasant Hill
925-646-6434
www.contra-costa.lib.ca.us

Branches throughout the county offer toddler and preschool story times and special children's events. The Danville, Lafayette, and San Ramon libraries are favorites.

PARENT RATING: ☆ ☆ ☆ ☆ ☆

Livermore Public Library
Civic Center Library
1000 S. Livermore Ave.
Livermore
925-373-5500
www.ci.livermore.ca.us/lpl.html

The main library and branches offer lap sits and preschool story times.

Oakland Public Library
510-238-7241 (Children's Services)
www.oaklandlibrary.org

Call Dial-a-Story, 510-597-5054, to enjoy a free three- to four-minute story for children of all ages. The Main Library and many branches offer story hours.

Pleasanton Public Library
400 Old Bernal Ave.
Pleasanton
925-931-3412 (Children's Services)
www.ci.pleasanton.ca.us

PARENT RATING: ☆ ☆ ☆ ☆ ☆

The library offers toddler and preschool story times and special children's events. "Great children's area," rave parents.

South Bay

Atherton Library
2 Dinkelspiel Station Ln.
Atherton
650-328-2422
www.pls.lib.ca.us

PARENT RATING: ☆ ☆ ☆ ☆

Parents rave about the toddler, preschool, and pajama story times.

Barnes and Noble Book Store
Hillsdale Mall
San Mateo
650-341-5560

Books Inc.
1375 Burlingame Ave.
Burlingame
650-685-4911
www.booksinc.net

Borders Books and Music
www.bordersstores.com

Popular children's story hours occur at many branches.

Burlingame Public Library
480 Primrose Rd.
Burlingame
650-342-1037
www.burlingame.org/library/

Both the main and branch library offer story times.

Hicklebee's Children's Books
1378 Lincoln Ave.
San Jose
408-292-8880
www.hicklebees.com

Kepler's Books and Magazines
1010 El Camino Real
Menlo Park
650-324-4321
www.keplers.com

Menlo Park Library
800 Alma St.
Menlo Park
650-858-3464 (Children's Desk)
www.pls.lib.ca.us
PARENT RATING: ☆ ☆ ☆ ☆

Palo Alto Children's Library
1276 Harriet St.
Palo Alto
650-329-2134
www.city.palo-alto.ca.us/library
PARENT RATING: ☆ ☆ ☆ ☆ ☆

The first freestanding public children's library in the U.S. features a Secret Garden behind the building. The library and its branches offer a plethora of children's events, plus ongoing story times.

Peninsula Library System
www.pls.lib.ca.us

This system is a consortium of 32 San Mateo County libraries. Check out the website to get information on, and link to, the following libraries:

- Atherton
  650-328-2422
- Belmont
  650-591-8286
- Brisbane
  415-467-2060
- Burlingame
  650-558-7400
- Daly City
  650-991-8074
- East Palo Alto
  650-321-7712
- Foster City
  650-574-4842
- Half Moon Bay
  650-726-2316
- Menlo Park
  650-858-3460
- Millbrae
  650-697-7607
- Pacifica
  650-355-5196
- Portola Valley
  650-851-0560
- Redwood City
  650-780-7061
- San Bruno
  650-616-7078
- San Carlos
  650-591-0341
- South San Francisco
  650-829-3865
- Woodside
  650-851-0147

Each of the branches offers children's programs. A parent favorite is the San Carlos Library's storytelling hour (**PARENT RATING:** ☆ ☆ ☆ ☆).

San Jose Public Library
180 W. San Carlos St.
San Jose
408-277-4874 (Youth Services)
www.sjpl.lib.ca.us

Story times for children of all ages happen regularly at the main library and branches.

Trains, Planes, Boats, and Automobiles

In honor of our sons, we present a special section devoted to their favorite hobby: anything that moves! As one parent told us, "Toddler boys love all types of street car, BART, and cable car rides." Believe it or not, even public transportation can be a glorious adventure to a toddler or preschooler who has never ridden a bus or train, not to mention taken a ferry ride on the Bay. If you have a baby, be sure to use a baby carrier (e.g., front carrier or sling) rather than a stroller, as navigating some methods of public transit with a stroller can be a nightmare. (Ferries, fortunately, are an exception, since ferry operators are used to accommodating bikers.)

San Francisco

BART

www.bart.gov

Bay Area Rapid Transit serves a large portion of the Bay Area with fast, usually clean trains. Kids under 4 ride free.

Caltrain

800-660-4287
www.caltrain.com

PARENT RATING: ☆ ☆ ☆ ☆

It may be only a commuter rail to adults, but to kids it's an adventure on a "real" train. Kids under 4 ride free. One of our favorite trips is San Francisco to Burlingame—short enough that boredom never sets in. A caution: getting on and off the train with a stroller can be a complicated proposition, so bring a lightweight, compact stroller or leave it at home.

Golden Gate Ferries

San Francisco Ferry Building
415-923-2000
www.goldengateferry.org

PARENT RATING: ☆ ☆ ☆ ☆ ☆

A much cheaper alternative to the Blue and Gold Fleet, these commuter ferries ply the waters between San Francisco and Sausalito or Larkspur. The boats are very comfortable and offer refreshments on board. Always dress warmly for a bay cruise if you want to go on deck for a view (which your children will certainly want to do!). The Ferry Building is also a great vantage point to see the boats come in and out, even if you never go aboard!

San Francisco Maritime National Historical Park

415-561-7100
www.maritime.org

PARENT RATING: ☆ ☆ ☆ ☆ ☆

This park includes:
◆ **USS-Pampanito**, a WWII submarine. Pier 45.
◆ **Maritime Museum.** Beach St. at the foot of Polk St. This museum features maritime artifacts.

- **Hyde Street Pier**. Foot of Hyde St. on Jefferson St. This pier is home to many historic maritime ships, including some from the turn of the nineteenth century. The center-piece is the three-hundred-foot 1886 sailing ship Balclutha.
- **Aquatic Park**. Picnic next to the museum (at the foot of Polk St.).

SS Jeremiah O'Brien Liberty Ship
Pier 45
415-441-3101
PARENT RATING: ☆ ☆ ☆ ☆
Kids ages 2 and up will enjoy touring this restored WWII Liberty Ship, which is berthed at Pier 32 but still cruises the Bay on special occasions.

North Bay

Traintown
20264 Broadway
Sonoma
707-938-3912
www.traintown.com
PARENT RATING: ☆ ☆ ☆ ☆ ☆
Even the very young will love riding the scaled-down steam train through ten acres of park, including a stop at the animal petting area. Other rides (except the carousel) are best for ages 3 and up. Parents may find the whole thing a bit cheesy, but kids seem to adore it. There is a snack bar on site, but we recommend try-ing one of the many lovely wineries nearby for lunch, or picnicking on Sonoma Square.

East Bay

Alameda-Oakland Ferry
510-522-3300
www.eastbayferry.com
- Alameda
  2990 Main St.
- Oakland
  Jack London Sq.

PARENT RATING: ☆ ☆ ☆ ☆ ☆
Ride the ferry from Alameda or Jack London Square to San Francisco's Ferry Building, Pier 39/Fisherman's Wharf, Pacific Bell Park, or Angel Island.

Diablo Valley Lines (Walnut Creek Model Railroad Society)
2751 Buena Vista Ave.
Walnut Creek
925-937-1888
This HO-scale model railroad club is open to the public on some weekends.

Jack London Water Taxi Service
510-839-7572
www.bushwacker.net/jlwatertaxi/
Inner harbor estuary tours, a water taxi service, and private charters are available on this small boat, which picks up and drops off passengers at several points in Oakland and Alameda.

Niles Canyon Railway
6 Kilkare Rd.
Sunol
925-862-9063
www.ncry.org
Part of the original transcontinental railway, this historic railroad has been preserved and reconstructed. Visitors may take a thirteen-mile train journey through the Niles Canyon.

Presidential Yacht Potomac
FDR Pier, foot of Clay St. at
Embarcadero
Oakland
510-627-1215
www.usspotomac.org
President Franklin D. Roosevelt's
Floating White House now rests at
Jack London Sq., where visitors may
climb aboard and explore, or even
take a cruise.

USS Hornet Museum
Pier 3, Alameda Point
Alameda
510-521-8448
www.uss-hornet.org
This WWII aircraft carrier has been
transformed into a museum where
you can tour the ship and see the

footprints marking Neil Armstrong's
first steps on land after his trip to the
moon. Bring a baby carrier, not a
stroller, as there are many stairs to
navigate.

South Bay

Billy Jones Wildcat Railroad
Oak Meadow Park
Los Gatos
408-395-7433
www.bjwrr.org
Take a one-mile-long railroad ride
around Los Gatos Creek, Oak Meadow
Park, and Vasona Park on a scale
train powered by turn-of-the-century
locomotives. Ride the 1910 carousel
across from the depot, accompanied
by music from a reproduction
Wurlitzer organ.

Other Amusements

You probably know of major attractions like Great America and Six
Flags, but there are some great hidden gems for younger children at
other local establishments. Many of these places offer great children's
birthday parties as well:

San Francisco

Basic Brown Bear Factory
444 DeHaro St.
800-554-1910
www.basicbrownbear.com
PARENT RATING: ☆ ☆ ☆ ☆ Tours
(designed, of course, to encourage
you to buy) include the tale of how
the teddy bear got his name, a walk
through the factory and demonstration of how bears are made, and a
time for each child to stuff, sew,
groom, and bathe his own bear (with
a little help from the factory staff).

It's entertaining for kids ages 2 and
up. Bears are fairly inexpensive, but
be sure to bring extra money for all
those cute clothes.

Build-A-Bear Workshop
www.buildabear.com
In this nationally franchised retail
store, your child can build his own
bear. Children may stuff their bears,
give them hearts, and then dress
them in myriad different outfits and
accessories. Children ages 3 and up
are welcome. See the website for
Bay Area locations.

Fisherman's Wharf and Pier 39

www.fishermanswharf.org or
www.pier39.com

PARENT RATING: ☆ ☆ ☆

Yes, it's touristy, but the wharf can be
fun if you hold onto your wallet and
go in the less-crowded early morning. Stick to the free sights, stroll the
mercifully flat Embarcadero from the
Ferry Building to Aquatic Park, and
ride the ferries, cable cars, and trolley cars. Parents recommend:

◆ **Blue and Gold Fleet Ferries.**
  Pier 41. (415-705-5555, www.
  blueandgoldfleet.com).
  PARENT RATING: ☆ ☆ ☆ ☆
  Tourist ferries go to Alcatraz
  Island, Sausalito, Tiburon,
  Alameda/Oakland, Vallejo, and
  Angel Island, see parks, above.

◆ **Alcatraz** (www.nps.gov/alcatraz).
  PARENT RATING: ☆ ☆ ☆ ☆
  Be sure to bring warm clothes
  and wear comfortable shoes.
  There is no food service on the
  island. Best for ages 3 and up.

◆ **Cable Cars.**
  PARENT RATING: ☆ ☆ ☆ ☆
  Two scenic lines (Powell/Hyde
  and Powell/Mason) terminate at
  Fisherman's Wharf, but you can
  also avoid the crowds of tourists
  and pick up the California St. line.

◆ **Carousel.** Pier 39.

◆ **Fire Engine Tours** (415-333-7077,
  www.fireenginetours.com).
  Expensive, but kids love this nar-
  rated seventy-five-minute ride
  from the Cannery on Beach St.
  through the Presidio, Fort Point,
  Golden Gate Bridge, Sausalito,
  and Union St. on a classic 1955
  Mack Fire Engine.

◆ **The Embarcadero.** Three miles of
  paved walkways along the waterfront make this a great stroller
  walk from Fisherman's Wharf to
  China Basin.

◆ **Restored Vintage Trolley Cars**
  (www.streetcar.org).
  PARENT RATING: ☆ ☆ ☆ ☆
  Twenty-five different antique
  trolleys imported from all over
  the world grace the F Line. Market
  St. to Embarcadero (Ferry
  Building) to Fisherman's Wharf.

◆ **Sea Lions** (415-705-5500). Droves
  of sea lions can be found on Pier
  39. Weather permitting, Marine
  Mammal Center volunteers lead
  free educational talks on weekends.

◆ **Street Performers.** Magicians,
  jugglers, comedians, and mimes
  hang out at Pier 39's "stage."

Pacific Bell Park (home of the San Francisco Giants)

24 Willie Mays Plaza
415-972-2000
www.sfgiants.com

PARENT RATING: ☆ ☆ ☆ ☆ ☆

What could be more fun than an
afternoon at the ballpark eating hot-
dogs and watching the splash landing special effects when the Giants
score a home run? The Giants' new
"intimate" stadium makes it much
easier for kids to follow the action.
Kids under age 2 are free, but kids
over 2 will enjoy it much more. The
miniature, scaled-down copy of the
park past the left field wall is a hit
with older kids when it's not too
crowded. Make it an adventure and
take Caltrain from the south or a
ferry from Marin or the East Bay.

Sony Metreon

4th and Mission Sts.

415-369-6000

www.metreon.com

PARENT RATING: ☆ ☆ ☆ ☆ ☆

In Sony's huge new indoor entertainment mecca you will find:

- **Sony Theaters.** There are fifteen movie screens, including the largest IMAX screen in North America.
- **Where the Wild Things Are.** Maurice Sendak's classic children's tale is brought to life in a walk-through interactive, hands-on exhibit. Children under age 3 may find the dark passages and monsters a bit loud and intimidating, though even the younger set will enjoy playing with the huge blocks, boat, and slide at the end of the tour. Many parents recommend simply browsing through the adjacent toy store!
- **In the Night Kitchen Café.** This is a great place to find sandwiches and pizza after you tour the Wild Things exhibit. Particularly if your children have been reading this book, they will love looking at the huge model of Mickey and his airplane suspended from the ceiling, and will point out the trains made of "bread loaves" circling near the ceiling.
- **The Way Things Work.** Inspired by David Macaulay's eponymous book of invention, this is a three-dimensional exhibit illustrating how everyday technology works.
- **Airtight Garage.** This high-tech arcade includes a fun "bowl the streets of San Francisco" virtual reality game. Games can be pricey.

- **Restaurants and shops**, including the Discovery Channel Store, are a sure hit.

Yerba Buena Gardens

4th and Howard Sts.

415-777-2800

www.zeum.org

PARENT RATING: ☆ ☆ ☆ ☆

A project of the San Francisco Redevelopment Agency to develop an entire city block as an urban destination for youth, the Rooftop at Yerba Buena Gardens now offers the following fun for kids:

- **Zeum.** This high-tech multimedia creative center is geared to older kids (ages 8 and up).
- **Carousel.** Kids of all ages love this restored 1906 carousel from San Francisco's former amusement park Playland-at-the-Beach.
- **Ice Skating and Bowling Center** (415-777-3727, www.skatebowl.com).
- **Playground.** The slides are quite steep for little children, but the 3-and-up crowd will love them. There is a large area for running, and our kids adore playing with th e little fountains throughout the rooftop.

North Bay

Redwood Empire Ice Arena and Charles Schulz Museum

1667 W. Steele Ln.

Santa Rosa

707-546-7147

www.snoopyshomeice.com

PARENT RATING: ☆ ☆ ☆ ☆

Known as "Snoopy's Home Ice" in Charles Schulz's home town, this arena offers special Puppy Practice sessions for children ages 12 and

319

under and their parents. Beginners can use chairs on the ice. The Schulz Museum is scheduled to open next door to the arena in summer 2002. See www.charlesmschulzmuseum. org/home.html or call 707-579-4452 for details.

East Bay

Berkeley Iceland Skating Rink and Skating School

2727 Milvia St.
Berkeley
510-647-1600
www.berkeleyiceland.com

This indoor skating rink offers tiny tots sessions.

Children's Fairyland

Lakeside Park
699 Bellevue Ave.
Oakland
510-452-2259
www.fairyland.org

PARENT RATING: ☆ ☆ ☆ ☆ ☆

Fairy tales come alive in this ten-acre outdoor theme park, a Bay Area tradition since 1950 that was recently renovated. Children may play in storybook exhibits incorporating fairy tales and nursery rhymes, watch daily puppet shows, and ride the train, the boats, the miniature Ferris Wheel, and the carousels. Be sure to buy a "magic key" to "unlock" the stories and nursery rhymes. All ages will enjoy the park, but it's especially fabulous for 2- and 3-year-olds. While there, take a walk through Lakeside Park to Lake Merritt and picnic around the lake. In the peak warm weather season, parents recommend going during the week as weekends

are very crowded. Parents say this "offbeat" park "delights children."

Dunsmuir Historic Estate and Gardens

2960 Peralta Oaks Ct.
Oakland
510-615-5555
www.dunsmuir.org

Stroll around the grounds of this fifty-acre historic estate with its thirty-seven-room nineteenth-century neoclassical revival mansion and farm area. Enjoy Family Sundays with puppet shows, music, and magicians. Look for special Christmas holiday events.

Pixieland Amusement Park

2740 E. Olivera Rd.
Concord
925-676-9612
www.pixieland.com

PARENT RATING: ☆ ☆ ☆ ☆

Pixieland (in one form or another) has been entertaining families since 1950. Kid-oriented rides are best for ages 3 and up. The train, antique cars, and carousel are favorites for younger children.

South Bay

Bonfante Gardens Theme Park

3050 Hecker Pass Hwy.
Gilroy
408-840-7100
www.bonfantegardens.com

Bonfante Gardens is a new theme park combining gardens, rides, and local history. The seventy-five-acre park includes a huge greenhouse garden, a steam train, a mine coaster, a rock maze, a boat ride through gardens, an antique car ride, and a restored 1927 carousel.

Family-Friendly Restaurants

Many families report that you need not entirely change your lifestyle after your baby arrives. While you won't likely be visiting Chez Panisse or the French Laundry with the baby, you don't need to stick to fast food. In addition to the well-known chains like Chevy's, Fresh Choice, Left at Albuquerque, and Johnny Rocket's, most restaurants in the Bay Area do their best to accommodate children. Parents advise bringing the little ones to brunch or lunch, rather than dinner, whenever possible; babies are less fussy during the day, and daytime meals are less formal. Dim sum is a particularly popular family outing. Several parents commented that big San Francisco hotel restaurants can be "very accommodating" since they are used to serving families. Ask your waiter to bring you a glass of hot water to heat bottles (safer than microwaving them), and order side dishes for kids if there is no children's menu. We also recommend bringing along small toys, crayons and coloring books, or sticker books to entertain toddlers during meals.

Local parents recommended the following restaurants for family-friendly dining:

San Francisco

Barney's Gourmet Hamburger
- 4138 24th St., 415-282-7770
- 3344 Steiner St., 415-563-0307

They offer hamburgers, great curly fries, and shakes.

Bill's Place
2315 Clement St.
415-221-5262
Hamburgers are a specialty, and there is a patio in back.

Café Muse
8th Ave. at Fulton
415-668-6873
This is a great place for a sandwich or coffee while enjoying Golden Gate Park.

Curbside Café
2417 California St.
415-929-9030.
This café is wonderful for brunch.

Giorgio's Pizza
151 Clement St.
415-668-1266
This neighborhood pizzeria is very tolerant of children! Kids love the pizza and the juke box.

Mel's Drive-In
- 2165 Lombard St., 415-921-2867
- 3355 Geary Blvd., 415-387-2255
- 1050 Van Ness Ave., 415-292-6537

This fifties flashback diner is open all night. Parents say it's "great for families" and "always a hit" with the kids.

Park Chow

1240 9th Ave.

415-665-9912

This is a great place for a casual bite after visiting Golden Gate Park or its museums. The menu has "virtually everything."

Bubba's Diner

566 San Anselmo Ave.

San Anselmo

415-459-6862

This diner has "great comfort food."

The Cantina

651 E. Blithedale

Mill Valley

415-381-1070

At this Mexican eatery, "they cater to kids while Mom and Dad can enjoy a beer."

Dipsea Café

- Mill Valley
  200 Shoreline Hwy., 415-381-0298
- San Rafael
  2200 4th St., 415-459-0700

This popular spot for breakfast and lunch (and now dinner in San Rafael) tends to be crowded on the weekends but offers crayons and a kids' menu.

Easy Street Café

- Larkspur
  574 Magnolia Ave., 415-924-9334
- San Anselmo
  882 Sir Francis Drake Blvd., 415-453-1984

This creole brunch spot caters to children. The San Anselmo location has a play area for kids.

Half Day Café

848 College Ave.

Kentfield

415-459-0291

This is a great place for breakfast or lunch with the kids.

LoCoco's Italian Pizzeria

638 San Anselmo Ave.

San Anselmo

415-453-1238

Pizza and traditional Italian fare are served here, and kids get crayons.

Taco Jane's

21 Tamalpais Ave.

San Anselmo

415-454-6562

This casual place has great Caribbean/Mexican food, outdoor seating, and a friendly, kid-loving staff.

Waypoint Pizza

15 Main St.

Tiburon

415-435-3440

They have excellent pizza, and children can sit at their own kid-sized picnic table.

Willow Street Restaurant and Brewery

812 4th St.

San Rafael

415-453-4200

You can enjoy a micro-brew while the kids entertain themselves with crayons and feast on great pizza.

Berkeley Bakery and Café
1561 Solano
Berkeley
510-527-2253
This is a great spot for breakfast with the kids.

Filippos Pastaria
1499 Solano Ave.
Albany
510-524-4300
They have wonderful pasta and are kid-tolerant.

Muffins, Muffins, Cookies and Beans
2711 Encinal Ave.
Alameda
510-865-7243
This bakery and coffeehouse serves pastries and sandwiches and features a separate playroom for kids with a VCR, TV, books, and toys aimed at kids under age 6.

Pete's Brass Rail and Car Wash
201 Hartz Ave.
Danville
925-820-8281
www.petesbrassrail.com
This pub-style restaurant offers micro-brews for the parents, and burgers, hot dogs, and PB&Js for the kids.

The Red Tractor
5634 College Ave.
Oakland
510-595-3500
They serve American food, such as macaroni and cheese, and supply crayons for kids.

Rick and Ann's
2922 Domingo Ave.
Berkeley
510-649-8538
This American cuisine spot has a great brunch, a kids' menu, and crayons.

Sweet Tomatoes
4501 Hopyard Rd.
Pleasanton
925-463-9285
They offer an all-you can eat, buffet-style lunch and dinner and special prices for kids during off hours.

Applewood Pizza
227 1st St.
Los Altos
650-941-9222
Kids will love the pizza.

Austin's
1616 W. El Camino Real
Mountain View
650-969-9191
This Texas barbeque restaurant features cowboy decor.

Christie's
245 California Dr.
Burlingame
650-347-9440
This is a great place for breakfast.

Late for the Train
150 Middlefield Rd.
Menlo Park
650-321-6124
They offer "California comfort food" in a warmly-decorated café.

Max's
1001 El Camino Real
Redwood City
650-365-6297
This New York-style deli café has a kid's menu featuring hot dogs and macaroni and cheese.

Peninsula Fountain & Grill
566 Emerson St.
Palo Alto
650-323-3131

This American diner, known as the "Creamery," serves comfort food and great shakes. Get there early on weekend mornings to get a spot in a booth.

Stacks
361 California Dr.
Burlingame
650-579-1384
This Burlingame institution serves breakfast and lunch, and provides crayons for kids.

Special Events for Kids

The Bay Area is home to many special events for kids, from concerts and theatrical productions to seasonal holiday extravaganzas. How do you find out what is happening around town? Try your local newspaper first. The *San Francisco Chronicle*'s weekend pink pages usually carry a good selection of family outings. The local family periodicals, *Bay Area Parent* and *Parents Press*, contain local calendars of events, and you can pick them up at any baby store for free. If you live in the South Bay, check out Palo Alto Online at www.paloaltoonline.com/paw/paonline/index.shtml. The site features a good listing of current local events and things to do for families. The best source for current events is usually your local mothers' club newsletter or website!

Below are some of our favorite ongoing and annual events for families:

CONCERTS AND THEATER

San Francisco and Bay Area-Wide

The Buddy Club
510-236-SHOW (7469)
www.thebuddyclub.com
This troupe offers children's shows in San Francisco, Marin, and the East Bay from October through April. You can also hire the performers for birthday parties and special events. The shows are geared to children ages 2-12 and their parents, and include magicians, jugglers, singers, clowns, ventriloquists, acrobats, puppeteers, and lots of audience participation.

Make*A*Circus

415-242-1414

www.makeacircus.org

For over twenty-five years, Make*A*Circus has been entertaining kids each summer with its audience-participation circus at locations all over the Bay Area for children ages 3 and up. The three-part performance includes a company show, workshops for audience members, and the grand finale community show in which children in the audience perform.

Young Performers Theatre

Fort Mason Center (Building C), Fl. 3
San Francisco

415-346-5550

www.ypt.org

This troupe offers a year-round program of seven children's theatrical productions. Child actors perform alongside adults.

North Bay

Luther Burbank Center for the Arts

50 Mark West Springs Rd.
Santa Rosa

707-546-3600

www.lbc.net

Family Shows target a range of age groups; some are for ages one and up, and others are for older children.

Rafael Film Center

1118 4th St.
San Rafael

415-454-1222

www.rafaelfilmcenter.org

This three-screen movie house features family film classic matinees one weekend of every month.

East Bay

Julia Morgan Center for the Arts

2640 College Ave.
Berkeley

510-845-8542

925-798-1300 (tickets)

www.juliamorgan.org

The Kaleidoscope Sunday Matinee series is perfect for families. It features multicultural music, theater, and dance events, some with local performers, and children's tickets are half-price.

Parkway Theater's Baby Brigade

1834 Park Blvd.
Oakland

510-814-2400

www.picturepubpizza.com

On Monday nights, parents may bring their babies (under age one) to this movie house and brew pub without fearing recrimination from fellow audience members. Babies are free. Pizza, sandwiches, pasta, beer, and wine are served.

South Bay

Children's Theater of Palo Alto

1305 Middlefield Rd.
Palo Alto

650-463-4970 (tickets)

Kids must be 8 years old to participate in the performances, but younger children will enjoy attending the shows, which tend to be classic musicals.

Peninsula Youth Theatre/
Children's Theatre in the Park
Mountain View Center for the
Performing Arts
500 Castro St.
Mountain View
650-903-6000
www.mvcpa.com
The City of Mountain View hosts a
variety of free family events, from
performances by the Peninsula Youth

Theatre to music from around the
world.

San Jose Children's Musical
Theater
1401 Parkmoor Ave.
San Jose
408-288-5437
www.sjcmt.com
This theater offers musical theater
training and performances by and
for kids.

Some of Our Favorite Seasonal Events

Check with your local Parks and Recreation Department for seasonal events. Many parks host Easter egg hunts, Earth Day celebrations, and Fourth of July extravaganzas. Your local shopping center is a good place to get a photo with Santa or the Easter Bunny. The 2-and-under crowd will likely run screaming from either of them, but you can always try! Local churches, synagogues, and Jewish Community Centers also host religious holiday events. Another fun fall or winter outing is a visit to a pumpkin patch or a tree farm, many of which have animals, hay rides, and candy for the kids. The best are located well outside the city, in Petaluma, Sebastopol, and Half Moon Bay. Below are some of our favorite events:

Cardoza Ranch
5869 Lakeville Hwy.
Petaluma
707-762-2065
PARENT RATING: ☆ ☆ ☆ ☆ ☆
This working ranch opens its doors
to pumpkin pickers come October,
with hay and pony rides, a playground, a train, and animal feedings.

Deck the Halls
415-552-8000 (San Francisco
Symphony)
Jointly sponsored by the Symphony
and Junior League, this popular

annual holiday concert is especially
designed for toddlers and preschoolers with plenty of singing for the
whole family.

Easter Parade on Union Street
San Francisco
415-885-1335
The merchants hand out candy and
sponsor entertainment and music.

Embarcadero Center Ice Rink
Justin Herman Plaza
4 Embarcadero Center
San Francisco
415-772-0700

PARENT RATING: ☆ ☆ ☆ ☆ This rink, open seasonally, is a beautiful spot to view the downtown holiday lights.

Goblin Jamboree, Bay Area Discovery Museum
Sausalito
415-487-4398
PARENT RATING: ☆ ☆ ☆ ☆ ☆
Each October the BADM offers a wonderful Halloween event for families, featuring games, candy, a train ride, entertainment, a haunted house, etc. Kids love to dress up! See above under "Museums" for full listing.

Lemo's Farm
12320 Hwy. 92
Half Moon Bay
650-726-2342
PARENT RATING: ☆ ☆ ☆ ☆
This is a pumpkin patch extravaganza with a pony ride, a wagon train ride, a hay ride, a petting farm, an air jumper, a haunted house, and, of course, you can pick your own pumpkins.

The Nutcracker
301 Van Ness Ave.
San Francisco
415-865-2000
This annual holiday production of the renowned San Francisco Ballet takes place each December. It's best for ages 3 and up; younger kids probably won't sit through the whole performance!

Teddy Bear Tea, Ritz-Carlton Hotel
600 Stockton St.
San Francisco
415-296-7465
PARENT RATING: ☆ ☆ ☆ ☆
Our 3-year-old loved sipping hot chocolate, singing carols, and sitting on the bear's lap during the holiday season.

Winter Lodge Ice Rink
3009 Middlefield Rd.
Palo Alto
650-493-4566
www.winterlodge.com
Strollers are allowed on the ice at this seasonal rink.

Traveling with Your Kids

If you are like us, you are probably dreading that first airline or long car trip with your baby. Here are some tips to make life easier:

◆ If traveling by air, pack only as much as you can handle on your own. You will have the baby, a diaper bag, a stroller and perhaps a car seat, so keep extra gear and clothing to a minimum, and plan to do laundry instead.

◆ Before you go, arrange for a portable crib at your destination. If you need to rent baby gear at your destination, try one of the rental companies listed in chapter 4. If you travel by car frequently, a portable crib or playpen is a good investment.

◆ Take lots of diapers in your carry-on for transit (as many as one per hour of travel time). Don't waste space in your suitcase for a week's supply of diapers, however, as you can probably pick up some upon arrival.

◆ Invest in a roomy, easy-to-use diaper bag. We liked the backpack version for traveling, since it freed our arms for the baby and other gear. Fill the diaper bag with a changing pad, diapers, wipes, diaper cream, disinfectant, emergency medications for baby (e.g., Tylenol), toys, a fold-up potty seat for older kids, a change of clothing for each child, a cell phone, and snacks. Only the most modern and roomy of planes contains a fold-down changing table in the bathroom, so you may be relegated to changing the baby in your seat (much to your neighbors' chagrin). We use disposable changing pads because who knows what you will find on airline seats and bathroom changing tables. Carry little plastic bags for dirty diapers.

◆ Toddlers love to carry their own backpacks or small, wheeled suitcases. Give your child a small pack filled with our favorite travel aids: a small white board for drawing, crayons and a coloring book, sticker books, and board books.

◆ When traveling with an infant by air, take an FAA-approved infant car seat. (Most car seats manufactured after 1981 are approved, and most are labeled as such; check your manual to be sure.) Get a Snap-n-Go™ or similar lightweight frame on wheels for the car seat and roll it and the baby right up to the gate, where you can check the frame (and the car seat as well if you don't have a seat for the baby). Car seats are not required for air travel, but they do make life easier with infants, who tend to be lulled to sleep as if they are in a car. If you don't have a seat for your baby on the plane, use a front carrier to keep the baby safely up against you (and to free your arms). You will still need to hold your baby during take-off and landing, however, as front carriers are not approved for such times.

◆ When traveling with a toddler by air, there are two schools of thought: Some like to take the toddler car seat (heavy as it is) on the plane because it restrains the child from moving around. Toddlers are notoriously adept at extricating themselves from regular seat belts. Others find the toddler seats terribly heavy and awkward to lug through the airport and maneuver onto the plane with all of the other stuff they are carrying. Don't expect any help from flight attendants in this regard. If they can, they leave the car seat at home and rent a car seat on the other end. Most major rental car agencies rent car seats for a minimal fee. Of course, if you are being met and picked up by someone upon arrival, you'll need a car seat in that person's car.

◆ An inexpensive umbrella stroller can be a lifesaver with a toddler in a busy airport. You can wheel it up and check it just as you get on the plane.

◆ Children under age 2 may ride free on most airlines as "lap babies," but we found that once our kids reached the age of mobility, it was worth buying them a separate seat. When booking airline tickets, ask for an infant discount. Most carriers offer half-price fares for children under age 2.

◆ If you can't afford a seat for your baby, try to book flights during off-peak hours of the day. Reserve the window and aisle seats for yourself and your spouse or partner, and ask the gate agent not to seat anyone between you. Chances are, no one will want to sit in your row with a screaming baby anyway!

◆ Avoid red-eye flights. You will be exhausted enough after a daytime flight, and the only thing worse than a normal red-eye flight is one with a screaming baby.

◆ If you are using a car seat, be forewarned that most airlines will make you put your baby in the window seat to avoid blocking egress to the aisle. If you are traveling alone, you will then be stuck in the middle seat. Try booking a window seat and an aisle seat, and hope no one will want to sit in your row! Or stick to planes with a 2-5-2 configuration, giving you an aisle and the baby the window.

◆ Many airlines have stopped preboarding families with young children, even pregnant women with kids! You can try pleading with a gate agent (good luck), but we've found it's more effective if you have a premier-type frequent flyer card for the airline or fly family-friendly airlines (e.g., Southwest).

◆ During take-off and landing, help your baby's ears clear by nursing or feeding him a bottle.

- Most airlines offer infant and child meals. Call ahead to reserve one for your child.
- The backpack of goodies should keep toddlers entertained during a flight, but in desperation we've found the airline's earphones to be a lifesaver. The airline movie is guaranteed to bore your kids, but if you or your partner carries a laptop computer, you can have a DVD movie festival right in your seat. DVDs and players are often available for rent in the airport.
- Several parents recommended Amtrak trains for short trips, citing benefits such as "large aisles, plenty of leg room, the dining car, and the motion lulling baby to sleep."

FAVORITE EASY VACATION SPOTS FOR BAY AREA FAMILIES

CALISTOGA

Try Calistoga Spa Hot Springs (707-942-6269), with four outdoor pools, or Indian Springs Resort (707-942-4913), with a "big, warm pool and a large grassy area for play." Parents can take turns getting treatments while kids play in the pool.

CAMPING

800-444-PARK (state park campground reservations)
www.cal-parks.ca.gov

A hint: wherever you camp with kids, make sure the car is not too far away in case you need to make a fast exit. Parents recommended the following parks:

- **Big Basin Redwoods State Park**, near Boulder Creek in the Santa Cruz Mountains, 800-874-8368 (reservations), 831-338-8861 (information). They rent wooden platform tents complete with all the necessary gear and even breakfast fixings, making it easy on families.
- **Bodega Dunes Campground**, Sonoma Coast State Beach, Hwy. 1, Bodega Bay, 800-444-7275. Comment: "A beautiful setting but close to home…a long beach to walk on."
- **Mt. Diablo State Park**, 96 Mitchell Canyon Rd., Clayton, 925-837-2525. Comment: "Views, views, views, and lots of rocks to scramble over." Try the Live Oak Campground near Rock City.
- **Samuel P. Taylor State Park**, West Marin, 415-488-9897. There are redwood groves and hiking, and it's a short drive to the Point Reyes area. Kids love scrambling over the hollowed-out ancient redwood trunks in the day-use area.

LAKE TAHOE

800-824-6348 or www.tahoefun.org (Lake Tahoe Resort Association)

- Some parents recommend "ski weekends at smaller resorts like Sugar Bowl (530-426-9000, www.sugarbowl.com) or Bear Valley (209-753-2301, www.bearvalley.com) and avoiding bigger, more crowded resorts like Squaw Valley and Alpine Meadows."
- On the other hand, Children's World at Squaw Valley (530-530-6985, www.squaw.com) is one of the few places where you can find ski lessons and day care for children as young as 2 years old! Squaw also has a large skating rink at the top of the tram.
- Parents say Diamond Peak (775-832-1170, www.diamondpeak.com) and North Star (530-562-1010, www.skinorthstar.com) resorts both have especially good kids' programs.
- Kids ages 5 and under ski free at most of the resorts, but keep in mind that you'll probably be shelling out money for child care, rental equipment, and ski lessons.
- As an alternative with very young children, "Try cross-country skiing...Mom and Dad can exercise with baby in tow." Royal Gorge Cross-Country Ski Resort (800-666-3871, www.royalgorge.com) features a Family Center where families can relax and change diapers, and starting at age 4 kids can enroll in the PeeWee Snow School.
- Don't forget summer in Tahoe, where you can enjoy sunny, warm beaches!

LAS VEGAS

www.golasvegas.cc (Tourist Bureau of Las Vegas)
Comment: "Amazingly great fun for kids for two to three days maximum...dolphins, shows, and sights."

MENDOCINO COAST

www.mendocinocoast.com (Mendocino Coast Chamber of Commerce)
Take the Skunk Train through the redwoods (California Western Railroad, 800-77-SKUNK), spend a day at the beach watching whales, or hike through one of the nearby state parks.

MONTEREY/CARMEL

www.monterey.com (Monterey Peninsula Visitors and Conventions Bureau). Comment: "A great weekend getaway."
- **Dennis the Menace Playground**
  Camino del Estero and Fremont (off Del Monte Ave.)
  Monterey
  Though its structures are a bit old (circa 1950), this playground is a perennial favorite because of its cartoon theme, steam engine, and lake with paddle boats.
- **Monterey Bay Aquarium**
  886 Cannery Row
  Monterey
  831-648-4800
  831-648-4937 (advance ticket sales)
  www.mbayaq.org
  PARENT RATING: ☆ ☆ ☆ ☆ ☆
  This enormous aquarium is a sure hit with kids. Don't miss the Splash Zone, a special rock and

reef exhibit for families. Full- or self-service dining is available in the café.

The area is home to many kid-friendly destinations, including Legoland, Sea World, the world famous San Diego Zoo, and the beach. If you can

afford it, stay at the full-service Hotel del Coronado (www.hoteldel.com or 800-468-3533) to appreciate it fully.

www.searanchrentals.com
Comment: "Renting a house is easy, you will get great R&R, and there are miles of beaches."

Birthday Parties

Before you will know it, the baby you swaddled only yesterday is on the verge of taking his first steps as well as celebrating his first birthday! What a milestone! There is something special about the first birthday, which often makes parents want to celebrate—after all, you've made it through the first year of parenthood. Many child development experts recommend a small gathering for the first birthday—following the old school rule of limiting the number of guests to the child's age. However, we know plenty of Bay Area parents (including ourselves) who pulled out all the stops for a big first birthday party for their little ones. They were great—but most of all, they were parties for the parents, as babies even at the big one year mark are far too young to realize what a birthday is all about.

There are many great locales and entertainers for children's birthdays in the Bay Area—a true testament to the Bay Area as a young family's metropolis! We have listed the entertainers according to where they are based or where they do most of their business (except San Francisco and the North Bay which we have combined under North Bay). Many entertainers serve the entire Bay Area. Also, most of the venues already mentioned in this chapter also host birthday parties. Here are some more ideas for children's birthday parties:

◆ **Celebrate at a kid-friendly restaurant.** Kid-friendly restaurants, such as pizzerias and ice cream parlors, make great venues for children's birthday parties for kids ages 2 and up.

◆ **Hire a storyteller.** A storyteller can be a real hit at kids' parties! Try calling your local bookstore or library for a recommendation.

- **Reserve space at a local park or playground.** If you want a simple party but don't want to host it (or simply can't!) at your home, reserving a park space is a great and economical alternative. Many parks also have a recreation room, which can come in handy in case of rain. Call your local Parks and Recreation Department for reservations and details. This is a popular option, so be sure to book as early as two to three months in advance!
- **Visit your local fire station.** This is always a great party theme for little boys, and a great venue for parents—as it is free! Most fire departments will be glad to give kids a tour of their station, and may let them climb on the trucks, try on the jackets and boots, and demonstrate how the hoses and ladders work.

TIPS FOR BABY'S FIRST BIRTHDAY

- Limit the number of guests so that excessive noise, stimulation, and confusion don't rouse the children too much.

- If the weather is nice, find an enclosed playground, keep the party very short (an hour and a half is enough), and don't plan any organized activity, other than having the kids play and eat some cake.

- Have two cakes—one that you serve your guests and another small one that you put in front of baby. This always makes very memorable moments and great photo opportunities! Both Safeway and Lucky stores will give you a free small cake for a baby's first birthday. Just bring in your baby's birth certificate a day or two ahead of time.

- If you are in a playgroup with many kids' birthdays during the same month, have one group birthday party and then have your own family's celebration on the actual birthday. (You can get away with this for the first couple of years!)

- If your child receives gifts, open them after guests leave.

All Star Showgrams

800-427-SHOW

PARENT RATING: ☆ ☆ ☆ ☆ ☆

Serving the entire Bay Area, All Star's performers will come to your house as almost any popular children's character and entertain your child and his or her guests with dances, games, balloons, face painting, magic, and party favors. Parents rave about the success and reliability of this company.

Jump For Fun

800-281-6792

www.jumpforfun.com

PARENT RATING: ☆ ☆ ☆

This national company is the world's largest maker of inflatable vinyl air jumpers. They rent 15x15 foot jumpers in various themes that hold up to ten children at a time. The company delivers and sets up the jumper. They leave the rest up to you, including supervising the kids.

San Francisco and North Bay

Boswick the Clown

415-665-1909

PARENT RATING: ☆ ☆ ☆ ☆ ☆

Parents and kids both love Boswick for being a real clown! He has an impressive clown resume, including having toured with Ringling Brothers and the Barnum & Bailey Circus. He specializes in juggling, magic, and making balloon animals.

Tim Cain

415-488-9204

www.timcain.com

PARENT RATING: ☆ ☆ ☆ ☆ ☆

You are sure to love this nationally renowned recording artist for children who will enliven your child's birthday party. Tim arrives at your home with his guitar in hand, ready to sing favorites or his original songs.

Flying Teapot Puppets

415-826-6926

www.flyingteapot.com

margaret@flyingteapot.com

The owner presents unique puppet shows in your home for birthdays for children ages 2-6. Her shows feature a full-size puppet stage, beautiful puppets, and live music and singing.

Kozy Klown

415-893-9542

A real clown who parents rave about —"fun family entertainment, including face painting, balloons, and tattoos."

Little Women's Tea Parties

415-566-9422

www.littlewomensteaparties.com

www.teapartyinabox.com

This company offers dress-up tea parties that feature pictures, games, crafts, and afternoon tea. Alternatively, they'll package and ship everything for the perfect tea party!

Miss Kitty (Judy Nee)

www.misskittysings.com

PARENT RATING: ☆ ☆ ☆ ☆ ☆

An award-winning vocalist, entertainer, and recording artist, Miss Kitty is guaranteed to present a fabulous show at your child's party. She features all the classic children's songs plus original compositions, encourages singing and dancing along with the music, and allows time for each child to take the mike. Book well in advance, as Miss Kitty is a very popular choice. See under Discovery Museum and Rainy Day Outings.

Penney the Clown
510-832-5696

www.penneytheclown.com

Penney can be a clown, fairy princess, or other fun character. She promises to add excitement to your child's party with magic, balloons, face painting, and dress-up.

Princess Polka Dot and Friends
415-461-1222

This popular children's entertainer sings, does magic tricks, has puppets, makes balloons, does face painting, tells stories, and more.

The Puppet Company
510-569-3144

www.puppetcompany.com

This professional puppeteer with over thirty years experience creates unique puppet shows that include classics and fables.

East Bay

The Birthday Magician
925-778-3757

This award-winning magician offers birthday party fun for the entire family that includes live doves, a cute bunny, and audience participation.

California Kids Jump
P.O. Box 15583

Fremont

800-543-7675

They rent large inflatable vinyl air jumpers.

Happy the Clown (Dub Blackwood)
510-525-0251

Happy is a "low-key" clown who promises a fun time for all.

Precious the Clown
510-594-1834

Precious will arrive at the party without her face painted and with the children's help she'll paint her face and transform herself into a clown.

The Puppet Company
See listing under San Francisco.

Twinkles
925-937-5457

Carla Winter offers birthday party entertainment for children ages one and up that includes music, song and dance, magic, face painting, animal balloons, juggling, and drawing caricatures.

Linda Zittel and the Magic Window Puppets
510-234-6266

This artist offers wonderful birthday party performances that feature storytelling with puppets, instruments, and finger puppet making for ages 2-7.

Aunt Willa's Pizza on Wheels

650-348-8865

www.pizzaonwheels.com

Aunt Willa makes and delivers delicious pizzas, drinks, green salad, and dessert to your door.

Babaloon & Tunes

888-339-7925 or 415-824-6725

www.babaloons.com

This company offers clowns or Teletubbies for all ages that perform balloon art, juggling, magic tricks, games, bubbles, singing and face painting.

Cosmo Jump

800-829-5867 or 650-570-5867

www.cosmojump.com

Cosmo Jump rents interactive inflatables, cotton candy machines, snow cone makers, and popcorn poppers.

Daffy Dave

650-326-3711

www.daffydave.com

Daffy Dave is goofy and wacky, but kids love him! Winner of the *Bay Area Parent's* 2000 Reader's Choice Award, he is one of the area's most sought after party entertainers.

D.W. Wilson's Ultimate Magic Show

650-369-9395

This magician has lots of experience in entertaining children, as he was part of the original Romper Room show.

Frankie & Her Live Animal Friends

650-592-7987

Frankie entertains and educates young birthday guests with live animals such as rabbits, snakes, tortoises and more.

Friendly Pony Parties and Barnyard Pals

650-738-0248

These pony rides and/or a barnyard zoo will come to your home for a unique and memorable party.

Happy Birds

408-268-0778

www.happybirds.com

Happy Birds offers unusual entertainment—they will bring a talented team of parrots to your home that plays basketball, rides bikes, talks, sings and roller-skates.

Lizard Lady

650-355-4105

http://home.onemain.com/~lizardlady

Lizard Lady offers unforgettable parties with her congenial reptiles.

Magic and Puppets

415-731-3898

Puppeteer Joe Hoffman has twenty-five years of experience and offers wonderful entertainment for children's birthday parties.

Magic Mike's Funhouse

408-244-7469

www.magictimeproductions.com

Mike offers a musical magic show that features juggling, ventriloquism, and surprises for party guests. He is a winner of a Parent's Choice Award for best show for parties in the Bay Area.

Miss Carol's Magical Puppetime

650-737-1286 or 650-342-9355
www.magicalpuppetime.com

Miss Carol features her handcrafted marionettes in a cabaret show of your choice. She has an impressive puppet collection of many familiar fairytale, nursery rhyme, and circus characters. Sing-alongs, magic, and face painting are also part of the party.

Mr. Magichead Productions

800-585-4554

Mr. Magichead and his bunny Lulu offer silly and memorable magic shows.

Most Unique Parties & Ponies

877-338-9130 or 831-338-9130
www.mostunique.com

This entertainer offers favorite costumed characters that feature magic, animals, puppets, games, music, face painting, and balloons. For extra special birthdays, a barnyard petting zoo and pony-cart rides are also available.

Pal Productions

650-355-0290

Pal Productions offers costumed characters that will entertain your party guests with dancing, games, and face painting. They serve most of the Bay Area.

Skates The Clown

650-365-1514
www.skatestheclown.com
www.qwikandeasy.com/balloons

Skates features magic, puppets, songs, games, balloon art, and face painting.

Celebrations by Jetta Jacobson

415-221-7199

An experienced early childhood educator and event planner, Jetta will organize and carry out your child's birthday party. She meets with you to learn about your child's interests and how to transform them into a memorable birthday celebration.

Everything But the Kids

925-258-1914

This group does everything from designing and sending out invitations to planning age appropriate entertainment such as music, art, face painting, cooking, tea parties and more.

It's a Piece of Cake

409 Lyon St.
San Francisco
415-929-1946
itsapieceofcake2000@go.com

This is a full-scale event and entertainment service for children, specializing in birthday parties. They offer stress-free party packages where every detail is handled from planning to clean up.

Sophie's Stress Free Soirees—Unique Parties Planned and Created by Your Children

228 Del Monte Ave.
South San Francisco
415-978-6651
www.instaparty.com

PARENT RATING: ☆ ☆ ☆ ☆ ☆

Sophie Maletsky offers a full-scale party-planning service where she takes children's ideas and transforms them into birthday fantasies.

On-Line Resources for Birthday Parties

www.birthdayexpress.com
Shop for themed party supplies, favors, activities, and more on this extensive website.

www.birthdayinabox.com
This website offers the convenience of ordering pre-printed or blank invitations, coordinating paper goods, games, party favors and personalized thank you notes in dozens of popular children's party themes.
PARENT RATING: ☆ ☆ ☆ ☆ ☆

www.iparty.com
Find all of your themed party paper goods on this website and have them sent to your door. They save you the trouble of looking for the exact theme your child wants—they have them all!

More Resources

◆ Bay Area Backroads with Doug McConnell, www.bayareabackroads.com. The website for this popular television show on KRON-TV Channel 4 includes a searchable database of past stories.

◆ www.gocitykids.com (national website with listings for outings and current events for children).

◆ Tricia Brown, *The City by the Bay: A Magical Journey Around San Francisco.* This is the Junior League's illustrated children's guide to San Francisco.

◆ Dierdre Honnold, *San Jose with Kids: A Family Guide to the Greater San Jose and Santa Clara Valley Area.*

◆ Karen Misuraca, *Fun with the Family in Northern California: Hundreds of Ideas for Day Trips with the Kids.*

◆ Clark Norton, *Fodor's Around San Francisco With Kids : 68 Great Things to Do Together.* This book has ideas for older children.

◆ Elizabeth Pomada, *Fun Places to Go with Children in Northern California.*

CHAPTER 9

IN SEARCH OF MARY POPPINS: Finding Competent Child Care

Sometime toward the end of your pregnancy, you will begin thinking about child care. Given the high demand for good quality child care in the Bay Area, it is never too early to address this issue. Do a little legwork before baby arrives, such as asking friends about their child care arrangements, interviewing individual child care providers, and visiting day care centers, and if you like one, registering for a space (yes, even before baby arrives)!

Of course, your child care needs will depend on your postpartum life. If you are returning to work full-time after a maternity leave, you will probably require full-time help. If you work at home, work part-time, or are involved in activities that require you to leave the house part of the day, you will likely need part-time child care assistance. Even if you aren't sure about your plans for returning to work, you will certainly want some help, ranging from regular support to occasional baby-sitting.

In this chapter we will share what we know about finding competent child care in the Bay Area. We will help you answer these questions and more:

- What are my child care options?
- What are the pros and cons of each type of child care?
- Where can I go to obtain good child care and what can I expect to pay for it?
- Who regulates the child care industry?
- How do I go about hiring a child care provider on my own?
- What are the legal issues involved in having someone work in my home?
- What are the best resources for finding baby-sitters?

California Child Care Licensing

In California, the Community Care Facilities Licensing Division of the Department of Social Services (DSS) (650-266-8843) licenses both day care centers and family day care homes. There are no state licensing requirements for in-home child care providers such as nannies and baby-sitters. Keep in mind that requirements for licensing a child care facility are minimal and basic, so the quality of licensed child care covers a wide spectrum.

However, license requirements do set some standards for the health and safe care of children by limiting the number and ages of children in the center or home. Additionally, a criminal record clearance through the Department of Justice and a "clean" Child Abuse Index Check, which indicates whether reports of suspected child abuse have ever been made against an individual, are required of all applicants and directors before a license is issued. All caregivers must also receive a tuberculosis clearance, and at least one person in the center or home must have fifteen hours of health care training, CPR, and first aid. By law, parents also have the right to drop in unannounced at any time at their child's center.

Day Care Centers

Day care centers, whether privately or publicly run, provide child care in a setting other than a home for large groups of young children (usually anywhere from 12-150 children). Most are open long hours (typically ten to twelve hours a day), year-round, and tend to follow local school year calendars in terms of holidays and breaks. Licensed day care centers are required to offer physical, activity-oriented and education programs, often in age-defined "classrooms," under adult supervision. Many day care centers do not offer care for infants (especially those under one year old), and those that do usually have a limited number of spaces (typically ten to twelve at most) due to state licensing requirements. Competition for these spaces can be keen. If you are planning on having your child attend a day care center before his or her first birthday, we urge you to contact and tour centers early in your pregnancy, as some centers have waiting lists as long as one to two years!

PROS AND CONS

One of the main advantages of day care centers (compared to in-home care) is reliability, since you are not dealing with one individual, but an organization of care providers. Many parents also appreciate that caregivers at day care centers are subject to a certain degree of accountability, since they are with others throughout the day, unlike an in-home caregiver. In addition, day care centers are usually open long hours and may be conveniently located in or near your workplace or neighborhood. Also, many parents appreciate the socialization with

---

How to Find Out about or File a Complaint against a Child Care Center or a Family Day Care Home

To find out if a child care center or family day care home you are considering has a complaint against them, you can call Community Care Licensing (650-266-8843) or your local California Childcare Resource and Referral Network agency (415-882-0234, main office), who will forward the inquiry to Community Care Licensing. Complaints and inquiries may be made anonymously.

other children that day care centers offer, as well as their structured nature, including scheduled program activities.

The disadvantages of day care include the necessity of transporting your child to and from the center. (If you think it is difficult getting yourself out the door early in the morning to make it to work on time, plan on at least doubling that time in order to get you and your baby dressed, fed, and out the door!) Also, many day care centers charge a fee when a parent is late picking up a child. Some parents dislike the fact that most centers follow established schedules (for feeding and napping, for example) which may or may not be compatible with your baby's natural rhythms. (On the other hand, many parents appreciate this and attribute the fact that their baby takes a bottle or naps at a certain time to their child's day care center.) In addition, day care centers can sometimes seem "institutional" in atmosphere, although it should be noted that many parents prefer such a setting to the quirks and unpredictability of family home care.

Since most day care centers are large and offer care for many children, your baby or child will have an increased exposure to other children's germs. If your child becomes sick, you'll have to make arrangements for backup care since most sick children are asked to stay at home. Also, in some day care centers, staff turnover can be high and care from various caregivers may affect your child's ability to adjust to the day care center. Finally, a day care center day can be a long one for a baby or young child to be in a non-home environment.

COSTS

Day care centers are either private, receiving little or no public funding, or are subsidized in varying degrees by public resources, including federal, state, and local funds. For many privately run centers, there are no subsidized spaces set aside for low-income families. For subsidized centers, however, the majority of spaces are generally set aside for lower income families, and fees are determined on a sliding scale. Requirements for these spaces vary according to the source of the funding. For instance, in some cases one parent is required to be working or in training. Competition for the subsidized spaces can be fierce.

Many day care center directors advise planning interim child care arrangements well before the baby is born, in order to cover child care needs while on a waiting list. Interim arrangements might include planning and budgeting for a longer maternity leave, having a relative or nanny take care of your child, or taking a full payment space while waiting for a subsidized one, if eligible.

CARE PROVIDER TRAINING, EDUCATION, AND QUALIFICATIONS

California state regulations require that all teachers (caregivers) working in day care centers have at least twelve units of Early Childhood Education (ECE), and teacher's assistants must have at least six units of ECE. Directors and site directors must have twelve units of ECE as well as three additional ECE units in administration. Teachers in subsidized centers are required to have a Children's Center Permit (twenty-four ECE units). Fingerprint and tuberculosis test clearance are required for all teachers.

LICENSING

In California, the Community Care Licensing Division of the Department of Social Services is the state regulatory authority that regulates child care. Regulations state that there must be thirty-five square feet of indoor space per child and seventy-five square feet of outdoor space per child. Centers in urban areas, such as San Francisco's financial district, often petition for a waiver of the outdoor space requirement since outdoor space is limited. Regulations also require one toilet and sink for every fifteen children.

Regulations require all equipment to be age appropriate, and daily planned activities must include quiet and active play, rest and relaxation, and support for toilet training.

Regulations for child-to-caregiver ratios vary according to whether the facility is subsidized or not and per the age of the children. In nonsubsidized centers, the maximum permitted child-to-caregiver ratios are as follows:

Infants (newborn-2 years): 4:1

Preschool (2-6 years): 12:1, or if the classroom has a caregiver and an aide, the ratio is 18:1

In subsidized centers, the maximum caregiver-to-child ratios are as follows:

Infants (newborn-2 years): 3:1 with a maximum of eighteen in one room

Preschool (2-6 years): 8:1 with a maximum of twenty-four in one room

Please note that regulations for non-subsidized centers do not include maximum numbers of children per classroom. For more information about day care licensing see www.ccld.ca.gov.

Family Child Care

Family child care refers to child care that is provided in a person's private home for a fee. The state of California considers care for two or more children from two or more families a family child care home and requires a license to operate as such. The license confirms that the caregiver and her home have met standards for childproofing, cleanliness, and child-to-caregiver ratios. While all family child care homes are required to be licensed, there are many that are not. In these cases, it may be that unlicensed homes don't meet the standards, or that the caregiver has decided not to apply for the license due to the expense. Just remember that while licensing can be a helpful indicator of quality child care, it is certainly not a guarantee.

In selecting a day care center or family child care home, try to visit at least a couple of times and observe how the children are cared for, and what their day is like (for instance, are they indoors all day, how much time is spent with the television on, are they read to, how are they fed—on demand or at set times, and so on). Also, talk to other parents whose children are cared for there, as well as those who no longer have their children there, if you can get access to this information.

PROS AND CONS

Many parents prefer the homey environment of family child care. Family child care offers consistency with caregivers since there are usually only one or two. Because care is provided in a home and space is more limited, there are usually fewer children than in day care centers. There is also a lower child-to-caregiver ratio than day care centers (see below), and many caregivers in family day care homes are experienced mothers with children of their own. Also, family child care is usually the least expensive form of child care (see below).

One of the most significant drawbacks to family child care for many parents is that the caregiver is not required to have any education or background in child development. And similar to a day care center, a license is granted largely based on the physical environment, rather than on how the children actually spend their day. Family child care also requires transporting your baby or child to the caregiver's home. Also, as with day care centers, backup care is needed if your child becomes sick, since family child care homes do not want ill children putting others at risk of infection.

COSTS

Family day care is usually the least expensive child care alternative (ranging from $7-15 per hour.)

CARE PROVIDER TRAINING, EDUCATION, AND QUALIFICATIONS

California state law requires all family day care home providers to complete fifteen hours of CPR and first aid, health, and safety training. A current tuberculosis clearance and finger print records are required for all adults residing in the home and for all adults who are present in

345

the home during the time children are in care. Unlike day care center teachers, they are not required to complete any ECE courses, although many providers voluntarily take ECE courses and/or have other qualifications gained through previous experience as teachers, nurses, or parents, for example.

LICENSING

In California, the Community Care Licensing Division of the Department of Social Services is the state regulatory authority that regulates family child care homes. A licensed home must meet health and safety standards, and cleared caregivers undergo a child abuse and criminal records check. Family child care homes can be licensed as either a small (six to eight children) or large (twelve to fourteen children) facility. A license limits the number and ages of children being cared for. See below for a summary of these restrictions. Also, when the caregiver has children of her own at home (which often is the case), they must be included in the overall number of children that she is licensed to care for.

Requirements for small family day care homes (which typically have one caregiver) include the following:

◆ If a family day care home is for infants only (newborn to twenty-four months), the caregiver's license restricts her to four infants and no other children.

◆ If licensed for six children, no more than three children may be under the age of twenty-four months.

◆ If licensed for eight children, no more than two may be infants (newborn to twenty-four months), and two must be at least six years old.

Large family day care homes are required to have a primary caregiver and a full-time assistant so that the ratio of children to caregiver is 6:1. In order to be licensed as a large family care home, the caregiver needs to have either been licensed for a small family care center for at least one year, or have experience with a day care center. The following restrictions apply to large family day care homes.

- If licensed for twelve children, no more than four may be infants (newborn to twenty-four months).
- If licensed for fourteen children, no more than three may be infants and two must be at least six years old.

In-Home Care

In-home care is exactly that—care provided in your home by either a nanny, au pair, or regular baby-sitter. In some cases, the caregiver may live with the family.

PROS AND CONS

Parents who choose this option often point to the one-to-one ratio and individual attention a child gets from a single caregiver. Recent research has shown that these considerations can be especially important for infants. In-home care also provides parents with the most flexibility with respect to their schedules, including the great convenience of not having to pack a child up for the day each morning and make it out the door on time with both of you dressed and fed! Also, if your child becomes ill, unlike a family care home or day care center, you typically can rely on your in-home caregiver to care for your child at home, unless, of course she becomes sick. Unlike a day care center that typically has a set schedule for feeding, napping, and playing for all of the children, with a single caregiver in your home, you set the schedule as well as rules for your baby's care. Also, having care provided in your home generally means that you decide who is going to care for your baby, unlike a day care center or family care home.

Care in your home includes care provided by a nanny, au pair, or other child care provider who either lives with you or who comes to your home on a regular basis, such as a regular baby-sitter.

A drawback to in-home care is being dependent on a single person's reliability and health, unlike with a larger organization such as a day care center. Loss of privacy, attachment issues (e.g., the "other mother" syndrome), possible language limitations (especially with au pairs), and less socialization with other children are also issues that should be carefully considered.

Other disadvantages include the higher cost compared to day care centers and family child care homes. Care in your home also means that you become an employer and are required to withhold taxes and possibly provide benefits such as health insurance and vacation time to your caregiver. Benefits typically include two weeks of paid vacation, seven paid holidays, and five sick days a year. In-home care providers are also unlicensed and unregulated, and therefore each applicant's background, credentials, and references must be thoroughly checked. Your provider will be unsupervised (at least part of the time) while providing child care, so thorough reference checks are crucial.

COSTS

The number one disadvantage of this form of child care (excluding au pairs) is that it is expensive ($12-25 per hour for live-outs, the average being $15-18 per hour, and $1,600-2,600 or more per month for a live-in, depending on the level of candidates' experience, education, and skills. Annual forty-hour week child care in the San Francisco Bay Area can range from $17,000-32,000 and up. Of course, child care at home can be much more cost effective if more than one child is being cared for, and some parents opt to share a nanny with another family. This is known as a sharecare arrangement.

CARE PROVIDER TRAINING, EDUCATION, AND QUALIFICATIONS

One of the biggest drawbacks about individual in-home care providers is that they are not legally required to have any particular training, education, or health and safety certification, such as CPR or first aid. Of course, if you are doing the hiring, you set the qualifications yourself. Also, many nanny agencies require their candidates to have various qualifications, including prior experience in working with babies and young children, specialized education and training in early childhood development, and CPR and first aid certification. Nannies who are placed through agencies are required by the state to undergo a background check through the Trustline registry, which includes fingerprinting and checking court records. If you hire a caregiver yourself, you may also ask her to register with Trustline. See under "Interviewing Candidates and Conducting Background Checks." In short, however, the onus of setting the standards for an appropriate caregiver and checking and verifying references and background fall on you or an agency.

LICENSING
Privately hired in-home childcare providers are legally exempt from licensing requirements.

HOW TO FIND COMPETENT CHILD CARE
Choosing child care is a laborious and emotionally intense task for any parent. We will give you an overview of the process here. Remember to give yourself plenty of time (at least four to eight weeks to hire a caregiver to come to your home and even longer to find a day care center or family day care home). We also suggest setting up a filing system for all the information you gather as you explore your child care options. There are lots of resources and experts out there to help you, but ultimately, your budget and values, and your child's personality, are the most important factors in selecting the best possible arrangement.

WORKSHOPS AND SEMINARS ON CHOOSING CHILD CARE
The Bay Area has several parenting centers that offer workshops and seminars that aim to guide you through the child care decision-making process. Here are the ones that parents shared with us. Because schedules and fees change, please call for current information.

Bananas
5232 Claremont Ave.
Oakland
510-658-0381
They offer a Choosing Infant Care
workshop on a regular basis. This
workshop helps parents understand
their options and provides support in
selecting appropriate care. Babies
are welcome.

Center for Creative Parenting
Pacheco Plaza
446A Ignacio Blvd.
Novato
415-883-4442
Sponsored by the Marin Child Care
Council, this center regularly offers a
seminar on how to choose quality
child care.

Alyce Desrosiers, LCSW
San Francisco
415-441-8447
Alyce is a licensed child psychotherapist who conducts seminars on
choosing in-home child care at several parent resource centers. She
also offers individualized services in
helping parents select a caregiver.

Parents Place
1710 Scott St.
San Francisco
415-359-2454
Parents Place regularly offers a
workshop entitled How to Choose a
Nanny in the San Francisco Bay
Area. This seminar is led by Alyce
Desrosiers, LCSW, who consults with
parents in helping them choose reliable caregivers for their children.

**Children's Council of San
Francisco**
575 Sutter St., 2nd Fl.
San Francisco
415-276-2900
The Council offers a Choosing Child
Care workshop on an ongoing basis.

Child Care Coordinating Council
700 S. Claremont, Ste. 107
San Mateo
650-696-8780
The council offers a workshop several times a year entitled Good
Beginnings...Choosing Child Care.

Below are some factors to consider in finding quality child care. Of course the best assessment is your own feeling about a place. The more comfortable you feel, the easier it will be to leave your child in someone else's care.

- *Fewer children to each adult.* Research suggests that quality child care depends on a low child-to-adult ratio so each child can receive individual attention. This is especially important for infants.
- *Consistency with caregivers* and a low turnover rate.
- *Caring individuals.* The caregivers should be warm and caring people who sincerely enjoy and understand children.
- *An environment that appeals to children.* The environment should be inviting to children and appropriate for the ages of the children in care.
- *Involvement of children.* Quality child care facilities engage and involve the children with age-appropriate activities, toys, and schedules. Caregivers interact with the children.
- *Parental involvement.* Parents should feel that they are partners with their caregiver.

SELECTING A DAY CARE CENTER OR FAMILY DAY CARE HOME

The Bay Area has hundreds of day care centers and family day care providers. If you are considering using a day care center, begin to explore your options while you are pregnant. It is not unusual to be placed on several waiting lists well before your baby arrives. Call child care resources and agencies in your area for referrals to licensed child care centers and family day care homes and set up appointments to visit them. This is your opportunity to educate yourself and to begin evaluating your options. It will be much more difficult driving around town, visiting centers, and meeting with directors when you have a newborn with you.

DAY CARE LICENSING OFFICES

California Department of Social Services—Community Care Licensing Division

www.ccld.ca.gov

The Community Care Licensing Division of the California Department of Social Services oversees the licensing of all child care facilities in California. Below is a list of local Community Care Licensing Offices in the Bay Area. Contact them for a listing of private and subsidized day care centers and family care providers in your neighborhood or near your place of work.

San Francisco and San Mateo

Peninsula District
801 Traeger Ave., Ste. 100
San Bruno
650-266-8843

This office licenses child care centers and family day care homes in San Francisco and San Mateo counties.

North Bay

Redwood Empire District
101 Golf Course Dr., Ste. A230
Rohnert Park
707-588-5026

This office licenses child care centers and family day care homes for Marin, Sonoma, and Napa counties.

Department of Health and Human Services

Marin County
Licensing Department
10 N. San Pedro Rd., Ste. 1002
San Rafael
415-499-7118

This office licenses child care centers and family day care homes for Marin County.

East Bay

Bay Area District
1515 Clay St., Ste. 1102
Oakland
510-622-2602

This office also licenses child care centers and family day care homes in Alameda and Contra Costa counties.

South Bay

San Jose District
111 N. Market St., Ste. 300
San Jose
408-277-1289 (family day care)
408 277-1286 (child care centers)

This office licenses child care centers and family day care homes in Monterey, San Benito, Santa Clara, and Santa Cruz counties.

CALIFORNIA CHILDCARE RESOURCE AND REFERRAL NETWORK

The California Childcare Resource and Referral Network is a coalition of largely state-funded agencies that are located in every county in California. Several of these agencies are known as the 4Cs– Community Childcare Coordinating Council. They assist parents in finding child care by maintaining databases of local caregivers (licensed family day care homes and day care centers). They make referrals only, and never recommend a provider. They track providers' licensing status, the languages they speak, the age groups they serve, their schedules, and the number of spaces available. They also provide child care subsidy assistance to low-income families either in training or in the work force, license preparation, training, and professional support to child care providers, child care resources and options for children with special needs, and advocacy, public education, and support to the child care community. Their services are free and are available to all parents and child care providers. Referrals are offered in English and Spanish either on the phone or during drop in times. The following is a list of state-funded child care resource and referral agencies in the Bay Area:

California Childcare Resource and Referral Network

Main Office
111 New Montgomery St.
San Francisco
415-882-0234
www.rrnetwork.org
PARENT RATING: ☆ ☆ ☆

Reviews ranged from "slightly better than the phone book" to "very helpful in directing me to family day care centers in my neighborhood." One frustration was that the network does not keep a current listing of which centers have openings and which do not.

The useful website contains a variety of information, such as tips on finding child care that suits your family, as well as recent legislation and policies impacting child care.

San Francisco

Children's Council of San Francisco

445 Church St.
415-343-3300 (referrals)
415-276-2900 (administration)
www.childrenscouncil.org
PARENT RATING: ☆ ☆ ☆ 1/2

The Council's Childcare Switchboard provides parents with free referrals for day care centers and family day care homes. The Referral Line data-

353

base has over eight hundred providers so referrals can be made to actual child care providers. Referrals are licensed but not screened. They also offer a child care resource room with child care referral listings, free workshops on choosing child care, a free newsletter, *The San Francisco Children's News,* and fingerprinting for child care providers.

Counselors are polite and helpful. A common complaint was that they do not do your homework for you. They stress that they offer referrals rather than recommendations (e.g., listing a day care source does not ensure its quality). However, many agreed that it is a good place to start a child care search. Where else can you get a list of all the licensed facilities in your work area or neighborhood? They also have a Bayview/ Hunter's Point office (1329 Evans St., 415-920-7280).

Wu Yee Children's Services
888 Clay St., Lower Level
415-391-4956 (referrals)
415-391-8993 (administration)

Marin Child Care Council
555 Northgate Ave.
San Rafael
415-472-1092 (administration)
415-479-CARE (referrals)
www.mc3.org

Community Childcare Coordinating Council (4Cs of Sonoma County)
396 Tesconi Ct.
Santa Rosa
707-544-3084 (referrals)
707-522-1410 (general information)
707-544-3077 (administration)
www.sonoma4cs.org
info@sonoma4cs.com

River Child Care Services
P.O. Box 16
Guerneville
707-887-1809 (referrals)
rcc@sonic.net

This office covers the Western Sonoma County/Russian River area.

Please note: Listings for Alameda County and Contra Costa County are separate.

ALAMEDA COUNTY

Community Childcare Coordinating Council (4Cs of Alameda County)
22351 City Center Dr., Ste. 200
Hayward
510-582-2182 (referrals for Hayward area)
510-790-0655 (referrals for Union City, Fremont, and Newark)
510-582-2182 (administration)

Bananas

5232 Claremont Ave.
Oakland
510-658-7101 (child care resources center)
510-658-0381 (child care referral)
www.bananasinc.org

PARENT RATING: ☆ ☆ ☆ ☆ ☆

A central clearinghouse for child care information and referrals for Alameda County, this office offers referrals for all types of child care, including day care centers, family day care, in-home care, shared care, and baby-sitters. They have lots of names of people looking for work, and will provide you with sample interview questions and contracts. They issue a quarterly newsletter that contains free listings mainly for shared in-home care in Alameda County. You can pick up a copy of this newsletter at Bananas' office, or subscribe by mail for $5. They offer a workshop on how to find infant child care, including a discussion of the various options. They also have a great parents' resource library, sponsor parenting/caregiver workshops, and produce a series of very popular and useful one-page handouts, on specific topics related to parenting and child development.

Child Care Links

1020 Serpentine Ln., Ste. 102
Pleasanton
925-417-8733 (referrals)
925-417-8740 (fax)
www.childcarelinks.org

This office provides child care referrals for southern and eastern Alameda County.

CONTRA COSTA COUNTY

Contra Costa Child Care Council

- Concord
  1035 Detroit Ave., Ste. 200,
  925-676-5442 (administration)
- Concord
  2280 Diamond Blvd., Ste. 500,
  925-676-5437 (referrals for central Contra Costa County)
- Antioch
  3104 Delta Fair Blvd.,
  925-778-5437 (referrals for eastern Contra Costa County)
- Richmond
  3065 Richmond Pkwy., Ste. 112,
  510-758-2099 or 510-233-KIDS
  (referrals for western Contra Costa County)

Four Cs Child Development Center for Subsidized Childcare

756 21st St.
Oakland
510-272-0669

Oakland Licensed Day Care Association

5730 Market St.
Oakland
510-658-2449

Please note: Listings for San Mateo County and Santa Clara County are separate.

SAN MATEO COUNTY

Child Care Coordinating Council of San Mateo County

700 S. Claremont St., Ste. 107
San Mateo
650-696-8787 (referrals)
650-696-8780 (administration)
www.thecouncil.net/

Choices for Children

111 N. Market St.
San Jose
408-297-3295
www.choiceforchildren.org

This private nonprofit agency largely manages subsidized funding for child care for low-income families.

SANTA CLARA COUNTY

Community Child Care Council of Santa Clara County (4Cs)

111 E. Gish Rd.
San Jose
408-487-0749 (referrals)
408-487-0747 (administration)
www.4c.org

City of Palo Alto Child Care and Family Services

Office of Human Services
4000 Middlefield Rd.

Palo Alto
650-329-2280

This office provides a reference list of licensed infant and toddler care centers in Palo Alto.

Palo Alto Community Child Care

3990 Ventura Ct.
Palo Alto
650-493-2361
www.paccc.com

This private nonprofit organization is not part of the Resource and Referral Network, but does offer a brochure on child care choices and accredited programs available in Palo Alto. They also manage subsidized funding for child care services for low-income families.

CHILD CARE CENTERS

The cost of child care centers is determined by several factors, including the age of your child (infants demand more care, and therefore are the most expensive), the quality and location of care, and whether corporate rates apply to you (some employers may subsidize their employees' child care costs or negotiate a better rate on their behalf). Expect to pay $900-1,400 per month for full-time infant care (this generally means infants up to twelve months old), around $700-1,000 for toddlers (usually ages two–three), and $700-950 for preschoolers (usually ages three–four). These rates are lower when corporate sponsorship fees apply, or when a day care center offers subsidized spaces. Subsidized spaces are determined on a sliding scale, depending on a family's income and eligibility. Fees are also less for part-time schedules (two or three days a week), but these schedules are often difficult to obtain. Finally, to apply and get on the waiting list of many child care centers, you need first to complete a registration form and submit it with a registration fee that is usually between $10-50.

There are hundreds of day care centers and family day care providers in the Bay Area. Keep in mind that some employers contract with corporate day care providers and offer use of a day care center exclusively to their employees. Often the day care center will be in the company's building. Check with your employer to see what arrangements they may offer. Competition for spaces in these programs is often keen, so apply early. If that is not an available option, however, here are a few day care centers, open to the community at large, that we have found. Most day care centers have fixed hours of operation, usually from 7 a.m.-6 p.m. and are open only on weekdays. Please call for specific hours. Because there are so many family care homes offering child care services, and because they may not necessarily be licensed, we have not listed any here. Please contact your local Resource and Referral Agency for a listing of licensed family day care providers near your home or workplace.

Children's Village
A Child Development Center of Catholic Charities

250 10th St.

415-865-2610

www.ccasf.org/

Ages: 3 months to 6 years

Child/caregiver ratio: 3:1 for infants, 4:1 for toddlers, 8:1 for preschoolers

Total number of children: 100

Children's Village opened in October 2000 and is one of the largest downtown child care centers. Funded by Catholic Charities, Children's Village is nondenominational. It is housed in a former elementary school and has an extraordinary natural setting, including pleasant gardens and a large outdoor playground—rarities for an urban day care center. They have two infant rooms, accommodating nine infants; two toddler rooms for twelve; and several preschool rooms of twenty-four each. Parents of newborns are urged to apply for a space on the waiting list even before delivery. They have a limited number of subsidized spaces.

Civic Center Child Care Corporation (C-5)

505 Van Ness Ave.

415-626-4880 (infant site)

Ages: 3-18 months

Child/caregiver ratios: 3:1 for infants, 3.5:1 for ages 19-24 months, and 4:1 for 25-36 months

Total number of children: 21

Located in the State of California Public Utilities Building, and close to the Civic Center, this day care center is open to the general public as well as state employees. C-5 prides itself on encouraging parental visits throughout the day. They also have a site for preschoolers (18 months to 5 years old) in the California State Building, 455 Golden Gate, 415-703-1277, where they have the capacity to take sixteen toddlers and twenty-five to thirty preschoolers.

Easter Seals Healthy Environments Child Development Center

95 Hawthorne St.

415-744-8754

PARENT RATING: ☆ ☆ ☆ ☆

Ages: 6 weeks to 5 years

Child/caregiver ratios: 3:1 for infants (under 12 months), 4:1 (12-24 months), 6:1 for toddlers (25-36 months), 10:1 for preschoolers (3-5 years)

Total number of children: 80-90

This popular day care center is located one block from Moscone Center. The center is at full enrollment most of the time, resulting in a substantial waiting list. Many expecting parents apply and pay the $50 registration fee to get their names on the waiting list as soon as they know their due date. Part-time and full-time spaces are also offered for infants two to three days a week. Since the Government Services Administration provides space and supplies, priority is given to families employed by the federal government.

Marin Day Schools

PARENT RATING: ☆ ☆ ☆ ☆

Ages: Varies depending on campus

Child/caregiver ratios: Generally, 3:1 for infants (under 12 months), 4:1 for one-year-olds, 11:1 for 2-year-olds, and 10:1 for ages 3-5 (Sherith Israel Campus has some variations, see below.)

Total number of children: varies depending on campus

This is one of the largest private non-profit day care centers and preschools in the area, with fourteen locations in San Francisco, Marin, and Redwood City. Some campuses take children as young as 3 months through 5 years, while others operate more as a pre-school, taking children beginning at 2 years old. See under "Favorite Local Preschools" in chapter 10. They offer year-round full-time and/or part-time care. They are notorious for being difficult to get into, especially for the infant day care programs at the downtown locations, and some of the pre-school programs. Your best bet is to get on the waiting list before your baby is born! These centers often contract with local companies that give employees and their children preference. Marin Day offers a limited number of "scholarships" to eligible families.

Spear Street Campus

220 Spear St.

415-777-2081

Ages: 3 months to 4 1/2 years old

Total number of children: 48

This campus offers an infant program for twelve and spaces for thirty-six older children. Corporate fees are available to PC World, Industry Standards, and Gap employees. Part-time spaces are available on a limited basis. Their facility includes a play yard, which is a rarity downtown.

Hills Plaza Campus

2 Harrison St.

415-777-9696

Ages: 3 months to 5 years

Total number of children: 52

This campus has an infant program for nine with a total of fifty-two children. Corporate fees are available to families employed by Gap, PC World, and Telespree. Part-time spaces are available on a limited basis.

San Francisco City Hall Campus

1 Dr. Carlton B. Goodlett Pl.

415-554-7560

Ages: 2 months to 5 years

Total number of children: 52

Located in City Hall, this campus largely serves families employed by the city. The infant program has a capacity of nine. Corporate rates are not available.

Fox Plaza Campus

1390 Market St.

415-554-3979

Ages: 2-16 months

Total number of children: 6 (At the time this book goes to press, they are planning on expanding to 12 children.)

This unique facility only takes six infants and shows preference for families working in the Fox Plaza building, mainly attorneys who work for the city.

Sherith Israel Campus (formerly California Street Campus)

2266 California St.

415-775-2211

Ages: 2-5 years

Child/caregiver ratios: 6:1 for 2-year-olds, 8:1 for 3-year-olds, and 9:1 for 4-year-olds and pre-kindergarten age.

Total number of children: 160

The first of the six San Francisco locations of Marin Day Schools, this campus primarily operates as a pre-school, taking children who are at least 2 years old by September of that school year. The two's program is for eighteen children. The overall facility serves 160 children, but since many of the preschoolers are on part-time schedules, typically there are no more than ninety to ninety-five children on-site at one time. See under "Favorite Local Preschools" in chapter 10.

Laurel Heights Campus

3333 California St.

415-775-2111

Ages: 3 months to 5 years

Total number of children: 84

This attractive facility was opened in 1999 and offers an infant program for twelve infants. Sixty percent of the spaces go to UCSF and USF families for whom corporate rates apply. Part-time spaces and fees are available.

South of Market Childcare at Yerba Buena Gardens

790 Folsom St.

415-820-3500

Ages: 3 months to 5 years

Child/caregiver ratios: 3:1 for infants, 4:1 for toddlers, and 8:1 for ages 4 to pre-kindergarten

Total number of children: 82

Opened in 1998, Yerba Buena is a large, attractive day care center. There is an infant program for six infants (3-18 months); a toddler program for twelve (18-36 months) and a preschooler program for sixty-four (3-5 years old). Competition for spaces in the small infant program is stiff. There also are a limited number of part-time spaces available. A subsidized program is located across the street at 366 Clementina St. (415-391-0389). Families must financially qualify as low-income families to participate in this subsidized program.

St. Nicholas Child Care Center

5200 Diamond Heights Blvd.

415-550-1536

Ages: 3 months to 5 years

Child/caregiver ratios: 4:1 for infants and 12:1 for toddlers and preschoolers

Total number of children: 85-90

St. Nicholas is a large child care center that has a full-time staff of fourteen. They offer care for an unusually large number of infants, serving thirty-six infants 3-24 months old. They also serve sixteen toddlers ages 2-3; twenty-one preschoolers ages 3-4; and sixteen preschoolers ages 4-5.

Bailey Iniece Infant Toddler Center

20 Ebbtide Ave.
Sausalito
415-332-5698

Ages: 3-36 months

Child/caregiver ratios: 4:1

Total number of children: 40

This center offers full-time care with an infant program for eight, ages 3-15 months. Fees are determined on a sliding scale.

Belvedere Tiburon Childcare Center

1185 Tiburon Blvd.
Tiburon
415-435-4366

Ages: 2-8 years

Child/caregiver ratios: 6:1 for 2-3 years old, 12:1 for ages 4-5 years old, 12:1 for kindergarten-age, and 14:1 for school age children

Total number of children: 94

The Belvedere Tiburon Childcare Center (BTCC) is a private, nonprofit organization offering full- and part-time child care for up to thirty-six children, 2 years and up, as well as a preschool program for children ages 3-5. The center also offers a drop in program on a space-available basis. Parents need to have visited the center and filled out the necessary paperwork to be eligible for the drop in program. All drop in arrangements are to be made at least a day in advance. BTCC has a large outdoor area that features a play ship!

The Kid's Place

50 El Camino Dr.
Corte Madera
415-927-0498

Ages: 6 weeks to 5 years old

Child/caregiver ratios: 4:1 infants (under 24 months) and 6:1 for ages 2-5

Total number of children: 50

This center offers full- and part-time infant, toddler, and preschool care, to age 5. The infant room has capacity for sixteen infants (from 6 weeks to 2 years old).

Canal Childcare Center

46 Louise St.
San Rafael
415-457-1444

Ages: 3-5 years

Child/caregiver ratios: 8:1

Total number of children: 18

Part of Community Action Marin (an umbrella organization providing support to low-income families), this popular child care center caters mainly to working, low-income families. The center also offers after school care for school age children. Fees are determined on a sliding scale.

Creekside Village School

1787 Grant Ave.
Novato
415-898-7007

Ages: 6 weeks to 4 years

Child/caregiver ratios: 4:1 (infants up to 18 months), 6:1 (18-24 months), 8:1 (2-year-olds), 10:1 (3-year-olds), 12:1 (4-year-olds), 14:1 (after school care)

Total number of children: 120

361

Located on a serene two-acre property, Creekside offers care for eight
infants ages 6 weeks to 12 months.
This center is also licensed for eighteen one-year-olds, and the rest of the
children are toddlers and preschoolers, up to age 4. Breakfast and a hot
lunch are included in their fees, as
well as special programs including
Spanish instruction twice a week and
music once a week. They offer flexible schedules, including part-time
care for as few as two days, or five-
hour days. The summer program
offers more organized outside activities and special entertainment.

Golden Poppy Preschool and Infant Center

50 El Camino Dr.
Corte Madera
415-924-2828
www.fs7.com/goldenpoppy/

Ages: 6 weeks to 6 years

Child/caregiver ratios: 3:1 for infants
under 12 months, 4:1 for ages 1-3,
6:1 for preschoolers (ages 3-6)

Total number of children: 130

PARENT RATING: ☆ ☆ ☆ ☆ ☆

This private day care center was
voted Marin's best Day
Care/Preschool by the *Pacific Sun*
from 1993-1999. Golden Poppy is
licensed for sixty children in the
infant and toddler center and 101
children in the preschool; however,
they keep their numbers considerably lower, with caregiver to children
ratios roughly twice of what the state
requires. They offer an infant and
toddler program for twent-eight children up to 2 years old that includes
twelve infants less than one year and
sixteen children between one and 2

years old. When children reach 2,
they go to the preschool. The preschool has eighteen 2-year-olds,
twenty-four 3-year-olds, and twenty-
four children ages 4-5 (pre-kindergarten). Golden Poppy offers full-
and part-time spaces, including two,
three, and four days of care a week,
as well as a morning program and an
extended care program. (These various schedules account for the overall
total number of children.)

Marin Jewish Community Center

200 N. San Pedro Rd.
San Rafael
415-479-2000

Ages: 3 months to 4 years

Child/caregiver ratios: 4:1 for infants
and young toddlers, 6:1 for toddlers,
and 7:1 for preschoolers

Total number of children: 140

Marin's JCC offers a popular infant
and toddler full-day care program,
known as kidcare. They offer care for
twelve infants from 3-24 months and
eighteen toddlers, ages 2-3. For children who are 3 years old by the early
fall, there is a preschool program and
extended care. Applications for day
care are taken throughout the year,
and parents are advised to apply
early.

Marin Lutheran Children's Center

649 Meadowsweet Dr.
Corte Madera
415-924-3792

Ages: 6 weeks to 2 years

Child/caregiver ratios: 4:1 for infants
and 6:1 for toddlers

Total number of children: 32

This center offers care for up to
twenty-two infants, although they

prefer to keep it to sixteen, from ages 6 weeks to 2 years. They also offer care for sixteen toddlers ages 18 months to 3 years. Part-time spaces are available on a limited basis, with a minimum of two full days a week.

Robin's Nest Pre-School

A popular and privately owned program, Robin's Nest was founded in 1985 in San Anselmo and now has five campuses in Marin and Sonoma counties. Admission is available year-round as class openings permit, offering a morning, midday, and full-day program at most locations. Each is licensed to serve a different number of children. The Windsor location is the only campus offering child care for eight infants, ages 14-24 months. Robin's Nest locations also offer three or four days of care per week as well as flexible hours, including a morning program.

◆ **Mill Valley**
70 Lomita Dr.
415-388-5999
Ages: 2-6 years
Child/caregiver ratios: 7:1 for 2-year-olds, 7.5:1 for 3-year-olds, and 9:1 for 4-year-olds
Total number of children: 40

◆ **San Anselmo**
100 Shaw Dr.
415-459-4355
Ages: 2-5 years
Child/caregiver ratios: 6:1 for 2-year-olds, 8:1 for 3-5 years
Total number of children: 60

◆ **Novato**
1990 Novato Blvd.
415-879-1990
Ages: 18 months to 6 years
Child/caregiver ratios: 5:1 for 18-36 months, 8:1 for 3-6 years
Total number of children: 42

◆ **Terra Linda**
1 Wellbrock Heights
San Rafael
415-479-4778
Ages: 18 months to 6 years
Childcare/caregiver ratios: 6:1 for 18 months to 3 years, 12:1 for 3-6 years
Total number of children: 36

◆ **Windsor**
9451 Brooks Rd.
707-838-0549
Ages: Newborn to 8 years
Childcare/caregiver ratios: 4:1 for newborns (up to 12 months), 6:1 for 13-36 months, 12:1 for 30 months to 8 years old
Total number of children: 120

Wee Care Children's Center

8 Olive St.
Mill Valley
415-388-2015
Ages: 4 months to 5 years
Child/caregiver ratios: 3.5:1 for 1 month to 2 years and 8:1 for 2-5 years
Total number of children: 28

This small, nonprofit child care center located in downtown Mill Valley, usually has a waiting list, so parents are advised to apply early.

Association of Children's Services

3021 Brookdale Ave.

Oakland

510-261-1077

Ages: 2 weeks to 5 years

Child/caregiver ratios: 3:1 for newborns to 2 years, 4:1 for 2-3 years, 8:1 for 3-5 years

Total number of children: 85

The *Oakland Tribune* recently voted the Association of Children's Services (AOCS) (which sounds like more than one but is actually a single center) the best day care center in Oakland. Parents say that on average, the staff is better educated than at most other centers, with each program directed by an experienced teacher with a B.A. or M.A. degree in early childhood development. Children over 30 months are expected to be part of the nursery school program. Depending on available space, you will either be notified of an opening or placed on the waiting list. If placed on the waiting list, it is recommended that you phone monthly to reconfirm your interest.

Bright Horizons Family Solutions

www.brighthorizons.com

One of the largest providers of employer-sponsored child care, Bright Horizons runs over 325 child care centers worldwide. Many of their child care centers only accept families from the employers with whom they contract. However, some of their centers are open to the community, but they give preference to families employed by the corporate sponsor of these sites.

◆ Garner Preschool

2275 N. Loop Rd.

Alameda

510-769-5437

Ages: 2-5 years

Child/caregiver ratios: 8:1 for 2-4 1/2 years and 10:1 for kindergarten-age

Total number of children: 200

◆ Planet Avant!

46885 Bayside Pkwy.

Fremont

510-413-7400

Ages: 6 weeks to 6 years

Child/caregiver ratios: 4:1 for 6 weeks to 18 months, 6:1 for 18 months to 3 years, 10:1 for ages 3-4 years, and 12:1 for 4-6 years old

Total number of children: 87

The corporate sponsor is Avant! Corporation and Sun Microsystems.

The Child Day School

See chapter 10. Call each campus for information on care for infants.

Child Education Center

1414 Sacramento St.

Berkeley

510-528-1414

Ages: 3 months to 5 years

Child/caregiver ratio: 3:1 for infants (3-13 months), 4:1 for toddlers (13 months to 2 years), 5:1 for 2-year-olds, 7:1 for preschoolers ($3^1/_2$-$4^1/_2$ years), and 8:1 for pre-kindergarden ($4^1/_2$-5 years)

Total number of children: Not available.

CEC is a nonprofit day care center with attractive grounds and light and airy classrooms. The center is located two blocks from the North Berkeley BART station. Founded in 1981 by a group of parents, the center's board of directors is made up entirely of parents. CEC offers many scheduling options and full- and part-time space and fees vary accordingly. See also chapter 10.

Clark Kerr Infant Center

2900 Dwight Way (Building 5A)
Berkeley
510-642-7031

Ages: 3 months to 3 years

Child/caregiver ratio: 3:1 for 3 months to 2 years and 4:1 for 2-3 years

Total number of children: 24

UC Berkeley's new child care facility opened in 1999 and primarily serves Berkeley faculty and staff families. They are licensed for twenty-four infants.

Cornerstone Children's Center

First Presbyterian Church
2407 Dana St.
Berkeley
510-848-6252

Ages: 6 weeks to 5 years

Child/caregiver ratio: 3:1 for infants up to 12 months, 4:1 for 1-2 years, 6:1 for 2-2^1/2 years, and 8:1 for 2^1/2-5 years

Total number of children: 88

This popular day care center usually has a waiting list of six to nine months. They offer care for 30 infants under 2 years and 58 children from 2-5 years.

Emeryville Child Development Center

1220 53rd St.
Emeryville
510-596-4343

Ages: 4 months to kindergarten-age

Child/caregiver ratios: 3:1 for under 12 months, 6:1 for 12-18 months, and 8:1 for 18 months to 5 years

Total number of children: 90

Emeryville's infant program has capacity for thirteen infants less than 18 months. While largely a private center, this facility offers a few subsidized spaces.

The Model School

2330 Prince St.
Berkeley
510-549-2711

Ages: 3 months to 5 years

Child/caregiver ratios: 3:1 for infants (3-14 months), 4:1 for toddlers (14-24 months), 5:1 for older toddlers (24-36 months), and 8:1 for pre-kindergarten ages

Total number of children: 90

The Model School is a leading day care and preschool. They embrace the teaching concepts of John Dewey and Maria Montessori, and parental participation is an important principle of the school. The child to caregiver ratios are considerably better than the standards set by the state of California.

Richmond Magic Years Children's Center

1221 Nevin Ave.
Richmond
510-970-7100

Ages: 3 months to 5 years

Child/caregiver ratios: 3:1 for infants (3-12 months), 4:1 for toddlers (13 months to 2 years), and 12:1 for preschoolers ($3^1/_2$-5 years)

Total number of childen: 86

Magic Years is a nonprofit, private day care center offering day care for sixteen infants under the age of 2 years, twelve toddlers ages 2-3 years, and two classrooms of fifteen preschoolers, ages 3-4. A limited number of part-time spaces are available, and families employed by the federal government take priority.

St. John's Infant Center

22717 Garber St.
Berkeley
510-549-9342

Ages: 3 months to $3^1/_2$ years

Child/caregiver ratios: 3:1 for 3-18 months, 4:1 for 18 months to $2^1/_2$ years, and 5:1 for $2^1/_2$-$3^1/_2$ years

Total number of children: 45

Largely subsidized by the church where it is housed, St. John's offers a popular child care program for up to forty-five children, including nine infants (up to 15 months old), and fifteen "wobbly walkers," ages 15 months and up. They also offer early bird hours for an additional fee. Fees are both full pay and subsidized, with the subsidized fees being determined on a sliding scale, depending on a family's income.

South Bay

Bright Horizons Family Solutions

See under East Bay.

◆ Bright Horizons at Cupertino

10253 N. Portal Ave.
San Jose
408-366-1963

Ages: 6 weeks to pre-kindergarten

Child/caregiver ratio: 4:1 for infants 6 weeks to 2 years, 5:1 for 2-3 years, and 8:1 for 3 years through pre-kindergarten-age

Total number of children: 24 infants (6 weeks to 24 months) and 72 children (ages 2 and up)

This center takes infants through preschoolers; the corporate sponsor here is Sun Microsystems.

◆ The Tamien Childcare Center

1197 Lick Ave.
San Jose
408-271-1980

Ages: 6 weeks to 12 years

Child/caregiver ratio: 3.5:1 for infants 6 weeks to 14 months, 4:1 for 14 months to 2 years, 6:1 for 2-$3^1/_2$ years, and 10:1 for ages $3^1/_2$-5 and school age children

Total number of children: 126

This center takes 111 infants through preschool ages; the remaining are school age children. The corporate sponsor here is the Valley Transportation Authority.

California ChildCare Centers, Inc.

◆ **San Mateo**
Crystal Springs E.C.E. Center
2145 Bunkerhill Dr.
650-572-1110
Ages: 2-5 years
Child/caregiver ratios: 12:1 for all ages
Total number of children: 36

◆ **Daly City**
South Gate Preschool
1474 Southgate Ave.
650-755-8422
Ages: 2-5 years
Child/caregiver ratios: 12:1 for all ages
Total number of children: 42

◆ **Millbrae**
Community Preschool
450 Chadbourne Ave.
650-652-4504
Ages: 2-5 years
Child/caregiver ratios: 12:1 for all ages
Total number of children: 36

◆ **Redwood City**
Redwood Children's Center
1445 Hudson St.
650-367-7374
Ages: 2-5 years
Child/caregiver ratios: 12:1 for all ages
Total number of children: 45

Childrens' Creative Learning Centers, Inc.

794 E. Duane Ave.
Sunnyvale
408-732-2500
www.cclinc.com

Ages: Varies depending on site
Child/caregiver ratios: Varies depending on site
Total number of children: Varies depending on site

Founded in 1992, Childrens' Creative Learning Centers (CCLC), prides themselves on providing affordable quality child care to employers and families nationwide. They are based in Sunnyvale and serve the Peninsula and South Bay with sites in Stanford, Los Altos, Sunnyvale, Atherton, and San Jose. A Palo Alto site is scheduled to open in 2003. Call for more information about each site or visit their website.

The Children's Pre-School Center

4000 Middlefield Rd.
Palo Alto
650-493-5770
Ages: Newborn to 5 years
Child/caregiver ratio: 4:1 for infants and toddlers (under 2 years), 6:1 for older toddlers (2-3 years), and 9:1 for preschoolers (3-5 years)
Total number of children: 150

Since its opening in 1984 as the first corporate-sponsored day care program in the Bay Area, the Children's Pre-School Center has developed into a nationally accredited program serving over two hundred families. Priority is given to employees of corporate sponsors, including Roche, ALZA Corporation, Cooley Godward, and SAP, Inc. The Children's Pre-School center offers care for infants to 5-year-olds. The Center usually has a substantial waiting list, especially for infants, as they only take eight babies. The toddler program (one-2 years) consists of groups no larger than twelve children. Corporate-sponsored fees and part-time options are available.

Early Horizons

Established in 1984, Early Horizons in Sunnyvale offers full- and part-time care, including three-quarter days, half days, and a preschool session. They also have a Los Altos campus serving children under 2 years old.

◆ **Sunnyvale**

1510 Lewistown Rd.

408-746-3020

Ages: 2 months to 10 years

Child/caregiver ratios: 4:1 for infants under 2 years; 6:1 for 2-year-olds, 10:1 for 3- and 4-year-olds, and 14:1 for ages 5 and up

Total number of children: 210

◆ **Los Altos**

201 Covington Rd.

650-941-2548

Ages: 2-24 months

Child/caregiver ratios: 4:1 for infants under 2 years and 6:1 for 2-year-olds

Total number of children: 84

Foster City Pre-School and Day Care Center

Charter Square Shopping Center

1064F Shell Blvd.

Foster City

650-341-2041

Ages: 2-6 years

Child/caregiver ratios: 7:1 for 2-year-olds and 12:1 for 3- to 6-year-olds

Total number of children: 135

Serving the Foster City area since 1973, Foster City Pre-School and Day Care Center offers full-time care and part-time options of either two or three days a week. No infant care is available.

Hoover Children's Centers

2396 Evergreen Dr.

San Bruno

650-871-5025

Ages: 2 months to preschool-age

Child/caregiver ratios: 3:1 for infants 2-12 months, 4:1 for infants 12-18 months, 6:1 for toddlers 18 months to $2^{1}/_{2}$ years, and 12:1 for preschoolers.

Total number of children: 75

Offering care to children since 1981, the Hoover Center was awarded "Best Day Care Center in San Mateo County" for 1998 and 1999 by *San Mateo Times* readers. The Hoover Center is a large full-service day care center offering parents many scheduling options. A $100 registration fee (which does not apply to the first month's tuition) must accompany your application.

Kids at Play Preschool and Infant Center

124 W. Latimer Ave.

Campbell

408-370-3745

Ages: 6 weeks to 6 years

Child/caregiver ratios: 4:1 for infants, 8:1 for toddlers (2-3 years), and 11:1 for preschoolers (4-5 years)

Total number of children: 36

This small privately owned center has recently opened an infant center, offering care to seven infants, age 6 weeks to 2 years. There is a sizable waiting list for the infant program.

Kids at Play also offers care for seventeen toddlers—nine 2-year-olds and eight 3-year-olds. There are also eleven preschoolers, ages 4-5 years.

Love N' Christian Care Daycare Center

2490 Middlefield Rd.
Palo Alto
650-322-1872
Ages: 2-6 years
Child/caregiver ratio: 10:1 for 2-year-olds and 12:1 for preschoolers, 3-5 years.
Total number of children: 6-70
PARENT RATING: ☆ ☆ 1/2

We have heard from parents that there is high turnover among the staff at this private day care center.

Marin Day Schools Redwood City Campus

403 Winslow St.
Redwood City
650-363-4939
Ages: 2 months to 5^1/$_2$ years
Child/caregiver ratio: 3:1 for 2-12 months, 4:1 for 1-2 years, 7:1 for 2-3 years, and 9:1 for 3-5 years
Total number of children: 92

This campus offers care for twenty-seven infants under the age of 2. See under San Francisco.

Palcare

945 California Dr.
Burlingame
650-340-1289
www.palcare.org
Ages: 3 months to 5 years
Child/caregiver ratio: 4:1 for infants, 6:1 for toddlers (ages 2-3 years), and 8:1 for preschoolers (ages 3-5 years)

Total number of children: 263

Palcare's flexible and unique hours cater to parents who have nontraditional or changing work schedules. Parents can request a customized schedule each month, rotating their days as their work schedule dictates. Fifty percent of Palcare's enrollment is reserved for families employed at the San Francisco Airport. Other special employers also have priority because of their annual contributions. Palcare offers care for two rooms of sixteen infants each, 3-24 months. They also offer two rooms of eighteen toddlers each, ages 2-3 years, and three large rooms of twenty to thirty preschoolers, ages 3-5 years. Palcare uses an unusual graduated rate system in which the hourly rates go down as you use more hours per month. Fees are based on your monthly hours and your child's age. In addition, there is an annual registration fee of $150 per child.

Palo Alto Community Childcare

3990 Ventura Ct.
Palo Alto
650-493-2361
www.paccc.com

This private nonprofit organization runs seventeen day care centers in the Palo Alto area, three of which take infants. Each center has its own name and license to operate. Call or visit their website for information on specific centers.

Well Infant Care Center (part of Under the Weather)

See under "Sick Child Care."

Sick Child Care

It's always smart to make arrangements for emergency and back-up care before you really need it. Typically, you need to have visited and registered with a center to receive backup or drop in care. Child Care Resource and Referral agencies in your county can help you find a family day care or day care center when you need temporary backup help with a sick child. Most nanny agencies also handle temporary sick child care. In addition, here are a few sick child care programs that we've heard about:

Wheezles and Sneezles

1108F San Pablo Ave.
Albany
510-526-SICK (7425)

Wheezles and Sneezles helps when your child has a mild illness that keeps a child out of school or child care, but is not serious enough to keep a parent home from work. The staff and an on-site nurse look after up to ten children a day (from infants to 12 years old). A registered nurse screens children as they come in each morning. A nurse on staff will administer the child's medication, offer them quiet activities, story time and of course, a scheduled nap. They also offer an in-home service for infants or children who are contagious or bedridden. Fees are reasonable and are on a sliding scale.

The "Get Well Room" at the Fairfax/San Anselmo Children's Center

199 Porteous Ave.
Fairfax
415-454-1811

This day care center offers care for mildly ill children ages 3 months to 10 years who are enrolled in the center as well as for those who are not. Prior registration and a visit to the center are prerequisites to using the service, as well as immunization records and a physician's report. All children who are not enrolled for child care at the center must be seen by their nurse or doctor each day that they attend the Get Well Room. To be seen, you need to call ahead and make an appointment in the period from 7:30-9:30 a.m., when the nurse is on-call. You can call the day before or that morning to schedule the appointment. If your child is seen by his or her own pediatrician, they can be taken in at any time during the day on a space-available basis. Generally, enrollment in the Get Well Room is limited to six children. They are open September to June. Fees are $17.50 for a half-day and $35 for a full day.

Under the Weather

2612 El Camino Real
San Mateo
866-455-5439
www.under-the-weather.com

This center specifically designed for mildly ill children welcomes children aged one month to 12 years. Children must be preregistered. The center is designed to prevent cross-contamination of illnesses while keeping in mind the developmental needs of a variety of age groups. They have three rooms, each designed for specific illnesses and symptoms. The children are assigned to a room and then placed in a group of children of similar age. A pediatric registered nurse, on the premises at all times, assesses each child upon arrival and throughout the day. An individualized plan of care is developed and implemented for each child. After a child is accepted into care, a pager is assigned to each parent so they can be contacted if needed. Family memberships as well as corporate memberships are available. In early 2002, Under the Weather opened a Well Infant Care Center at the same address in San Mateo. It accomodates eight infants ages 2 months to 2 years. At presstime, Under the Weather is considering plans to open another sick child care facility in Santa Clara.

Drop In Child Care

What do you do when your primary child care arrangement is unavailable for a day or so? Perhaps your nanny is sick, the day care center is closed, or the weather is bad—backup or drop in care is what you need!

ChildrenFirst

- San Francisco
  Bank of America Building
  555 California St.
  415-392-7531
- Palo Alto
  3 Palo Alto Sq.
  3000 El Camino Real
  650-493-3777

PARENT RATING: ☆ ☆ ☆ ☆ ☆

Parents who work for participating companies can take advantage of a relatively new backup day care, run by ChildrenFirst, the only national company that exclusively specializes in backup child care. Exclusively corporate sponsored, ChildrenFirst offers care for *well* children from 12 weeks to 12 years of age. Parents must first register their children by bringing current medical records, photos of your family, and insurance and pediatrician information. Parent comments: "A very professionally run facility." "I was impressed with the report of my son's day that I received when I picked him up. It told me exactly what he did, what activities and toys he played with, and what he ate, how long he napped, and so on."

Core Group

See under "Baby-sitting Services and Resources."

Marin Day Schools

Backup Relief Child Care
199 Fremont St.
San Francisco, 415-331-7766

This backup relief child care center, run by one of San Francisco's largest day care and preschools, works through corporate sponsorship. Participating companies purchase slots for their employees and their families. Please call for more information and to find out whether your or your spouse's company participates in this program.

Strawberry Children's Day Center

118 E. Strawberry Dr.
Mill Valley, 415-388-3940

PARENT RATING: ☆ ☆ ☆

Part of Strawberry's Recreation Center, the Children's Day Center offers drop in care for children 18 months to kindergarten. In order to participate in this program, you need to schedule an interview with your child at the center to do the necessary paperwork and meet with one of the caregivers. After this interview you are placed on a waiting list, which we've heard is reasonable. The first time you drop off your child, you are asked to stay with your child and get your child used to the center. The fee is $5 an hour, and you may use the center up to twelve hours a week.

Hiring an In-Home Care Provider

Hiring someone to take care of your child in your home while you are at work is an overwhelming task, both emotionally and practically. Basically, you have two choices—conduct the search yourself or enlist the support of an agency. For a fee an agency will provide you with appropriate candidates and will do the initial screening such as confirming their legal status (that candidates are eligible to work in the United States) and ensuring that the candidates have previous professional experience, including checking references. Since nannies are typically women, in this book we refer to a nanny as a "she". Please note, however, that male nannies do exist—approximately three percent of the nanny work force in the Bay Area are males.

CONDUCTING THE SEARCH YOURSELF

With in-home care, the search and selection process for the right caregiver is obviously critical. There are myriad books, experts, and other resources available (a few are mentioned in this chapter or listed in the bibliography). One source we found particularly helpful is *Finding a Nanny for Your Child in the San Francisco Bay Area*, by Alyce Desrosiers.

We heard from many parents how they went about conducting their search for an in-home child care provider; these are some of the basic steps that they took. Of course, there are other ways to conduct a search too. And no matter how systematized many parents are about collecting and analyzing information about prospective candidates, many say that they really just "knew" when they found the provider who was right for them. The process is as much an art as a science. One mother described it as a kind of "gestalt," and another described it as akin to dating, and said "you know when you've met her." Even so, most parents will agree that while instincts are helpful, a well-planned strategy and search method will help you make your ultimate decision with confidence.

Writing a Job Description

If you decide to conduct the search yourself, you'll first need to write a job description. The job description should include caregiving responsibilities (including the age of your child or children and where you live), housekeeping responsibilities (if any), and hours, and list the salary range and benefits. You may also want to include specific qualifications such as training, education, and prior experience as well as legal status, languages spoken, CPR and first aid certification. Before writing the job description, you should assess your schedule and your child's daily routine (which of course will be changing from month to month if your child is an infant) to best articulate the requirements of the position. When writing the job description, be as specific as possible.

Announcing your job opening

Get the word out through family, friends, and colleagues, and via newspapers, bulletin boards at local parenting organizations, local colleges, and various children and parenting centers. Some centers, such as Parents Place in San Francisco and Bananas in the East Bay, have entire walls devoted to bulletin boards for parents and potential nannies to place ads. You can also ask about placing your ad in churches and temples or schools, especially nursing schools. Be as specific as possible in your ad in terms of what you need (such as days, hours, language skills, and other qualifications). This may help reduce the volume of unqualified callers.

BULLETIN BOARDS AND BINDERS WITH CHILD CARE LISTINGS

The Bay Area has many child care bulletin boards and parenting centers that maintain binders, all which provide the opportunity for parents seeking child care and child care providers seeking employment to connect with one another. Many offer this as a public service while others charge a nominal fee for posting your ad. Beware that most of the organizations that host such bulletin boards only do that—they offer no screening, recommendations, or referrals of the candidates. Still, if you are willing to do all the screening and reference checks, these information sources can be a parent's best friend:

Alliance Francaise

1345 Bush St.

415-775-7755

This well-known French language school hosts a bulletin board with a variety of items, including some child care ads, typically of bilingual nannies and baby-sitters.

Day One

3490 California St., 2nd Fl., Ste. 203 (entrance on Locust)

415-440-Day1 (3291)

www.dayonecenter.com

This wonderful state-of-the-art parent resource center offers free referrals in binders for nannies, as well as other care providers, including childbirth and postpartum care doulas.

Natural Resources

1307 Castro St.

415-550-2611

PARENT RATING: ☆ ☆ ☆ ☆ ☆

Natural Resources is a pregnancy, childbirth, and parenting center that offers all sorts of resources, products, and services to parents, including a regular newsletter that includes some child care provider listings. Your best bet is to go there and look through the binders with current listings of nannies and baby-sitters seeking employment; parents say that they are great resources!

Parents Place

1710 Scott St.

415-359-2454

www.parentsplaceonline.org

PARENT RATING: ☆ ☆ ☆ ☆

Parents Place, a Jewish and Family Children's Services program, has the most extensive child care resource bulletin board in town! While overwhelming at first, a large board lists available nannies and baby-sitters seeking employment. For a nominal fee, you can place an advertisement on pre-printed index cards with your particulars (days and times needed, and the number and ages of your children). There is no screening of candidates, although some of the nannies have also joined up with nanny agencies. They also have an electronic bulletin board on their website. Comments: "Really hit or miss...our first nanny was great, not worthwhile since." "Good, but not always updated." "Great resources, but you have to filter through a lot of chaff and need to check references carefully."

Peek-a-Boutique

1306 Castro St.

415-641-6192

This popular children's resale shop hosts a community bulletin board containing some child care ads.

California Pacific Medical Center

Newborn Connections

3698 California St.

415-600-BABY (2229)

The Perinatal Education and Lactation Center has a small bulletin board of items of interest to new parents, including some child care ads.

Center for Creative Parenting
Pacheco Plaza
446A Ignacio Blvd.
Novato
415-461-8323
This full service parenting center hosts a bulletin board offering a variety of items of interest for new parents, including child care.

Jewish Community Center
200 North San Pedro Rd.
San Rafael
415-479-2000
This center has a large bulletin board with postings of nannies looking for employment and vice versa.

Parents Place Marin
600 5th Ave.
San Rafael
415-491-7959
Parents Place Marin moved into a new building in 2002, where they offer more services and programs, including a large bulletin board that features advertisements for nannies and baby-sitters. The aim is to have a similar size board with as many postings as their popular San Francisco location.

Canal Community Alliance
91 Larkspur St.
San Rafael
415-454-2640
415-454-3967 fax
The Canal Community Alliance, a social service organization that aims to help low-income residents in the Canal neighborhood of San Rafael, has a bulletin board that contains postings and notices for various employment opportunities.

Bananas
5232 Claremont Ave.
Berkeley
510-658-7101 (child care resources center)
510-658-0381 (child care referral)
PARENT RATING: ☆ ☆ ☆ ☆ ☆
Bananas is a nonprofit child care referral agency for Alameda County residents. You will get better information and be less frustrated if you visit Bananas rather than call. They have cards with child care provider's information (such as address, schedule, and available space) that you can match up to maps, which they have there.

Peninsula Parents Place
410 Sherman Ave.
Palo Alto
650-688-3040
They have a child care bulletin board that includes child care wanted and offered, including shared care opportunities. Preprinted index cards are provided for you to complete, describing the job, and posted. If you wish to place an ad, you need to go in person, as information is not taken over the phone.

YMCA
3412 Ross Rd.
Palo Alto
650-856-9622
They have a good bulletin board with ads for baby-sitters and nannies.

> **TIP:** Many mothers' groups produce newsletters for their members that contain useful classifieds for sitters, nannies, and other forms of child care. In most cases, other moms place the ads, recommending people who have worked for them. One of the best child care classified sections that we've seen among such newsletters is that of the *Neighborhood Parents Network* (formerly Neighborhood Moms), based in the East Bay. Call 510-527-MOMS to inquire about membership and their newsletter.

NEWSPAPERS

Newspapers are another great way to advertise your child care needs. Both nannies in need of work and parents in need of child care advertise in these papers. However, do your homework—screen carefully and check references thoroughly. If you decide to run an ad, be as specific as possible about the days of the week and times and the age(s) of your child or children. You might also set up a voice mailbox where you reiterate your specific criteria and urge people to only leave a message if they meet your criteria.

San Francisco

El Mensajero, 415-821-3224
France Today, Journal Francais, 415-921-5100
Hokubei Mainichi, 415-567-7323
Irish Herald, 415-752-7977
Marina Times, 415-928-1398
Noe Valley Voice, 415-821-3324
The Philippine News, 800-872-3000
Potrero View, 415-824-7516
San Francisco Chronicle, 415-777-7777

North Bay

The Ark Newspaper, 415-435-2652 (Tiburon)
Classified Gazette, 415-457-4151 (San Rafael)
Family News, 415-492-1022
Marin Independent Journal, 415-883-8666 (Novato)
Marin Scope Newspapers (*Marin Scope, Mill Valley Herald, Twin City Times, Ross Valley Reporter, News Pointer*), 415-289-4040, ext. 25

Napa Valley Register, 707-226-3711

Pacific Sun Weekly, 415-383-4500

San Francisco Chronicle,
415-777-7777

Vallejo Times Herald, 707-255-8456

East Bay

Contra Costa Newspapers
(Montclarion, Piedmonter,
Berkeley Voice, Contra Costa
Times, San Ramon Valley Times,
West Coast Times, Oakland Hills
El Cerrito Journal, Alameda
Journal), 510-339-8777

East Bay Express, 510-540-7500

The Daily Planet, 510-841-5600

The Oakland Tribune, 800-595-9595

UC Berkeley Daily Californian,
510-548-8300

South Bay

El Observador, 408-543-2944

Los Altos Town Crier, 650-948-9000

Pacifica Tribune, 650-359-6666

Palo Alto Weekly, Mountain View
Voice, and The Almanac,
650-326-8210

Palo Alto Daily News, 650-327-6397,
ext. 301

San Jose Mercury News,
408-920-5111

San Jose Metro, 408-298-8000

San Mateo Daily Journal,
650-344-5200

San Mateo Times, 650-348-4459

Stanford Daily Newspaper,
650-723-2555

BEST WEBSITES FOR CHILD CARE SEARCHES

Bay Area Sitters

www.bay-area-sitters.com

This free message board for the Bay
Area helps connect parents and nannies and baby-sitters.

Child Care Net

www.childcarenet.com

This is an on-line child care search
engine for Santa Clara County, with
information provided by 4Cs of Santa
Clara County.

Careguide

www.careguide.net

Who would think that a national website could be useful for finding child
care resources? This one is! It maps
day care centers, providers, and

nanny agencies according to your
locale, and in some cases provides
details about facilities and programs. A
great place to start a child care search.

The Child Care Action Campaign

www.childcareaction.org

This website is packed with information on how to find affordable day
care, what each state is doing to
improve child care, and more.

craigslist

www.craigslist.org

This is a free community-based bulletin board. Look under child care for
job listings.

Department of Social Services, Community Care Licensing

http://ccld.ca.gov/docs/links.htm#childcare

This California Social Services Department website offers all sorts of valuable information about finding child care, including links to other sites that will provide you with names and numbers of day care and family care centers in your area.

Edaycare

www.edaycare.com

A leading on-line application service provider for child care providers in the Silicon Valley, this site helps child care providers and parents find each other. This website also has a search engine that locates day care centers by typing in a zip code.

NannyBank

www.NannyBank.com

NannyBank allows you to post and search for your nanny and baby-sitter needs on this extensive website.

Needbabysitter

www.needbabysitter.com

This website matches teenage baby-sitters and adult age nannies to appropriate child care opportunities through an anonymous and exclusive-use message board (where parents share contact information with only those sitters who they may be interested in hiring).

Parents Place

San Francisco

See under "Bulletin Boards and Binders with Child Care Listings"—San Francisco.

UC Berkeley Parents Network

http://parents.berkeley.edu

(by the end of 2002, this website will be replaced by www.parentsnet.org)

PARENT RATING: ☆ ☆ ☆ ☆ ☆

This extensive site offers more advice and recommendations than you'll ever need on almost every aspect of parenting. You can sign up to receive the on-line newsletter, where you can post child care want ads on the parent-run e-mail list. Parents frequently post available caregivers that they personally recommend. Originally intended for parents who either work or are students at UCB, the list has grown to include many others who live in the Berkeley area.

4nannies

www.4nannies.com

Serving San Francisco, you pay a fee of $189 to have access to an on-line directory of hundreds of nannies looking for immediate employment. Candidates' resumes expire after thirty days. You arrange and run background checks yourself (about $100 per applicant).

Legal Child Care Issues

Remember that if you hire in-home care, you may be deemed an employer and be subject to various federal and state laws. We have listed some things you should know as an employer, but be sure to check with a legal or tax professional when you hire—laws are always changing!

- California law requires you to pay an employee a minimum wage of $6.75 per hour.
- If you pay a single caregiver $1,300 or more in a calendar year, you are considered an employer and are required by the IRS to pay federal and state employment taxes. (See IRS publication #926.)
- The Internal Revenue Service's Kit 942 includes everything you need for domestic employees. Call 800-TAX-FORM (800 829-3676).
  - ⬥ Publication 503: Child and Dependent Care Expenses
  - ⬥ Publication 923: Employment Taxes for Household Employees
  - ⬥ Form 942: Employer's Quarterly Tax Return for Household Employees
  - ⬥ Publication 15, Circular E: Employer's Tax Guide
  - ⬥ Form 941 or 940 EZ: Federal Unemployment Tax
- Household employers are required to file IRS Schedule H with their personal income tax return. They can either make estimated tax payments using IRS 1040 ES estimated tax payment voucher, or they can elect to have additional federal income taxes withheld and file schedule H at the end of the year with their own personal income tax form.
- In-home employees may ask you to withhold state income taxes from their paychecks and forward it to their state. This is not a requirement but something you may discuss with your employee.
- An employee must be provided with a W-2 form for the previous year's earnings by January 31.
- As an employer, you must verify the identity and legal status of your employee and pay employment taxes. Both you and the caregiver are required to sign a Form I-9 from the U.S. Department of

Justice Immigration and Naturalization Service verifying that the employee is eligible to work in the United States. These forms require that you, the employer, have your employee submit to you relevant documentation of her identity and employment eligibility in the U.S. You may obtain this form by calling the Immigration and Naturalization Service at 800-870-3676 and ordering the Handbook for Employers (Form M-274) which includes Form I-9. You will also need to contact the Internal Revenue Service and ask for Publication #926, the Household Employer's Tax Guide, at 800-TAX-FORM. You may also download this publication off the IRS website at www.irs.gov/pub/irs-pdf/o926.pdf.

◆ All employers in the state of California are required to report information about new employees to the California New Employment Registry at 916-657-0529.

◆ The state of California requires that you provide your caregiver with worker's compensation insurance. (Contact your insurer about coverage under an existing homeowner's insurance or tenant's insurance policy. Alternatively, the California State Compensation Insurance Fund may be reached at 415-974-8000.) Also, talk to your insurer about potential liability if your caregiver is watching someone else's child in your home. If your caregiver will be driving, you'll need to confirm she has adequate insurance coverage if she is using her car. (If driving your car, she'll need to be added to your policy.)

INTERVIEWING CANDIDATES AND CONDUCTING BACKGROUND CHECKS

THE TELEPHONE INTERVIEW

As you receive calls from prospective candidates responding to your ad, use the telephone to screen applicants. This will help save you from wasting invaluable time by meeting with inappropriate people. If possible, set aside a quiet time (when baby is napping) to return calls so that you can focus your attention on the applicants. As you speak with each one, describe the responsibilities, hours, and days needed to see whether these suit the applicant. Then ask the applicant about their qualifications, previous work experience, why they are looking for work right now (and why they left their most recent position), CPR and first aid certifications, and salary expectations. You may also want to ask whether or not they have tuberculosis and hepatitis certificates.

Some parents find it helpful to have a form that they have prepared in advance, and use it throughout the interviewing process, to help develop a profile on each candidate. Others are more comfortable just talking on the phone and taking notes as they go along. If you decide to use a form, it might include the following categories for you to fill in with the information you collect as you go through the interviewing process with each candidate:

◆ Name, address, telephone number, and e-mail address
◆ Education, experience and training
◆ Legal status
◆ Health and safety certificates
◆ Description of last position and reasons for leaving
◆ Gaps in employment
◆ Jobs that didn't work and why
◆ Personality and fit with your child
◆ Understanding of children
◆ Ability to communicate with you
◆ Child care approaches and philosophies (for instance, whether she embraces feeding on demand or on schedule, how comfortable she is with handling breast milk (if applicable), how she handles a crying baby, how she feels about having your child nap on a regular schedule, and so on.)
◆ Approach to discipline

If you are interested in an applicant, request the names of the applicant's three most recent employers. Unlike other jobs that you may have hired for, you will want to check references at the beginning of this process rather than at the end. If she cannot provide you with references, don't even consider her.

MEETING AND INTERVIEWING POTENTIAL CAREGIVERS

After the telephone interview and screening of potential candidates, and reference checks, schedule a round of initial interviews in person. Ask each candidate to bring copies of her resume, visa (if applicable), certificates, and licenses. Use this interview to evaluate applicants' work experience, personality and character, and fit with your child. If your child is one year old or younger, you may want to consider having the first interview without your child so that you can focus your attention on the applicant. Invite back those candidates you are most comfortable with and impressed by for a second interview.

During the second interview continue your previous discussion. Have your candidate meet your child and observe their interaction. You may want your spouse or partner to meet the candidate at this time as well. After this interview, you should be down to one or two potential candidates. Invite them back for a third and final interview where you continue to assess their overall match with your child. This interview may be a half-day working interview where you offer to pay the applicant for her time.

CHECKING REFERENCES

Check references carefully. Make sure they are authentic. Also, if an applicant tells you that a recent employer has moved away and has an unlisted number, request other references from that job (such as a neighbor who may have known the family she worked for). For each reference get the following information:

◆ Full name
◆ How the applicant knows the reference
◆ Current address
◆ Current work and home telephone numbers

CONDUCTING BACKGROUND CHECKS

The TrustLine Registry
800-822-8490
www.TrustLine.org

Conducting a background check can confirm that a candidate is who she says she is and has no history of substantiated child abuse or neglect on record in California. TrustLine is the California state registry of in-home child care providers who have passed a background screening. The screening includes a review of records of criminal convictions and substantiated allegations of child abuse and neglect maintained by the California Department of Justice. It also screens for records of any federal crimes maintained by the Federal Bureau of Investigation. If nothing disqualifying comes up, the individual is listed as "cleared" and is placed on the TrustLine registry. If a nanny or potential nanny tells you that she is TrustLine registered you should call 800-822-8490 for confirmation.

Ideally, the Trustline screening process would be completed before, or immediately after, the nanny has started work. However, this process takes longer than expected due to the volume of applications. Plans for a new computer system are in the works to speed up at least the non-FBI portions of the check to one week. Another of the shortcomings of the TrustLine process is that a nanny is registered and listed on TrustLine as soon as she clears the California checks which can take up to three to four months. Since the FBI check takes even longer (sometimes up to a year and a half), a nanny can initially clear the California portion of the screening and be TrustLine registered before the FBI check is completed.

In operation since 1989, TrustLine is managed by the California State Department of Social Services (CDSS). CDSS contracts with the California Child Care Resource and Referral Network to provide access to the database through a toll-free number, listed above. Roughly ten percent of those undergoing background checks do not clear, some because of repetitive misdemeanors, but some because of very serious criminal convictions including murder and kidnapping. Staff at the TrustLine office will tell you only if your candidate doesn't clear the background check, not why, because of confidentiality laws. Since 1994, nanny agencies are required by California state law to initiate the TrustLine process upon placement of a nanny in a position. Some agencies pay for this service, which costs $124.

Nannies, au pairs, and baby-sitters hired outside a nanny agency are not required to register with TrustLine, but you may certainly ask your candidate to do so. Who pays for this service is negotiated between you and your nanny. The nanny or baby-sitter will need to complete a one-page application form and have her fingerprints taken. Call to request the application form and to find out where your nanny can go to get fingerprinted. Applicants need a California driver's license, California I.D. card, a state-issued photo I.D. from a state other than California, or an Alien Registration Card (green card) to register.

PRIVATE BACKGROUND INVESTIGATIONS

There are also private companies that specialize in conducting background checks for nannies and other in-home caregivers.

PFC Information Services
6114 La Salle Ave., Ste. 638
Oakland
510-653-5061
www.pfcinformation.com

This public filing service works nationally with nanny agencies and parents to provide comprehensive background checks of caregivers. Owned by Lynn Peterson, a former owner of a nanny placement agency, the service is more comprehensive than the state-mandated TrustLine registry. They cover criminal records for felonies and/or misdemeanors in any jurisdiction or state; DMV reports for suspensions, license revocations, and moving violations (including DUIs); credit reports verifying an applicant's prior addresses and employment, and identifying excessive debts or collections; and a Social Security Scan, which verifies an applicant's Social Security number. PFC Information Services, Inc. has a very strong reputation. They pride themselves on providing details that TrustLine does not. Their searches are done manually, which they believe is more thorough than a computer search. This check takes roughly three to seven days to complete

and the basic package costs $140. Nannies must provide a signed authorization to run a background check. Call to receive these forms. Five to seven percent of PFC's background checks for nannies come back showing significant negative items on a nanny's record.

Know Your Nanny
20 Oxford Rd.
Jackson, NJ 08527
800-454-2062
www.knowyournanny.com

Know Your Nanny assists parents all over the United States with the process of screening, hiring, and monitoring in-home child care providers, including offering background checks and renting and selling surveillance equipment such as the "nanny cam" (these allow you to see how your nanny and child spend the day).

Paula Drake Investigations
P.O. Box 51622
Palo Alto
650-857-9465
www.siliconvalleypi.com

Ms. Drake offers thorough background checks for nannies as well as nanny camera surveillance.

FINAL DETAILS

Once you have hired a caregiver, you are required by the INS to confirm your caregiver's identity and employment eligibility. In order to do this you will need Form I-9 from the INS (employment eligibility form), which explains what documents (e.g., passport, visas, and a driver's license) your caregiver needs to submit to you. See above under "Legal Child Care Issues."

As a final step, you may want to draft and sign an agreement. Such an agreement clarifies roles, responsibilities, and expectations, and can prevent misunderstandings. It may also include a trial period, allowing either party to terminate the agreement within a certain period of time. Other things that you may include in such an agreement include the following:

- Term of employment (beginning date and ending date)
- Work schedule
- Specific duties
- Compensation and pay schedule
- Benefits (such as medical, vacation, and telephone use). Some parents find it to their benefit to provide health insurance for their caregivers, since it is often viewed as an incentive for caregivers to provide long-term care. Basic health insurance for caregivers can cost anywhere from $68-220 monthly.
- Conditions and terms for termination
- Confidentiality regarding personal and family information
- Performance review dates and frequency

Nanny Tax and Payroll Services

As an employer of an in-home child care provider, you are responsible for taking care of the related payroll and tax matters. You are responsible for complying with IRS and state tax laws, attending to payroll issues such as sick, vacation and personal time tracking, and preparing and filing taxes for your care provider. Since these details can be time consuming, some families opt for professional assistance in this area. Here are a few resources that we've heard about:

Accuchex
365 Bel Marin Keys Blvd.
Novato
415-883-7733
This company specializes in household payroll and tax services, and will do quarterly filings.

Breedlove and Associates
701 South Capital of Texas Hwy., Ste. C 1312
Austin, TX 78746
888-273-3356
PARENT RATING: ☆ ☆ ☆ ☆ ☆
Breedlove is a national company specializing in domestic employer tax and payroll services. Currently they have over five hundred Bay Area clients and work exclusively with families and file quarterly household taxes. Comment: "Extremely helpful, always calls back and are available to answer questions."

California State Employment Development Department
1825 Sacramento Dr., Ste. 401
San Francisco
415-929-5700
This agency offers free seminars on payroll and tax issues for domestic employers. You may also obtain the state-required registration forms for new employees here.

Crown Bookkeeping and Payroll Services
1733 Woodside Rd., #205
Redwood City
650-365-5005
This agency offers domestic employer tax and payroll services.

Essentia Software
888-999-1722 or 601-582-0669
www.essentia-soft.com
This company offers NannyPay 99, a Windows 95/98/NT payroll program designed to calculate your nanny's taxes.

Express Tax Services
390 8th St.
Oakland
510-451-1833

Gibbs Bookkeeping and Tax Service
346 Grand Ave.
Oakland
510-893-8304

Greenberg and Greenberg
2090 Chestnut St.
San Francisco
415-775-9503
This is a small, local tax service whose clients are mainly neighborhood businesses and families.

GTM Associates
16 Computer Dr. W.
Albany, NY 12205
888-432-7972
www.gtmassociates.com
PARENT RATING: ☆ ☆ ☆ ☆ ☆
Although located in New York state, GTM provides household payroll and tax services all over the country and is a recognized leader in its field. They provide free over-the-phone advice and have a resourceful website that features a "nanny tax resource center."

Home/Work Solutions
2 Pidgeon Hill Dr., #210
Sterling, VA 20165
www.4nannytaxes.com/
They are one of the nation's leading providers of household payroll and employment tax preparation services, specializing in nanny tax compliance. Parents rave about their website!

Internal Revenue Service
800-829-1040 (24-hour recording)
800-829-3676 (forms and publications
www.irs.gov
The IRS publishes a Household Employers Tax Guide that provides all the forms you need for household employment tax matters. You can also download this publication from their website.

One Stop Payroll
620 Contra Costa Blvd., Ste. 215
Pleasanton
800-788-2088
This company offers domestic employer tax and payroll services.

SurePay
1880 Pleasant Valley Ave.
Oakland
877-787-3729
Although located in the East Bay, this company primarily serves clients in San Francisco, including domestic employers.

Insurance and Financial Products for Nannies

Eisenberg Associates
1340 Newton Centre
Newton, MA 02459
617-964-4849 or 800-777-5765
This official insurance representative of the International Nanny Association offers short-term and permanent health insurance, life insurance, disability coverage, and so on.

Nanny Agencies and Resource Centers

In return for a fee, agencies can take care of most of the search process for you. They typically ask you to provide them with information on your ideal caregiver by filling out a detailed questionnaire that includes job description details such as salary, responsibilities, and hours. Based on this information, they provide you with candidates that they prescreen. They may do basic research that includes background checks of criminal records, legal status, and language proficiency. They also usually contact references and may provide you with a set of written comments based on telephone interviews of the candidate's previous employers. Most agencies require their nannies to make at least a one-year commitment when placed with a family.

Many agencies also offer other related services, including accountants to handle nanny tax issues and advice on salaries, vacation policies, and other benefits. Beware that agencies may present you with candidates who are unwilling to have their income reported to the IRS. While some agencies offer advice and work with nannies and parents to find a solution to these issues, others leave parents and nannies to work out the question of compliance with tax and employment laws. As an aside, we've been told that the San Francisco Bay Area has one of the highest percentages of parents who pay employment taxes on their nannies' salaries.

Basic registration fees to initiate a nanny search with an agency range from free up to $350. This fee, if any, starts the process along with the completion of the agency's detailed questionnaire and/or interview that assists the agency in providing candidates to you. You then interview the agency-supplied candidates. Salaries are typically negotiated between you (the employer, rather than the nanny agency) and the candidate. Agencies usually charge a flat referral fee when you hire one of their candidates. This fee may be based on a certain number of weeks of the nanny's salary, or a percentage of her salary (12.5 percent is the current rate). Typically, placement fees range from $3,000-3,600 in the Bay Area, depending on the firm and whether you are looking for full- or part-time help. Nanny agencies typically prefer exclusivity but cannot legally demand it. While it may be expensive to sign up with more than one agency, you will get a larger selection of candidates if you do so, although some overlap.

Most agencies offer a trial period (which varies but is often one to two weeks) before parents make a hiring decision. If a parent hires a nanny and it doesn't work out for whatever reason (e.g., whether she leaves or whether you let her go), most nanny agencies offer either a credit policy towards finding a replacement or a refund for a portion of the placement fee.

The nanny agency industry is unregulated. However, many of the larger nanny agencies are members of the member-run Bay Area Nanny Agencies Association (BANAA). BANAA seeks to ensure that members conduct their businesses ethically and work towards informing one another about issues pertinent to the child care industry. BANAA members need to be in business for at least three years and are voted in by fellow members based on their business practices. BANAA membership generally means that an agency takes its business seriously. There are also the International Nanny Agency Association (that any agency may join) and the Alliance of Professional Nanny Agencies. Both host an annual conference and have members nationwide.

The following agencies and centers can help locate live-in and live-out, permanent or temporary care. Please note that most nanny agencies service more counties than the one in which they are based. This is particularly true of the San Francisco-based agencies, many of which service the entire Bay Area.

San Francisco

Aunt Ann's Agency (In-House Staffing)
www.in-housestaffing.com
• San Francisco
  2722 Gough St., 415-749-3650
• Daly City
  198 Los Banos Ave., 650-757-2000
Placements: A full range of domestic staff, including full- and part-time nannies, baby nurses, and postpartum care providers.
Registration fee: None.
Placement fee: For a full-time nanny, 12.5 percent of a nanny's gross annual salary; the same for part-time nannies, except with a $1,000 minimum.

BANAA member: Yes.
PARENT RATING: ☆ ☆ ☆ ☆ ☆
A well-established, private family-owned business, Aunt Ann's was founded in 1958 and offers a full range of domestic staffing including full-time or part-time nannies and baby nurses. Aunt Ann's serves the entire Bay Area and requires applicants to be experienced adults with at least one year of child care experience. Candidates are TrustLine registered upon placement, with no additional fee for this service. References are checked and CPR training is offered. Aunt Ann's requires no registration fee (one of the very few that doesn't), as they believe that you shouldn't have to pay before

a service is rendered. Nannies caring for one child typically get between $15-18 an hour in San Francisco, $13-18 in the East and North Bay, and $15-20 on the Peninsula and in the South Bay. Aunt Ann's has a refund policy that guarantees a pro-rated return of your placement fee should your needs change in the first 120 days of employment. Aunt Ann's also offers temporary placement of nannies. Placement fees for this service are 35 percent of the nanny's total earnings. As an extra bonus, Aunt Ann's will gladly meet with you in person to discuss your child care needs. Comments: "Professional, reliable, first-class service."

Bay Area 2nd Mom, Inc.

See description under South Bay.
415-346-2620

Natural Resources

See description under "Bulletin Boards and Binders with Child Care Listings"—San Francisco.

PARENT RATING: ☆ ☆ ☆ ☆ ☆

This organization offers free referrals and resources for child care.

Town and Country Resources

(formerly Town & Country Nannies and Mothers in Deed)
www.tandcr.com
- San Francisco
  1388 Sutter St., Ste. 904, 415-567-0956
- Palo Alto
  425 Sherman Ave., Ste.130,
  650-326-8570

Placements: A full range of domestic staff, including live-in or live out, full- or part-time nannies, baby nurses and postpartum care providers.

Registration fee: $250

Placement fee: 12.5 percent of the nanny's gross annual income, with the same fee for part-time help, although with a $1,500 minimum. For temporary or short-term help, 35 percent of the overall pay for that period.

BANAA member: Yes.

PARENT RATING: ☆ ☆ ☆

Offering service throughout the Bay Area since 1982, Town and Country is one of the city's largest nanny placement agencies. Reviews about the quality of nannies and staff were mixed although they are still a Bay Area standby. Comments: "I had great luck with Town and Country." "Expensive, but efficient, thorough, and gracious."

North Bay

Nannies of the Valley Placement Agency

3212 Jefferson St., #373
Napa
707-251-8035

Placements: Nannies only.

Registration fee: $250

Placement fee: $1,350 for full-time nannies and $1,000 for part-time.

BANAA member: No.

Nannies of the Valley offers comprehensive nanny placement in Sonoma, Napa, and Marin counties. Prior to interviewing appropriate candidates, half of the placement fee is due, with the remaining fee due before a hired nanny starts work. This placement fee includes a free replacement should your nanny not work out in the first ninety days. Nannies of the Valley also offers on-call services that are designed to provide parents with quality nanny care for short-notice occasions such as illnesses, vacations, or other last minute needs. A one-year subscription for access to prescreened nannies for on-call needs is $400 a year or $250 for six months, not exceeding nine hours of care per week. (For care between nine and fifteen hours per week, a subscription fee is $600 per year or $450 for six months.)

Rent-A-Parent
1640 Tiburon Blvd.
Tiburon
415-435-2642

Placements: Temporary and permanent nannies and baby-sitters, including on-demand service.

Registration fee: None.

Placement fee: The placement fee for a full-time nanny equals six weeks of gross salary, with a minimum of $2,000 for full-time placements and $1,400 for part-time placements. For baby-sitters, the placement fee is 35 percent of the caregiver's total fee with a minimum fee of $20 per day for temporary or call-on-demand placement. There is also a $10 service charge for same-day placements.

BANAA member: Yes.

PARENT RATING: ☆ ☆ ☆

Serving Marin County since 1984, reviews about the quality of the nannies and staff were mixed. Rent-a-Parent offers a full refund plan within the first three months for any reason.

East Bay

Be-In-Our-Care Nanny Agency
www.beinourcare.com
- Walnut Creek
  31 La Mesa Ln., 925-933-2273
- Oakland
  5737 Thornhill Dr., Ste. 203, 510-339-3380

Placements: Nannies only.

Registration fee: None

Placement fee: For a full-time or part-time live-out nanny, five weeks of a nanny's annual gross salary (typically $1,800 for full-time nannies and $800 for part-time).

BANAA member: Yes.

This very well established nanny agency was founded in 1985 and specializes in placing nannies in the East Bay.

A Nanny Connection
P.O. Box 1038
Danville
925-957-0358 or 866-957-0358

Placements: Full- or part-time, live-in or live-out, permanent or temporary nannies.

Registration fee: None.

Placement fee: One month of the nanny's salary (or $1,000, whichever is greater) for full-time nannies (more than twenty hours a week), and one month's salary (or $600, whichever is greater) for part-time nannies (less than twenty hours a week).

BANAA member: No.

PARENT RATING: ☆ ☆ ☆ ☆ ☆

With sixteen years of experience in the childcare business, A Nanny

Connection offers professional customer service-oriented assistance in placing nannies in the East Bay. All nannies are experienced, CPR certified, tuberculosis certified, TrustLine registered upon placement, and have references. After you complete an application, they will set up interviews for you. Placements are guaranteed for three months or you are entitled to another search free of charge or half of your money back.

Bay Area 2nd Mom, Inc.

510-595-1535 or 888-926-3666
See description under South Bay.

Moms Away

1015 Keith Ave.
Berkeley
510-559-9195

Placements: Nannies only.

Registration fee: None.

Placement fees: One month of the nanny's salary, with a minimum of $1,800 for a full-time live-out or live-in nanny, and $800 minimum for a part-time nanny.

BANAA member: Yes.

Servicing the entire East Bay area for ten years, this small agency places prescreened and experienced nannies as full- or part-time help. References are checked along with driving and court records. A one-year commitment is required from nannies.

Nannies Limited

11717 Murietta Ct.
Dublin
925-803-1040

Placements: Full-time, part-time, live-in, or live-out nannies.

Registration fee: None.

Placement fee: The placement fee for a full-time, live-out or live-in nanny is equivalent to one month of the nanny's salary or $1,600, whichever is greater, plus $124 for TrustLine registry. The placement fee for a part-time, live-out or live-in nanny is equivalent to one month of the nanny's salary, plus $124 for TrustLine. Temporary placement fees are prorated based on the nanny's length of service, and a summer placement fee is a one time flat fee of $500.

BANAA member: No.

Nannies Limited has been helping families find nannies appropriate for their needs since 1991.

The Nanny Network, Inc.

712 Bancroft Rd. #216
Walnut Creek
925-256-8575
www.nannynet.net

Placements: In-home permanent, temporary, full-time, and part-time nannies to Contra Costa and Alameda counties.

Registration fee: None.

Placement fee: $1,800 for a full-time nanny (more than twenty-five hours a week) and $1,000 for a temporary nanny (working from one to ninety days, either part-time or full-time). Placement fees for a temporary nanny (working from one to ninety days, either part-time or full-time) are $15 a day for live-out and $25 a day for live-in.

BANAA member: No.

PARENT RATING: ☆ ☆ ☆ ☆ ☆

The owner started this business after her own experience of hiring a nanny in 1992. Parents love the fact that this agency makes house calls and can come to your home to explain their services and do the initial paperwork. Comment: "Fast, personalized service."

South Bay

Bay Area 2nd Mom, Inc.

644 Towle Pl.
Palo Alto
650-858-2469 Peninsula/South Bay
510-595-1535 East Bay
415-346-2620 San Francisco/North Bay
www.2ndmom.com

Placements: Nannies and baby nurses.

Registration fee: $350

Placement fee: The placement fee for a full-time nanny is $2,500 (or 15 percent of the nanny's salary, whichever is greater), and $2,000 (or 15 percent, whichever is greater) for part-time nannies who work under twenty-five hours a week.

BANAA member: Yes.

PARENT RATING: ☆ ☆ ☆

Serving the entire Bay Area since 1987 with offices in San Francisco, Emeryville, Campbell, and Palo Alto, 2nd Mom offers screened and experienced nannies and baby nurses, including permanent full-time and part-time nannies; live-ins and live-outs; temporary nannies for one week to three months; on-call nannies for last-minute sick baby care, cancellations, newborn baby care, and weekend and overnights as well as single night occasions. This nanny agency received mixed reviews as to the quality of nannies and their staff. On-call service for well or sick child care is $18-33 per hour depending on the age and number of children. Their on-call sick child care services received excellent reviews.

California Nanny Network

4100 Moorpark Ave.
San Jose
650-321-6942 Peninsula office
408-260-9125 South Bay office
www.cananny.com

Placements: Nannies only.

Registration fee: $75

Placement fee: Placement fees for live-in and live-out nannies are six weeks of the nanny's gross salary. An additional placement fee for temporary help is $25 a day.

BANAA member: No.

Serving the South Bay through San Jose for live-in, live-out, and temporary care, the California Nanny network offers comprehensive family and nanny matching with a one-year guarantee. They serve all of California for live-in help. All nannies undergo thorough background checks. The refund policy states that within the first thirty days a free replacement nanny is offered, or 50 percent of your fee is credited toward a new search. The registration fee for temporary care is $225, entitling you to access a pool of temporary nannies for a year.

Connie's Household Management

122 2nd Ave., Ste. 214
San Mateo
650-344-0111

Placements: Nannies and baby nurses.

Registration fee: None.

Placement fee: 80 percent of one month of the nanny's salary.

BANAA member: No.

Serving South San Francisco to San Jose, Connie's offers full-time nannies and baby nurses, including weekends and overnights.

Just Ask Nanny

P.O. Box 620538
Woodside
650-328-1925

Having worked twenty-six years as a nanny, the owner of this business consults on any child care issue and provides child care referrals. She serves the entire Peninsula, except San Francisco and San Jose.

Kidz Biz Nanny Search

1277 Linda Mar Shopping Center, #318
Pacifica
650-738-0848

Placements: Permanent, part-time, full-time, and temporary nannies down the Peninsula (from San Francisco to Mountain View and Palo Alto).

Registration fee: None.

Placement fee: 11 percent of a nanny's annual gross salary.

BANAA member: No.

The owner of this agency is a working mother and was previously a nanny for ten years. All nannies undergo thorough background checks, a reference check, a driving record check, fingerprinting for TrustLine registry, CPR certification, tuberculosis testing, and verification of legality to work in California. Hourly rates range from $10-20 per hour for the care of one child depending on the nanny's background and education. They offer no refunds, but do offer a thirty-day guarantee or a 100 percent credit for another nanny search.

South Bay Nannies and Nurses Registry

P.O. Box 28931
San Jose
408-236-3494

Placements: Nannies, nurses, and mother's helpers.

Registration fee: $175

Placement fee: The referral fee for a permanent placement is $2,500 (or 12 percent of the nanny's total salary, whichever is greater), and for a temporary placement it is $2,000 (or 30 percent of the nanny's total wage, whichever is greater).

BANAA member: Yes.

In business for more than thirty years, South Bay Nannies and Nurses is a full-service placement agency for live-in and live-out nannies, nurses, mother's helpers, and housekeepers, and also offers occasional, temporary, and on-call placements, including sick child care. They place one-third of their nannies in permanent positions, one-third in temporary positions, and one-third in on-call jobs.

Stanford Park Nannies

www.spnannies.com

- Menlo Park
  1050 Chestnut St., Ste. 207,
  650-462-4580
- Los Gatos
  236 N. Santa Cruz Ave., #102 B,
  408-395-3043

Placements: Nannies and baby nurses.

Registration fee: $150

Placement fee: 12 percent of a nanny's annual salary.

BANAA member: Yes.

PARENT RATING: ☆ ☆ ☆ ☆ ☆

Serving San Mateo and Santa Clara counties since 1990, Stanford Park Nannies offers exceptional nanny and baby nurse placement services.

The owners have more than seventeen years of combined nanny referral experience. All nannies must make a one-year commitment and have at least two years of experience. Nurses and nannies are available part-time or full-time, live-in or live-out. The agency does complete background checks, fingerprinting, and driving history and insurance checks. In the event of termination during the first twelve months of employment, a partial credit of the original fee is applied toward a future search.

Town and Country Resources

425 Sherman Ave., Ste. 130
Palo Alto
650-326-8570

See description under San Francisco.

Au Pair Agencies

Au pairs are young adults from outside the United States who provide live-in child care in exchange for a stipend, room and board, and the opportunity to spend a year in the United States. They are an affordable option for in-home child care and many parents appreciate exposing their children to a foreign culture and language. However, most au pairs lack the experience and credentials of nannies and come to this country first and foremost for the cultural experience. For this reason, many professionals in the child care industry believe that an au pair is best used as a "support person" in a "busy" home where one parent does not work full time outside the home, and should not be intended for exclusive child care for extended periods of time. United States Department of State regulations state that an au pair must be offered her own room and cannot work more than ten hours a day and forty-five hours a week. Agencies typically screen candidates, and parents often conduct telephone interviews to find the best match.

Au Pair Care
2226 Bush St.
San Francisco, CA 94115
800-4-AUPAIR or 415-434-8788
www.aupaircare.com

Au Pair In America
River Plaza
9 W. Broad St.
Greenwich, CT 06902
203-399-5000
www.aifs.com

Go Au Pair
6965 Union Park Center., Ste. 100
Midvale, UT 84047
800-574-8889 or 801-255-7722
www.goaupair.com

Au Pair USA/InterExchange
161 6th Ave.
New York, NY 10013
800-287-2477 or 212-924-0446
www.interexchange.org

EF Au Pair
One Education St.
Cambridge, MA 02141
800-333-6056 or 617-619-1100
www.efaupair.org

United States Department of State
Exchange Visitor Program Office
301 4th St., SW
Washington, DC 20547
202-401-9810

Baby-sitting Services and Resources

Even if you decide not to work outside the home, you will probably need some regular help. Moreover, you will, at least occasionally, want to have some life away from your child! A baby-sitter is a great option when a full-time nanny is too much for your needs or your budget. Average hourly rates for sitters in the Bay Area range from $10-17 for one child and $12-20 for care for two or more children, depending on where you live and the sitter's experience and background. Many sitters and agencies have a four-hour minimum.

There are many Bay Area baby-sitting resources. The most important things to remember are to check references and trust your instincts in hiring a mature individual who can handle your child's needs.

San Francisco

American Child Care Service Inc.
508 California St., #500
415-285-2300

This service offers short-term, temporary child care primarily serving the out-of-town visitor who needs in-room baby-sitting services in a hotel. There is a transportation fee of $5 and an additional transportation fee of $10 after midnight.

A Bay Area Child Care Agency

758 San Diego Ave.
Daly City
650-991-7474

PARENT RATING: ☆ ☆ ☆

Serving San Francisco County and the Peninsula, this agency offers professional nannies, baby nurses, and temporary last-minute placement calls. They cater more to the out-of-town visitor staying in a hotel, but do offer local in-house placements. Every baby-sitter is a mature adult. Rates are $8 an hour for a minimum of four hours plus a transportation fee of $8 after 8 p.m. for up to two children from one family. There are additional charges for more children. Comment: "You'll get someone, but she may not be exactly what you want; screen first."

California College of Arts and Crafts

1111 8th St.
415-703-9500
415-621-2396 fax

Fax your job description to the attention of "Student Life" and it will be posted on the college's bulletin board for job opportunities.

City College of San Francisco

Student Career Services
50 Phelan Ave.
415-550-4346
415-550-4400 fax
www.ccsf.org/career/employer

Mailed or faxed job announcements to the office of Cooperative Work are sent to the Child Development Department and all nine campuses. You may also submit an ad via their website.

The Core Group

2616 Jackson St.
415-567-0568
www.thecoregroup.org

PARENT RATING: ☆ ☆ ☆ ☆ ☆

In 1998 a business-savvy University of San Francisco graduate set up a personal concierge service offering child care among other services such as catering, cooking, party help, and computer assistance. The "core" of many San Francisco parent's baby-sitting services, fees are $12 per hour for one child and $15 per hour for two. They serve the entire Bay Area. Extra charges for driving time and tolls apply. Sitters are also available for overnight stays which run $85 for a weeknight and $95 for a weekend night. The Core Group prides itself on offering baby-sitters who are college students or graduates with child care experience, and who are professional and reliable. In addition to the hourly rates, $35 per month allows you to use any service the group offers for that thirty-day period. The cancellation policy requires notice forty-eight hours in advance or you pay a $25 fee.

Enterprise for High School Students

3275 Sacramento St.
415-896-0909

This well-respected organization places high school students in domestic and other jobs. All students are required to take a workshop to participate in the program. Students must show proof of a C average or better to qualify for the program and must provide a letter of recommendation from an academic teacher.

Natural Resources

See description under "Bulletin Boards and Binders with Child Care Listings"—San Francisco. They offer referrals for baby-sitters.

San Francisco State University Career Center

1600 Holloway Ave.
415-338-1111
415-338-2979 fax

This career center will post your job description on its website and send it out to one thousand potential candidates. The fee for each listing is $17. Alternatively, for free, fax or mail your listing to be placed in the job binder and on the job hotline. Job listings are placed in binders for one week. Interested students will call you. Or, record an ad on the hot line; The fee is $5 for the first minute and $2 for each additional minute. The Career Center does not screen students.

University of San Francisco

2130 Fulton St.
415-422-6216
415-422-6470 fax

PARENT RATING: ☆ ☆ ☆ ☆

The Career Services Center will fax or mail you a current list of students interested in baby-sitting or part-time nanny positions. Requests are free and are generally processed that day. Students are usually in their early twenties with varying amounts of child care experience. The Career Center does not do any screening. Alterntively, fax your ad and it will be placed in the job binder the next business day. Or, post your ad on-line for $25 for thirty days by calling 800-999-8725 (Monster Track). The USF School of Nursing also maintains a bulletin board on the 1st floor of Cowell Hall where slightly more mature students advertise their availability. The bulletin board is called "Students with Cars Looking for Work." You need to go there in person to get listings or to post an ad. Comment: "Fast turn around, but you do the work of background checks and interviews."

North Bay

Dominican College

Student Development Office
50 Acacia Ave.
San Rafael
415-457-4440
415-257-1399 fax

College of Marin, Career Center

835 College Ave.
Kentfield
415-457-8811 (Career Center)
415-457-3896 (Career Center fax)
415-485-9369 (Early Childhood Education Department)

Nannies of the Valley Placement Agency

See description under "Nanny Agencies and Resource Centers"—North Bay.

Napa Valley Community College

2277 Napa Vallejo Hwy.
Napa
707-253-3050 (Career Re-entry and Job Placement)
707-253-3089 fax (Attention: Jessica)

Novato Mothers Club

Novato Unified School District
1015 7th St.
415-458-3203
www.novatomothersclub.com

PARENT RATING: ☆ ☆ ☆ ☆ ☆

This club offers various programs and play groups for new mothers, including a baby-sitting co-op, which many parents rave about!

Rent-A-Parent

See description under "Nanny Agencies and Resource Centers"—North Bay. Almost half of their placements are on-call/on-demand placements in Marin.

Star Belly Child Care Services

3505 Sonoma Blvd. #200
Vallejo
707-557-9268

PARENT RATING: ☆ ☆ ☆

Star Belly is synonymous with on-call, short-notice, and short-term baby-sitting needs serving Marin, San Francisco, and the East Bay. Hourly rates range from $12-20, depending on the ages and number of children. For placement of regular baby-sitters, there is a one-time fee of $100. In addition, for $60 per month, you have unlimited access to on-call sitters. All child care providers are CPR certified and have been fingerprinted. Some really liked Star Belly while others did not. Comment: "Good for on-call, last minute needs."

Sonoma State University

1801 E. Cotati Ave.
Rohnert Park
707-664-2196 (Career Services)
www.sonoma.edu/sas/crc

Post your job advertisement on their website.

Tamalpais High School, Student Career Services

700 Miller Ave.
Mill Valley
415-388-3292
415-380-3506 fax

Redwood High School, Student Career Services

395 Doherty Dr.
Larkspur
415-924-3616

East Bay

Bananas

See under "Bulletin Boards and Binders with Child Care Listings"—East Bay.

Bay Area Sitters Unlimited

See description under Sitters Unlimited—South Bay.

Contra Costa Community College

Student Development Office
2600 Mission Bell Dr.
San Pablo
510-235-7800
510-231-0327 fax

Diablo Valley College

Job Placement Office
321 Golf Club Rd.
Pleasant Hill
925-685-1230, ext. 2206
925-691-7538 fax

Merritt Community College

12500 Campus Dr.
Oakland
510-531-4911
510-434-3825 fax
www.merritt.edu

Mail or fax baby-sitting job descriptions to the career services department, attention Catherine Thur.

Mills College

5000 MacArthur Blvd.
Oakland
510-430-2069
510-430-3235 fax
www.mills.edu

Mail or fax your job description to the career center. Your listing will be posted for free for thirty days.

Saint Mary's College

1928 St. Mary's Rd.
Moraga
925-631-4380
925-631-1468 fax
kacole@stmarys-ca.edu

PARENT RATING: ☆ ☆ ☆ ☆

Parents find the job board a great help here for finding baby-sitting help. Either fax or e-mail your job advertisement.

University of California, Berkeley

2537 Haste St.
Berkeley
510-642-1827
510-642-8033 fax

Fax your baby-sitting job description to the child care services department.

South Bay

A Bay Area Child Care Agency

See description under San Francisco.

Cañada Community College

Student Career Center
4200 Farm Hill Blvd.
Redwood City
650-306-3457
800-999-8725 (Jobtrack)
650-306-3457 fax
www.jobtrack.com

Fax announcement to be placed in a binder, or for a small fee record your job announcement on their Jobtrack telephone service listing.

Foothill Sitter Agency

408-732-3143

In business for over thirty years, Foothill provides screened baby-sitters. There is a four-hour minimum, and the average hourly charge is $8-10 an hour. You pay the sitter directly and the sitter pays an agency fee. There is also a transportation charge of $4-5.

College of Notre Dame Career Center

1500 Ralston Ave.
Belmont
650-593-1601
650-508-3715 fax

They have a bulletin board of jobs and a binder with child care opportunities for students. Fax your job description.

Additional Helpful Websites on Child Care

www.iamyourchild.org (Parenting site)

www.nccic.org (National Childcare Information Center)

www.parentsplace.com (Parenting site)

www.ivillage.com (Women's site)

www.parentsoup.com (Parenting site)

www.zerotothree.org (Parenting site for information on infants and toddlers)

www.childcareaware.org (Contains useful information for parents choosing child care)

www.childcareaction.org (Contains a myriad of information concerning current child care advocacy issues)

College of San Mateo
Career Services Center
1700 W. Hillsdale Blvd.
San Mateo
650-574-6571
650-574-6680 fax
They will fax or send you a job description form. Completed forms are placed in an employment binder for one month at no charge.

Skyline College
Career Center
3300 College Dr.
San Bruno
650-738-4337
Job descriptions received by mail are posted for thirty days for free. Or, for $15 your listing can be placed on a 24-hour automated job line for both Skyline College and San Francisco State University.

Stanford University
The Worklife Office
Main Quad (Building 310)
Stanford
650-723-2660
This office provides a list of baby-sitters, primarily for weekends and evenings.

Peninsula Sitters Agency
10370 Prune Tree Ln.
Cupertino
408-255-1291
In business for over thirty years, Peninsula sitters offer baby-sitting services to the Peninsula and South Bay area on an on-call basis. Rates are $10-12 an hour for one child, with an additional $5 fee for transportation. All sitters are licensed and bonded, and many work in preschools or day care centers.

Sitters Unlimited

1286 Arnold Ave.
San Jose
408-452-0225
www.sittersunlimited.com

Sitters Unlimited is a national baby-sitting service with franchises across California and Hawaii. In business since 1979, the San Jose office caters to the out-of-town visitor who needs child care or has local occasional needs. Hourly rates are $12 per hour for one child (four hours minimum). An additional dollar per hour is added for each additional child, up to four. Clients must also pay the sitter's transportation charges, usually $3-6. There is an additional $10 fee for a temporary sitter home visit.

South Bay Nannies and Nurses

See description under "Nanny Agencies and Resource Centers"— South Bay.

CHAPTER 10

CHOOSING A PRESCHOOL YOU'LL LOVE
(and Getting In)

Given the competitiveness of the Bay Area preschool admissions process, we might have put this chapter at the beginning of the book. That way, the first thing you would do after your pregnancy test comes back positive would be to sign up your unborn child for preschool. In all seriousness, while the process is competitive, it's not quite that bad, and we do not want to create even more stress in a situation already too stressful. So we've chosen to put this chapter where it belongs, at the end of the book, after you have had some time to get to know your child and his or her needs (and yours). This chapter will answer the following questions and more:

◆ What are the different types of preschools?
◆ What should I look for in choosing a preschool?
◆ How do we get into the schools we want?
◆ Which preschools in my area do other parents recommend?

What Type of Program Should I Choose?

Here is a basic rundown of the different types of schools, but the best way to decide what is right for your child is to visit various schools and see for yourself how they work.

A **developmental** program focuses on play as a vehicle for learning. While not completely eschewing academics, these schools believe that it's too early for kids to absorb a heavy dose of reading, writing, and arithmetic. Instead, learning is accomplished through group play, with a sprinkling of the alphabet, numbers, colors, and science and nature thrown in where appropriate. Activity areas often include blocks, dramatic play (e.g. playing house), books, and arts and crafts. Programs for younger children are less structured than those for older kids, but all usually include a circle time for social interaction, music, and stories. These schools emphasize a low student-to-teacher ratio with a fairly small number of children in the classroom. Children are usually grouped by age. Probably the majority of preschools today espouse some variant of the developmental philosophy.

An **emergent** curriculum is developmentally based, but responsive to the needs and interests of the children. For example, the children may be studying trees and become interested in building a tree house. Rather than sticking to the daily curriculum plan, the teacher may allow the children to pursue that interest.

Two other variants on the developmental model include **High/scope** and **Reggio Emilia**. In the Piaget "high/scope" theory, teachers encourage children to plan and implement their own lesson plans for the day. Reggio Emilia, named for the Northern Italian region where the theory developed, refers to a project-based curriculum in which children develop their own ideas for the projects.

It's best to visit a **Montessori** school to see the Montessori method in action. Montessori classrooms are set up very differently than developmental classrooms. When you walk in, you will notice the noise level is considerably lower. Materials are organized on shelves in an orderly manner, without a lot of clutter. Students are given opportunities to complete individual, self-directed projects at their own pace, and teachers provide lessons designed to take advantage of childrens' individual "sensitive periods" in which they are receptive to learning. Lessons range from practical life to sensory skills to language and math; all are designed to foster a good work ethic and individual growth. Classes are a mix of older and younger children, with the older children helping to teach the younger ones. Classes are usually larger, with a higher student-to-teacher ratio, than in developmental schools. (This is because the program is student-directed rather than teacher-directed.) Maria Montessori, an Italian educator working with underprivileged children in the early 1900s, originated the method. Modern Montessori schools are affiliated with either the American Montessori Society (AMS) or the Association Montessori Internationale (AMI). AMS schools do not follow the original Montessori method as strictly as AMI schools. Note, however, that Montessori schools do not need to be affiliated with either organization, or any organization, to call themselves Montessori schools. As a result, schools are organized in many different ways, and it is best to visit each school to see how the philosophy is implemented. Montessori schools tend to be more expensive than developmental programs because children usually attend school five days per week and the school day runs into the afternoon.

An **academic** preschool reflects its name: it focuses on instilling the basic academic subjects to prepare children for elementary school. The teacher usually initiates projects, and children work in groups. This approach is popular in some foreign countries (France, for instance) and is used in a sprinkling of schools in the U.S. as well, though its popularity is waning in the U.S. as older preschool students sometimes burn out. Even developmental preschools include some academic aspects, however. Academic schools tend to be more expensive than developmental programs.

A **Waldorf** school, based on the work of turn-of-the-century educator Rudolf Steiner, encourages creativity in young children as a vehicle for intellectual growth and development. Learning is hands-on rather than through academics. In addition, children are taught to respect their teachers, because Steiner believed that such admiration would motivate children to learn. Waldorf schools usually emphasize the arts, interaction with the natural environment, use of wooden rather than plastic toys, and little or no television at home. Classes are a mix of older and younger children.

A **cooperative** or parent participation nursery school is not so much a theory of learning as a way of organizing and running a school.

Parents run cooperative schools; they teach in the classroom (helped by a few professional teachers), maintain the school, administer policies, and so on. Generally, cooperative preschools incorporate a developmental philosophy since teachers are lay persons without formal training. Cooperative schools are also usually less expensive than other preschools, and most provide great community-building opportunities. Parents must, however, be prepared to devote the necessary time to the school, which may be difficult for working parents or those with younger children at home.

Religious schools are affiliated with a particular church or synagogue. The curriculum may be developmental or academic with the addition of some religious traditions. Programs run the gamut from including compulsory chapel to teaching biblical stories to simply celebrating certain holidays or festivals. Be sure you are comfortable with whatever traditions are celebrated in a religious program (and with the possible lack of diversity among the students).

Foreign language schools seek to teach a second language to students at a very young age by either a partial or total immersion method. Children are believed to be receptive to learning other languages during the preschool years. Schools vary in the amount of English taught; some include instruction in English for part of the day, while others exclude English entirely. These schools tend to have longer school days and place more emphasis on academics than traditional nursery schools.

What to Look for in a Preschool Program

Here are some things to look for when you are evaluating different preschool programs:

◆ **Licensing requirements**. The California Department of Social Services licenses preschools and enforces minimum quality and safety standards. The licensing requirements are basically the same as for day care facilities. In fact, the state classifies preschools as "day care centers." To get a license, a preschool must meet the requirements listed in chapter 9 for day care licensing: ample space, facilities, equipment, teacher and director qualifications, and so on.

To check whether your preschool is licensed or to get a list of local licensed facilities, contact the California Department of Social Services' Community Care Licensing Division, listed in chapter 9.

♦ **Accreditation.** The National Association for the Education of Young Children (NAEYC), the largest national organization of early childhood educators, conducts an extensive national voluntary accreditation process for early childhood education programs, including preschools. Accredited preschools must meet certain quality standards. Not surprisingly, very few schools make the grade. To find out more about accreditation or to obtain a list of accredited preschools, contact:

NAEYC
1509 16th St., NW
Washington, DC 20036-1426
202-232-8777
www.naeyc.org

♦ **Ratio and teachers.** The NAEYC and the American Academy of Pediatrics recommend that the ratio of students to teachers be no more than 5:1 for 2-year-olds, 7:1 for 3-year-olds, and 8:1 for 4- and 5-year-olds. Two- and 3-year-olds should be in groups of no more than ten to fourteen children, and 4- and 5-year-olds should be in groups of no more than sixteen children. Look for teachers with at least an associate's degree or higher in early childhood education, and a low turnover of teachers from year to year. Make sure

---

HELPFUL WEBSITES FOR GENERAL INFORMATION ABOUT CHOOSING PRESCHOOLS

♦ iparenting.com website at http://preschoolerstoday.com/resources/daycarechecklist.htm (handy checklist and form for jotting notes about each school).

♦ Babycenter.com website at www.babycenter.com/general/6007.html (questions to ask each school).

♦ www.babycenter.com/childcare/preschoolguide (preschool-related articles and advice).

the relationship between the students and the teachers is positive and that teachers are warm and nurturing.

◆ **Safe and nurturing environment.** Of course, we would all like our preschools to have campuses the size of Stanford. To be realistic, however, look for at least the space required for licensing (thirty-five square feet of space per child in a classroom and a fenced outdoor play area with seventy-five square feet of space per child). Facilities should be clean, cheerful, and arranged at a child's eye level. Children should be within a teacher's line of sight at all times. Diaper-changing facilities and bathrooms should be sanitary. Activities, equipment, and toys should be stimulating, inviting, and age appropriate. The program should encourage self-direction and problem solving, as well as communication between the children. There should be time for both structured and unstructured activity. Ultimately, the most important criterion in choosing a program is whether it is a safe, loving environment. Ask yourself whether the school will nurture your child's self-esteem, encourage him or her to thrive and develop in positive ways, and stimulate a love of learning.

◆ **Location.** The preschool day is fairly short (usually under three hours in traditional programs), making location critical. If by the time you get home from dropping your child at school, you need to turn around and head out to pick him or her up again, the school is too far away. Attending a local school also allows your child to meet other neighborhood kids with whom he or she may attend kindergarten.

◆ **Extended care.** Working parents may need extended care in the early mornings or afternoons. If so, choose a program that is flexible, preferably one that allows you to sign up for such care at the last minute in case of emergency. Parents warn, however, not to expect a Harvard curriculum, or even one approaching the regular school day, during extended care hours. Accept it for what it is: glorified day care.

◆ **Potty training.** In general, schools only offering programs for children ages 2 years, 9 months and up require children to be potty trained because they are not usually licensed for diaper-changing facilities. Programs for younger children usually do not require children to be potty trained.

◆ **Cost**. Preschool tuition varies greatly and depends on the type of school and number of hours your child attends. Cooperative schools tend to be the least expensive and averaged around $2,000 per school year (assuming a ten-month year) in 2002. Developmental, emergent, and religious schools with half-day programs tend to be mid-range in price, varying from $2,500 per year for two-day programs to $6,000 per year for full-week programs. Schools with extended day programs can be even more expensive, up to about $10,000 per year. At the top of the chart are Montessori and academic programs. Both tend to have long school days and full weeks, so the cost can be $10,000-12,000 or more per year.

QUESTIONS TO ASK WHEN VISITING PRESCHOOLS

◆ What is the school's philosophy?
◆ Is the school licensed? Accredited?
◆ Who are the teachers? What sort of training do they have?
◆ What is the turnover of teachers each year? (Look for stability.)
◆ What is the student-to-teacher ratio? How large are the classes?
◆ Are students grouped by age or in multiple-age groups?
◆ What is a typical day's schedule? Are there opportunities for outdoor play? Creative play? Imaginative play?
◆ How much time do students spend in individual play and in group play?
◆ Is extended care available?
◆ Does a child need to be toilet trained?
◆ Do parents meet with teachers to discuss students' progress?
◆ How does the school handle discipline or set limits? How does it handle conflicts between children?
◆ Are there outings or field trips?
◆ How are parents involved in the school?
◆ What is the security policy?

◆ What is the procedure for dropping off and picking up a child? Is parking or a drop-off zone available? (This is particularly critical in crowded areas of San Francisco and Oakland.)

◆ How and when does the school make its admissions decisions?

◆ (If relevant) What elementary schools do graduating students attend?

The Admissions Process

So how do you get your child into a preschool? Here is a synopsis of the Bay Area preschool admissions process from start to finish:

1. **Make a list of schools.** First, you need to decide where to apply. Make a list of criteria, and then a list of schools meeting your needs. Start by asking friends, neighbors and colleagues where they send their children to school. The favorite preschools identified by parents completing our surveys (see below) also provides a starting point for finding a school. Additional resources for identifying schools include the following:

◆ The NAEYC website (www.naeyc.org) features a searchable database of accredited schools. No information about the schools other than addresses and telephone numbers is provided, but it's a place to start.

◆ In San Francisco, consult *Finding a Preschool for Your Child in San Francisco*, by Lori Rifkin, Vera Obermeyer, and Irene Byrne. The book lists many city schools together with information provided by each school.

◆ In the East Bay, check out The Neighborhood Parents Network's *Preschool Directory*, a detailed compilation of schools published annually. To order, go to www.parentsnet.org or contact Neighborhood Parents Network, P.O. Box 8597, Berkeley, CA 94707, 510-527-6667.

◆ East Bay Moms, a Berkeley-Oakland parents' group, publishes a *Preschool and Child Care Program Directory* with a limited selection of schools. To order, go to www.eastbaymoms.com or write to East Bay Moms, 6000 Contra Costa Rd., Oakland, CA 94618.

◆ Attend a public preschool preview night for your area, usually held in the fall or winter. Representatives from local preschools are available to answer parents' questions and provide brochures. (Sadly, some of the most popular San Francisco preschools are so oversubscribed that they don't attend.) **PARENT RATING:** ☆ ☆ ☆ ☆ "At least it's an opportunity to meet the directors in person and get all of the brochures at once without having to call around." The following organizations sponsor public preschool preview nights:

◇ **San Francisco**: Parents' Place San Francisco, a program of Jewish Family and Children's Services, hosts a San Francisco Preschool Preview Night in February, 415-359-2454. Parents' Place also periodically offers a class on choosing a preschool in San Francisco (**PARENT RATING:** ☆ ☆ ☆ ☆).

◇ **Marin**: Parents' Place Marin hosts a Marin Schools Night Fair in October, 415-491-7959.

◇ **Berkeley/Oakland**: Neighborhood Parents Network hosts a Preschool Fair in December, 510-527-6667.

◇ **Contra Costa County**: Pleasant Hill/Walnut Creek Mothers' Club hosts a Contra Costa Preschool, Childcare and Parenting Fair in February, 925-939-6466.

◇ **Livermore/Pleasanton/San Ramon**: The Amador Mothers' Club hosts a Tri-Valley Preschool Fair, www.amadormothersclub.com.

◇ **San Mateo County**: The Peninsula Family YMCA in San Mateo hosts a preschool preview night in February, 650-286-9622.

◇ **Palo Alto**: Parents' Place Palo Alto periodically offers a class on choosing a preschool, 650-688-3040.

◆ Attend your local mothers' group's preschool preview night, which is even better than a public preschool night. Fellow mothers will give you personal insights into local preschools. See chapter 6 to contact the group in your area. **PARENT RATING:** ☆ ☆ ☆ ☆ ☆ "This is the kind of invaluable inside information you won't get from the preschools themselves!"

◆ In the East Bay, visit the UC Berkeley Parents Network's website, http://parents.berkeley.edu, for frank parent feedback about local preschools. (UC Berkeley Parents Network is merging with Neighborhood Parents Network. Its website will be changed to

www.parentsnet.org by the end of 2002.) **PARENT RATING:** ☆ ☆ ☆ ☆ ☆
"Great insider tips!"

◆ For a directory of parent cooperative preschools, check out the website of the California Council of Parent Participation Nursery Schools, www.ccppns.org.

◆ To find a Montessori school in your area, consult the North American Montessori Teachers' Association website, www.montessori-namta.org.

◆ A comprehensive list of Bay Area Jewish preschools can be found on the Jewish Bulletin of Northern California's website, www.jewishsf.com/resource/chap7.html.

A word on feeder schools: Do "feeder schools" exist and does your child really need to attend one? Yes and no. While all the educational "consultants" will deny the existence of feeder schools, we have noticed that in San Francisco certain preschools send more of their graduates to the top private elementary schools than do other preschools. Those feeder preschools tend to be the ones with longer waiting lists and more competition for admission. That does not mean, however, that *no* children from other preschools get in to private elementary schools, and you'll ultimately be happier at a preschool you like rather than one you choose simply to get your child into a particular elementary school. If you plan to send your child to a private elementary school, particularly in San Francisco, you should find out what preschools that elementary school's students attended. Check with friends who have children in private elementary school and find out where their kids went to preschool. (Elementary schools usually won't tell you and preschool directors may be a bit optimistic about their "in" status with elementary schools.) If you are sending your child to the local public elementary school, relax. Don't worry about going to the most popular preschool. Just find one that is safe, stimulating, and a good fit for your child.

2. **Start the Application Process.** Certain very popular schools have long waiting lists, particularly those in San Francisco, but also a few of the suburban schools. Many preschools (especially in the city) say they accept students based solely on the date of application and

gender of the child. If you want your child to attend any of these schools, get on waiting lists as soon as you can. Sometimes, as ridiculous as this sounds, you can (and should) actually sign up while you are still pregnant! Most schools, however, will not put a child on a waiting list until the child is born. It's a good idea to apply to all of the schools you are interested in as early as possible to increase your chances of admission, if the application date is a basis for admission.

On the other hand, some schools don't look at the application date at all. Rather, they set a deadline to apply (usually in December before the year of entry), and accept students based on an application, sometimes a parent interview, and other criteria such as having diversity and a gender and age balance in a class-room, as well as enthusiasm and interest. (Reality check: We sus-pect—and anecdotal evidence backs this up—that this "selective" admission process really boils down to whether the director likes you and "who you know." After all, it's difficult to interview two-year-olds!) In Berkeley, for example, very few schools maintain waiting lists based on order of application. If these schools are your choice, apply as soon as your child is old enough to have a clear-ly defined personality and needs.

Still other schools (e.g., in the Burlingame/San Mateo area, and in publicly run schools in other areas) accept students by lottery. In that case, just make sure you submit your application by the dead-line, then cross your fingers.

Another problem with the early application approach is that the programs you apply to may not end up being appropriate for your child as a preschooler. Perhaps, for example, you applied to schools with structured programs, but your child needs a more playful environment. Or (like us), you may move to a different neighborhood between birth and preschool, making your early applications moot. At a nonrefundable $50 fee per application, consider your applications carefully.

Call the schools to get brochures and applications. Write a letter to accompany each application, explaining why you want your child to attend the school. Some schools require a detailed written application in which you are asked everything from your educational plans for your child to how you handle discipline. Use the opportunity to your advantage. While many schools claim they base decisions solely on date of application, we have found that directors are more likely to give spaces to parents they like and children they know will attend the school if admitted.

3. **Take a tour**. Call the schools early in the fall of the year prior to your desired date of entry. Tour season is usually September through January. A few schools provide tours only to parents of admitted students, but most offer public open houses or individual tours for interested parents. This may be your only chance to see a school in session, so take advantage of the tour and ask the director all your questions. Take time to observe a class in action. Do the students seem happy, engaged, and enthusiastic? Do the teachers provide appropriate stimulation and supervision? Is the facility clean and safe? If you toured the school while you were pregnant or when the child was first born, go back again to make sure you still like the school. Teachers come and go, facilities move, and curriculums get revised.

4. **Follow up**. After you have toured several schools, try to prioritize your list. If you have a favorite, write to the director and tell him or her that the school is your first choice. It's also a nice idea to write each of the directors a thank-you letter for providing the tour, especially if it was an individual tour. Call each school to ascertain your child's place on the waiting list and his or her chances of admission, particularly as admission time grows nearer. Convey your enthusiasm to the director. After all, many schools don't rely solely on the numbers in choosing whom to admit. Nonprofit schools, in particular, are always looking for signs that parents will actively participate in the school if their children enroll. And, of course, directors prefer to fill a class with children whose parents are committed. Finally, to gain a better perspective of what it's like to attend the school, talk to parents of students at the school— often the school will provide you a list of available parents, if you don't know any.

5. Make a Decision. Most preschools notify applicants of admissions decisions between January and March for September admissions. Typically parents have only a week or two to decide whether to accept the spot (by putting down a hefty nonrefundable deposit). It is critical for you to prioritize your list of schools ahead of time, should you be so lucky as to get into more than one place. Ultimately, it comes down to choosing a school that fits with your family's needs and your child's personality. Parents have told us time and again that they were much happier when they followed their instincts rather than the herd. Remember, even if you don't get into a school in March, openings often arise before the school year begins, as families move or change plans.

Favorite Local Preschools

While our surveys revealed a core group of parents' favorite preschools in each region of the Bay Area, the list below is far from comprehensive, and the fact that a certain preschool is not on the list is no indication of its quality. And be aware that some of the schools listed, especially in San Francisco, are so popular that they are almost impossible to get into, given the number of applications and the small class sizes. As one parent drily remarked, it was harder to get his child into certain preschools in the city than it was for him to get into graduate school. While this process can be trying, keep your sense of perspective by remembering: This is only preschool! Consider all of the schools that appeal to you, not just the most popular ones. There *is* a preschool out there for everyone. Location may be the most important criterion of all for busy families, so we've further subdivided the list into neighborhoods within each region. Note that the ratio listed after each preschool refers to the child-to-adult ratio for that school or class. Please also note that ages listed in decimal form, such as 2.9 years, means two years, nine months and is often how schools express age eligibility for their classes.

PACIFIC HEIGHTS/ COW HOLLOW/MARINA

Calvary Presbyterian Church Nursery School

2515 Fillmore St.

415-346-4715

Ages: 3-5 years

Schedule: Mornings, five days a week. Extended care available.

Ratio: 10:1

Philosophy/other: Founded in 1955, the school offers a developmental curriculum in a church-affiliated preschool. Art and music abound. The play yard is on the roof. Students attend chapel once a week during the second year of school, but the school incorporates religious traditions of all types.

Admission: By date of application and observation of the child. There is a very long wait list (at least three years) with preferences for siblings and church members.

PARENT RATING: ☆ ☆ ☆ ☆ ☆

Parents love the school, its art and music programs, and its small size and close community, but report it is difficult to get in unless you are a member of the church or have some other connection. They say the school is "very successful" in getting its children into kindergarten.

Cow Hollow Preschool

St. Mary the Virgin Episcopal Church

2325 Union St.

415-921-2328

Ages: 2-3 years

Schedule: Mornings only, two to three days a week. No extended care.

Ratio: 3:1

Philosophy: Founded in 2000, this cooperative nonsectarian preschool is designed especially for children too young for many traditional preschool programs. A developmental curriculum includes socialization, skill development, art and music.

Admission: By date of application, with preference for siblings, children of alumni, and members of St. Mary's Church.

PARENT RATING: ☆ ☆ ☆ ☆

Parents call this small, new co-op a great "gap filler" for children who are too young for traditional preschool programs. The facility is "great" and the professional teachers "very involved."

Little Gators Preschool

3149 Steiner St.

415-346-8608

Ages: 2-5 years

Schedule: Mornings or afternoons, two or three days a week. No extended care.

Ratio: 7:1

Philosophy/other: This private nonprofit preschool offers a developmental curriculum with weekly themes, including music, art, games, stories, cooking, dance, introduction to letters and numbers, social studies, science, computer, and motor skills. There is a small outdoor area.

Admission: By application but not necessarily by date applied. Emphasis is on local neighborhood and interest level of parents.

Parents liked the "cozy" class size and loving feel of the school, and praised the involved director. They report the school feels somewhat like a family day care.

The Little School
1520 Lyon St.
415-567-0430
Ages: 2-6 years
Schedule: Mornings or afternoons, two to five days a week. Extended care available.
Ratio: 7:1
Philosophy/other: This private non-profit school has a developmental philosophy. The curriculum includes music and movement, art, and free play. There is time for individual play and group activities. Children stay with the same group during their entire education at the school.
Admission: By application prior to deadline and attending an orientation meeting. Admission is very selective and diversity-oriented, with criteria such as gender, age, special needs, and ethnicity taken into consideration. The date of application no longer has any bearing on admissions, but siblings receive preference.

Parents reported the school takes early childhood education "very seriously." The facility is "top-notch," with an innovative design featuring generous-sized outdoor and indoor play areas. Parents praised the "creative" play and "unusual" projects encouraged by the teachers.

Marin Day Schools
2266 California St.
415-775-2211
www.marindayschools.org
Other SF campuses: Hills Plaza, 2 Harrison St.; Spear St., 220 Spear St.; Laurel Heights, 3333 California St.; City Hall, 1 Dr. Carlton B. Goodlett Pl.
Ages: 2-6 years (other campuses accept younger children)
Schedule: Open all year. Mornings, afternoons, or all day with extended care available.
Ratio: 6:1 (2-year-olds); 8:1 (3-year-olds); 9:1 (4-year-olds)
Philosophy/other: The developmental curriculum incorporates play, math and reading, music and art, and motor skills, with different themes for each month. Other campuses in San Francisco include day care for younger children.
Admission: By date of application, with preference for siblings. Each campus gives preference to certain groups from whom they lease space or have corporate affiliations.

Parents were very pleased with the flexible scheduling (including accommodating last-minute requests for extended care), the school's "excellent" communication with parents and "professional" attitude (including a special annual presentation on kindergarten admissions), and the "theme" approach to the curriculum.

St. Luke's School
1755 Clay St.
415-474-9489
Ages: 2.6-5.9 years

Schedule: Mornings or afternoons, three to five days a week. No extended care.

Ratio: 9:1

Philosophy/other: This structured, NAEYC-accredited program balances between academic instruction, social interaction, and artistic expression. The school is located in St. Luke's Episcopal Church. The academic curriculum includes grace and courtesy, music and movement, art, cooking, ballet, gymnastics, French, social studies, reading, and stories.

Admission: By date of application and by interview, with preference for siblings. Tours are by invitation only. In recent years, only parents who applied very early (i.e., during pregnancy) or had ties to the school were able to get their children into this school.

PARENT RATING: ☆ ☆ ☆ ☆ ☆
Parents report that the school presents a "positive environment" where students are very "well-disciplined" and emerge ready for kindergarten, owing to the "academic" orientation. The school has a very good reputation for getting its graduates into private elementary schools.

LAKE STREET/RICHMOND/ SUNSET

Jewish Community Center of San Francisco
The Presidio
1808 Wedemeyer Way
415-292-1283
www.jccsf.org
Ages: 2-6 years
Schedule: Mornings, two to five days a week. Extended care available.

Ratio: 6:1

Philosophy/other: This developmental, "Reggio Emilia" project-based curriculum is influenced by the Jewish heritage, incorporating Jewish values, customs, and holidays. Music, drama, art, dance, gym, and storytelling specialists make regular visits. Children enjoy a large outdoor play yard and take supervised "nature walk" in the Presidio. Older children enjoy fieldtrips. There are two other smaller S.F. campuses.

Admission: By application date and other considerations (e.g., parental enthusiasm and interests).

PARENT RATING: ☆ ☆ ☆ ☆ ☆
"Great" art program and "professionally-run" school with "active" director. Parents emphasized the school's afternoon enrichment programs (ballet, sports, gymnastics, swimming, and art).

Lakeside Presbyterian Center for Children
201 Eucalyptus Dr.
415-564-5044
Ages: 2.6-6 years
Schedule: Mornings or afternoons; two, three, or five days a week. Extended care available.

Ratio: 7:1

Philosophy/other: NAEYC accredited, this developmental program has a Christian orientation and is affiliated with the Lakeside Presbyterian Church. The curriculum includes daily art projects and songs and games.

Admission: By interview visit with parents and child.

Parents report the classrooms are "large," outdoor equipment "great" and projects "creative." Most of the students' families "are not members of the church," and there is not a "heavy dose" of religion. Parents are expected to participate "quite a bit" in the school events.

Lone Mountain Children's Center

The Presidio
1806 Belles St.
415-561-2333

Ages: 2.7-5.3 years

Schedule: Mornings or afternoons; two, three, or five days a week. No extended care.

Ratio: 8:1

Philosophy/other: This private, non-profit school offers a developmental and experiential curriculum with a focus on the uniqueness of each child and exposure to different ways of thinking. Older classes are organized around curriculum units. Children rotate through activities during the school day in small groups.

Admission: By date of application relative to the child's date of birth, with preference for siblings and children of alumni. All who apply while pregnant are grouped at the top of the list. The school tries to achieve a gender balance. Parents are not invited to visit the school until their child is admitted.

PARENT RATING: ☆ ☆ ☆ ☆ ☆
Parents call the school "extremely nurturing" and "focused" on the children. The school has an "excellent" reputation for getting children into private elementary schools. Children have the same teachers throughout their years at the school, so teachers "really get to know the children."

Montessori Children's House of the West Coast

25 Lake St.
415-922-9235

Ages: 2.9-5.11 years

Schedule: Open all year, half or full days. Extended care available.

Ratio: 6:1

Philosophy/other: The nonsectarian, Montessori curriculum focuses on communication skills. Parents must volunteer eighteen hours per year for the school. Students take daily walks in nearby parks and regular field trips.

Admission: By application and interview. Parents are encouraged to submit an application six to twelve months in advance of the expected date of enrollment.

PARENT RATING: ☆ ☆ ☆ ☆

150 Parker School

150 Parker Ave.
415-221-0294
www.onefiftyparker.org

Ages: 2.9-6 years

Schedule: Mornings or afternoons, five days a week. Extended care available.

Ratio: 6:1

Philosophy/other: This public non-profit corporation is run by a board of parents and the director. Founded in 1954, the school features a developmental, experience-based curriculum with a focus on the natural environment, including fine and gross motor skills, music, creative arts, social skills, and preparation for academics.

Admission: By "educational considerations and date of inquiry." The school seeks diversity in admissions.

PARENT RATING: ☆ ☆ ☆ ☆ ☆

This is a small program with a "great" director and outdoor space. The school takes a "holistic" approach to the child. Children can "float" to different areas of interest during free play periods.

Peter's Place Nursery School

227 Balboa St.

415-752-1444

Ages: 2.9-5 years

Schedule: Mornings or afternoons; two, three, or five days a week. Lunch program but no extended care.

Ratio: 7:1

Philosophy/other: This private non-profit school offers a developmental curriculum focusing on encouraging confidence and self-esteem in each child. The school has a small setting in a renovated building with an outdoor area in the backyard.

Admission: By application date with preference for continuing students, siblings, and children with special needs. The school tries to balance gender in each class.

PARENT RATING: ☆ ☆ ☆ ☆ ☆

Parents appreciate the small size of the school and the low teacher turnover rate, allowing teachers to focus on each child.

Temple Emanu-El Preschool

2 Lake St.

415-751-2535, ext. 118

www.emanuelsf.org

Ages: 2-5.6 years

Schedule: Mornings, three to five days a week. Extended care available.

Ratio: 6:1

Philosophy/other: The developmental curriculum in this NAEYC-accredited school incorporates Jewish values and traditions. Children spend time with a mixed age group for a part of the day, and then move to small groups. Additional programs include storytelling, music and movement, and Friday Shabbat. Outdoor play is held in an atrium area.

Admission: By date of application, with preference for Temple members.

PARENT RATING: ☆ ☆ ☆ ☆ ☆

There is a "strong" religious component to the program, with non-Jewish children welcome but only Jewish traditions taught. Parents report that the school has an "excellent" director, "extremely well-educated" teachers, and a good reputation for getting children into private kindergartens.

WESTERN ADDITION/ HAIGHT ASHBURY/ COLE VALLEY

Chinese-American International School (CAIS)

150 Oak St.

415-865-6000

www.cie-cais.org

Ages: 3 years to 12th grade

Schedule: Full school day, five days a week. Extended care available.

Ratio: 8:1

Philosophy/other: This private non-profit independent school offers a bilingual immersion Mandarin Chinese/English Montessori program.

Prior Chinese is not required. Students spend half of each day with an English teacher and half with a Mandarin Chinese teacher. The curriculum includes Montessori lessons, everyday life skill experiences, auditory and speaking skills, storytelling, music, games, and after-school enrichment classes.

Admission: By tour, application, parent interview, and evaluation visit.

PARENT RATING: ☆ ☆ ☆ ☆

Parents seeking to send their children to CAIS for elementary school are encouraged to apply to the preschool program. Ninety percent of the students are from non-Mandarin speaking households. Parents are "very involved" in the school.

French-American International School (FAIS)

150 Oak St.
415-558-2060
www.fais-ihs.org

Ages: 3.9 years to 12th grade

Schedule: Full school day, five days a week. Extended care available.

Ratio: 10:1

Philosophy/other: This private independent school offers a structured, bilingual French-English program. Prior French is not required. The curriculum meets French and state of California requirements. Students spend 80 percent of their time with a French teacher and 20 percent with an English teacher in the early grades.

Admission: By campus visit, application, and interview (with an emphasis on a child's auditory and language development skills and a shared philosophy of family and school).

PARENT RATING: ☆ ☆ ☆ ☆

Parents report the preschool is "excellent" and "more structured" and "intensive" than the average preschool. Parents seeking to enroll their child in the FAIS elementary school are encouraged to apply to the pre-k program. The school offers "great facilities," and it attracts a "very diverse" student population.

Pacific Primary

1500 Grove St.
415-346-0906

Ages: 2.5-6 years

Schedule: Flexible. Open all day, all year.

Ratio: 10:1 or 7:1, depending on age of child.

Philosophy/other: This developmental, open-ended curriculum emphasizes creative arts. The school celebrates diversity among its families. Designed to meet the needs of working parents, it serves breakfast, lunch, and snacks.

Admission: By application and interview (with preference for siblings). The school seeks a diverse population and welcomes children with special needs. Admission is very selective.

PARENT RATING: ☆ ☆ ☆ ☆

Parents raved about the active dramatic program that culminates in a school play at the end of the year. Parental involvement is required.

NOE VALLEY/MISSION/ SOUTH OF MARKET

Parents report that despite an influx of families to Noe Valley, the neighborhood remains tremendously underserved in terms of preschools. Many popular programs have closed or relocated in recent years. With demand so high, Noe Valley parents are advised to look early!

Children's Day School

333 Dolores St.
415-861-5432
www.cds-sf.org

Ages: 3.4 years to 5th grade

Schedule: Full school day, five days a week. Extended care available.

Ratio: 6:1

Philosophy/other: This private non-profit independent school has an inquiry-based, project-based, multi-cultural curriculum. They focus on teaching respect for diversity and each child's individual needs and background. The curriculum includes environmental education and Spanish, and the school features a farm and organic garden on an acre of land, as well as specialists in art, music and movement.

Admission: By application, interview, and visit to the school. Admission is selective, based on the applicant's "social, emotional, and cognitive development." Admissions are rolling, but applicants are encouraged to apply before February for September entry.

PARENT RATING: ☆ ☆ ☆ ☆ ☆

It's a "unique" setting with a farm and garden in the heart of the Mission. Parents especially appreciate the school's multicultural emphasis and extended hours to accommodate working parents.

Eureka Learning Center

• 464 Diamond St., 415-648-0380
• 551 Eureka St., 415-821-3422

Ages: 2.6-5 years

Schedule: Mornings, five days a week. Extended care available.

Ratio: 5:1

Philosophy/other: This NAEYC-accredited, developmental program is based on "real life" activities, including art, woodworking, dance, dramatic play, language, music, natural science, math and field trips.

Admission: By date of application, with preference for siblings and consideration for gender balance and diversity. There is a several-year-long waiting list, so parents are encouraged to apply early.

PARENT RATING: ☆ ☆ ☆ ☆ ☆

The school has a reputation as "the best" in Noe Valley. Parents also appreciate the outdoor play opportunities.

The Preschool

Baja Noe Valley
415-285-5327
www.ThePreschool.com

Ages: 2.6-5.6 years

Schedule: Mornings, five days a week. Lunch program, but no extended care.

Ratio: 5:1

Philosophy/other: This NAEYC-accredited, developmental program with mixed-age groups includes art, music, dance, stories, cooking, gardening, Spanish, math, science and nature.

Admission: By date of application, with preference for siblings and consideration of gender and age balance. School contacts parents for tours when openings arise.

PARENT RATING: ☆ ☆ ☆ ☆
Parents appreciate the "nurturing" environment of this small school.

The San Francisco School
300 Gaven St.
415-239-5065
www.sfschool.org
Ages: 3 years to 8th grade
Schedule: Full school day, five days a week. Extended care available.
Ratio: 11:1
Philosophy/other: The curriculum in this private, independent, nonprofit school is a developmental and Montessori mixture. The school encourages diversity among students, and teachers are trained in the Montessori method.
Admission: By application and a family interview.

PARENT RATING: ☆ ☆ ☆ ☆ ☆
This "structured" preschool program provides an entrée into the excellent elementary school. Admission is very selective.

| North Bay |

SOUTHERN MARIN

Belvedere Hawthorne Nursery Schools
415-435-1661
• Belvedere
  Cove Road Pl. (nursery school)
• Tiburon
  145 Rock Hill Dr. (pre-k)

Ages: 2.6 years to pre-k
Schedule: Mornings; two, three, or five days a week. Extended care available.
Ratio: 8:1
Philosophy/other: Founded in 1939, this nonprofit corporation is the oldest independent nursery school in Marin County. The curriculum includes social and motor skills, listening, following directions, problem solving, art and music, nature, science, math, crafts, puppetry, stories, and play. They also offer a "Time for Twos" program with parent participation.
Admission: By date of application, with priority for siblings. In 2001, there was a two-year waiting list.

PARENT RATING: ☆ ☆ ☆ ☆
Parents love this "very popular" and "traditional" school. They advise applying as early as possible.

Marin Day Schools
• Mill Valley
  10 Old Mill St., 415-381-4206
• San Rafael
  1123 Court St., 415-453-9822
• Tiburon
  445 Greenwood Beach Rd., 415-381-3120
See San Francisco listing.

Strawberry Preschool/Tamalpais Preschool
• Tiburon
  240 Tiburon Blvd., 415-388-4437
• Mill Valley
  410 Sycamore Ave., 415-388-4286
Ages: 2.9 to pre-k

Schedule: Mornings; two, three, or five days a week. Extended care available.

Ratio: 9:1

Philosophy/other: These "sister" nonprofit nonsectarian preschools offer a developmental curriculum. The NAEYC-accredited programs include math and reading readiness, arts and crafts, sensory motor games, music, drama, cooking, carpentry, outdoor play, gardening, science and nature study.

Admission: By date of application (with preference for siblings).

PARENT RATING: ☆ ☆ ☆ ☆ ☆

Parents appreciated the "excellent" facilities, "very enthusiastic" and "committed" teachers, and the "traditional preschool" approach. They recommend applying early for this "very popular" program, as waiting lists often close several years in advance.

CENTRAL MARIN

Children's Cottage Cooperative Nursery School

2900 Larkspur Landing Cir.
Larkspur
415-461-0822

Ages: 2-4 years

Schedule: Mornings, two, three, or five days a week. Extended care available.

Ratio: 4:1

Philosophy/other: This cooperative preschool is located in an historic cottage built in 1891. The school was founded in 1949 and is NAEYC accredited.

Admission: By date of application, with preference for siblings and alumni. Parents must visit the school to be put on the waiting list.

PARENT RATING: ☆ ☆ ☆ ☆ ☆

Parents praised the low student-teacher ratio and "nurturing" teachers. The cottage and play yard feature an abundance of fun activities for children, from costumes to water and sand play. "Kids are never bored" at this school, say parents.

Marin Day Schools (San Rafael campus)

See listing under Southern Marin.

Marin Enrichment

Bacich School Campus
25 McAllister Way
Kentfield
415-461-4395

Ages: 2.9-5 years

Schedule: Mornings; two, three, or five days a week. No extended care.

Ratio: 7:1

Philosophy/other: This school features an emergent developmental curriculum with arts, science, music, and storytelling, designed to prepare children for kindergarten. The school uses Bacich kindergarten's playground.

Admission: By date of application and visit to the school.

PARENT RATING: ☆ ☆ ☆ ☆ ☆

Parents praised the "intimate" class size and excellent, "diverse" teachers who are "committed" to the children.

Marin Jewish Community Center

200 N. San Pedro Rd.
San Rafael
415-479-2000, ext. 8041
www.marinjcc.org

Ages: 2.9-5 years

Schedule: Mornings; two, three, or five days a week. Extended care available.

Ratio: 10:1

Philosophy/other: The school features an "enriching Judaic curriculum," including reading, math readiness, science, social studies, gymnastics, music, aquatics, art, drama, and cooking. Teachers are trained to "recognize each child as a unique individual." There are parent participation programs for younger toddlers.

Admission: Registration begins on the first business day in January for the September session. Parents reportedly line up early in the morning to secure a spot, as the program is extremely popular.

PARENT RATING: ☆ ☆ ☆ ☆ ☆
Parents laud the facility as "top-notch," with access to a pool and other JCC programs. Although the classes are large (forty children), parents think the program is "excellent."

Marin Montessori School

5200 Paradise Dr.
Corte Madera
415-924-5388
www.marinmontessori.org

Ages: 2 years to 8th grade

Schedule: Mornings or full school day, five days a week. Extended care available.

Ratio: 5:1 (toddler); 12:1 (primary)

Philosophy/other: This private non-profit school features an AMI-accredited program with much "self-direction" and little "play" involved. The curriculum includes traditional Montessori subjects along with mathematics, language, geography, geology, botany, zoology, physical science, music, and art.

Admission: By application and interview with parent and child (with preference for siblings and children with previous Montessori experience). Parents must commit to keep their children in the program through kindergarten.

PARENT RATING: ☆ ☆ ☆ ☆ ☆
The school has "fabulous" facilities, with "spacious, clean" classrooms and a large "sunny" playground and garden right on the Bay.

Marin Primary and Middle School

20 Magnolia Ave.
Larkspur
415-924-2608
www.mpms.org

Ages: 18 months to 8th grade

Schedule: Flexible. Open all day, all year.

Ratio: 6:1 (toddlers); 8:1 (preschool)

Philosophy/other: Founded in 1975, this nonprofit school offers a developmental curriculum focusing on each child's best method of learning. There are specialists in art and music, field trips, and elective classes in gymnastics, piano, dance, and computer.

Admission: By application and interview with parents. The school seeks to balance classes by gender, birth dates, schedule desired, and "other pertinent information received from the parents." Preference is given to siblings and children of staff.

PARENT RATING: ☆ ☆ ☆ ☆ ☆
Parents like the small (six-month) age span in the younger classes to help "ease the transition" to school. They praise the school's "extensive" resources and facilities, including a library and spacious playground, as well as the "flexible" scheduling.

The Mountain School
50 El Camino Dr.
Corte Madera
415-924-4661
Ages: 2.9-5 years
Schedule: Mornings; two, three, or five days a week. Extended care available.
Ratio: 10:1 or 12:1, depending on age of child.
Philosophy/other: This nonprofit, Waldorf-inspired preschool and kindergarten was founded by parents. The curriculum focuses on developing children's imaginations through songs, stories, and puppetry.
Admission: By application. Admission is selective (not by date of application).

PARENT RATING: ☆ ☆ ☆ ☆
This is a very popular "alternative" school with a focus on art and drama.

Ross Valley Nursery School
689 Sir Francis Drake Blvd.
Kentfield
415-461-5150
Ages: 2.9 to pre-k
Schedule: Mornings or afternoons; two, three, or five days a week. No extended care.
Ratio: 7:1
Philosophy/other: The developmental curriculum in this NAEYC-accredited school includes art, music, stories, circle time, outdoor play, and cooking. Children break into smaller groups for group time.
Admission: By date of application (with preference for siblings). Applications accepted from birth.

PARENT RATING: ☆ ☆ ☆ ☆ ☆
Probably the most popular developmental program in the Ross Valley, this school enjoys an excellent and long-standing reputation in the community. Currently parents must apply very early in a child's life to obtain admission. Parents praised the "warm" atmosphere and "involved" parents at this "traditional" nursery school. The outdoor area was completely renovated in 2001.

San Anselmo Preschool
121 Ross Ave.
San Anselmo
415-453-3181
www.sananselmopreschool.org
Ages: 2.5 to pre-k
Schedule: Mornings or afternoons; two, three, or five days a week. Extended care available.
Ratio: 7:1

Philosophy/other: This nonprofit school offers a developmental curriculum focusing on science and the environment. There are numerous small live animals on the premises, and a courtyard with a roof overhang for rainy days. Large classes divide into smaller groups for part of the day.

Admission: Applications are accepted up to one year in advance. After returning students reenroll, admissions begin by order of application.

PARENT RATING: ☆ ☆ ☆ ☆
Though the program is large, parents noted the ability of the children to "self-direct" their play in one of several adjoining rooms (e.g. science, art, or reading). Parents report the staff is "diverse" and appreciated the "unique" science and nature approach.

Trinity Preschool and Kindergarten

333 Woodland Ave.
San Rafael
415-453-4526
www.trinitypreschool.com

Ages: 2.9-5 years

Schedule: Mornings, two to five days a week. Extended care available.

Ratio: 7:1 (3-year-olds); 10:1 (4-year-olds); 8:1 (pre-k)

Philosophy/other: This nonprofit school affiliated with the Lutheran Church offers a Christian oriented developmental program. Students attend chapel one day a week and learn Bible stories and songs. The curriculum includes weekly themes, language skills, science, music, arts and crafts, and nature studies.

An after-school program includes gymnastics, dance and music.

Admission: By date of application.

PARENT RATING: ☆ ☆ ☆ ☆ ☆
Parents call the teachers "proactive" and "tuned in" to each child's needs. The facility is "spacious and bright" with a nice view of the hills, and the outdoor playground was completely renovated in 2001.

NORTHERN MARIN

Creekside Village School of Novato

1787 Grant Ave.
Novato
415-898-7007
www.creeksidevillageschool.com

Ages: 6 weeks to 5 years

Schedule: Flexible. Open all day, all year.

Ratio: 4:1 (newborn-2 years); up to 12:1 for older children, but usually smaller.

Philosophy/other: This day care center and school offers a developmental program. There is a large outdoor area, and breakfasts, lunches and snacks are included.

Admission: By application as space becomes available.

PARENT RATING: ☆ ☆ ☆ ☆
Parents appreciate the "flexible" hours and committed staff.

Montessori School of Novato

1466 S. Novato Blvd.
Novato
415-892-2228
Ages: 2-6 years
Schedule: Flexible. Open all day, all year.
Ratio: 12:1
Philosophy/other: This AMI accredited private school offers a traditional Montessori curriculum with practical life exercises, sensorial materials, and math and language.
Admission: By date of application, with preference for siblings. The school also tries to balance genders and ages.
PARENT RATING: ☆ ☆ ☆ ☆ ☆

St. Francis Preschool

967 5th St.
Novato
415-892-2597
www.skyfamily.com/stfrancis/
Ages: 2.9-5 years
Schedule: Two or three mornings a week. Lunch program but no extended care.
Ratio: 7:1
Philosophy/other: This developmental nonprofit preschool is affiliated with an Episcopal Church, but the program does not include any religious teaching. The curriculum includes pre-reading, pre-math, art, literature, music, nature, science, and dramatic play. The school also offers a program for toddlers and parents.
Admission: By date of application, with preference for siblings and toddler program graduates.
PARENT RATING: ☆ ☆ ☆ ☆

BERKELEY

Berkeley Hills Nursery School

1161 Sterling Ave.
Berkeley
510-849-1216
Ages: 2.6-5 years
Schedule: Mornings, three to five days a week. Extended care available.
Ratio: 7:1
Philosophy/other: This private, nonprofit preschool offers a developmental curriculum. A typical day involves two individual choice periods (one indoors and one outdoors) and a group time for ideas, songs, plays and stories.
Admission: By date of application while balancing gender and age.
PARENT RATING: ☆ ☆ ☆ ☆ ☆
Located near a park in a woodsy residential area, this is a "traditional" nursery school with "experienced" directors and "nurturing" teachers.

Berkeley Montessori School

2030 Francisco St.
Berkeley
510-849-8341 (preschool)
510-849-8340 (admissions)
www.bmsonline.org
Ages: 3 years to 8th grade
Schedule: Full school day, five days a week. Extended care available.
Ratio: 12:1
Philosophy/other: Founded in 1963, this AMS-affiliated school's curriculum includes traditional Montessori learning plus environmental education, music, art and drama.

Admission: By parent tour, application, and student interview. Candidates are evaluated for academic, social and emotional skills.

PARENT RATING: ☆ ☆ ☆ ☆

Parents say children are "polite" and "well-behaved" and can really "focus" on individual projects. Teachers are "creative" with good ideas for projects.

Child Education Center

1414 Sacramento St.
Berkeley
510-528-1414

Ages: 3 months to 5 years

Schedule: Flexible hours, three or five days a week. Extended care available.

Ratio: 3:1 to 8:1, depending on age of child.

Philosophy/other: This private non-profit school and day care center offers a developmental curriculum, including art, music, motor skills, nature, walks, field trips, computers, dance and swim classes, cooking and drama. The program emphasizes language development.

Admission: By interview, tour, and date of application.

PARENT RATING: ☆ ☆ ☆ ☆

This school features a "close-knit community of parents," with "lots" of parent involvement. "Great director, great teachers, supportive of kids and parents," said parents.

Dandelion Cooperative Nursery School

941 The Alameda
Berkeley
510-526-1735

Ages: 2.9-5 years

Schedule: Mornings, two to five days per week. Extended care available.

Ratio: 4:1

Philosophy/other: This NAEYC-accredited, cooperative preschool offers a play-based curriculum. Parents work at the school the same number of days per month as the child attends school per week. Classrooms mix ages except at circle time.

Admission: Parents may submit an application after visiting the school in the fall prior to the year of entry. Admissions begin in February on a first come, first served basis.

PARENT RATING: ☆ ☆ ☆ ☆

Parents "become a real community" by working in the preschool. They report that the head teachers provide great consistency.

Duck's Nest Preschool

- Berkeley
  1411 4th St., 510-527-2331
- Oakland
  4498 Piedmont Ave., 510-428-0901

Ages: 2 years to pre-k

Schedule: Mornings, three, four, or five days per week. Extended care available.

Ratio: 6:1 to 9:1, depending on child's age.

Philosophy/other: This school offers a developmental curriculum with monthly themes. The program includes garden and animals, art, music, movement, and enrichment classes.

Admission: Attend open house in February and submit an application.

PARENT RATING: ☆ ☆ ☆ ☆ ☆

Parents "love it." They say teachers are "experienced" and kids "are happy" and have "a lot of fun" while "actually learning" at the same time. The facilities are "clean and well-kept" and parents are "very involved."

The Gay Austin School

1611 Hopkins St.
Berkeley
510-526-2815

Ages: 2-4 years

Schedule: Mornings or afternoons; two, three, or five days. Extended care available.

Ratio: 5:1 to 8:1, depending on age of child.

Philosophy/other: Founded in 1956, this private school features a developmental curriculum, including art, music, math, science, and language.

Admission: By date of application (priority deadline is the end of January).

PARENT RATING: ☆ ☆ ☆ ☆ ☆

Parents praised the "small" size of this "traditional" preschool with a "close-knit community of parents."

Hearts Leap School

2638 College Ave.
Berkeley
510-549-1422

Ages: 2-5 years

Schedule: Full school day, four or five days a week. Extended care available.

Ratio: 6:1 to 9:1, depending on child's age.

Philosophy/other: This school has an emergent, developmental curriculum that includes play, creative arts, science, literacy, and motor skills. The multicultural program takes a problem-solving and conflict-resolution approach to discipline.

Admission: By application and tour. The school does not encourage a waiting list, but parents may apply early.

PARENT RATING: ☆ ☆ ☆ ☆

Parents praised the "enthusiastic" teachers and "great new facilities" with spacious outdoor yard. "Not a day care-type facility...this is a real school."

Montessori Family School

1850 Scenic Ave.
Berkeley
510-848-2322
www.montessorifamily.com

Ages: 3-12 years

Schedule: Mornings or full day, five days a week.

Ratio: 11:1

Philosophy/other: This AMS-affiliated school features multiage classes and a traditional Montessori curriculum with the addition of art, movement, music, and grace and courtesy. Special interest classes are offered after school.

Admission: By classroom observation, date of application, and student visit. The school tries to balance genders and ages in the classroom.

PARENT RATING: ☆ ☆ ☆ ☆

Parents say the school produces "well-disciplined" kids and has "trained, experienced" teachers.

Step One Nursery School and Kindergarten

499 Spruce St.
Berkeley
510-527-9021

Ages: 2-6 years

Schedule: Mornings, three to five days a week. Extended care available.

Ratio: 6:1 or 7:1, depending on child's age.

Philosophy/other: This nonprofit school offers an emergent, developmental curriculum. Parents are expected to contribute fifteen hours a year.

Admission: By date of admission (with preference for siblings and families of cultural and racial diversity). The school balances ages and genders.

PARENT RATING: ☆ ☆ ☆ ☆ ☆

"Great" facility and "experienced," "caring," "long-time" teachers with "diverse" student body, say parents. Teachers "really pay attention to each child. They truly know my kids and love them." Parents recommend getting on the waiting list "very early" as the school is very popular.

OAKLAND

Duck's Nest Preschool

See listing under Berkeley.

Lakeshore Children's Center

3534 Lakeshore Ave.
Oakland
510-893-4048

Ages: 2.9-6 years

Schedule: Full day, five days a week. Open all year.

Ratio: 8:1 or 10:1, depending on child's age.

Philosophy/other: This nonsectarian school's developmental curriculum emphasizes conflict resolution and multiculturalism. Activities focus on developing social, emotional, creative, physical, cognitive, and life skills, and include a lot of free play. Outside teachers provide lessons in Spanish, gymnastics, music, dance and sign language.

Admission: By parent visit and date of application.

PARENT RATING: ☆ ☆ ☆ ☆

Parents are "very enthusiastic" about the self-described "Peace Academy," a long-time school with "diverse" students, "consistent" faculty and a "warm atmosphere."

Lakeview Preschool

515 Glenview Ave.
Oakland
510-444-1725

Ages: 2.9-5 years

Schedule: Open all year. Full school day, two to five days a week. Extended care available.

Ratio: 5:1

Philosophy/other: Founded in 1971, this private preschool has a multicultural emphasis with celebrations from around the world. The curriculum includes Spanish, music, science, movement, stories, art, and cooking.

Admission: By parent visit, application, and interview with child. Decisions are made on the basis of the child's age, gender, readiness, diversity, schedule desired, fit between the family's and the program's objectives, and the date of application.

PARENT RATING: ☆ ☆ ☆ ☆

Parents appreciated the "diversity" in students and program.

Mills College Children's School

5000 MacArthur Blvd.
Oakland
510-430-2118

Ages: 3 months to 5th grade

Schedule: Mornings or full days, five days a week.

Ratio: 1:1 and 2:1 (infants and toddlers); 4:1 (preschoolers)

Philosophy/other: This NAEYC-accredited laboratory school is staffed by a head teacher and student teachers from Mills College. The curriculum is developmental, and there are multiage classrooms. Established in 1926, this is the oldest campus laboratory school on the West Coast.

Admission: By tour and application. Admission is selective. "We strive for classrooms with a balance of boys and girls, a range of ages, and diversity."

PARENT RATING: ☆ ☆ ☆ ☆ ☆

Parents call the school "excellent" and "fabulous." Head teachers have master's degrees and "tons" of experience. Students have access to Mills College facilities, including dance and swimming classes.

Montclair Community Play Center

5815 Thornhill Dr.
Oakland
510-339-7213

Ages: 3-5 years

Schedule: Mornings, five days a week. Extended care available.

Ratio: 4:1

Philosophy/other: Founded in 1933, this nonprofit, parent-owned cooperative offers a developmental curriculum based on parent involvement, antibias, and conflict resolution. They also offer a toddler program with parent participation.

Admission: By attendance at January open house, application, and tour, with preference for alumni and then toddler program graduates. The school strives to create diversity and a balance of genders and ages in admissions.

PARENT RATING: ☆ ☆ ☆ ☆

"Lots of work" for the parents, but a "tight-knit" community and an "excellent" program, say parents.

Temple Sinai Preschool

2808 Summit St.
Oakland
510-451-2821
www.templesinaipreschool.org

Ages: 2-5 years

Schedule: Mornings, three to five days a week. Extended care available.

Ratio: 4:1 or 7:1, depending on child's age.

Philosophy/other: This Reform Jewish preschool offers a developmental program with Jewish traditions. The school is open to children of all religions.

Admission: Current preschool families receive first preference in admissions, then Temple Member families, and then non-Temple Member families by date of application.

PARENT RATING: ☆ ☆ ☆ ☆
Parents had nothing but praise for the "long-time" staff and "kid-focused" program with its "well-equipped playground" and "supportive" parent community.

LAFAYETTE/MORAGA/ ORINDA

The Child Day Schools
- Antioch
  112 East Tregallas Rd., 925-754-0144
- Lafayette
  1049 Stuart St., 925-284-7092
- Moraga
  372 Park St., 925-376-5110
- Pleasanton
  883 Rose Ave., 925-462-1866
- San Ramon
  18868 Bollinger Canyon Rd., 925-820-2525

Ages: Infant to kindergarten (available programs may vary)

Schedule: Half or full days, five days a week. Open all year.

Ratio: 4:1 to 10:1, depending on child's age.

Philosophy/other: This NAEYC-accredited private school features a High/scope developmental curriculum. The rooms are organized into specific learning areas through which children rotate. Teacher-child interaction emphasizes teacher support rather than control.

Admission: First come, first served.

PARENT RATING: ☆ ☆ ☆ ☆ ☆
The campuses are individually run, so programs and ratings may vary. Parents at the Lafayette campus had high praise for the director and appreciated the flexible scheduling.

They say the school hires "great staff" who tend to stay.

Growing Tree Pre-School
1695 Canyon Rd.
Moraga
925-376-8280

Ages: 18 months to 5 years

Schedule: Mornings or full school days, one to five days a week. Extended care available.

Ratio: 4:1 to 12:1, depending on child's age.

Philosophy/other: This NAEYC-accredited school offers an emergent play-based curriculum. The youngest group focuses on cognitive learning, the middle ages rotate through activities, and the pre-kindergarten program introduces letters and numbers.

Admission: By date of application.

PARENT RATING: ☆ ☆ ☆ ☆
Parents praise the small classes, newer facilities, and relatively structured program. They say the codirectors are very involved, and advise parents to apply early as this is a very popular program.

Old Firehouse School
984 Moraga Rd.
Lafayette
925-284-4321

Ages: 4 months to 5 years.

Schedule: Mornings or full days. Extended care available.

Ratio: 3:1 to 9:1, depending on child's age.

Philosophy/other: The individualized, emergent curriculum draws on the Reggio-Emilia philosophy and emphasizes literacy. Recent projects have included creating a dinner party, a spaceship, a doll hospital, and a jungle video. Each child is assigned to the same teacher throughout his or her years at the school.

Admission: By application, with consideration of gender and age balances, schedule requested, and parental support of the school.

PARENT RATING: ☆ ☆ ☆ ☆

Located in an old fire station, the school gets high praise for its "innovative" curriculum and incentive bonus program to retain qualified teachers. The playground includes hills, a deck, a garden, a pagoda, an enchanted cottage, a tricycle track, and a sand and water play area.

The Orinda Preschool (TOPS)

10 Irwin Way
Orinda
925-254-2551
www.topsonline.org

Ages: 2-5 years

Schedule: Mornings; two, three, or five days a week. Extended care available.

Ratio: 5:1

Philosophy/other: Founded in 1938, this NAEYC-accredited parent cooperative preschool and kindergarten has a developmental curriculum. The transitional kindergarten program includes math, science and literacy activities.

Admission: By date of application (with preference for current and alumni families).

PARENT RATING: ☆ ☆ ☆ ☆

Parents say this school is "lots of fun." This is a popular program so apply early.

St. Mark's Nursery School

451 Moraga Way
Orinda
925-254-1364

Ages: 2.9-4 years

Schedule: Mornings, two or three days a week. Lunch program but no extended care.

Ratio: 8:1

Philosophy/other: Founded in 1962, this school offers a developmental program with a lot of free play and small group time.

Admission: By date of application.

PARENT RATING: ☆ ☆ ☆ ☆

Parents praise this school's "warm" atmosphere and "very traditional" program.

St. Stephen's Nursery School

66 Saint Stephen's Dr.
Orinda
925-254-3770

Ages: 2-4 years

Schedule: Mornings, two or three days a week. Lunch program but no extended care.

Ratio: 4:1 (2-year-olds) or 8:1 (3- and 4-year-olds)

Philosophy/other: This school offers a developmental program with a structured schedule of free play and circle time. The school is affiliated with the Episcopal Church, but the curriculum does not include religious content other than holiday celebrations and saying grace.

Admission: By date of application, with priority registration for current families, siblings, and church members.

PARENT RATING: ☆ ☆ ☆ ☆ ☆

Parents praised the intimate size, long-time director and staff, "wonderful" art teacher, and involved families.

Seedlings Preschool

49 Knox Dr.
Lafayette
925-284-3870

Ages: 6 months to 4 years

Schedule: Full school day, two or three days a week. Extended care available.

Ratio: 3:1 to 8:1, depending on child's age.

Philosophy/other: This NAEYC-accredited program is affiliated with, and located in, the Lafayette-Orinda Presbyterian Church. The developmental curriculum includes art, math, science, music, motor skills, language, and practical life skills, as well as Christian traditions.

Admission: First come, first served, with priority for current families, siblings, and members of the church.

PARENT RATING: ☆ ☆ ☆ ☆ ☆

"Great reputation" and "excellent facilities," say parents.

ALAMO/DANVILLE/ PLEASANTON/LIVERMORE

The Child Day Schools

See listing under Lafayette/Moraga/ Orinda.

Creative Learning Center

120 Hemme Ave.
Alamo
925-837-4044

Ages: 2.9 years to kindergarten

Schedule: Mornings, afternoons, or full school days, three or five days a week. Extended care available.

Ratio: 5:1 to 8:1

Philosophy/other: Located in an old house surrounded by huge trees, the school offers a developmental curriculum, including art, language, drama, science, math, woodworking, music and movement, health, nature, social studies, computer, and field trips. Parent participation is encouraged.

Admission: By date of application.

PARENT RATING: ☆ ☆ ☆ ☆ ☆

Parents praised the school's philosophy of "socialization" rather than "strict academic drills," and "respectful" staff who "do a great job at resolving conflict and redirecting the children to more appropriate activities."

The Dorris-Eaton School

1286 Stone Valley Rd.
Alamo
925-837-7248

Ages: 3-5 years

Schedule: Mornings or afternoons; two, three, or five days a week. Extended care available.

Ratio: 10:1 (some classes are smaller)

Philosophy/other: This private school offers a developmental curriculum including basic reading and math, art, music, movement, and motor skills.

Admission: By date of application beginning a year in advance of entry, with priority for continuing families and siblings.

PARENT RATING: ☆ ☆ ☆ ☆

"Warm, attentive, experienced staff."

Gingerbread Preschool

4333 Black Ave.
Pleasanton
925-931-3430
www.ci.pleasanton.ca.us

Ages: 3-5 years

Schedule: Mornings or afternoons; two to four days a week. No extended care.

Ratio: 8:1

Philosophy/other: Run by the City of Pleasanton, this preschool offers a developmental curriculum of themed units, including music and movement, dramatic play, art, natural sciences, literature, and math.

Admission: By lottery, with priority for currently enrolled families, then Pleasanton residents, then non-residents.

PARENT RATING: ☆ ☆ ☆ ☆

Parents lamented that the program lasts for only two hours each day!

Shining Light Preschool

4455 Del Valle Pkwy.
Pleasanton
925-846-2588

Ages: 3-5 years

Schedule: Mornings or afternoons, two to four days a week. No extended care.

Ratio: 4:1 (3-year-olds) or 6:1 (4-year-olds)

Philosophy/other: This Christian, parent cooperative preschool is affiliated with the Valley Community Church. The school also offers a limited number of noncooperative spots. The developmental curriculum includes monthly themes and letters, building character and Bible time,

special events and field trips, crafts, science, cooking, fine motor skills, and music and movement.

Admission: By date of application.

PARENT RATING: ☆ ☆ ☆ ☆ ☆

Parents praised the small classes and "fun way of teaching." "The director is excellent...my child has developed wonderful skills."

Stratford School

3201 Camino Tassajara
Danville
925-648-4900
www.stratfordschools.com

Ages: 2.9-4 years

Schedule: Mornings or afternoons; two, three, or five days a week. No extended care.

Ratio: 10:1 or 12:1, depending on age of child.

Philosophy/other: This private, independent school offers an academic curriculum, including phonics, mathematics, music, art, and science. During SMART (Stratford Math and Reading Time), teachers use puppets and visual aids to teach the alphabet and numbers.

Admission: First come, first served, based on space available and grade level readiness (with priority for siblings).

PARENT RATING: ☆ ☆ ☆ ☆ ☆

"A relative newcomer with a great reputation," say parents. "Very academic and very structured and the program is very well-rounded . . . . Great preparation for kindergarten."

Sycamore Valley Day School

1500 Sherburne Hills Rd.
Danville
925-736-2181
www.svds.com

Ages: 2-6 years

Schedule: Mornings or full school days; two, three, or five days a week. Extended care available.

Ratio: 10:1 (2-year-olds); 12:1 (3- and 4-year-olds); 14:1 (pre-k)

Philosophy/other: The developmental curriculum features art, reading awareness, science, math, small and large motor skills, physical fitness, field trips, and music.

Admission: By application and evaluation by the director.

PARENT RATING: ☆ ☆ ☆ ☆

South Bay

BURLINGAME/SAN MATEO/HILLSBOROUGH

First Presbyterian Church Nursery School

1500 Easton Dr.
Burlingame
650-342-8326

Ages: 2-4 years

Schedule: Mornings, two to four days a week. No extended care.

Ratio: 3:1 (2-year-olds); 6:1 (3-year-olds); 7:1 (4-year-olds)

Philosophy/other: Founded in 1964, this nonprofit cooperative preschool is affiliated with the church. The curriculum is play-based and the school is NAEYC accredited.

Admission: By date of application, with priorities for church members, current families, siblings of graduates, and graduates of the toddler class.

PARENT RATING: ☆ ☆ ☆ ☆ ☆

Little Wonders

225 Tilton Ave.
San Mateo
650-348-0736

Ages: 9-33 months

Schedule: Two-hour classes meet once a week.

Ratio: 1:1 (parents must accompany children)

Philosophy/other: This nonprofit, non-sectarian cooperative school offers an unstructured program including free play, snack, discussion, and music.

Admission: Priority registration is for current and alumni families. New families must visit the school and register by the deadline (usually April) to be entered in a lottery for admission.

PARENT RATING: ☆ ☆ ☆ ☆ ☆

Peninsula Jewish Community Center Preschools

650-591-4438
www.pjcc.org
- Belmont
  2440 Carlmont Dr.
- Foster City
  800 Foster City Blvd.
- Redwood City
  Temple Beth Jacob,
  1550 Alameda de las Pulgas

Ages: 2-5 years

Schedule: Mornings (Belmont and Redwood City) or full day (Foster City). Extended care available.

Ratio: 7:1

Philosophy/other: The developmental theme-based curriculum in these NAEYC-accredited schools includes music, movement, art, and holiday celebrations. Shabbat is celebrated each week. Enrichment classes in music, cooking, ballet, swimming, drama and science are also available. There are also parent participation programs for younger children.

Admission: After reenrollment occurs in February for currently enrolled families and siblings, the general public is admitted on a first come, first served basis.

PARENT RATING: ☆ ☆ ☆ ☆ ☆

St. Matthew's Episcopal Day School

16 Baldwin Ave.
San Mateo
650-342-5436
www.stmatthewsonline.org

Ages: 3 years to 8th grade

Schedule: No extended care.

Ratio: 9:1

Philosophy/other: Private independent school.

Admission: Admission is selective and based on an application and interview. Priority is given to siblings, church members, and children of alumni.

PARENT RATING: ☆ ☆ ☆ ☆

PALO ALTO/MENLO PARK

Bing Nursery School

850 Escondido Rd.
Stanford
650-723-4865

Ages: 2-5 years

Schedule: Mornings or afternoons; two, three, or five days a week. Minimal extended care.

Ratio: 4:1 to 8:1, depending on child's age.

Philosophy/other: Founded in 1966, this NAEYC-accredited university laboratory school features a developmental curriculum, including art, music, language, computers, building, gardening, and animal care. Both professional teachers and Stanford students teach.

Admission: By date of application with priority to: current students and siblings; children of Stanford faculty, students and staff; siblings of Bing alumni; and children of Stanford alumni. The school also strives to balance genders, ages, and ethnicities, and to accommodate special needs.

PARENT RATING: ☆ ☆ ☆ ☆ ☆

Probably one of the most famous preschools in the country, the school is housed in a a 13,000-square-foot building on a four-acre campus. Each light-filled preschool room has its own half-acre outdoor area, with covered patio areas for rain. Admission is "very competitive."

Kirk House Preschool (Menlo Park Presbyterian Church)

1148 Johnson St.
Menlo Park
650-323-8667
www.mppc.org

Ages: 3-5 years

Schedule: Mornings or afternoons, two or three days a week. No extended care.

Ratio: 6:1 or 7:1, depending on age of child.

Philosophy/other: Founded in 1953, this nonprofit preschool affiliated with the church offers a developmental, theme-based curriculum. The program includes Christian teachings and Bible stories, as well as art, science, and music.

Admission: By date of application (with priority for church members).

PARENT RATING: ☆ ☆ ☆ ☆ ☆

Ladera Community Church Preschool

3300 Alpine Rd.
Portola Valley
650-854-0295
www.ladera.org

Ages: 2-5 years

Schedule: Mornings or afternoons, two or three days a week. No extended care.

Ratio: 4:1 or 5:1, depending on age of child.

Philosophy/other: Founded in 1966, this NAEYC-accredited, nonprofit preschool offers a developmental curriculum with no religious education in the classroom.

Admission: By visit to the school and application. Priority is given to children of church members, then to currently enrolled families, then to alumni families, and then to date of application. The school tries to balance genders in each class.

PARENT RATING: ☆ ☆ ☆ ☆

This is a small program with wonderful outdoor space.

Palo Alto Friends Nursery School

957 Colorado Ave.
Palo Alto
650-856-6152

Ages: 3-4 years

Schedule: Mornings or afternoons; two, three, or five days a week. No extended care.

Ratio: 5:1 to 8:1, depending on age of child.

Philosophy/other: This nonprofit, nonsectarian cooperative nursery school is sponsored by the Friends Meeting. The curriculum is play-based, involves free choice, and includes creative activities. The emphasis is on social and emotional skills rather than academics.

Admission: The waiting list opens ten months prior to entry. Admission is first come, first served.

PARENT RATING: ☆ ☆ ☆ ☆ ☆

Pre-School Family (Palo Alto Unified School District)

4120 Middlefield Rd.
Palo Alto
650-856-0833
www.paadultschool.org/preschool

Ages: newborn to 4 years

Schedule: Mornings, one to four days a week. Parents attend once a week with their children, as well as meet two to three times per month for discussion classes. No extended care.

Ratio: 2:1 or 3:1, depending on age of child. Children under 2 are accompanied by parents.

Philosophy/other: A parent education program of the school district, this NAEYC-accredited, cooperative preschool was founded in 1946 and offers a developmental curriculum.

Admission: After priority registration for currently enrolled students in March, public registration is held in April on a first come, first served basis.

PARENT RATING: ☆ ☆ ☆ ☆

Ta'Enna Preschool (Albert L. Schultz Jewish Community Center)

655 Arastradero Rd.
Palo Alto
650-493-0563, ext. 245
www.paloaltojcc.org

Ages: 2.6-5 years

Schedule: Mornings; two, three, or five days. Extended care available.

Ratio: Not available.

Philosophy/other: The NAEYC-accredited, developmental curriculum features songs, music, art and play. The school celebrates Shabbat and Jewish holidays. Students may also take extracurricular enrichment classes. They also offer parent participation classes for younger children.

Admission: First come, first served.

PARENT RATING: ☆ ☆ ☆ ☆ ☆

Trinity School

650-854-0288, ext. 119
www.trinity-mp.org
- Menlo Park
  330 Ravenswood Ave. (Angus Hall and Trinity Hall campuses)
- Portola Valley
  815 Portola Rd. (Christ Church campus)

Ages: 3 years to 5th grade

Schedule: Mornings; two, three, or five days a week. No extended care.

Ratio: 9:1

Philosophy/other: This NAEYC-accredited, Episcopal day school offers an emergent curriculum in three locations.

Admission: Applications are accepted a year in advance of entry. Admission is by priorities (siblings, parish members, diversity and age balance are all factors) not by date of application.

PARENT RATING: ☆ ☆ ☆ ☆ ☆
Admission is very selective to this "very popular" program.

Woodland Preschool

360 La Cuesta Dr.
Portola Valley
650-854-9068
www.woodland-school.org

Ages: 2 years to 8th grade

Schedule: Open all year. Flexible hours and extended care available.

Ratio: 12:1

Philosophy/other: This private independent day school on a ten-acre campus offers an academic curriculum that includes language arts, French, art, music, drama, and gymnastics.

Admission: By application and evaluation visit of child to school.

PARENT RATING: ☆ ☆ ☆ ☆

Woodside Parents' Nursery School

3154 Woodside Rd.
Woodside
650-851-7112

Ages: 18 months to 5.9 years

Schedule: Mornings or afternoons, one to five days a week. Lunch program but no extended care.

Ratio: 1:1 (toddlers, parents participate), 4:1 (preschool, ages 3-4 years), or 5:1 (pre-k)

Philosophy/other: This NAEYC-accredited, nonprofit cooperative preschool offers a developmental curriculum including art, science, reading, and music.

Admission: By date of application.

PARENT RATING: ☆ ☆ ☆ ☆ ☆

Reported to be "a lot of work" for the parents, but well worth it.

LOS ALTOS, SAN JOSE AND SOUTH

Jewish Community Center of Silicon Valley Preschool

14855 Oka Rd.
Los Gatos
408-358-5939
www.sanjosejcc.org

Ages: 2-5 years, with optional parent co-op for 2-year-olds

Schedule: Mornings; two, three, or five days for regular preschool. Extended care available.

Ratio: 5:1 (2-year-olds), 8:1 (3-year-olds), or 9:1 (4-year-olds)

Philosophy/other: This developmental program features "hands-on" experiences in Judaic studies, science and math, art, music, movement, drama, stories, and cooking. Jewish culture and Shabbat are celebrated, but children of other religions are welcome. Afternoon enrichment classes are available.

Admission: By date of application.

Los Altos United Methodist Church Children's Center

655 Magdalena Ave.
Los Altos
650-941-5411
www.laumc.org

Ages: 2-5 years

Schedule: Mornings or afternoons; two, three, or five days a week. Extended care available.

Ratio: 5:1 to 8:1 depending on child's age.

Philosophy/other: This developmental program is Christian based and church affiliated but open to all.

Admission: First come, first served, with priority for returning students, siblings and church members.

PARENT RATING: ☆ ☆ ☆ ☆ ☆

This is a new facility with a long waiting list.

Mariposa Montessori

408-266-LOVE
www.mariposamontessori.org
• Los Gatos
  16548 Ferris Ave.
• San Jose
  1550 Meridian Ave.

Ages: 2.5-6 years

Schedule: Mornings or afternoons; two, three, or five days a week. No extended care.

Ratio: 7:1 or 8:1, depending on child's age.

Philosophy/other: The campuses of this Montessori school are located on church property but the program is nonsectarian.

Admission: By date of application.

PARENT RATING: ☆ ☆ ☆ ☆ ☆

Montecito School

1468 Grant Rd.
Los Altos
650-968-5957
www.montecitoschool.com

Ages: 2-5 years

Schedule: Mornings or afternoons; two, three, or five days a week. Extended care available.

Ratio: 8:1

Philosophy/other: Founded in 1962, this private preschool offers a developmental curriculum emphasizing social skills, motor development, coordination, auditory and visual skills, following directions, and enhancing attention span. The school is part of the National Wildlife Federation "Schoolyard Habitat" program.

Admission: By date of application.

PARENT RATING: ☆ ☆ ☆ ☆ ☆

This is a long-standing parent favorite on a beautiful wooded campus with animals. There is a long waiting list, so apply early.

Stratford Schools

www.stratfordschools.com
• Los Gatos
220 Kensington Way, 408-371-3020
• Sunnyvale
1196 Lime Dr., 408-732-4424

See listing under East Bay—Alamo/Danville/Pleasanton/Livermore.

Bibliography

CHAPTER 1

American College of Obstetricians and Gynecologists. *Planning for Pregnancy, Birth & Beyond*. 2nd Ed. New York: Penguin Books, 1997.

American Society for Reproductive Medicine. *Third Party Reproduction: A Guide for Parents*. American Society for Reproductive Medicine, pamphlet, 1996.

California Employment Development Division. *Certified Nurse Midwives and Licensed Midwives*. California Occupational Guide No. 555, 1995.

California Employment Law Center. *Family/Medical Leave*. Pamphlets, The *Law At Work* series.

California Employment Law Center. *Pregnancy Discrimination*. Pamphlets, *Your Rights At Work* series.

California Pacific Medical Center. *Information about Cord Blood Banking for Expectant Parents*. California Pacific Medical Center, pamphlet, November 1996.

Clapp, Diane N. *Selecting an Infertility Physician*. RESOLVE, Fact Sheet 16, June 2000.

Eisenberg, Arlene, Heidi Murkoff, and Sandee Hathaway. *What to Expect When You're Expecting*. New York: Workman Publishing, 1996.

Equal Rights Advocates. *Family and Medical Leave and Pregnancy Issues*. Equal Rights Advocates, pamphlet.

Held, Nancy, Teresa Corrigan, Jonna Schengel, Alison Horton, and Jeannie Karel Pimentel. *Healthy Pregnancy Guide*. San Francisco, CA: California Pacific Medical Center, 1998.

National Adoption Information Clearinghouse. "Adoption: Where Do I Start?" National Adoption Information Clearinghouse website, Fact Sheet AB-0006A, www.calib.com/naic.

National Adoption Information Clearinghouse. "Intercountry Adoption." National Adoption Information Clearinghouse website, Fact Sheet AB-0009A, www.calib.com/naic, June 2000.

RESOLVE. *Assisted Reproductive Technologies*. RESOLVE, Fact Sheet 33, July 2000.

RESOLVE. *Overview of Adoption*. RESOLVE, Fact Sheet 1, May 2000.

RESOLVE. *Regulation of Infertility Clinics and Laboratories*. RESOLVE, Fact Sheet 32a, 1997.

U.S. Department of Labor, Employment Standards Administration. *The Family and Medical Leave Act of 1993*. Fact Sheet No. 028.

Williams, Constance. "What's a Doula?: A Brief Discourse on the Latest Innovation in Birth Care." Birthways website, www.birthways.org.

CHAPTER 2

Baby Steps: East Bay Trails to Enjoy with Babies on Board website, http://home.earthlink.net/~natashab/NMbabysteps.html.

Bay Area Moms website, www.plumsite.com/bayareamoms/outandabout/naturetrails/.

Byrne, Helen. *Exercise After Pregnancy, How to Look and Feel Your Best*. Berkeley, CA: Ten Speed Press, 2001.

East Bay Moms Newsletter. March 2000.

Ginsburg, Marsha. "Stroll Through History." *San Francisco Examiner*, 18 July 2001.

Kukula, Kathryn. "Yoga For You." *American Baby*, December 2000.

Penny, Vicki. "Mommy and Me Workouts." *Golden Gate Mothers Group Newsletter*, October 2001.

San Francisco Bay Area Hiker website, www.bahiker.com/.

Sherry Reinhardt's Support Services for Mothers website, http://users.lmi.net/sherryr.

"Take a Hike." *Bay Area Parent*, May 2000.

Torassa, Ulysses. "Stretch and Deliver." *San Francisco Chronicle*, 13 January 2002.

UC Berkeley Parents Network website, http://parents.berkeley.edu.

Urban Baby website, http://urbanbaby.com/.

CHAPTER 3

Fields, Denise and Alan. *Baby Bargains*. 3rd Ed. Boulder, CO: Windsor Peak Press, 1999.

CHAPTER 4

Carber, Kristine M. "Just for the Kids." *San Francisco Examiner Magazine,* 13 August 2000.

Fields, Denise and Alan. *Baby Bargains*. 3rd Ed. Boulder, CO: Windsor Peak Press, 1999.

Lipman, Susan Sachs. "Second-Hand But First-Rate, The Ultimate Guide to Bay Area Children's Resale Stores." *Parents Press,* February 2000.

Mos, Leanne. "Chasing Baby." *San Francisco Chronicle,* 10 November 2001.

Oppenheim, Joanne and Stephanie. *Oppenheim Toy Portfolio.* New York: Oppenheim Toy Portfolio, Inc., 2002.

Urban Baby website, http://urbanbaby.com/.

CHAPTER 5

Doulas of North America website, www.dona.org.

Dunnewold, Anne, Ph.D., and Diane G. Sanford, Ph.D. *Postpartum Survival Guide.* Oakland, CA: New Harbinger Press, 1994.

Kapp, Diane. "Mother's Little Helpers, Doulas Making Life Easier for Pre and Postpartum Women." *San Francisco Chronicle,* 18 November 2001.

Kleinman, Karen R., M.S.W., and Valerie D. Raskin. *This Isn't What I Expected.* New York: Bantam Books, 1994.

Placksin, Sally. *Mothering the New Mother: Your Postpartum Resource Companion.* New York: Newmarket Press, 1994.

Town and Country Resources website, www.tandcr.com.

Underwood, Anne, Ana Figueroa, Joan Westreich, and Tara Pepper. "Motherhood and Murder." *Newsweek,* 2 July 2001.

CHAPTER 6

Bay Area Parent, March 2001-February 2002.

Parents Press website, www.parentspress.com/.

CHAPTER 9

Adrade, Ana. *Infant to Five, A Comprehensive Guide for Parents Looking for Childcare.* The Wolf Pack Family Child Care, pamphlet, 1998.

Bananas, Inc., A Childcare Resource and Referral Agency. Pamphlets, *Choosing Childcare* series, 2001-2002.

Bay Area Parent, *March 2001-February 2002.*

California Childcare Resource and Referral Network website, www.rrnetwork.org/.

California Department of Social Services. *Facts You Need to Know about Licenses for Childcare Facilities.* Pamphlet, 1999.

California Department of Social Services, Community Care Licensing Division website, http://ccld.ca.gov/.

Children's Council of San Francisco. *Choices in Childcare.* Pamphlet, 2000.

Desrosiers, Alyce. *Finding a Nanny for Your Child in the San Francisco Bay Area.* San Francisco, CA: Pince-Nez Press, 2001.

Desrosiers, Alyce. *Choosing In-Home Childcare, A Parenting Guide.* Pamphlet, 1999.

Eisenberg, Arlene, Heidi Murkoff, and Sandee Hathaway. *What to Expect the First Year.* New York: Workman Publishing, 1996.

Go City Kids website, www.gocitykids.com.

Held, Nancy, Teresa Corrigan, Ann Kosistky-Haiman, and Diane Goldman, *Choosing Childcare Guide.* California Pacific Medical Center, pamphlet, 1998.

Raffin, Michele P. *The Good Nanny Book: How to Find, Hire, and Keep the Perfect Nanny for Your Child.* Berkeley, CA: Berkeley Publishing Company, 1996.

UC Berkeley Parents Network website, http://parents.berkeley.edu.

Urban Baby website, http://urbanbaby.com/.

CHAPTER 10

Neighborhood Parents Network. *Preschool Directory.* 2000-2001 Ed. Berkeley, CA: Neighborhood Parents Network, 2000.

Rifkin, Lori, Vera Obermeyer, and Irene Byrne, *Finding a Preschool for Your Child in San Francisco.* San Francisco, CA: Pince-Nez Press, 2000.

About the Authors

Now a full-time mom, **Stephanie Lamarre** formerly practiced intellectual property law in several private and governmental positions. She is a graduate of Princeton University and Stanford Law School.

Stephanie moved to the Bay Area in 1989, and lived on the Peninsula and in San Francisco before moving to Marin County, where she lives with her husband, David, three-year-old son, Jack, and baby daughter, Elise. She is an active member of various North Bay parenting groups and a supporter of Pixie Park, a children's cooperative park.

Michelle Keene was formerly a World Bank consultant, and executive with the U.S. Environmental Protection Agency, where she specialized in pollution issues. She is a graduate of Bowdoin College and holds an M.A. from The Fletcher School of Law and Diplomacy at Tufts University.

Michelle has lived in San Francisco since 1998, relocating from the East Coast just three months before the birth of her first child. She lives with her husband, Mark, and two sons, three-year-old Michael and baby Maximilian. She currently serves on the steering committee of the Golden Gate Mothers' Group, the city's largest mothers' group.

Michelle and Stephanie met in 1999 as they struggled to adapt to life after their first babies were born. They quickly realized the need for a guide to parenthood in the San Francisco Bay Area, found there was none. . .and the idea for this book was born. They have spoken to Bay Area mothers' groups about transitioning from professional life to life at home, entrepreneurial ideas for working from home, and the many Bay Area baby resources included in *Babies by the Bay*.

Index

More Wildcat Canyon Press Titles...

The Mother's Companion: A Comforting Guide to the Early Years of Motherhood
Here's a book as delightful to hold (*almost*) as a newborn baby, and friend as true as any for every new mother.
TRACY MARSH WITH SHARON HAUPTBERGER AND LISA BRAVER MOSS
ILLUSTRATED BY AMANDA UPTON —$20.00 Paper over Boards

Life after Baby: From Professional Woman to Beginner Parent
An emotional compass for career women navigating the unfamiliar seas of parenthood.
WYNN McCLENAHAN BURKETT —$14.95 Paperback

Twin Stories: Their Mysterious and Unique Bond
A fascinating exploration of what it's like to be a twin.
SUSAN KOHL —$13.95 Paperback

Soaring Solo: On the Joys (Yes, Joys!) of Being a Single Mother
Companionship, comfort, and reassurance for women with the most difficult—but rewarding—job of all: being a single mom.
WENDY KELLER —$13.95 Paperback

The Courage to be a Stepmom: Finding Your Place Without Losing Yourself
The first book to focus on the unique emotional and psychological needs of the stepmother.
SUE PATTON THOELE —$14.95 Paperback

The Worrywart's Companion: Twenty-one Ways to Soothe Yourself and Worry Smart
The perfect gift for anyone who lies awake at night worrying.
DR. BEVERLY POTTER —$12.95 Paperback

Available at bookstores and fine retailers nationwide.
To order any of these titles, just call us toll free at: 1-800-247-8850